VOLUME 21   NUMBERS 2–3   2015

Queer Inhumanisms

Edited by Mel Y. Chen and Dana Luciano

Books in Brief

Figure 1. Laura Aguilar, *Grounded #114*, 2006, digital.
Courtesy of Laura Aguilar and the UCLA Chicano Studies Research Center

Introduction

HAS THE QUEER EVER BEEN HUMAN?

Dana Luciano and Mel Y. Chen

*W*hat can be said about the photograph at left? At first glance, viewers will likely recognize the larger background object as a boulder: rough textured, sand colored, partly in shadow, surrounded by desert brush and blue sky. The smaller figure in the foreground presents more of a challenge. It both resembles and differs from the boulder; both share similar asymmetrically oval outlines, but the texture of the foregrounded figure is smoother, more like human skin. Upon noting the hair at the top and the cleft of the buttocks below, the viewer might begin to see this as a human body, seated on the ground, facing away from the camera. One cannot easily categorize the figure: sex, gender, race, age are obscured by its position. And many of the conjectures that one might make about this body as "simply" a body—for instance, that it is curled frontally inward and that it possesses arms and legs hidden by this pose—depend on assumptions about what a "proper body" looks like and what it can do.[1]

The photograph, *Grounded #114* (2006), is the work of Laura Aguilar, a Chicana lesbian photographer from San Gabriel, California, whose lens tends to focus on nonnormative bodies and on members of marginalized groups.[2] Her specialization in portraiture, especially self-portraiture, locates her work, as Laura Pérez observes, on a "terrain of contestation for women of color," as they must "peel away racialized and gendered associations . . . that their bodily appearance triggers in Eurocentric ways of seeing."[3]

Since the mid-1990s, Aguilar's work has given complex interpretation to Perez's "terrain of contestation" by incorporating land as part of that challenge.

GLQ 21:2–3
DOI 10.1215/10642684-2843215
© 2015 by Duke University Press

In this work, Aguilar poses nude in "natural" settings, sometimes accompanied by other women, though more often alone, aligning her body with features of the landscape. Her outdoor photographs are often read by critics as gestures of defiance, flaunting, in a natural setting, the kind of body—fat, brown, queer—that is treated, in dominant culture, as at once a secret and a spectacle. In *Grounded #114*, from the artist's first color series, Aguilar seems to mold her body into an echo of the boulder behind her—the pose concealing sex and gender, obscuring race, and making even her status as human difficult, at first, to discern. As in other feminist self-portraits, the female body refuses either to open itself to appropriation by the viewer or to position itself as the object of the male gaze.[4] Ironically, though, Aguilar performs this refusal not by intensifying her apparent status as subject (through, say, a defiant facial expression or virtuosic posturing) but by turning away from the demand for recognition within the circle of humanity.[5] By mimicking a boulder, Aguilar enters the very nonhuman fold where some would place her, effectively displacing the centrality of the human itself.

We take up Aguilar's boulderish turn away from the demand for full humanity as a way to explore the overlap between queer studies and the rising critical interest, across the humanities and social sciences, in nonhuman objects. This turn toward the nonhuman insists, at minimum, that we view the boulder in the photograph not as "mere" backdrop or landscape but as equally important, equally in need of inquiry. In light of the social "invisibility" of Aguilar's (human) subjects, this insistence might seem an outrage: why look away from the already overlooked or advantage the inanimate over the dehumanized? Yet *Grounded #114*'s self-portrait beckons us to follow this turn, to take seriously the possibilities of subjecting oneself to stone. There is something compelling about the symmetry of the two figures in this portrait, something that asks us to consider the suggestively queer connections between flesh and stone, between human and nonhuman. One might frame Aguilar's boulder mimicry as protective camouflage, or a form of reverence, or even an in/organic identification; the same minerals occur in both bodies, after all. Yet when discussing this image, neither of us, from the perspectives of our own scholarship, could ignore the possibility that it stages a kind of mating dance.[6] The connections and contrast between the two bodies—one flesh, one rock—come off as undeniably sexy; the pinkish-brown of Aguilar's skin against the brownish-beige of the rock, the roughness of its surface against the smoothness of hers, caress the eye, catalyzing a tactile erotics. The folds of her flesh counterpoint the dents in the stone, both marking textured, touchable bodies. Her skin brings out a softness in the stone; the boulder lends her body an air of durability.

Victoria Martin characterizes an earlier series of Aguilar's landscape nudes as possessing "much sensuality" but "no overt sexuality."[7] This seems true of *Grounded #114* as well, but only, perhaps, because we tend to think of sexuality in terms of human or animal genital relations. If we think, more broadly, of the constitutive pleasure and potentiality of forms of corporeal communing, then we might well consider this image a sexual one, following, not without irony, on the queer theoretical insistence that we *denaturalize* the kind of "sex" that lies at the center of deployments of sexuality.[8] To say, as Amelia Jones contends of Aguilar's landscape photography, that the "boundaries between human and nonhuman melt away," that there is no clear division between the natural world and the human body, is also to say that there is no natural law to oppose to human deviance, since nature cannot be posited as other than and prior to humans.[9] And lifting that prohibition, in turn, multiplies not only the possibilities for intrahuman connection but also our ability to imagine other kinds of trans/material attachments. Thus humans, as Jeffrey J. Cohen proposes, might indeed be understood as desiring stone, because of its semblance to us and because of its radical difference. Stone, queerly, ignites longing for "a world more capacious than the small one we too often think we inhabit."[10]

And yet stone's time, as Cohen also points out, is not our own. This is invoked in the contrast between the two figures in *Grounded #114*. As we suggested earlier, to view Aguilar as *posing* like the boulder is to understand her body's position as both willed and temporary—and that of the boulder as unwilled and permanent. But the boulder's shape, whether or not we call it willed, is likewise temporary—though the duration of that "posture" may be millions of years. In the gap between the presumed mutability of a fleshly body and the stillness of stone, we may also glimpse the vulnerability, the ephemerality of that body compared with the stability and durability of the boulder. In the American Southwest, the photograph's location, its invocation of temporal contrast, has political as well as geological and ontological valence; this desert terrain belongs to a region overlaid with histories of occupation, of settlement, displacement, colonization, and genocide, as well as of attachment, identification, aspiration, and political and cultural reimagination.[11] These histories are not invoked directly in *Grounded #114*, though they hover just beyond the frame. Aguilar's inhuman intimacy with an occupied landscape might be read as recalling the presence of these pasts, the objectification of indigenous populations. Conversely, her determined alignment with this space could signal a mode of decolonization, a pictorial manifestation of Cherríe Moraga's Queer Aztlán.[12]

The connection between the terrain of the nonhuman and these human histories and possibilities shows that giving attention to the boulder's potential agency within the image need not negate or marginalize concerns relating to Aguilar's identity. Critical attention to the active force of the nonhuman has emerged within scholarship usually understood as concerned with "identity" or "social location." Like Moraga, Gloria Anzaldúa envisions a mode of resistance, *mestiza* consciousness, that links marginalized subjects to the land, not just symbolically but materially. This intimate and physical connection to the nonhuman, in the form of the exteriorized land and the interiorized "Shadow-Beast," results in what Carlos Gallego terms the "onto-epistemology" of Anzaldúa's New Mestiza.[13] Importantly, mestiza consciousness is born *both* of an awareness of dehumanization—"the queer," Anzaldúa observes, "are the mirror reflecting the heterosexual tribe's fear: being different, being other and therefore lesser, therefore sub-human, in-human, non-human"—and of a deliberate transgression of the boundaries of the human.[14] To follow Aguilar's turn toward the boulder, then, is not to turn away from questions of objectification or dehumanization; it is, rather, to consider how these questions already anticipate the contemporary "nonhuman turn"—to examine, contra Jones, not how the "boundaries between human and nonhuman melt away" but how those categories rub on, and against, each other, generating friction and leakage. And it is also to ask about other forms, other worlds, other ways of being that might emerge from the transmaterial affections suggested in the photograph. When the "sub-human, in-human, non-human" queer actively connects with the other-than-human, what might that connection spawn?

The query that launched our work on this special issue, "Queer Inhumanisms," was a simple one: has the queer ever been human? At a moment when scholars are grappling with the question of whether humanity has a future, we were drawn toward the question of its queer pasts. Many of queer theory's foundational texts interrogate, implicitly or explicitly, the nature of the "human" in its relation to the queer, both in their attention to how sexual norms themselves constitute and regulate hierarchies of humanness, and as they work to unsettle those norms and the default forms of humanness they uphold. Anzaldúa viewed dehumanization as an opportunity to reconstruct what it means to be human. The humanity of her New Mestiza is not rigid, bounded, and pure but flexible, multiple, and fluid, composed not only of different identities but different entities, different materialities. For Anzaldúa, we are multiple not only symbolically but, as Mikko Tuhkanen observes, biologically, ontologically, spatiotemporally: as Anzaldúa writes, "You're all the different organisms and parasites that live on your body and also the ones who live in a symbiotic relationship to you. . . . So who are you? You're not one single entity.

You're a multiple entity."[15] In the same year that saw the publication of Anzaldúa's landmark *Borderlands/La Frontera: The New Mestiza* (1987), Leo Bersani, in "Is the Rectum a Grave?," also challenged the ideal of the bounded individual, the integral "self," which he viewed as a potential license for violence. Opposing attempts to redeem sex, he proposed, instead, that we allow sex to become what we most fear, a site for the "breakdown of the human itself."[16] Sex, that is, was valuable precisely as it did violence to the human as violent form, as it shattered the idealized self. Monique Wittig's provocative 1978 assertion that lesbians are not women because of their nonparticipation in the regulatory schemes that uphold heterosexualized gender was extended, in a 1991 essay by Cathy Griggers, to the contention that the lesbian body exemplified the machinic or cyborgian condition of the (post)human body.[17] Sandy Stone's 1991 "posttranssexual" provocation asserted that "the disruptions of the old patterns of desire that the multiple dissonances of the transsexual body imply" worked to produce "a myriad of alterities, whose unanticipated juxtapositions hold what Donna Haraway has called the promises of monsters—physicalities of constantly shifting figure and ground that exceed the frame of any possible representation."[18] And in their introduction to the 1995 collection *Posthuman Bodies*, Judith Halberstam and Ira Livingston observed, "Sexuality is a dispersed relation between bodies and things. . . . What is bodily about sex? What is sexual about sex? What is gendered?"[19] In these formulations and others, the figure of the queer/trans body does not merely unsettle the human as norm; it generates other possibilities—multiple, cyborgian, spectral, transcorporeal, transmaterial—for living.[20]

More recent queer scholarship amplifies these efforts to chart the damage done by the human as norm and to alter or replace it as form. In *Aberrations in Black* (2004), for instance, Roderick Ferguson extends the interrogation of the "human" as a technology of racialization (a question taken up by Frantz Fanon, Hortense Spillers, Sylvia Wynter, and others) to show how black subjects' citizenship, morality, and even humanity is made dependent on their submission to sexual regulation.[21] Analyses of queer temporality examines the part that various time schemes played in the production of the human and its subhuman and inhuman others. Lee Edelman, in *No Future*, outlines sexuality, the site of the meaningless, mechanistic, and inhuman drive, as implacably opposed to the optimistic futural narratives developed on behalf of the sentimentalized Child.[22] Edelman's call to "insist on enlarging the inhuman" instead of demanding recognition as humans is taken up in a different critical register by Elizabeth Grosz. For Grosz, the inhuman is not posited in opposition to the human but issues from the proliferation of difference: the "inhuman work of difference [is] the ways in which difference stretches, transforms, and opens up any identity to its provisional vicissitudes, its shimmering self-variations that enable it to become other than what it is."[23] Departing from the inhuman, Jasbir Puar, in *Terrorist Assemblages*, considers the construction of the *unhuman* as a tactic of control society. Extending the unlegal, rather than illegal, status of the detainee, Puar speculates on the withdrawal, rather than regulation, of identity categories and other markers of legibility from these bodies, rendering them unintelligible as humans.[24] The unhuman takes its place as one exemplar of the biopolitical shift from disciplinary to control society, as power works increasingly through the permeation of material bodies, instead of through discrete, identity-marked subjects legible against a standard of humanity.

The increasing urgency of ecological and climatological damage has also pushed many queer critics to move past what Stacy Alaimo describes as a long-standing reluctance to appeal to "nature," partly because both "nature and 'the natural' have long been waged against homosexuals, as well as women, people of color, and indigenous peoples."[25] As Catriona Mortimer-Sandilands and Bruce Erickson contend in their introduction to the collection *Queer Ecologies*, queer environmental thought might begin precisely from the conjunction of an idealized "nature" as a tool to discipline sexual and gender dissidents, and the debasement and exploitation of material nature.[26] Queer ecocriticism also takes up an understanding of ecology as naming not the idea of the "natural world" as something set apart from humans but a complex system of interdependency. Hence, as Tavia Nyong'o argues, ecology offers an apt framing for "the environment of counter-cultural communal life, musicking, and polymorphous sexuality," such as that developed in Samuel R. Delany's 1979 memoir *Heavenly Breakfast*.[27] Delany's speculative fiction, along with that of Octavia Butler, Larissa Lai, Joanna Russ, and many others, has long served as a rich source of queer posthumanist provocation, a site for imagining other, possibly queerer, worlds. As Nyong'o demonstrates, though, a queerly materialist reframing of ecotheory can also enable us to discover those worlds within our own.

The question of whether the queer, for queer theory, has ever been human must, then, be answered, not equivocally but deliberately, yes and no. *Yes*, because this sustained interrogation of the unjust dehumanization of queers insistently, if implicitly, posits the human as standard form, and also because many queer theorists have undeniably privileged the human body and human sexuality as the locus of their analysis. But *no* because queer theory has long been suspicious of the politics of rehabilitation and inclusion to which liberal-humanist values lead, and because "full humanity" has never been the only horizon for queer becoming. We might see the "yes/no" humanity of the queer less as an ambivalence about the human as status than as a queer *transversal* of the category. The queer, we could say, runs across or athwart the human. As Eve Kosofsky Sedgwick reminds us, "The word 'queer' itself means across—it comes from the Indo-European root *-twerkw*, which also yields the German *quer* (transverse), Latin *torquere* (to twist), English *athwart*."[28] To say that queer transverses the human is to understand their relation as contingent rather than stable: it needs to be read up from particular situations, not proclaimed from above.

Our hope, in this special issue, is to set the two terms of our title—"Queer Inhumanisms"—both alongside and athwart one another. "Queer Inhumanisms," that is, does not declare an identity so much as it stages an encounter, one that seeks to discover what each of its terms might do to the other. The encounter with the inhuman expands the term *queer* past its conventional resonance as a container for human sexual nonnormativities, forcing us to ask, once again, what "sex" and "gender" might look like apart from the anthropocentric forms with which we have become perhaps too familiar. At the same time, the deliberate twist given the reclaimed epithet "queer" in late twentieth-century queer activism and analysis—the way it gestures, at once, toward a history of abuse and marginalization and an aspirational expansiveness—prompts us to recall two inflections of "inhuman," the dynamic sense that Grosz employs and the one that invokes indifference and brutality. The scholarship presented in this issue travels between these two inflections, keeping in mind both the promise and the costs of the call to move "beyond" the human.

This special issue emerges at a moment that is witnessing a broad-based shift across the humanities and social sciences affecting both objects and methods—a shift that is coming to be known as "the nonhuman turn."[29] The phrase points to an increasing tendency to question our automatic recourse to the human as both the center of our analysis and the ground of any epistemology. Areas of thought usually associated with the nonhuman turn include affect studies, assemblage theory, speculative realism and object-oriented ontology, actor-network theory, techno-posthumanism, animal studies, environmental studies and ecocriticism, and the new materialisms.[30] These widely disparate domains all share a conviction that the "human" (at least as traditionally conceived) has unjustly dominated and unduly limited the horizon of critical thought, even in the work of structuralist and post-structuralist thinkers who sought to de-emphasize the centrality of human agency and intentionality. For despite their identification as antihumanist, both structuralism and post-structuralism (often designated as the "linguistic" and "cultural" turns, respectively, remained, in the view of many thinkers associated with the nonhuman turn, irredeemably anthropocentric insofar as they privileged (human) epistemology over ontology, language over matter, "representation" over "realism."

"The human," in this body of work, is usually associated with the Enlightenment subject, C. B. MacPherson's possessive individual, and/or "Man" as glossed in Michel Foucault's *The Order of Things*: he is rational, bounded, integral, sovereign, and self-aware. This is the figure to whom rights and citizenship are granted; this is the default figure that grounds and personifies norms of behavior, ability, and health; this is the figure around which we ordinarily construct notions of political and social agency.[31] Posthumanism and other anthro-decentric modes of thought extend the critique of this figure outlined by twentieth-century anti-humanisms.[32] Alongside this normative and masculinized sense of the "human," through, we want to point to two other inflections of the term. The first is an affective one: the often-feminized subject of sympathy, defined by the capacity for emotional attachment to others. To be "human," in this sense, is to feel for others, to love and to grieve and to respond to the suffering of others. This mode of humanness, aligned with the ideal of humaneness, grounds most liberal and sentimental appeals to justice as a way to remediate damage.[33] This figure of the human is less bounded than the first; indeed, its function has often been to make tolerable the damage inflicted by possessive individualism. Yet while a certain openness is demanded of "humanity" in this guise, it must still be effectively self-regulated, limited in scope and function—and hence, although it is frequently rendered as feminine, it remains as normatively white as the figure of Man.[34]

In addition to this implicitly hetero-gendered pair, the cognitive-rational and the sympathetic-emotional figures of the human, we note a third sense, one increasingly invoked in the context of climate change: that of the human as species. Undergirded by evolutionary thought, the human as species is both aligned with and hierarchically differentiated from other forms of life. Insofar as it appeals to biology and to processes of growth, habituation, and reproduction, the sense of the human as species seems to manifest a more material connection between humans than those established through emotional interdependence or cognitive similarity. For this reason, it offers both the idea of an immutable, natural reality outside human control, cited, for example, in claims about competitiveness and violence as founded in "human nature" or the prohibition of homosexuality as "unnatural," and an evocation of unfolding, of progressing, which has been taken up in numerous ways, from Karl Marx's appeal to the "life of the species" as precisely what is thwarted by capitalism to the visions of superiority (often based on white racial purity) devised by eugenicists. The human as species, then, is both materially "here" (and hence vulnerable to "degeneration" or extinction) and speculative, not yet "here." This temporal duality obtains for the other forms of the human as well: they refer at once to a putative "fact" of (human) nature, the way things *are*, and an ideal, a standard to aspire to, the way things *should be*. It is this latter aspect of the "human" that has enabled it to become a resource for critique. As Zakiyyah Iman Jackson points out, for instance, the work of decolonial critics such as Fanon, Wynter, and Aimé Césaire attends rigorously to the gap between the figure of Western Man and the humanist ideal—a gap in which outrages like colonialism and slavery loom large.[35]

Each of these inflections of "human" has been taken up, in recent anthrodecentric scholarship, in ways that elaborate not simply a critique of old forms but an awareness of new frames. Analyses of neoliberalism show how fantasies of possessive individualism and sovereign agency have worn thin in a new labor economy; theories of affect call attention to the impersonal nature of affect, as opposed to the putatively personal implications of "emotion"; and critical discussions of the commercialization of "life itself" illuminate the breaking down of beliefs in species individuality.[36] In this light, the nonhuman turn marks, for many critics, not a venture "beyond" the human but a new mode of critical realism, a recognition that the nature of "reality" itself is changing as power moves away from the individual. The emergence of what late-Foucauldian and Deleuzian critics frame as "control society," they argue, requires a critical lens capable of determining how, as Puar explains, "societies of control tweak and modulate bodies as matter," rather than as humans or subjects.[37] Yet recognizing this, as Puar adds, does not mean wholly abandoning the ethical investments and methodological frameworks that drove ostensibly "human-centered" fields of inquiry based in identity and social location. Though the emergence of control society historically follows that of "disciplinary" society, the latter has not been transcended; it remains not only copresent but deeply imbricated with the former. Hence the form of the "human" remains with us partly as a means of disciplinary dehumanization and regulation, exclusion, and/or marginalization, tactics that, as Puar points out, remain primary vectors of control for "some bodies—we can call them statistical outliers, or those consigned to premature death, or those once formerly considered useless bodies or bodies of excess."[38] The mattering of the body is not, then, inherently a posthuman condition, insofar as humanness and its constitutive parts remain a material as well as ideological force.

For other scholars, the ethical dimension of the nonhuman turn is paramount. Jane Bennett's *Vibrant Matter*, for instance, posits an expanded political ecology as the effect of closer attention to the vitality and agency of all matter.[39] For Bennett, refusing to acknowledge the vitality of the nonhuman is not only shortsighted but ethically "wrong," and making things right—"highlighting the common materiality of all that is"—will both deflate the overblown human ego and open new possibilities for thought and action.[40] In *Meeting the Universe Halfway*, Karen Barad argues that an understanding of agency as enacted or "intra-active" rather than the property of any singular subject or object does not obscure but rather heightens human accountability, developing a sense of responsibility that goes far beyond one's individual "acts" to a recognition of one's agential entanglement in "the larger material arrangements of which 'we' are a 'part.'"[41] The ethical dimension of the nonhuman turn also emphasizes the possibilities for anthrodecentric generativity. Barad insists on the importance of "elaborating feminist and queer understandings of world-making where humans and nonhumans and the divide between them are not hard-wired into political analyses."[42] José Esteban Muñoz's conception of the "brown commons" likewise opens a transmaterial space devoted to "a process of thinking, imagining otherwiseness." Deliberately minoritarian, defiantly queer, this "commons of brown people, places, feelings, sounds, animals, minerals, flora and other objects" refutes the form of the individual in favor of "a movement, a flow, an impulse, to move beyond the singular and individualized subjectivities."[43]

The critics we have drawn from above, in order to explicate the stakes of anthro-decentric thought as both a lens for critical realism and a mode of queer world-making, all share critical orientations drawn from feminism, critical race studies, disability studies, and elsewhere. They are all set in motion, that is, by particular forms of dissatisfaction with the way things are, often founded on histories of neglect, oppression, or injury. This particularity calls attention to a tension between universalizing and locating impulses in both anthro-decentric and queer thought, a tension that parallels the divergent senses of the reclaimed term *queer* itself—as primarily a tool of incessant unsettling, restless refusal of all forms of identity, or as an extensible collection or assemblage of overlapping and mutually imbricated forms of gendered, sexual, and other corporealized dissidence. Muñoz's brown commons specifically foregrounds the latter; the "sense of brownness" that bonds the commons is both a history of damage and devaluation and a response thereto, a "smolder[ing] with . . . life and persistence."[44] This emphasis on histories of damage is in keeping with one consistent provocation across the diffuse and multiple body of work that we seek to name, imperfectly, by "queer theory": its emergence as a response to precarity. Queer theories grounded in woman and lesbian of color feminism, for instance, draw on thinkers who observed with Andre Lorde, that their subjects were "never meant to survive."[45] The trajectory of queer theory that locates its origins in critical response to the AIDS pandemic also necessarily understands queer survival as far from a given. (Indeed, as Neel Ahuja observes in this volume, early queer-theoretical responses to AIDS, such as Bersani's 1987 essay, prefigure contemporary critical concerns with extinction.) Eve Kosofsky Sedgwick's oft-cited essay "Queer and Now" opens with the assertion "I think that everyone who does gay and lesbian studies is haunted by the suicides of adolescents."[46] Queer theory, then, emerges from an understanding of queer life as precarious life.[47]

We are not attempting, in pointing to this history, to reserve queer theory for LGBTQI-identified people or topics. Nor are we insisting that queer theory must always remain "faithful" to its moment of emergence; this, in our view, would hypostasize a living and lively body of thought. Rather, we are marking a specific kind of situation—a desire to persist in the face of precarity—as the primary catalyst for queer thought in general. That situation, moreover, is particularly generative for queer inhumanist thought, since the intensification of precarity in particular contexts tends to push putatively "human" subjects to the critical edge of that category. (It is therefore no accident, we think, that many of the most generative queer critiques of the human have emerged from queer of color critique and transgender studies.) Queer ecology and many other queer engagements with the nonhuman also emerge, in the contemporary context, as a response to precarity, as the effects of climate crisis extend that condition to encompass all of humanity, and numerous other species as well. *All* life, we might say, is now precarious life. For some, the global nature of the crisis points to a need to return to universalizing frames of thought, producing demands for a species-based response even among thinkers historically suspicious of universality.[48] Similar claims resonate across many areas of thought associated with the nonhuman turn regardless of their conscious alignment with climate questions, as though the post-post-structuralist identity of the turn necessitated an impatience with or outright refusal of particularizing claims. Locatedness and historical specificity, privileged grounds for post-structuralism, are complicated by the adjustments in scale said to be necessary to think beyond the confines of the human.

The inclination to vastness in much of this work—in particular, in speculative realism, object-oriented ontology, and some new materialisms—leads some of its critics to designate it with terms like "the new cultural geology" or "the new infinity."[49] This extrahuman vastness is complemented, Jordana Rosenberg argues, by a hyperbolized attention to smallness, which they name the molecular. For Rosenberg, the ontological fascination with "particulate matter" conflates an effect of power (the aforementioned penetrative operation of power in control society) with a mode of resistance.[50] Drawing on Andrea Smith's scholarship, they suggest that its recent uptake in queer theory reproduces and extends the problems associated with "subjectless critique," which, as Muñoz, David Eng, and J. Jack Halberstam explain, demands a "continuous deconstruction of the tenets of positivism at the heart of identity politics."[51] Subjectless queer critique, in this sense, aligns itself with the aforementioned inflection of "queer" as a tool of incessant unsettling. Yet as Smith points out, this insistence on unsettling may well mask the queer subject's status as a settler subject, as well as enable the covert retention of a normative whiteness.[52] Recent critical attention to matter and materiality, Rosenberg argues, extends Smith's concerns as it installs the molecular as "the pre-eminent 'subjectless subject'" of ontologically-oriented theory."[53] Or, we might say, the nonhuman turn revives subjectlessness as *humanlessness.*

In this light, the palpable resistance by many critical race, feminist, and queer thinkers to posthumanism and/or the nonhuman turn is not the effect of some recalcitrant or retrograde attachment to the human. Rather, it illuminates a concern over the critically and politically limiting effects of much recent critical insistence on the "positive," of calls to turn away from "critique" as such. If posthumanism, as Jackson suggests, fails to examine the locations of its own appeals to universalism, it risks precisely the failures that Césaire identified over half a century ago in a humanism covertly centered on the figure of Western Man.[54] Charges that speculative thought, in particular, has neglected generations' worth of scholarship on gender, race, and sexuality have been partly answered in the recent embrace of feminist and queer theory by object-oriented ontologists.[55] Still, an uneven attention to race and related axes of dehumanization persists in many of these fields of study, as several contributors to this special issue remark. In light of this unevenness, recent appeals by some object-oriented and speculative thinkers to a limited range of queer theorists in order to affirm the fundamental queerness of the nonhuman or the ecological may, ironically, diminish the potential of speculative thought, insofar as the isolation of queerness from other contexts risks a form of queer exceptionalism that is, as Puar shows, uncritically aligned with Western discourses of modernity and progress.[56] Along with evading a certain critical responsibility, the distancing of social justice concerns based around race or gender from thinking about the non- or posthuman (on the basis that these categories reinstall an "anthropocentric" point of view) may well foreclose in advance some of the new formations that the nonhuman turn hopes to uncover. We cannot determine in advance what qualities normally cited as "human" will turn out to have expanded purchase.

For this reason, we are wary of divorcing "queer" thought entirely from located histories of precarity, of reducing "queerness" to simply a movement of thought, or of affirmation or negation. If we accept the framing of the nonhuman turn as a move "beyond" the merely human concerns of identity and alterity, we overlook how the very possibility of making a distinction between human and non-human has, historically, been constructed by the kind of actions and processes that we have named dehumanization. Amid the contested valorizations of "new" and "old" materialisms, we must also question whether consensus should or can be found in the very meanings and cosmological stations for that multivariate concept going by the name of "human." In an age of scientific modernity which both hollows out and levels the "human," an anticolonial understanding rejects unthought projections of the temporalized and geopolitical hierarchies that sustain settler and other imperialisms today. A number of critiques have prepared us to be wary of a presumptively universal "human" isolate from which a "beyond" or a "post" is possible, in part because of what is ontologically transcribed into that universal human.[57] Many indigenous thinkers, in particular, show that various indigenous ontologies not only consider many "inanimate" entities to be alive, sentient, and agential, but also to have relational capacity "akin to *personhood*." The combination of colonial governance, spiritual imperialisms, and dominant ontologies leads to a realm of contestations; an indigenous critique of the biopolitical collapse of individuated humanness on the one hand and personhood on the other could have significantly broader ontological ramifications than the secularized and componential logics of, say, "animal rights." In this view, despite their titular resemblance, we might differentiate the mainstream scientifically based logic of interspecies understanding of Temple Grandin and Catherine Johnson's *Animals Make Us Human* from the colonial inculcation and peaked awareness of spiritual transformation in Muscogee poet Joy Harjo's *How We Became Human*, or the solidification of sexual systems in relation to the adjudication of personhood in Mark Rifkin's *When Did Indians Become Straight? Kinship, the History of Sexuality, and Native Sovereignty*.[58] The task remains, then, how to forge connections between these divergent histories, how to think on more than one scale, how to remain responsive to the continuing historical urgency of particular or located crises at the same time as we face new universal or diffuse ones.

We have thus far privileged the term *nonhuman* despite its distance from our own title, "Queer Inhumanisms." We have not done so out of any affinity for "nonhuman" per se; it presents itself here by virtue of its familiarity, as a common descriptor of the focus of new critical developments. The term is not without its problems, though; it seemingly invites us to choose sides and perhaps to turn, even if polemically or temporarily, away from the human as such. Noreen Giffney and

Myra Hird's considered reconfiguration of the term, in contrast, in their ground-breaking 2008 collection *Queering the Non/Human*, transforms the false binary (human/nonhuman) into an occasion for critical thought. As they point out, "Recognizing the nonhuman in every trace of the Human also means being cognizant of the exclusive and excluding economy of discourses relating to what it means to be, live, act or occupy the category of the Human."[59] The slash through non/human, then, attempts to recollect and foreground the very histories of dehumanization too often overlooked in celebratory posthumanisms. "Inhumanisms," in our view, performs a similar kind of work through its homonymic echo. Resonating against "inhumane," inhuman points to the violence that the category of the human contains within itself. Yet it also carries a sense of generativity—inhuman not simply as category, as a spatial designator or the name of a "kind" of being, but as a process, an unfolding. This latter sense is especially pronounced within Deleuzo-Guattarian thought. Jeffrey Cohen and Todd Ramlow contend that the Deleuzian inhuman "opens the body to all kinds of positive possibility, to numerous invitations for reinvention and becoming."[60] Our titular embrace of "inhumanisms" follows the aspiration of becoming-minoritarian, though as the *s* at its end indicates, it does not necessarily align this aspiration with an embrace or advocacy of Deleuzian method or thought; indeed, the call to *become* resounds against numerous invocations of queerness as an unfolding, from Anzaldúa to Sedgwick to Muñoz. It might, in fact, have more precisely matched our inclinations had we chosen *a-human* (as in agnostic to the human as such). In the end, though, we chose *inhuman* for its dual temporal and historical resonances, since we do not as yet foresee a form of the inhuman that liberates itself entirely from histories and processes of dehumanization, nor one that does not risk falling back into them.

For any field or concentration as yet provisional, there are risks—of omission, of premature foreclosure—in putting forward a selection of essays that demonstrate a common character. We note, for instance, that certain partially overlapping areas are less represented in our dossier and essays: indigenous studies, non-US-originated authorship, or a diversity of theories of the transnational. Any of these returns us to the ongoing question about the narrowness of queer theory's referents. Our motivation in coordinating this selection, however, has never been coverage, but provocation. We thus open with the most kaleidoscopic, gestural formation, a dossier consisting of eleven compact pieces by writers both familiar and potentially new to *GLQ* readers, including J. Jack Halberstam, Jinthana Haritaworn, Myra Hird, Zakiyyah Iman Jackson, Eileen Joy, Uri McMillan, Jasbir K. Puar, Susan Stryker, Kim TallBear, and Jami Weinstein. Among them, too, is José Esteban

Muñoz, who sent us his first draft not long before his death in early December 2013. Given how deeply generative his work has been for us in conceptualizing this issue, we are grateful to have permission to feature his entry in the form that he sent it. We especially admire his ability to draw new materialist and object-oriented thought away from themselves, to catalyze, despite a predominant lack of attention to race in these fields, a conception of race that is at once materialist and speculative, ecological and active, defiantly minor and joyously collective, and deeply queer.

While we initially requested that our dossier writers relate their current work to the theme of queer inhumanisms, with the idea of giving form to its notional scope, we also asked them to imagine being part of a conversation. Looking around at their scholarly and activist surroundings, some go a step further: they rework, indict, suggest, reflect, or even launch a polemic. Readers will note speculation and celebration, as well as warning and reminder, meticulous critique and sweeping rejoinder. The collective dossier sets the tone for the breadth of ethical and conceptual reaches of a queer inhumanism that challenges that familiar opposition of the "new" and the "old" by jumping into—rather than acceding to—the multiply temporal fray of so many forms of scholarship, activism, and politics.

In the first essay, Tavia Nyong'o puts the lie to posthuman innocence—or the timeless neutrality of the posthuman wild—by inquiring after the mechanics and process of fabulation in the film *Beasts of the Southern Wild* (dir. Benh Zeitlin; 2012), in which a young girl named Hushpuppy, a "returning" extinct European species, the aurochs, and the "rewilded" site of the Bathtub play prominent roles.[61] Through these figures, Nyong'o traces not only queer relations within the internal politics and narrative of the film but also the relation to actual places that inspired its director, as well as to a fictional-autobiographical play on which it is based. The gendered, racial, and other discrepancies and shifts found among these sites are not, Nyong'o claims, an arbitrary and thus defensibly opaque part of the creative process, but neither should they be resolved as "real" to "fiction" or "original" to "derived." Rather, they can be plumbed as meaningfully equivocating "incompossibles" whose telling flickerings hint that it is a sovereign's invested projections, drawing on "the primitive vitality of a native terrain," that might underlie an otherwise alluring "dream of a rewilded, ecological cinema" that this film represents to so many.

Turning to material craft and what she calls the pedagogical potential of mathematical art projects such as *Crochet Coral Reef* (a collective fabric art project based on the artists' rendering of nondominant mathematical formulas) to instill "felt" being, Jeanne Vaccaro examines the promise for transgender of the handmade, validating craft's place in gender while refusing to repeat the analogical collapse that is often made of the two. Instead, Vaccaro focuses on the crafted nature of transgender while rejecting either a closed reading of transgender or the reductive and hostile accusation of mechanistic displacement and obvious seams that might have inspired Susan Stryker to reclaim Frankenstein as a site for her transgender rage. For Vaccaro, it is "feeling" that works to suture the human site of gendered knowing and the inhuman site of reef ecologies: "The handmade is a methodology and its intervention a felt method, a look at the ordering . . . of bodily knowledge."

If Vaccaro poses the handmade as the epistemology of the transgender ordinary, Eunjung Kim begins with ontology: "Can objectification . . . offer a new way to challenge the exclusionary configurations of humanity that create otherness?" Assessing the hidden limits of a disability studies perspective in which human dignity must be affirmed for disabled people, Kim critiques the collusion of the "ethical positioning of proximity to humanness" and ability-based criteria for human being and worth. Instead, in her reading of the 2006 Korean film *I'm a Cyborg, but That's OK*, Kim examines the potential of nondegraded, expanded objecthood, wherein the objectness of a female factory worker—Donna Haraway's cyborg exemplar—is literalized and augmented, and she deploys that objecthood for survival and mutual benefit. Kim's objected-subjects thus *unbecome human*, loosening the violent holds between value, humanness, agency, ability, and life. In the process, the dehumanization that might be attributed to life in the factories is defamiliarized, though not denied.

To further plumb the ironies of the inhuman, Jayna Brown's essay examines ramifications of the biologization of human matter in which "not all bodies are scientized in the same way." Cancer patient Henrietta Lacks's unusually resilient, queerly reproductive cancer cells were turned into a billion-dollar cell line. Not forgetting the double irony—the nonirony, that is—of the strange vitality attributed to "black" life and of its use as raw material, Brown nevertheless wishes to separate understandings of the plasticity of life, in which the behavior of cells can surprise and confound us, from its common partner, eugenics. A close look at the thinking of H. G. Wells and Julian Huxley reveals complex racialization, colonialist fantasy, and imperial interest couching narratives of tissue, cell, and, ultimately, the human. And yet "we"—black, queer, and disabled people—"are less ethically bound to honor the boundaries of a bodily sovereignty never granted to us." And this, despite the lack of any appreciable economic return to Lacks's family until recently, motivates Brown's invitation to consider even Lacks's cells as more than either the scientific boon or the site of racial deprivation that they have been understood to be; they are also plasticity's victorious exemplar.

Like Brown, Harlan Weaver notes that nonhuman scenes are not absent of racial history. His essay on pit bull intimacies is careful to mark homonormative whiteness's "engulfment" of race-analogical logics in queer liberal (and nonqueer) advocacy for pit bulls. Thinking microcosmically and with intra-action, Weaver examines the potential of a generous form of intimacy not bound to stable kinship and permitting of cross-species encounters, one that he calls "intimacy without relatedness." As he writes, in the animal shelter, "momentary, fleeting contacts described in touches, tastes, movements, and shared rhythms I describe are promisingly, improperly, and queerly inhuman." Weaver asks whether the potential of this queer inhumanism must necessarily be extinguished by the political closures around race analogy, homonormativity, and class in pit bull politics. He answers tentatively: perhaps not, provided that the theory and practice of the thick complexities of interspecies worlds he describes be equally invested in navigating such troubled histories.

The intimate interspecies scene that animates Neel Ahuja's essay aims less at the microcosmic (even though one of his participants is the mosquito) and more at the mutual entanglement of human and mosquito species in a setting of climate change, whose mobile constitutions render species natures partial and historicizable, rather than timeless. Observing that the climate crisis "presses queer theory for a planetary account of reproduction" in a way that troubles any queer posture against reproduction, Ahuja further argues that such a planetary account cannot ignore the all-too-tempting "xenophobic rendering of the environmental parasite." Taking the human as assemblage, and arguing for a dissolution of Manichaean accounts of the (mosquito) parasite/host pair in view of the human settler's own parasitic nature, Ahuja produces a queer inhumanism of both "interspecies entanglement and reproductive displacement."

Our final essay, by Karen Barad, emphasizes in its very form the conceptual experiment that queer inhumanism represents, given that that concept is both multiply produced within the pages of this issue, and a long way, if ever, from settling. Unsettling, in fact, is characteristic of Barad's revisionary approach to matter, given that it is so often imagined as stable, solid, contiguous. Serving as the bookend, in this issue, to both Nyong'o's retreat from the stabilization of reality versus fiction as a mode of analysis and his engagement with Hushpuppy's irresolvably conflicted "virtualization," Barad's experiment here is to take up, with marked enthusiasm, imagination as a partner to materiality, thereby releasing investments on originary fabrics and predictable developmental temporalities. Narrating the role of electricity in the formation of an embryo, Barad points to "material imaginings, electrical flirtations signaling connections-to-come," unsutured to what seems to emerge concretely. The virtual, then, for Barad, is an ontologically inde-terminate ubiquity, a "dance of indeterminacy." This makes matter itself—in its own restless self-engagement and in its substantive nothingness—more a ques-tion of the transmaterial. Turning toward trans*'s to meditate on its human locus, Barad wonders: "Can we (re)generate that which was missing in fleshiness but materially present in virtuality?" Inspired by dossier participant Susan Stryker's "Transgender Rage: My Words to Victor Frankenstein," Barad insists that a denat-uralization of nature—and its own "transembodiment" — leads auspiciously to the undoing of universality, the very universality that couches the human and its effects.

There is something about both the provocative disparities among the pieces in this volume and the queer inhuman itself that suggests unpredictability. Though we might say that there is a growing conviction about likely and actual disasters (reproductive and otherwise) that calls up crisis thinking, this conviction seems couched in a larger, ranging sense of wonderment vis-à-vis rapid changes of scale in climate discourse. These affective frictions, we feel, are also the queer inhu-man. They find affinity with Muñoz's gesture toward an unknowable yet resolutely accessible utopia, aligned more with horizon and imagination than with ideologi-cal closure. Returning to Laura Aguilar's *Grounded #114*, the photograph's distal enmeshment of body and stone, stone and body, the ensuing tenuousness of catego-rization in the face of ontological relativity, the drag and cause of a world-weary set of human denigrations, and the erotic pull to a future that we cannot witness, lead us to speculate that one consequence of Muñoz's utopian gesture might be the pos-sibility, for us humans, of approaching the outer reaches of inhuman identification, from a place—humanity—we know too well and then not at all.

Notes

We would like to express our deepest thanks to *GLQ*'s editors for their support and guidance, and to Jennifer V. Nguyen for invaluable research assistance.

1. As scholars in disability studies have shown, what body parts are deemed pres-ent, missing, essential plays a critical part in the calculus of reading images. For a disability-theoretical meditation on the supposedly "incomplete" statue of Venus de Milo, see Lennard Davis, "Visualizing the Disabled Body: The Classical Nude and the Fragmented Torso," in *Enforcing Normalcy: Disability, Deafness, and the Body* (London: Verso, 1995). Davis observes the paradox whereby one woman's disability renders her repugnant in the eyes of others, while a clearly disabled ("armless" and "variously mutilated") woman's body in the form of Venus de Milo is considered an

ideal of Western beauty. He writes: "If . . . disability is a cultural phenomenon rooted in the senses, one needs to inquire how a disability occupies a field of vision, of touch, of hearing; and how that disruption or distress in the sensory field translates into psycho-dynamic representations" (128).

2. Chon A. Noriega, "Clothed/Unclothed," *Aztlán: A Journal of Chicano Studies* 33, no. 2 (2008): 1. For studies of Aguilar's photography, in addition to the works cited below, see Yvonne Yarbro-Bejerano, "Laying It Bare," in *Living Chicana Theory*, ed. Laura Trujillo (Berkeley, CA: Third Woman, 1998), 277–305; Astrid M. Fellner, "Subversive Bodily Acts: The Photography of Laura Aguilar," in *Body Signs: The Latino/a Body in Cultural Production*, ed. Astrid M. Fellner (Vienna, Austria: Lit Verlag, 2011); Daniel Perez, "Chicana Aesthetics: A View of Unconcealed Alterities and Affirmations of Chicana Identity through Laura Aguilar's Photographic Images," *LUX: A Journal of Transdisciplinary Writing and Research from Claremont Graduate University* 2, no. 1 (2013), scholarship.claremont.edu/lux/vol2/iss1/22. Thanks to Gino Conti and J. Jack Halberstam for pointing us to this image and to Aguilar's work in general.

3. Laura Pérez, *Chicana Art: The Politics of Spiritual and Aesthetic Altarities* (Durham, NC: Duke University Press, 2007), 281.

4. Amelia Jones, "Performing the Other as Self: Cindy Sherman and Laura Aguilar Pose the Subject," in *Interfaces: Women, Autobiography, Image, Performance*, ed. Sidonie Smith and Julia Watson (Ann Arbor: University of Michigan Press, 2002), 93.

5. Alison Kafer makes a similar argument in her reading of Riva Lehrer's painted portrait of Eli Clare, a disability theorist and poet. Clare is pictured crouching, knee touching ground, in a forest scene, a branch emerging from inside his shirt. Kafer writes: "In fact, 'person' and 'plant' are not so easily distinguished, as evidenced by the young sapling emerging from Clare's chest. The painting is breathtaking in its conjuring of an entire ecosystem, one in which human is inextricably part of nature. Its power also lies in its mythology, in its blending together of environmental, disability, and gender politics. Clare isn't connecting with nature in order to be cured of his allegedly broken body, but is rather locating that body in space and time. He's not getting rid of the tremor but locating it, grounding it; it's as much a part of his body as the tree" (*Feminist, Queer, Crip* [Bloomington: Indiana University Press, 2013], 146–48).

6. In recent work, we have each addressed the animacy and the allure of nonhuman objects, including stone. See Mel Y. Chen, *Animacies: Biopolitics, Racial Mattering, and Queer Affect* (Durham, NC: Duke University Press, 2012); Dana Luciano, "Geological Fantasies, Haunting Anachronies: Eros, Time, and History in Harriet Spofford's 'The Amber Gods,'" *ESQ: A Journal of American Renaissance* 55, no. 4 (2009): 269–303; and Luciano, "Sacred Theories of Earth: Matters of Spirit in William and Elizabeth Denton's *The Soul of Things*," "After the Post-Secular," special issue, *American Literature* 86, no. 4 (2014): 713–36.

7.   Victoria Martin, "Laura Aguilar at Susanne Vielmetter Los Angeles Projects," *Artweek* 31, no. 5 (2000): 24.

8.   Michel Foucault, *The History of Sexuality, Volume One: An Introduction,* trans. Robert Hurley (New York: Vintage Books, 1990).

9.   Jones, "Performing the Other as Self," 93.

10. Jeffrey J. Cohen, "Queering the Inorganic," in *Queer Futures: Reconsidering Ethics, Activism, and the Political,* ed. Elahe Haschemi Yekani, Eveline Killian, and Beatrice Michaels (Surrey, UK: Ashgate, 2013), 149–65.

11. A segment of this history can be mapped through Aguilar's own family, whose residence in California's San Gabriel Valley can be traced back several generations, preceding the US claim to the territory. But if recognized life-forms such as "family" can sometimes claim a duration longer than nations, nations also uproot, even obliterate, life-forms (family, tribe, nation); the Mexican claim to this land was likewise that of an occupying power. An earlier self-portrait, *Three Eagles Flying* (1990), makes this claim more explicitly as it depicts Aguilar's nude body hemmed in and bound by US and Mexican flags. One of her best-known works, *Three Eagles Flying* is often read as a statement about cultural identity. But in light of Aguilar's later alignment of her body with the very land to which both nations, in turn, laid claim, we might extend its purview to histories of spatial occupation (as a considered approach to cultural identity in any context touched by powered interests might itself do). On this photograph, see especially Luz Calvo, "Embodied at the Shrine of Cultural Disjunction," in *Beyond the Frame: Women of Color and Visual Representation,* ed. Neferti X. M. Tadiar and Angela Y. Davis (New York: Palgrave Macmillan, 2005), 207–18.

12. Cherríe Moraga, "Queer Aztlán: The Re-formation of Chicano Tribe," in *Queer Cultures,* ed. Deborah Carlin and Jennifer DiGrazia (New York: Pearson, 2004), 224–29.

13. Gloria Anzaldúa, *Borderlands/La Frontera: The New Mestiza* (San Francisco: Aunt Lute Books, 2012), 40; Carlos Gallego, *Chicana/o Subjectivity and the Politics of Identity: Between Recognition and Revolution* (New York: Palgrave, 2011), 74.

14. Anzaldúa, *Borderlands/La Frontera,* 40.

15. Gloria Anzaldúa, quoted in Mikko Tuhkanen, "Queer Hybridity," in *Deleuze and Queer Theory,* ed. Chrysanthi Niganni and Merl Storr (Edinburgh: Edinburgh University Press, 2009), 96.

16. Leo Bersani, "Is the Rectum a Grave?," *October* 43 (Winter 1987): 221.

17. Monique Wittig, *The Straight Mind: And Other Essays* (Boston: Beacon, 1992); Cathy Griggers, "Lesbian Bodies in the Age of (Post)Mechanical Reproduction," *Postmodern Culture* 2, no. 3 (1992), muse.jhu.edu.proxy.library.georgetown.edu/journals /postmodern_culture/v002/2.3griggers.html. See also Griggers (as Camilla Griggers), "Phantom and Reel Projections: Lesbians and the (Serial) Killing Machine," in *Posthuman Bodies,* ed. Judith Halberstam and Ira Livingston (Bloomington: Indiana University Press, 1995), 162–76.

18. Sandy Stone, "The Empire Strikes Back: A Posttranssexual Manifesto," in *Body Guards: The Cultural Politics of Gender Ambiguity*, ed. Julia Epstein and Kristina Straub (New York: Routledge, 1991), 280–304. See also Susan Stryker, "My Words to Victor Frankenstein above the Village of Chamounix: Performing Transgender Rage," *GLQ* 1, no. 3 (1993): 237–54, and Karen Barad's discussion of that essay in this issue.

19. Judith Halberstam and Ira Livingston, "Introduction: Posthuman Bodies," in Halberstam and Livingston, *Posthuman Bodies*, 8.

20. "Viral," special issue co-edited by Patricia Clough and Jasbir K. Puar, *Women's Studies Quarterly* 40, nos. 1-2 (2012). On transcorporeality, see Stacy Alaimo, *Bodily Natures: Science, Environment, and the Material Self* (Bloomington: Indiana University Press, 2010), where she elaborates the concept in relation to chemical sensitivity.

21. Roderick Ferguson, *Aberrations in Black: Toward a Queer of Color Critique* (Minneapolis: University of Minnesota Press, 2004); see also Judith Butler, *Undoing Gender* (New York: Routledge, 2004); and Butler, *Precarious Life* (London: Verso, 2004).

22. Lee Edelman, *No Future: Queer Theory and the Death Drive* (Durham, NC: Duke University Press, 2004).

23. Elizabeth Grosz, *Becoming Undone: Darwinian Reflections on Life, Politics, and Art* (Durham, NC: Duke University Press, 2011), 91.

24. Jasbir Puar, *Terrorist Assemblages: Homonationalism in Queer Times* (Durham, NC: Duke University Press, 2007), 158.

25. Stacy Alaimo, "Eluding Capture: The Science, Culture, and Pleasure of 'Queer' Animals," in *Queer Ecologies: Sex, Nature, Politics, Desire*, ed. Catriona Mortimer-Sandilands and Bruce Erickson (Bloomington: Indiana University Press, 2010), 51.

26. Catriona Mortimer-Sandilands and Bruce Erickson, eds., introduction to Mortimer-Sandilands and Erickson, *Queer Ecologies*, 5.

27. Tavia Nyong'o, "Back to the Garden: Queer Ecology in Samuel Delany's *Heavenly Breakfast*," *American Literary History* 24, no. 4 (2013): 747.

28. Eve Kosofsky Sedgwick, *Tendencies* (Durham, NC: Duke University Press, 1993), xii. We note that in other linguistic accounts, its etymology remains inconclusive.

29. The designation "nonhuman turn" emerged relatively recently and gained popularity in the wake of a conference bearing that title, held in 2013 at University of Wisconsin–Milwaukee's Center for 21st Century Studies. Other common designations include the "ontological turn," the "material turn," and the "postlinguistic turn."

30. In addition to works directly discussed in this introductory essay, other recent scholarship at the intersection of queer and various aspects of the non/human includes, in "thing theory," Scott Herring, *The Hoarders: Material Deviance in American Culture* (Minneapolis: University of Minnesota Press, 2014); in phenomenology, Sara Ahmed, *Queer Phenomenology: Orientations, Objects, Others* (Durham, NC: Duke University Press, 2006); in affect and assemblage theory, Alexis Shotwell, *Against Purity: Liv-*

ing in Compromised Times (Minneapolis: University of Minnesota Press, forthcoming); Rebekah Sheldon, "Somatic Capitalism: Reproduction, Futurity, and Feminist Science Fiction," *ADA: A Journal of Gender, New Media, and Technology* 3 (2013), adanewmedia.org/2013/11/issue3-sheldon/; Julian Gill-Peterson, "The Technical Capacities of the Body: Assembling Race, Technology, and Transgender," *TSQ: Transgender Studies Quarterly* 1, no. 3 (2014): 402–18; Aimee Bahng, "Transpacific Futures: Regenerative Productivity and Salt Fish Assemblages in the Era of Genetic Modification," in "Fictions of Speculation," ed. Hamilton Carroll and Annie McClanahan, special issue, *Journal of American Studies* (forthcoming); in animal studies, Eva S. Hayward, "Spider City Sex," *Women and Performance* 20, no. 3 (2011): 225–51; Hayward, "Enfolded Vision: Refracting *The Love Life of the Octopus*," *Octopus: A Journal of Visual Studies* 1 (Fall 2005): 29–44; Alice Kuzniar, *Melancholia's Dog: Reflections on Our Animal Kinship* (Chicago: University of Chicago Press, 2006); Carla Freccero, "Figural Historiography: Dogs, Humans, and Cynanthropic Becomings," in *Comparatively Queer*, ed. Jarrod Hayes, Margaret Higonnet, and William J. Spurlin (New York: Palgrave, 2010), 45–67; and Christopher Peterson, *Bestial Traces: Race, Animality, Sexuality* (New York: Fordham University Press, 2012); in ecotheory, Claire Colebrook, *Death of the PostHuman: Essays on Extinction*, vol. 1 (Ann Arbor, MI: Open Humanities Press, 2014); Colebrook, *Sex after Life: Essays on Extinction*, vol. 2 (Ann Arbor, MI: Open Humanities Press, 2014); Nicole Seymour, *Strange Natures: Futurity, Empathy, and the Queer Ecological Imagination* (Urbana-Champaign: University of Illinois Press, 2013); Robert Azzarello, *Queer Environmentality: Ecology, Evolution, and Sexuality in American Literature* (Burlington, VT: Ashgate, 2012); and Elena Glasberg, *Antarctica as Cultural Critique: The Gendered Politics of Scientific Exploration and Climate Change* (New York: Palgrave Macmillan, 2012). Other oft-cited texts of the nonhuman turn include Donna Haraway, *The Companion Species Manifesto: Dogs, People, and Significant Otherness* (Chicago: Prickly Paradigm, 2003); Patricia Ticento Clough, ed., *The Affective Turn: Theorizing the Social* (Durham, NC: Duke University Press, 2007); Bill Brown, ed., *Things (a Critical Inquiry Book)* (Chicago: University of Chicago Press, 2004); Diana Coole and Samantha Frost, eds., *New Materialisms: Ontology, Agency, and Politics* (Durham, NC: Duke University Press, 2010); Steven Shaviro, *Post-Cinematic Affect* (London: Zero Books, 2010); Jussi Parikka, *Insect Media: An Archaeology of Animals and Technology* (Bloomington: Indiana University Press, 2010); Bruno Latour, *Reassembling the Social: An Introduction to Actor-Network-Theory* (Oxford: Oxford University Press, 2007); Jane Bennett, *Vibrant Matter: A Political Ecology of Things* (Durham, NC: Duke University Press, 2010); Levi Bryant, Nick Srnicek, and Graham Harman, eds., *The Speculative Turn: Continental Materialism and Realism* (Melbourne: re-press, 2011); Graham Harman, *Tool-Being: Heidegger and the Metaphysics of Objects* (Chicago: Open Court, 2002); Levi R. Bryant, *A Democracy of Objects* (Ann Arbor: MPublishing, University of Michigan Library, 2011); Quentin Meillassoux, *After Finitude: An Essay on the Necessity of Contingency* (London: Continuum, 2008); Ian Bogost, *Alien Phenomenology, or What It's Like to Be a Thing* (Minneapolis: University of Minnesota Press, 2012); Michel Serres, *The Parasite*, trans. Lawrence R. Scherer (Minneapolis: University of Minnesota Press, 2007); and Isabelle Stengers, *Cosmopolitics I and II*, trans. Robert Bononno (Minneapolis: University of Minnesota Press, 2010–11).

31. For further elaboration of located notions of the "human" and "human rights," see David L. Eng, Teemu Ruskola, and Shuang Shen, eds., *China and the Human: Part I: Cosmologies of the Human* and *China and the Human: Part II*, special issues, *Social Text*, nos. 109 and 110 (2011).

32. See Cary Wolfe, *What Is Posthumanism?* (Minneapolis: University of Minnesota Press, 2009); and Rosi Braidotti, *The Posthuman* (New York: Polity, 2013). Wolfe cautions that the term *posthumanism* does not imply a historical overcoming of the human, as some invocations—he cites N. Katherine Hayles's *How We Became Posthuman: Virtual Bodies in Cybernetics, Literature, and Informatics* (Chicago: University of Chicago Press, 1999)—seem to suggest; rather, he argues, posthumanism "comes both before and after humanism" as a critical and conceptual intervention as well as a historical moment (*What Is Posthumanism?*, xv).

33. See Lauren Berlant, "The Subject of True Feeling: Pain, Privacy, Politics," in *Cultural Pluralism, Identity Politics, and the Law*, ed. Austin Sarat and Thomas R. Kearns (Ann Arbor: University of Michigan Press, 1999), 49–84; Dana Luciano, *Arranging Grief: Sacred Time and the Body in Nineteenth-Century America* (New York: New York University Press, 2007).

34. On the whiteness of the sentimental subject, see Julie Ellison, *Cato's Tears and the Making of Anglo-American Emotion* (Chicago: University of Chicago Press, 1999); and Kyla Schuller, "Taxonomies of Feeling: The Epistemology of Sentimentalism in Late-Nineteenth-Century Racial and Sexual Science," *American Quarterly* 64, no. 2 (2012): 277–99.

35. Zakiyyah Iman Jackson, "Animal: New Directions in the Theorization of Race and Posthumanism," *Feminist Studies* 39, no. 3 (2013): 669–85. See also Alexander Weheliye, *Habeus Viscus: Racializing Assemblages, Biopolitics, and Black Feminist Theories of the Human* (Durham, NC: Duke University Press, 2014) for an extended consideration of Wynter's and Spillers's contributions to critical analyses of the human.

36. Lauren Berlant, *Cruel Optimism* (Durham, NC: Duke University Press, 2011); Brian Massumi, *Parables for the Virtual* (Durham, NC: Duke University Press, 2002); Nikolas Rose, *The Politics of Life Itself: Biomedicine, Power, and Subjectivity in the Twenty-First Century* (Princeton: Princeton University Press, 2006).

37. Jasbir K. Puar, "'I Would Rather Be a Cyborg Than a Goddess': The Becoming-Intersectional of Assemblage Theory," *philoSOPHIA* 2, no. 1 (2012): 63.

38. Puar, "'I Would Rather Be a Cyborg Than a Goddess,'" 63.

39. Bennett, *Vibrant Matter.*

40. Bennett, *Vibrant Matter,* 122.

41. Karen Barad, *Meeting the Universe Halfway: Quantum Physics and the Entanglement of Matter and Meaning* (Durham, NC: Duke University Press, 2007), 178.

42. Malou Juelskjær and Nete Schwennesen, "Intra-Active Engagements—an Interview with Karen Barad," in *Kvinder, Køn og forskning/Women, Gender, and Research* 1–2 (2012): 12.

43. José Esteban Muñoz, "The Brown Commons: The Sense of Wildness" (paper presented at the annual convention of the American Studies Association, San Juan, Puerto Rico, November 16, 2012).

44. Muñoz, "Brown Commons."

45. Audre Lorde, "The Transformation of Silence into Language and Action," in *Sister Outsider: Essays and Speeches* (New York: Ten Speed Press, 2012), 42.

46. Eve Kosofsky Sedgwick, "Queer and Now," in *Tendencies* (Durham, NC: Duke University Press, 1993), 1. Jasbir Puar's "Coda: The Cost of Getting Better: Suicide, Sensation, Switchpoints" points to the mechanisms of divergence between certain lives of value—those gay youth whose lives will get better—and the deaths of other young queers, such that the elaboration of one produces the elaboration of the other. At the same time, she asks questions that estrange conventional identity from itself; a theory of affect might yield "switchpoints" that reveal surprising alignments, in this case between "perpetrators" and their "victims" (*GLQ* 18, no. 1 [2011]: 149–58).

47. See Judith Butler, *Precarious Life: The Powers of Mourning and Violence* (London: Verso, 2004).

48. For instance, Dipesh Chakrabarty observes that human survival now demands a return to the universal even as he queries how to "relate to a universal history of life—to universal thought, that is—while retaining what is of obvious value in our postcolonial suspicion of the universal?" ("The Climate of History: Four Theses," *Critical Inquiry* 35, no. 2 [2009]: 219–20).

49. Chris Nealon, "The New Infinity," *Mediations: Journal of the Marxist Literary Group* 29, no. 1 (2015); see also Mark McGurl, "The New Cultural Geology," *Twentieth Century Literature* 57, nos. 3–4 (2011): 380–90. As Nealon observes, the positioning of hermeneutic or historical-materialist analysis as insufficient to address larger-than-human concerns reiterates a critique of human hubris that has strong roots in Christian, and specifically Catholic, doctrine, though it presents itself as nondenominational.

50. Jordana Rosenberg, "The Molecularization of Sexuality," *Theory and Event* 17, no. 2 (2014), muse.jhu.edu/login?auth=0&type=summary&url=/journals/theory_and _event/v017/17.2.rosenberg.html.

51. Judith Halberstam, José Esteban Muñoz, and David L. Eng, "What's Queer about Queer Studies Now?," *Social Text,* nos. 84–85 (2005): 2.

52. Andrea Smith, "Queer Theory and Native Studies: The Heteronormativity of Settler Colonialism," *GLQ* 16, nos. 1–2 (2010): 52.

53. Rosenberg, "Molecularization of Sexuality."

54. Aimé Césaire, *Discourse on Colonialism,* trans. Joan Pinkham (New York: Monthly Review Press, 1972); see also Zakiyyah Iman Jackson, "Animal: New Directions in the Theorization of Race and Posthumanism," *Feminist Studies* 39, no. 3 (2013): 669–85.

55. See Timothy Morton, "Queer Ecology," *PMLA,* 125, no. 2 (2010): 273–82; Levi Bryant, "Of Parts and Politics: Onticology and Queer Theory," *Identities* 16 (2011): 13–28; Katerina Kolozova, Michael O'Rourke, and Ben Woodard, eds., *Speculations of the Other Woman: New Realisms in Feminist Philosophy* (Brooklyn, NY: Punctum Books, forthcoming). Much new materialist thought has aligned itself with feminism since the mid-1990s. As Sara Ahmed argues, however, this body of work's tendency to define itself against the "anti-materialist" inclinations of post-structuralist feminists may present a reductive picture of the latter, resulting in the erasure or forgetting of "how matter matters in different ways, for different feminists, over time" ("Imaginary Prohibitions: Some Remarks on the Founding Gestures of the 'New Materialism,'" *European Journal of Women's Studies* 15, no. 1 [2008]: 36).

56. Puar, *Terrorist Assemblages,* 77.

57. See, e.g., Anthony Appiah, "Is the Post- in Postmodernism the Post- in Postcolonial?," *Critical Inquiry* 17 (1991): 336–57.

58. Temple Grandin and Catherine Johnson, *Animals Make Us Human: Creating the Best Life for Animals* (Boston: Houghton Mifflin Harcourt, 2010); Joy Harjo, *How We Became Human: New and Selected Poems, 1975–2001* (New York: Norton, 2002); Mark Rifkin, *When Did Indians Become Straight? Kinship, the History of Sexuality, and Native Sovereignty* (New York: Oxford University Press, 2010).

59. Noreen Giffney and Myra Hird, eds., *Queering the Non/Human* (Burlington, UK: Ashgate, 2008), 7–8.

60. Jeffrey J. Cohen and Todd Ramlow, "Pink Vectors of Deleuze," *Rhizomes* 11–12 (Fall 2005–Spring 2006), www.rhizomes.net/issue11/cohenramlow.html. See Gilles Deleuze and Félix Guattari, *A Thousand Plateaus: Capitalism and Schizophrenia,* trans. Brian Massumi (Minneapolis: University of Minnesota Press, 1987), esp. 26–38.

61. Lucy Alibar and Benh Zeitlin, *Beasts of the Southern Wild,* directed by Benh Zeitlin (2012; Beverly Hills, CA, 20th Century Fox Home Entertainment).

THEORIZING QUEER INHUMANISMS

THE SENSE OF BROWNNESS

José Esteban Muñoz

*M*y recent writing has revolved around describing an ontopoetics of race that I name the sense of the brownness in the world. Brownness is meant to be an expansive category that stretches outside the confines of any one group formation and, furthermore, outside the limits of the human and the organic. Thinking outside the regime of the human is simultaneously exhilarating and exhausting. It is a ceaseless endeavor, a continuous straining to make sense of something else that is never fully knowable. To think the inhuman is the necessary queer labor of the incommensurate. The fact that this thing we call the inhuman is never fully knowable, because of our own stuckness within humanity, makes it a kind of knowing that is incommensurable with the protocols of human knowledge production. Despite the incommensurability, this seeming impossibility, one must persist in thinking in these inhuman directions. Once one stops doing the incommensurate work of attempting to touch inhumanity, one loses traction and falls back onto the predictable coordinates of a relationality that announces itself as universal but is, in fact, only a substrata of the various potential interlays of life within which one is always inculcated.

The radical attempt to think incommensurate queer inhumanity is a denaturalizing and unsettling of the settled, sedimented, and often ferocious world of recalcitrant anti-inhumanity. Queer thought is, in large part, about casting a pic-

GLQ 21:2–3
DOI 10.1215/10642684-2843323
© 2015 by Duke University Press

ture of arduous modes of relationality that persist in the world despite stratifying demarcations and taxonomies of being, classifications that are bent on the siloing of particularity and on the denigrating of any expansive idea of the common and commonism. Within the category of human intraspecies connectivity, we feel the formatting force of asymmetrical stratifications both within humanity and outside it. The incommensurable thought project of inhumanity is the active self-attunement to life as varied and unsorted correspondences, collisions, intermeshings, and accords between people and nonhuman objects, things, formations, and clusterings. In trying to render a sense of brownness, a term that is indebted to the histories of theorizing blackness and queerness, it is incumbent to attempt to attune oneself to the potential and actual vastness of *being-with*.

DECOLONIZING THE NON/HUMAN

Jinthana Haritaworn

I am approaching the call in this special issue, to think through the "promises or limitations of the nonhuman," at several crossroads. First, as a recent settler of color who moved to Turtle Island at a time of Indigenous resurgence, I am challenged to fundamentally revisit European paradigms of race, gender, and the non/human. Here, the oft-invoked binaries of male/female and human/nonhuman are more than post-structuralist textbook conundrums. There is a keen awareness of how colonial attempts at dispossession, displacement, and genocide have targeted Indigenous peoples in their apparent failure to subjugate land, women, children, and gender-nonconforming people, and in their lack of proper distinctions between genders and species.[1] Leanne Betasamosake Simpson writes: "You use gender violence to remove Indigenous peoples and their descendants from the land, you remove agency from the plant and animal worlds and you reposition aki (the land) as 'natural resources' for the use and betterment of white people."[2]

Refusing a view of colonialism as in the past, Indigenous feminist, queer, transgender, and Two Spirit thinkers have traced the shifting manifestations of gender violence and environmental violence, from reservation and residential school systems to contemporary regimes of adoption and foster care, policing, and the epidemic rape and murder of Indigenous women, Two Spirit, and LGBT people, which are in turn linked to resource extraction and ongoing land theft.[3] Besides highlighting the significance of cis-heteropatriarchy and anthropocentrism to settler colonialism, they have underlined the defense of the land and the revaluing of traditional gender relations as central strategies of decolonization.[4]

Second, as a result of both chance and choice, my disciplinary investments have shifted from queer studies to environmental studies (my new institutional home) and critical ethnic studies (an emerging formation that has produced interesting interventions on the intersection of gender, race, and the nonhuman).[5] All these epistemic formations have privileged some genres of the in/human over others. For example, environmental studies often foregrounds nonhuman beings as proper environmental objects. Humans appropriately remain in the background, as the protectors of a "nature" that is decidedly nonhuman and must, if anything, be protected from humans that are marked as environmentally destructive.[6] Injecting a good dose of humanism into my teaching, and placing the in*ter*human—as Katherine McKittrick (following Sylvia Wynter) characterizes the relationship between "Man and his human Others" alongside the inhuman, seems crucial in such an institutional context.[7]

The antihumanism of my field is of course not neutral but part of a protectionist narrative that remaps "nature" or "the wilderness" colonially. This colonial landscape at some times ignores, at others actively paves the way for, the dehumanization of improperly environmental actors who are profiled through their lack of proper appreciation of and respect for nature. Writers on environmental racism have highlighted how poor people of color, Indigenous people, and people in the global South are punished and pathologized for their improper engagement with nature/animals, namely, for survival and sustenance rather than recreation or companionship.[8] At the same time, these populations are forced to bear the harmful effects of the extraction of resources, the siting of hazardous facilities, the dumping of toxic wastes, and other forms of environmental violence. For Indigenous peoples in particular, this ironically reflects a lesser segregation from the land and a greater proximity to nonhuman beings. The need to go beyond a simple analytic of anthropocentrism is highlighted by the fact that Indigenous peoples have had to fight to stay on and live off their lands, to continue to hunt and fish, for example, against both developers and environmentalists.[9] The costs and benefits of uneven development are thus distributed unequally: those whose subjugating and overconsumptive stance to "nature" causes the greatest pollution are not the ones who pay its price.[10] Those who are paying it, meanwhile, are labeled anti-environmental.

In making sense of this "greening of hate," I am struck by its parallels with gay imperialism or queer regeneration, as I describe the confluence of formerly degenerate bodies with formerly degenerate times and places, whose "recovery" coincides with the expulsion of populations that inhabit space pathologically.[11] Just as racialized and colonized populations have been targeted as (then) too queer and (now) not queer-friendly enough, they have also been targeted as (then) too close to nature and (now) destructive of it. Indeed, the moral deficiencies of the global poor are conceived sexually and environmentally, according to neoliberal cosmopolitan standards of "progress" and "diversity." Thus, in contexts of racism, colonialism, and genocide, "anti-environmental" populations are profiled and controlled through their excessive fertility and failed heterosexuality.[12] It seems important, then, to forge accounts of the nonhuman that actively interrupt the creation of deficient and inferior surplus populations that are distinguished by their monocultural, criminal, patriarchal, homophobic, and anti-environmental dispositions.[13]

In thinking through queer inhumanism, I am struck by the celebratory uptake of the nonhuman in queer scholarship, where morbidity, monstrosity, and animality have become objects of queer regeneration and nostalgia for more murderous times and places.[14] This is complicated by writings on racism and colonialism that highlight starkly uneven life chances and vulnerabilities to "premature death."[15] How do inhuman "orientations" intersect with different proclivities toward life and death?[16] For whom might identifying with the nonhuman be too risky a move? It once again seems important to consider the uneven terms on which bodies interpellated as "queer" or as "racialized" are sorted into various biopolitical and necropolitical molds.[17] For example, the ability to embrace death presumes an ascendant subject already anchored in the realm of life.

It is thus essential to interrogate the nonhuman alongside the dehumanization of "Man's human Others" and to understand what disposes them to becoming animal's other (or object's other). There is a certain temptation to scapegoat critical race theorists as anthropocentric, correlationist dupes of the species binary with an irrational investment in humanity and a lack of acknowledgment that objectification and animalization remain necessary objects of investigation.[18] How do we steer clear of yet another loop of "vulgar constructionism"?[19] To quote an anonymous grad student, the turn to animal studies at times reflects a desire for an "Other that doesn't talk back."

Meanwhile, as Zakiyyah Jackson shows, theories of posthumanism and animal studies have much to learn from critical race studies.[20] Black people in particular have been treated as both animalistic and cruel toward animals. Reviewing Michael Lundblad's *Birth of a Jungle*, and drawing on Aimé Césaire, Frantz

Fanon, Sylvia Wynter, and others, Jackson discusses how nineteenth-century humane discourse understood "blackness as inferior to both 'the human' and 'the animal.'"[21] Contemporary variations on this theme include Morrisey's statement that "the Chinese are a subspecies" given their "treatment of animals," and current moves to ban halal slaughter as especially inhumane.[22]

A more productive entry point might be to interrogate anthropocentrism as a colonial discourse that in turn requires decolonizing. There is now a resurgence of methodologies that open up possibilities for relating to nonhuman objects and beings beyond strict spatial and categorical separations.[23] If we are interested in recovering things and beings that are continually rendered disposable as a result of colonial capitalism and cis-heteropatriarchy, why not start with anticolonial accounts of the world that have a long history of resisting both human and nonhuman erasure? Such a nonhuman turn—which would naturally be allied to Indigenous sovereignty and self-determination—would have the potential to tackle anthropocentrism and dehumanization simultaneously, as relational rather than competing or analogous paradigms.[24] Following objects around this way may well lead us to altogether different objects, and worlds.

IN/HUMAN WASTE ENVIRONMENTS

Myra Hird

The major concern of my research is waste and environments. The plural *environments* calls us to both the delineations required to understand ourselves as exterior to others (whether human or inhuman, organic or inorganic) and to imagine spaces and times in, and of which, we are part. For the past decade or so, I have been interested in, and writing about, bacteria.[25] In important ways, bacteria push humanist suppositions further than studies of animals. Animals, as Lynn Margulis liked to remind us, are "big like us" and are more easily amenable to anthropogenic ways of apprehending and assimilating them into lifeworlds that we recognize. Bacteria trouble our familiar forms of communication, identity, sociality (community organization), reproduction, sexual reproduction, movement, metabolism, and just about everything else. But what is perhaps most disquieting (and therefore interesting) is that we remain utterly dependent on these ancestors who not only created us but also now sustain our environments. After all, it is the relationships that bacteria formed with earth's original nonlife that mark the shift from Hadean to Archean and precipitated what we now call "the environment."

In previous writing, I have tried to challenge the heteronormativity (among other things) that plagues neo-Darwinism. Specifically, I have examined neo-Darwinism's assertions about the origins of sexual difference and the "place" of sex, gender, and sexuality in nature. We may push heteronormativity quite far by paying attention to animal practices of sex, sexual difference, and sexuality, but when we attend to the bacteria that (literally) make up our bodies, we are hard-pressed to sustain the categories or vocabularies on which discussions of queer or other studies depend. As such, queer studies may want to consider how focused on sex, sexual difference, and sexuality it needs, or desires, to be. Perhaps, indeed, sexual difference, sex, and sexuality are not the main story of life or the geo-bio world of which we are a part.[26]

Elsewhere I have argued that the inhuman may be put to work in queering Western cosmologies, but is not in itself (devoid of relationality) queer.[27] This dovetails Jin Haritaworn's important suggestion in this special issue that we learn more about and reflect upon black studies, indigenous studies, and environmental racism to challenge neoliberal governance and the assimilation of identities and lifeworlds that do not conform to Western forms of neocapitalism, including heteronormativity's rejection and/or assimilation of queer. In my current research, I am exploring the complexities of neoliberal southern Canadian and northern Inuit lifeworlds as they intersect through waste issues in Nunavut's capital, Iqaluit. Iqaluit's waste is a rich example of Donna Haraway's "world-making."[28] Prior to European contact, Inuit produced little, if any, material waste. Now, Iqaluit is the highest waste-producing community in the north of Canada (Canada is the highest waste-producing country in the world).[29] A unique set of structures and practices govern Iqaluit's waste landscape: neocolonialism, government policies, treaty rights, corporate interests, socioeconomic issues, climate change, language, globalization, and the material characteristics of waste and the northern landscape.

For the most part, waste in Canada's southern municipalities is managed in terms of what Isabelle Stengers calls a "validating," "verifying," or "engaging" public who are invited to participate in consultation exercises with industry and government aimed at approving one or another waste management technology.[30] Stengers describes the move from an "ignorant public" in need of educating to "consensus building" and other forms of public engagement as an "Empty Great Idea" that "will not work" because this public is always already contained and managed around capitalist, neoliberal, and scientific parameters.[31] Stengers suggests that the "small, precarious" possibility of an "objecting minority" who "in the very process of their emergence" produces "the power to object and to intervene in matters which they discover concern them."[32] Although there are certainly long-standing plans afoot to engage Inuit people as a public, so far they have failed, and waste in Iqaluit, and other communities in Nunavut, is left in plain sight on the landscape. Still in its infancy, this case study responds to Haritaworn's provocation to engage other knowledges with queer theory. I have much to learn from a cosmology uniquely oriented to time and space, from in/human animal generation and transformation, and from a public for which, perhaps, waste is not a metaphor for colonialism but *is* colonialism.

OUTER WORLDS:
THE PERSISTENCE OF RACE IN MOVEMENT "BEYOND THE HUMAN"

Zakiyyah Iman Jackson

It is now common to encounter appeals for movement beyond "the human" in diverse scholarly domains, yet the temporal and spatial connotations of this "beyond," let alone destinations, are often underexamined. Perhaps the precipitous resurgence of the "beyond" in recent years is precisely owed to its performative gesture and routinized deployments having become a beguiling habituation, a seductive doxa effectively eluding the imperative of renewed reflexivity.[33] Contra the beguiling appeal of the "beyond," I would ask: What and crucially *whose* conception of humanity are we moving beyond? Moreover, what is entailed in the very notion of a beyond? Calls to become "post" or move "beyond the human" too often presume that the originary locus of this call, its imprimatur, its appeal, requires no further examination or justification but mere execution of its rapidly routinizing imperative. In the brief space I have here, I want to caution that appeals to move "beyond the human" may actually reintroduce the Eurocentric transcendentalism this movement purports to disrupt, particularly with regard to the historical and ongoing distributive ordering of race—which I argue authorizes and conditions appeals to the "beyond," maybe even overdetermining the "beyond's" appeal.

I have argued elsewhere that, far too often, gestures toward the "post" or the "beyond" effectively ignore praxes of humanity and critiques produced by black people, particularly those praxes which are irreverent to the normative production of "the human" or illegible from within the terms of its logic. Rather than constitute a potentially critical and/or generative (human) outer world to that of Man, potentially transformative expressions of humanity are instead cast "out of the world" and thus rendered inhuman in calls for a beyond that take for granted Man's authority over the *entire* contested field pertaining to matters "human."[34] Thus praxes of humanity illegible from *within* the logic of Man are simply rendered void or made to accord with Man's patterned logics by acts of presupposition—any excess or remainder disavowed.[35]

Moreover, one cannot help but sense that there is something else amiss in the call to move "beyond the human": a refusal afoot that could be described as an attempt to move *beyond* race, and in particular blackness, a subject that I argue cannot be escaped but only disavowed or dissimulated in prevailing articulations of movement "beyond the human." Calls for movement "beyond the human" would appear to invite challenges to normative human identity and epistemic authority; one might even say that they insist rather than invite, calling into question intransigent habits of identification—at least when these challenges are posed in the name of the nonhuman. However, given that appositional and homologous (even co-constitutive) challenges pertaining to animality, objecthood, and thingliness have long been established in thought examining the existential predicament of modern racial blackness, the resounding silence in the posthumanist, object-oriented, and new materialist literatures with respect to race is remarkable, persisting even despite the reach of antiblackness into the nonhuman—*as blackness conditions and constitutes the very nonhuman disruption and/or displacement they invite.*[36]

What "the beyond's" rising momentum largely bypasses is a more comprehensive examination of the role of race in "the human's" metaphysics, or the philosophical orientation of Man. Given Man's historical horizon of possibility— slavery, conquest, colonialism—the Western metaphysical matrix has race at its center in the form of a chiasmus: the metaphysics of race ("What is the 'reality' of race?") and the racialization of the question of metaphysics ("Under whose terms will the nature of time, knowledge, space, objecthood, being, cause and effect come to be defined?"). In other words, the question of race's reality has and continues to bear directly on hierarchies of knowledge pertaining to the nature of reality itself. According to Man's needlessly racially delimited terms, the matter of racial being purportedly does the work of arbitrating epistemological questions about the meaning and significance of the (non)human in its diverse forms, including animals, machines, plants, and objects. Though the notoriously antiblack pro-

nouncements of exalted figures like G. W. F. Hegel, Immanuel Kant, or Thomas
Jefferson (for instance) mark neither the invention of metaphysics nor its conclu-
sive end, the metaphysical question of race, and that of blackness in particular as
race's status-organizing principle, marks an *innovation* in the governing terms of
metaphysics, one that would increasingly purport to resolve metaphysical questions in terms of relative proximity to the spectral figure of "the African female."[37]
Whether machine, plant, animal, or object, the nonhuman's figuration and mattering is shaped by the gendered racialization of the field of metaphysics even as
teleological finality is indefinitely deferred by the processual nature of actualiza-
tion or the agency of matter. Thus, terrestrial movement toward the nonhuman is
simultaneously movement toward blackness, whether blackness is embraced or
not, as blackness constitutes the very matter at hand.

   The question of the "beyond" not only returns us to the racialized metaphysical terrain of orders of being, temporality, spatiality, and knowledge — it
reveals that we have never left. Put more directly: precisely what order of metaphysics will we use to evaluate the being of "the human," its temporal and spatial
movement, absence or presence? The "beyond" marks (racial/ized) metaphysics'
return, its *longue durée* and spectropoetics, such that race, particularly blackness, is precisely tasked with arbitrating fundamental questions of orientation. [38]
This is the case even when we turn to mathematics and science for adjudication. I
argue that to suggest otherwise disavows both Western mathematics and science's
discursivity and the (imperial) history of these idioms' iterability *as discourse.*[39]
While I would not argue that a "physical law," for instance, could be reducible to
the machinations of human language, I am arguing that when one mobilizes the
language of "law" or "properties" it says much about the location of the speaker
and the discursive terms of the meeting of matter and meaning.[40] Thus, a call for
movement in the direction of the "beyond," issued in a manner that suggests that
this call is without location, and therefore with the appearance of incognizance
regarding its situated claims and internal limits, returns us to a Eurocentric transcendentalism long challenged.

   "Movement beyond the human" may very well entail a shift of view away
from "the human's" direction; however, accomplishing this effort will require an
anamorphic view *of* humanity, a queering of perspective and stance that mutates
the racialized terms of Man's praxis of humanism, if it is to be movement at all.
Such movement demands a redirection of the euro(andro)(anthropo)centric terms
through which perspective is understood, necessitating a disruption of (certain)
humans' efforts *to direct and monopolize the internally divided field of perspective.*
Here perspective would not arise from beyond the imperatives of viewpoint and

judgment, but *as position* or the entanglement of judgment and viewpoint. This alternative movement, a transvaluation of the human, will require a change in the underlying structure of Man's being/knowing/feeling "human" in a manner such that we no longer make any reference to the transcendentalist conception that many are eager to move beyond.[41]

INHUMANIST OCCUPATION: PALESTINE AND THE "RIGHT TO MAIM"

Jasbir K. Puar

Contemporary geopolitics of colonialism, occupation, and warfare challenge a conventionally humanist life/death opposition and elucidate the need for inhumanist analyses to make sense of what is biopolitically at stake, especially because war machines already work by manipulating the registers of the inhuman. I have been tracing the use of maiming as a deliberate biopolitical tactic on the part of Israel in the occupation of Palestine, especially as it manifested during the 51 days of Operation Protective Edge during the summer of 2014. Medical personnel in both Gaza and the West Bank reported mounting evidence of "shoot to cripple" practices of the Israeli Defense Forces (IDF), noting an increasing shift from using "traditional means" such as tear gas and rubber-coated metal to disperse crowds to "firing at . . . knees, femurs, or aiming for their vital organs."[42] The (illegal) use of flechettes and "dum dum" bullets that fragment and splinter in bones, often causing crippling for life; the policy of calorie restrictions; the bombing of numerous hospitals and a disability center; the destruction of the main electric power plant in Gaza; the flattening of homes, schools, and mosques; the targeting youth and children; and the likely use of white phosphorous, all have added greater dimension to the tactic of debilitating both bodies and infrastructures.

These practices indicate the extension of the "right to kill" claimed by states in warfare into what I am calling the "right to maim." Maiming as intentional practice expands biopolitics beyond simply the question of "right of death and power over life"; maiming becomes a primary vector by which biopolitical control is operated in colonized space, modulating not only the foldings between life and death but also human and inhuman. I am not arguing that Israel claims the actual "right" to maim in the way they claim a right to self-defense and a right to kill in warfare. I am arguing instead that by ignoring international protocol regarding medical neutrality (which Israel is bound to by the Geneva Conventions), bombing hospitals, emergency vehicles and medical personnel, preventing timely transport for ill and injured patients to medical care, and attacking crucial civilian infrastructures that provide ministrations, food, water, and electricity, Israel is covertly enacting the right to maim even as it promotes itself as attempting to avoid civilian casualties. As the death toll of Palestinians soared this summer in comparison to Israeli deaths, with 2131 Gazans killed, 501 of them children, much less spectacular and rarely commented upon yet potentially more damaging were the number of injured civilians, totaling over 10,918.[43] If slow death is conceptualized as primarily through the vector of "let die" or "make die," maiming functions as "will not let die" and "will not make die."

This relation of death to debilitation is signaled in this statement from Maher Najjar, the Deputy General of Gaza's Coastal Municipalities Water Utilities (CMWU):

> There is no water reaching any of the houses right now. We're facing a real catastrophe. Sewage pumps cannot work because the power plant has been destroyed, so we have sewage flooding the streets of Gaza. We can't assess the extent of damage as we can't even go out without risking our lives right now. . . . We have the total collapse of all essential services and there's nothing we can do about it. Believe me, it would be better if the Israelis just dropped the nuclear bomb on Gaza and get done with it. This is the worst ever assault on the Gaza Strip.[44]

Expressed here is the conviction that debilitation is a fate worse than death—death is preferable to disability—a stance that contravenes the human rights model of disability. Why maiming is especially striking in this historical moment is because in the face of the rise of disability as a recognized vulnerable identity in need of state and global human rights protections, seeking to debilitate or to further debilitate the disabled, contrasts heavily with the propagation of disability as a socially maligned condition that must be empowered to and through a liberal politics of recognition.

What kind of sovereignty is being articulated when the right to kill is enacted as the right to disable, to target both bodies and infrastructure for disablement? In part by masquerading as a "let live" vector (the IDF policy of we shoot to maim, not to kill, is often misperceived as a preservation of life), biopolitical maiming also poses as "let die" when in fact it acts as "will not let die." In this version of attenuated life, neither living nor dying is the aim. Instead, "will not let die" replaces altogether the coordinate "make live" or "let die."

This shoot to maim but not kill vector meshes well with the principle of "collateral damage," which condemns yet does not punish the unintentional killing of civilians. Nadia Abu El-Haj writes that Israeli allies "say that the Israeli army wages war with moral integrity. It doesn't target civilians. It never intends to kill them. It even warns Gazans when an attack is coming so they can get out of harm's way."[45] Abu El-Haj probes the question of "unintentionality," arguing that "most civilian deaths in urban counterinsurgency warfare may be 'unintentional,' but they are also predictable."[46] But the discussion on intentionality leaves another possibility unspoken: while the intent behind civilian deaths may be indiscernible, debatable, or absolutely transparently obvious, what may well be intentional is the activity of maiming—injuries leading to permanent debilitation that remain uncalculated within the metrics of collateral damage. As a term that emerges in 1961, and signals the "debt" of war, that which should be avoided and must be paid back, why does collateral damage disarticulate death from debilitation?

Maiming thus functions not as an incomplete death, or an accidental assault on life, but as the end goal in the dual production of permanent disability via the infliction of harm and the attrition of the life support systems that might allow populations to heal. Disablement is used to achieve the tactical aims of colonialism, not just a by-product of war, of war's collateral damage. Disablement functions on two levels: the maiming of humans within a context that is completely resource-deprived and unable to transform the cripple into the disabled; and the maiming of infrastructure in order to transform the able-bodied into disabled through the control of calories, water, electricity, health care supplies, and fuel.

The productivity of maiming—will not let/make die—is manifold. This vector, "will not let/make die" keeps the death toll numbers seemingly low on Israel's side while still depopulating the territory, as the dying after the dying, perhaps years later, would not count as a war death alongside the immediate and quick administration of war deaths. Where do the numbers of "collateral damage" end and the demarcation of "slow death" begin? As it loops into the "make live" vector, for example, debilitation becomes extremely profitable for the humanitarian aid sectors that will take on the "rehabilitation" of Gaza in the aftermath of war; many who stand to profit are Gulf states and NGO actors who are embedded in corporate economies of humanitarianism, and certainly, it must be said, Hamas and the Palestinian Authority. As a public health crisis, Gaza now represents an extension, perhaps even a perversion, of Foucault's management of health frame, as the crisis feeds into models of disaster capitalism. Thus one interpretation here is that the debilitation of Gazans is not simply capitalized upon in a neoliberal economic order that thrives on the profitability of debility, but that Gazans must be debilitated in order to make (their) life (lives) productive. In this regard, along with the right to maim, Israel is exercising a sovereign "right to repair."

IMPROBABLE MANNERS OF BEING

Eileen Joy

Although, like many scholars, I have drawn on and been inspired by the thought of many scholars working in the humanities (in different disciplines and varied theoretical modes, ranging from ethical philosophy to deconstruction to queer studies to posthumanism to critical antihumanisms to speculative realism, and beyond), one piece in particular has haunted my study and, for better or worse, has provided the impetus for all my work—on the posthuman, on the queer, and on reforming institutional life and developing practices to hopefully help to sustain intellectual misfits and vagabonds not always readily welcomed within the academy: an interview that Michel Foucault gave to the French gay press in 1981, titled "Friendship as a Way of Life." In this interview, Foucault wondered aloud if our problem today was that we had "rid ourselves of asceticism," yet "it's up to us to advance into a homosexual ascesis that would make us work on ourselves and invent . . . a manner of being that is still improbable."[47] In David Halperin's formulation of Foucault's thinking at this time, this project of ascesis would be a continual process of becoming-queer: "an identity without an essence, not a given condition but a horizon of possibility, an opportunity for self-transformation, a queer potential," which I would also name as a posthuman potential—one that resonates with the late thought of Eve Kosofsky Sedgwick when she was thinking about intermediate ontologies (such as the weather) in Marcel Proust and how his novels produce and comment on surprise, refreshment, and new ("celestially nourishing") relationalities.[48]

    This work on the self that one "happily never attains," which is also a concern for and care of the self, importantly has something to do with freedom as well—a term not often associated with Foucault's thought, especially by those who oversimplify his entire oeuvre as being only about the ways in which various structures and techniques of power produce knowledge and individuals, with apparently no escape route out of the power-knowledge nexus. Yet much of Foucault's late writings were precisely concerned with "the definition of practices of freedom" and ethics as "the conscious practice of freedom"—with freedom here to be distinguished from the idea of liberation (the setting free of selves that have supposedly always been there and were simply repressed, in hiding, etc.). For Foucault, freedom was "the ontological condition of ethics," and ethics is "the form that freedom takes when it is informed by reflection."[49] And what this also means is that, for Foucault (as well as the late classical writers, such as Epictetus, Seneca, and Marcus Aurelius, whom he was reading at the time), ethics is a practice (an ascetics, or set of *exercises*) of freedom that revolves around the fundamental imperative: "Take care of yourself." One of the tragedies, I would argue, of social and cultural life in the present (and of gay life, more narrowly), is that we have never really taken up, collectively, Foucault's call to work on ourselves in order to invent improbable manners of being, new modes and styles of living, polymorphous affective intensities, and new relational virtualities and friendships. Some of us have devoted much of our lives to cultivating new relational modes and the company of misfits (an agonistic yet joyful venture, to be sure, in which we exult in the exquisite difficulties of becoming-with-others), but when I reread Foucault's 1981 interview, as I often do, I mourn that, as Adam Phillips has written, we have "not had the courage of [our] narcissism"—we have not found "a version of narcissism that is preservative at once of survival and pleasure," which "would be to have the courage of one's wish for more life rather than less."[50] Thus, in my own career, I have tried to answer Foucault's call, both by delineating the traces of and possibilities for these "improbable modes" in literary and historical texts, and also by developing new para-institutional modes for intellectual, cultural, and social work.

For myself, the posthuman and the queer are, and always have been, importantly enmeshed with, and even coeval to, each other. As a medievalist (and one whose work has often been concerned with intellectual history), I am very interested in tracing what might be called the fragmentary and incomplete documents of the fractal archives of thought, and I think that the homosexual, the gay, the queer, and the posthuman have been dancing with each other for a long while, in different ways, and this is probably because historically (and as is also true with other categories of supposed "difference," such as race, gender, ethnicity, class, etc.), so many marginalized groups have always been "less than human," and there are two ways (well, really more, but for discussion's sake . . .) to deal with this: one is the activist path where you fight back for more rights as a fully fledged human, and the other is the (perhaps) more theoretical-academic (and risky heterotopic) path where you decide to take the marker of "less than human" as an opportunity to finally bid the human adieu and start inventing those "improbable" virtualities and "diagonal lines" that Foucault talked about in his 1981 interview (this also accounts for some of the antagonisms within and beyond the academy for those working on rights-based activism and those who are supposedly living in some theoretical aerie of posthuman thought—a simplification, of course, and also, there go a whole series of woefully missed encounters). It is worth noting the article by Jeffrey J. Cohen and Todd R. Ramlow in *rhizomes*, published in 2005–6, "Pink Vectors of Deleuze: Queer Theory and Inhumanism," where they wrote that Gilles Deleuze's "greatest challenge to queer theory is something that seems almost recidivist in his work: his animism, his belief that the entire world constitutes a non-anthropomorphic, infinitely connective machinery of desire."[51] But why, more particularly, is this a challenge to queer theory? For Cohen and Ramlow, it is because (at least at the time that they wrote their essay) queer theory has sometimes been circumscribed within a "merely human frame," but I would suggest, again, that the queer and the nonanthropomorphic have always been importantly entwined and that the queer is always pushing against the limits of not just the "merely" but also the "overdetermined" human.

It is precisely the intersection—or is it a fractal coastline?—between connective desire, the queer, and what might be called the space of posthuman interbeing where I locate my own desires, professionally and personally. Especially in my para-academic activist work with the BABEL Working Group (since 2004) and now also with punctum books and punctum records (since 2011), the key has been in crafting a queer and posthumanist politics that is fully intent on creating new para- and out-stitutional spaces in which anything at all might unfold that otherwise could not find a means, mode, or space for expression. My projects connected to these groups aim for queer natality, monstrous births, and all manner of becomings. This is to labor for new spaces beyond the traditional human (and humanist) spheres (such as the humanities or the university), but that are still tied to those spaces if we believe, and I do, that so-called humanistic inquiry is still critical to the projects of freedom and becoming-otherwise, and that the human, however partially, still remains as an important and highly localized site of awareness and articulation, and also as a platform for new forms of love and affection that might be generative of new modes of being, not just for ourselves, but for others who are wayward, lost, abandoned, and so forth. In terms of my written scholarship— especially lately, to craft new modes of "weird reading" under the aegis of object-oriented and speculative realist thought—the queer and the posthuman are fully operative as well, because a large part of my project is to produce readings of literary texts outside humanist-centered, historicist frames of reference in order to (hopefully) unleash any literary text's potential for becoming-otherwise. Part of my interest in speculative realism and object-oriented ontology is precisely because I see the (acid trip) modes of thought opened in these intellectual realms as possible allies in rewiring the sensorium of reading with an eye toward increasing the pleasures and enjoyment of not just reading but of a heightened contact with the world itself, in all of its extrahuman (yet still co-implicate) vibrations. This is to ultimately affirm a pluralism of being and worlds—a move both queer and political, human and beyond the human at once.

OBJECTHOOD, AVATARS, AND THE LIMITS OF THE HUMAN

Uri McMillan

New materialists' calls to upend the hierarchical orderings of humans, nonhuman objects, and things has, unfortunately, not held as true for a truly radical "reorder of things" in the balkanized academy; this is especially true of the bounded disciplinary cells that continue to separate much of posthumanist thought from theories of racial embodiment.[52] In this vein, I concur with Zakiyyah Iman Jackson in her critique of the failure to interrogate critical race studies in much of new materialist thought and the resultant and ongoing violence of such an occlusion, particularly when theorizing blackness has long required considering existential questions of life and death, the limits of humanity, and a stultifying thingness. After all, as Alexander G. Weheliye notes in his discussion of Jamaican writer and cultural theorist Sylvia Wynter, "Within the context of her work, it is the human—or different genres of the human—that materializes as the object of knowledge in the conceptual mirror of black studies." Thus, in Wynter's work (as well as that of Hortense Spillers), the dismantling of Man as the universal human—a distinction that gains traction through its very barring of those designated as nonhumans or not-quite-humans (particularly black subjects and especially black women)—surfaces as sine qua non to the praxis of black studies.[53] The deaths of Eric Garner and Michael Brown at the hands of (at the time of this writing, unindicted) police officers—on July 17, 2014, and August 9, 2014, respectively—belie all too clearly the effects of these cleavages to those denied the spoils of full per-sonhood. Meanwhile films and novels grouped under the rubric of Afrofuturism consider questions of blackness, space, and time (and repeatedly, science)—while also rebuking the primacy of Western civilizations, they offer striking possibilities for pushing new materialisms into questions (both earth-based and interplanetary) of diaspora, nation, and futurity.[54] Meanwhile, building on all this work, Hershini Bhana Young elegantly pushes posthumanism into the realm of the sonic and visual art, via the nineteenth-century performer Thomas Wiggins (a.k.a. "Blind Tom") and the "fungible cyborgs" of the artist John Jennings. She argues that the sonic enables "a staging of the black subject as both within and outside of moder-nity, as excluded from traditional liberal discourses of the human and therefore having a special relationship with the category of post-human."[55] In this way, she suggests, the black subject—made, historically, to be both object and person—is prosthetic and human, flesh and machine. In short, theories of "object life" are at their most fecund, productive, and expansive when considered *with*, rather than *instead* of, black cultural studies.[56]

Objecthood, like queer theory itself, slips across several disciplinary gene-alogies. Objecthood is emerging as a concept in queer theory through its intertwin-ing with material culture. Scott Herring, in a recent essay on hoarding, and Drew Sawyer, in an essay on Crisco, provocatively fuse queer studies and thing theory. The former's attention to sexual nonconformity and the latter's focus on material objects combine to produce a *queer objecthood*, attuned to matter gone deviant.[57] Thus queer objecthood here encompasses the queer object relations inherent in excessive accumulation as well as the perverse uses of Crisco's viscosity for fry-ing *and* fucking. In a much different register, the writings of Frantz Fanon, Aimé Césaire, and Hortense Spillers, while distinct, coalesce in their suggestion that the most brutal effects of chattel slavery and colonization were their joint efforts to deny black diasporic subjects full access to "being."[58] While none of the three foreground the term *objecthood*, the terms that they *do* use, most explicitly Cés-aire's *thingification*, index the forceful disciplining of these subjects into a dif-ferent type of humanity, a lesser-than-human. It is this legacy of black abjection and the abhorrent queering of subjectivity that both Darieck Scott and Christina Sharpe take up.[59] While Scott recuperates Fanon, both make use of queer theories of shame and pleasure's intertwinings to discuss the "monstrous intimacies" of slavery and the pleasures-in-abjection that very well may be the wellsprings of what it means to be postslavery subjects.[60]

In my own work, I seek to bridge the chasm between a dehumanizing objecthood, on the one hand, and an embodied self-possession, on the other, by reimagining objecthood as a performance-based strategy that challenges notions of what constitutes black subjectivity. *Performing objecthood*, I argue, is a process that enables black women to transform themselves into art objects. Performing objecthood is a world making, one that envisions the capacity for agency in, paradoxically, becoming and performing as an object.[61] The performers I discuss in my forthcoming book *Embodied Avatars* activate objecthood in several ways across time: in collaboration with prosthetic technologies and freak show theatrical conventions in the nineteenth century, conceptual art-based performance works and art world activism in the twentieth, and black camp and video art in the twenty-first.[62] Performing objecthood, whether in the Great Exhibition of 1851 in London or in the streets of 1970s New York City, is not the negation of art (à la Michael Fried) but a potent leitmotif of black performance art.[63]

If these black women performers seem ancillary to our discussions here, I caution that they are not; they are indeed participants, albeit overlooked, in the dense relationalities and ecologies that these new materialisms seek to point us toward. I want, in other words, to push past the too-easy assertion that a vital materialism will act as a safety net for those at the very bottom of personhood.[64] I ask us to consider these performers as actors who work with the proverbial muck of these queered object relations; they create sets of performances with high political stakes, whether to escape from the grasp of chattel slavery in 1849 or to subversively critique the racism of white feminists in 1980. And they persist in doing so via the provocative use of avatars. *Avatar*, a term from Hindu mythology, is derived from the Sanskrit word *avatara*; its translation denotes the descent of a deity to earth in order to be reincarnated in a human form. Entering the English language at the end of the eighteenth century, it eventually acquired a much more banal, technological meaning. The word *avatar* was first used in 1985 to describe virtual persona, specifically a graphic representation of a person—a humanlike figure, usually—controlled by a person via a computer.[65] Taken together, these two seemingly divergent meanings gesture toward how avatars both duplicate and *displace* the human.

I redeploy both connotations of avatar—spiritual reincarnation and second selves—in the use of black performance art; I use it as an analytic that, at once, captures the shared manipulation of alterity by these cultural subjects, the transubstantiation of these performances across different representational forms and their abilities to shift across time.

Avatars suggest a slippage between the "other" and us, a reaching beyond the limits of where our bodies supposedly end. In this formulation, the "subject" is not a bounded entity but a permeable one. Ann Weinstone terms this an *avatar body*, or a "zone of relationality" in which "the categories of self and other are rendered undecidable."[66] I describe the manipulation of avatars by black women as a repeated tactic of multiplying the self, circumventing limits on how and where to *do* one's body. And their porousness, across the subject-object line as well as time itself, is useful for our discussion of queer inhumanism. They are utile in thinking through what it means to be (and to partially reject) "human," and they pivot in directions (be they disciplinary or ontological or temporal) not yet possible to map, let alone perceive. Exceeding delineations between the past and the present, slipping between the real and the virtual, and violating zones between objecthood and subjecthood, avatars suggest the paradoxical powers inherent in willfully alienating oneself from the limits of the human.

TRANSING THE QUEER (IN)HUMAN

Susan Stryker

My very first article, "My Words to Victor Frankenstein above the Village of Chamounix," published here in *GLQ* twenty years ago, addressed questions of transgender embodiment and affect through the figuration of (in)human monstrosity. I have stayed close ever since to the themes and approaches laid out in that initial work, and have noted with interest how current queer critical attention to the nonhuman world of objects, and to the weird potential becomings of vital materialities and matterings, resonate with the concerns I addressed back then.

At the time, my goal was to find some way to make the subaltern speak. Transsexuals such as myself were then still subordinated to a hegemonic interlocking of cissexist feminist censure and homosexual superiority, psycho-medical pathologization, legal proscription, mass media stereotyping, and public ridicule. The only option other than reactively saying "no we're not" to every negative assertion about us was to change the conversation, to inaugurate a new language game. My strategy for attempting that was to align my speaking position with everything by which "they" abjected us. It was to forgo the human, a set of criteria by which I could only fail as an embodied subject. It was to allow myself to be moved by the centrifugal force pushing me away from the anthropocentric, to turn that expulsive energy into something else through affective labor, and to return it with a disruptive difference. I embraced "darkness" as a condition of interstitiality and unrepresentability beyond the positive registers of light and name and reason, as a state of transformable negativity, as a groundless primordial resource. As I said then, "I feel no shame in acknowledging my egalitarian relationship with non-human material being. Everything emerges from the same matrix of possibilities."[67] Speaking as-if Frankenstein's monster—an articulate, surgically constructed (in)human biotechnological entity—felt like a clever, curiously cognizable, strategy for speaking as a transsexual, for talking back to hegemonic forces and finding a way around.

I like to put parentheses around the "in" in (in)human because what appeals to me most about monstrosity as I have lived it is its intimate vacillation with human status, the simultaneously there-and-not-there nature of a relationship between the two. (In)human suggests the gravitational tug of the human for bodies proximate to it, as well as the human's magnetic repulsions of things aligned contrary to it. It speaks to the imperiousness of a human standard of value that would measure all things, yet finds all things lacking and less-than in comparison to itself; at the same time, it speaks to the resistance of being enfolded into the human's inclusive exclusions, to fleeing the human's embrace. (In)human thus cuts both ways, toward remaking what human has meant and might yet come to be, as well as toward what should be turned away from, abandoned in the name of a better ethics.

Over two decades, I have worked to establish transgender studies as a recognized interdisciplinary academic field by editing journals and anthologies, organizing conferences, making film, conducting historical research, training students, hiring faculty, and building programs. My goal has been to create venues in which trans-voices can be in productive dialogue with others in ways that reframe the conditions of life for those who—to critically trans (rather than critically queer) Ruth Gilmore's definition of racism—experience "the state-sanctioned or extralegal production and exploitation of group-differentiated vulnerability to premature death" because of their gender nonnormativity.[68] This, for me, has been an "other conversation" that becomes possible when monsters speak. I consider working to enable more felicitous conditions of possibility for more powerful acts of transgender speech to be vital work that nevertheless carries many risks: it can bring too much that might better remain wild to the attention of normativizing forces, produce forms of gender intelligibility that foreclose alternatives and constrain freedom, consolidate identities in rigid and hierarchized forms, police discourses through institutionalization, and privilege some speakers over others. Yet I still believe that advancing transgender studies within the academy is a risk worth taking, if we bring our most radical visions of justice with us as we try to create something new, something better than the past has bequeathed us. I see the positive work of building transgender studies as one way to address half of the (in) human problematic: to abolish what "human" historically has meant, and to begin to make it mean otherwise through the inclusion of what it casts out (without, of course, abjecting something else in the process).

At the same time, in the (in)human problematic's other dimension, I am eager to make work with as much distance from the anthropic as possible. This is what I have tried to explore in the other half of my working life, through my involvement with the Somatechnics Research Network. Coined by a group of inter-disciplinary critical and cultural studies scholars at Macquarie University in Syd-ney who were inspired by Nikki Sullivan's brilliant deconstructive work on body modification, *somatechnics* emerged as a shorthand label for a robust ontological account of embodiment as process.[69] Its conversations draw on Maurice Merleau-Ponty's phenomenology of the body as sedimented habitual practices, as well as on rich Australian traditions of feminist philosophies of the body, and critical stud-ies of whiteness, race, and (post)coloniality.[70] Its ethical stance draws much from Jean-François Lyotard's *differend* and Emmanuel Levinas's stranger at the door, while its welcoming of strangeness owes much to queer and crip sensibilities.[71]

As a portmanteau word (*soma*, body, + *technics*, tools or techniques), somatechnics seeks to name the mutually constitutive and inextricably enmeshed nature of embodiment and technology, of being(s) and the means or modes of their (or its) becoming. Like Donna Haraway's "natureculture," somatechnics dispenses with the additive logic of the "and" to signify the nonseparateness of phenomena that are misrepresented as the conjunction of separable parts.[72] It plays along-side the Derridean "always already" of embodiment's technologization, as well as Bernard Stiegler's notion of the body's "originary technicity." At the same time, somatechnics provides a name for the "whole intermediary cluster of relations" that Michel Foucault tells us traverses the capillary spaces linking the anatamo-political and biopolitical poles of biopower, that constitute a nexus of techniques of subjective individualization and techniques of totalizing control of populations.[73] It is the circuitry, and the pulse, through which materiality flexes itself into new arrangements.

Jami Weinstein is right to point out that somatechnics can carry forward a humanist remainder to whatever extent it concerns itself solely with people. But why must our interest in bodies be confined to human bodies alone? Following Giorgio Agamben, we can acknowledge that within the metaphysics of Western biopolitics, the human emerges precisely where bare biological life (*zoe*) is simultaneously captured by the political order (*polis*) to potentiate as the *good life* while also being excluded as *mere life*, the life shared with animals and other entities in the kingdom of the living.[74] The threshold of biopolitical viability thus opens in two directions. Somatechnics, as a frame of reference in which body+milieu+means-of-becoming are constantly trading places and trying on each other's clothes, has the capacity to render the human nothing more than a local instantiation of more fundamental processes under special conditions. If transgender looks back to the human with the goal of making it something else, somatechnics faces a posthuman future.

In these repeated trans-movements across the cut of (in)human difference, we find a potential for agential intra-action through which something truly new, something queer to what has come before, begins to materialize itself.

AN INDIGENOUS REFLECTION ON
WORKING BEYOND THE HUMAN/NOT HUMAN

Kim TallBear

The multiple projects within my knowledge production repertoire are constituted of threads of inquiry woven and looping in multiple directions, away from and back into the growing fabric. A new project always begins inside the coming together of another. It is thus difficult to name discrete research efforts. But let me attempt to describe a few of them as they might cohere under the label "queer (in)human-isms." Although to be clear, from an indigenous standpoint, my work should not be seen as queering indigenous practice. Rather it should be seen as a twenty-first-century indigenous knowledge articulation, period.[75] I produce knowledge in concert with other indigenous thinkers both inside and outside the academy with the goal of supporting expanded notions and practices of indigenous self-determination. This is not to say that all indigenous thinkers will agree with my particular indigenous knowledge claims. We are diverse thinkers. On the other hand, my intellectual work might be seen to queer whitestream disciplinary think-ing and ontologies in the United States.

My work, which is also newly intelligible within a "queer inhumanisms" framework, stretches back to 1994–2001. During those years I worked as an environmental planner and policy specialist for US tribal governments, national tribal organizations, and federal agencies on projects related to waste management at the federal nuclear weapons complex. In addition to funding technical and policy work related to nuclear waste cleanup, the Department of Energy had begun funding human genome mapping research around 2000. The indigenous peoples' research institute I worked for at that time won a DOE grant to facilitate workshops with tribal program managers and community members to assess the implications for US indigenous peoples of human genome mapping. Via work related to remediating contamination of nonhuman communities by humans during the Cold War, I stumbled into forms of inquiry that I continued in graduate school and which involved "purity" and "contamination" narratives involving not "the environment" but human bodies and populations.

Of course my new fields of inquiry related to human genome research on indigenous peoples' bodies cannot sustain a separation between human and non-human. But at that moment in 2000, I saw myself shifting from working on projects related to human-on-less-privileged-human and human-on-nonhuman relations (the contamination of tribal communities and their lands by white-controlled corporations and federal facilities) to a project related to the objectifying and exploitation by a more powerful group (scientists and colonial universities and federally funded researchers) of a set of less powerful humans (indigenous peoples) in the course of human genome research. I remember being confused as to why and how I was making such a transition. I was terribly fascinated with the mapping of the human genome and implications for indigenous peoples. Perhaps, I asked myself, I was not sufficiently directed or committed in my previous work as an environmental planner? I wanted to be a committed environmental thinker, a form of work that combined both pragmatic, sometimes approaching activist, sensibilities with scientific and theoretical knowledges. Perhaps I was a humanist (human exceptionalist?) after all. Doubts in hand, I could not stop myself from taking what I thought was a new intellectual path. But from my vantage point in 2014, I see but one circuitous path through multiple intellectual cultures and communities to arrive at a place where the line between human and nonhuman becomes nonsensical. I work at these complex intersections.

1. The coconstitution of human genome diversity research concepts and practices with concepts of race, indigeneity, and indigenous governance of science. This is my longest-standing project and resulted in a monograph, *Native American DNA: Tribal Belonging and the False Promise of Genetic Science*, published in September 2013 by the University of Minnesota Press. The book treats the politics of race and "population" that

inform contemporary genome research on indigenous populations, particularly how different parties (scientists themselves, DNA test consumers, and family tree researchers) use DNA concepts to rescript concepts of Native American identity and history. The book ends with a look at how Native American tribes and Canadian Aboriginal peoples have sought to govern genome science research, thus producing some of the world's most innovative bioethical interventions. I also advise multiple scientists and biomedical ethics centers on genomics and indigenous peoples' governance. I hope to expand my advising work to indigenous communities that are grappling with DNA testing for enrollment and with potential genome research involving their citizenries. I recently advised, for example, the Constitutional Reform Committee of the Red Lake Nation (Red Lake Band of Chippewa Indians) in Minnesota. In addition to the book, this research has also resulted in a half-dozen peer-reviewed publications and several policy commentary and op-ed pieces. In addition, I have presented several dozen talks on this research at universities and science museums; at humanities, social science, and genome science conferences; and to indigenous governance and genome policy audiences in the United States, Canada, Australia, New Zealand, and the UK. I have also done nearly two dozen media interviews on radio and television in the United States, Canada, Great Britain, and Sweden.

2. Pipestone materiality and relations. Ceremonial pipes—called "peace pipes" in US popular culture—are sacred to Dakota, Lakota, and Nakota peoples (often called "Sioux"). Pipes and other objects are carved from pipestone, or "catlinite," as it was named by science, a soft yet durable stone that is deep red in color. Indigenous carvers have longed viewed the quarries in southeastern Minnesota as a prime source of the stone. In 1937 the US National Park Service created Pipestone National Monument in response to white settler encroachment on the quarries. Today, the US Park Service governs quarrying at the site, allowing only Native Americans belonging to federally recognized tribes to quarry there. It also operates a visitors' center with public access where Dakota carvers of pipes and other objects demonstrate their skills for park visitors daily.

My previous work on the cultures and politics of Native American DNA research paves the way for an examination of pipestone, a material with, as I describe below, legendary status as an artifact of "blood" of a people. A shared narrative, that of the vanishing or dying Native, has framed the response to mul-

tiple literal and figurative bodies—indigenous bodies, the land, and the indigenous body politic—by the state. Like bioscientists in the twentieth and twenty-first
centuries with their imperative to bleed indigenous peoples before it was too late,
a nineteenth-century Euro-American painter and early twentieth-century geolo-
gists and government agents saw the place where the red stone lies as an artifact
of a waning culture and time. They produced a "National Monument" to conserve
it. US Park Service pamphlets from the Pipestone quarry represent pipes as arti-
facts, as craft objects, and detail the history of white incursion in the area and the
regulatory response of the US government. They also reference the site's geologic
uniqueness. Such regulatory and material histories are important to our contemporary understanding of the Pipestone site.

   But like producing indigenous biological samples that come to stand for living peoples, making monuments and doing science risk deanimating the red stone.
From a Dakota standpoint, the pipestone narrative is one of renewed peoplehood.
A flood story tells of the death of a people and the pooling of their blood at this
site, thus resulting in the stone's red color and its description as sacred. The stone
is sometimes spoken of as a relative. Unlike with blood or DNA, pipestone does
not possess a cellular vibrancy. Yet without it, prayers would be grounded, human
social relations impaired, and everyday lives of quarriers and carvers depleted of
the meaning they derive from working with stone. Just like indigenous people who
insist on their continuing survival and involvement with their DNA, indigenous
quarriers and carvers, medicine people, and everyday people who pray insist on
living with the red stone daily. And they make decisions—some of them seen as
compromised—about how to best work with the vibrant objects of their attention.
Just as some indigenous people agree to engage in research or commercial activities related to DNA, others sell pipestone jewelry and craft pieces to earn a living
while also holding the stone and pipes carved from it as sacred. In this research,
which I have just begun, I investigate via archival research, interviews, and participant observation in the visitors' center and in the quarries (I am a member of a
federally recognized tribe) the extent to which the blood red stone and indigenous
relationships with it have been frozen in time or facilitated in more lively ways by
both the state and by indigenous peoples' ongoing engagement with the site into
the twenty-first century. The book produced from this research will engage the
Pipestone site and the stone itself from multiple standpoints and narratives: indigenous, regulatory, and scientific.

   3. Indigenous, feminist, and queer theory approaches to critical "animal
   studies" and new materialisms. The Pipestone project is set within this
   broader research agenda in which I have recently begun to theorize in the

area of indigenous, feminist, and queer theory approaches to animal studies and the new materialisms. In 2011 I co-organized with the Science, Technology, and Society Center at UC Berkeley a symposium on indigenous and other new approaches to animal studies, an already critical field in which thinkers dismantle hierarchies in the relationships of "Westerners" with their nonhuman others. I was also part of another UC Berkeley symposium in 2012 on the new materialisms where I did a talk on the role of indigenous thought. Both symposia helped mark a space for the role of indigenous thought in these related and burgeoning areas of contemporary social theory and new ethnographic practices. They also helped network me with other scholars who likewise see the advantages of inserting indigenous thought and practices into these academic conversations. The recent move to "multi-species ethnography" applies anthropological approaches to studying humans and their relations with nonhumans—beings such as dogs, bears, cattle, monkeys, bees, mushrooms, and microorganisms. Such work is both methodologically and ethically innovative in that it highlights how organisms' livelihoods are coconstituted with cultural, political, and economic forces. But the field has starting points that only partially contain indigenous standpoints. First of all, indigenous peoples have never forgotten that nonhumans are agential beings engaged in social relations that profoundly shape human lives. In addition, for many indigenous peoples, their nonhuman others may not be understood in even critical Western frameworks as *living.* "Objects" and "forces" such as stones, thunder, or stars are known within our ontologies to be sentient and knowing persons (this is where new materialisms intersects with animal studies). Indigenous approaches also critique settler colonialism and its management of nonhuman others. These and other newer approaches clearly link violence against animals to violence against particular humans who have historically been linked to a less-than-human or animal status.

4. Indigenous thought and the politics of nature and sexuality. Following conversations with critical animal studies and new materialisms scholarly communities, I have most recently become interested in the overlap between constructions of "nature" and "sexuality." This includes a foray into "queer ecologies" literature (which will increasingly inform my graduate teaching) that queers environmental scholarship and, conversely, greens queer theory. I throw into the mix a greening of indigenous queer theory. As I challenge Western politics of nature, it has become clear that I cannot avoid a similar analysis of sexuality. Nature and sex have both been defined according to a nature-culture divide. With the rise of scientific authority and management

approaches, both sex and nature were rendered as discrete, coherent, troublesome, yet manageable objects. Both are at the heart of struggles involving ideas of purity and contamination, life and death, but which only scientifically trained experts or rational subjects (read historically white, Western men) have been seen as fit to name, manage, and set the terms of legitimate encounter. There are common challenges to democratizing the science and representations surrounding both concepts. Again, indigenous thought has something to offer. I plan to conduct humanities-based and ethnographic inquiry around this topic. I am interested in how indigenous stories—I may start with Dakota stories—speak of social relations with nonhumans, and how such relations, although they sometimes approach what we in the West would call "sex," do not cohere into "sexuality" as we know it in Western modernity. Our traditional stories also portray nonhuman persons in ways that do not adhere to another meaningful modern category, the "animal." They feature relationships in which human and nonhuman persons, and nonhuman persons between themselves, harass and trick one another; save one another from injury or death; prey on, kill, and sometimes eat one another; or collaborate with one another. Our stories avoid the hierarchical nature-culture and animal-human split that has enabled domineering human management, naming, controlling, and "saving" of nature. I expect that such theoretical work in indigenous environmental and sexuality studies will link back to support applied thinking about how to democratize environmental science practices and regulation in much the same way that my social theoretical work around the genome sciences links back to applied thinking on how to construct new bioethical frameworks that incorporate indigenous thought, both "traditional" and "modern."

5. Constituting knowledge across cultures of expertise and tradition: indigenous bioscientists. With National Science Foundation (NSF) funding, in 2011 and 2012 I conducted anthropological fieldwork with indigenous bioscientists to examine how they navigate different cultures of expertise and tradition, both scientific communities and tribal communities. I also focus on scientists-turned-regulators and other policymakers in government agencies and in professional organizations who act as culture and policy brokers between indigenous and scientific knowledge communities. I am particularly interested to see if there are cross-fertilizations of genomics and indigenous knowledges and values as the field and laboratory are made more diverse. Do new research questions, theories, methods, and governing arrangements emerge when indigenous peoples act as researchers and not simply as subjects?

POSTHUMOUSLY QUEER

Jami Weinstein

Critical Life Studies (CLS) strikes at the heart of the dilemma that contemporary critical theory has been circling around: namely, the negotiation of the human, its residues, a priori configurations, the stubborn persistence of humanism in structures of thought, and the figure of life as a constitutive focus for ethico-political and onto-epistemological questions. Despite attempts by many critical theorists to demonstrate the inadequacy of the concept of the Human to account for and respond to ongoing social injustices and global crises, hasty attempts to repudiate humanism (and organicism) *tout court* and devise more adequate theoretical concepts have overlooked the fact that the humanistic concept *life* is preconfigured or immanent within the supposedly new conceptual leap. The concept life is maintained as an unchallenged premise and a non-negotiable given—above all, life itself is valued and must be preserved and protected.

In a clever articulation that evokes the emphasis on purity, Elaine L. Graham formulates these universals under the guise of "ontological hygiene."[76] This concept underscores the extent to which, as Jin Haritaworn argues, we must "forge accounts of the queer non-human that actively interrupt the creation of deficient and surplus populations" (p. 6 Dossier), those contaminated or impure identities that fall outside the purview of the humanist subject. This subject is, of course, the one positioned as the (imagined, unmarked) norm, the barometer against which all others are measured in order to determine the extent to which they would be considered human. In other words, the Other gets figured as an immutable, *a priori* alterity. Since what is deemed human is only such in virtue of being positioned as a negation in that binary alterity schema, humanism delineates a normative standard of legibility by which all others are read, assessed, controlled, disciplined, and assigned to fixed and hierarchical social statuses. And this administration of norms is the justificatory linchpin of often violent practices of exclusion, discrimination, and oppression.

Purity discourses have been deployed in many an oppressive politics and to a certain extent provide the motivation for moving from identity politics to queer politics. Likewise a plethora of theorists have endeavoured to re-envision the ontological binaries that reinforce these discourses. Donna Haraway, for example, strives to figure this difference differently by reconceptualizing multiplicity outside binary configurations and challenging "the 'sanctity of life'" concealed in the "anxiety over the pollution of lineages." She argues that purity claims are xenophobic and are "at the origin of racist discourse in European cultures as well as at the heart of linked gender and sexual anxiety."[77] Similarly, in my recent work, I refer to what I call *The New Wild West* in order to gesture toward how the underlying ontological assumptions about the human and the life that allegedly constitutes it is a particularly Western model. The phrase is also meant to capture how vital risk management strategies have transformed alongside politics and ontologies of the human. The current focus on microbes, hygiene, sanitizing, purity—for example, children being doused with hand sanitizer dozens of times a day—epitomizes this shifting landscape. In other words, hand sanitizing becomes the new "duck and cover" in tandem with modulations that both transfigure biopolitics into micro-biopolitics and control societies, and refashion notions of the bounded, autonomous, penetrable human into a human that is porous, invisibly invaded, and itself a potential biological threat. This New Wild West motif resonates both with the sanitized, pure, hygienic vision of the 1950's North American housewife and with the tropes of so many racist, colonial, and missionary programs. Consider the "one drop rule," anti-miscegenation/racial purity campaigns, and any number of so-called "civilizing" practices of colonizers and missionaries.

Microbes, like queers, women, and people of color, both disturb and reinforce established notions of purity and ontologically hygienic portraits of the human and its handmaiden, life. However, as Myra Hird argues, bacteria are not: "amenable to anthropogenic ways of apprehending and assimilating . . . into lifeworlds that we recognize. Bacteria trouble our familiar forms of communication, sociality (community structure), reproduction, sexual reproduction, movement, metabolism, and just about everything else" (p. 8 Dossier). It is partly following Hird that I have shifted my focus to the remnants of humanism buried in the concept *life itself.* We could say that life as we know it is a habit—one that strictly frames the limits of who gets interpreted as Human, and one that must be nervously reiterated in order to reinforce those limits. As such, it may be more apt to talk in terms of the *posthumous* than posthuman, inhuman, or nonhuman, thus deframing the manifold investments in life, breaking the habit, and refuting humanism more exhaustively. Posthumous life pushes the envelope by exposing the legacies of humanism still haunting us in the specter of life—even in our posthuman theories and analyses.

We must, however, heed Zakiyyah Iman Jackson's caution, "that appeals to move 'beyond the human' may actually reintroduce the very Eurocentric transcendentalism [we] purport to disrupt" (p. 11 Dossier). Bearing this in mind, it is important to highlight that, while the concept of posthumous adds "death of life" to the lineage of pronouncements that include the "death of God" and "death of Man," it does so in order to inflect the vestigial humanism lingering in the shared, and often veiled, allegiance to a nonnegotiable, proto-figure *life*, even among non-Eurocentric, non-heteronormative critical positions (i.e., the ontological turn, the affective turn, new materialism, neovitalism, somatechnics, and women, gender, feminist, trans, queer, critical race, postcolonial, posthuman, and animal studies). Further, by adopting the assemblage I have named *critical life studies*, we can effectively queer those very academic identities (turns and studies) that have in effect become the "LGBTQI" of academe. By refiguring the notion of life critically—outside the orbit and primacy of the human and vigilante to its inheritances and organic forms—critical life studies aims to thus foster a more expansive, less sectarian, *queer* engagement with critical theory.

Claire Colebrook explains that theory, "far from being an academic enterprise that we can no longer afford to indulge, is the condition and challenge of the twenty-first century or age of extinction: 'we' are finally sensing both our finitude as a world-forming and world-destroying species, and sensing that whatever we must do or think cannot be confined or dictated by our finitude."[78] Indeed, in the face of this sense of annihilation, there is a resurgence of research directed toward issues of life—albeit a *bios theoretikos*, or theories of particular lives. Might we not gesture instead to a *zoe theoretikos*, or theories of life itself not locatable in particular bodies or objects, not pluralizable, as we are propelled to consider the world without humans, without life?

In conclusion, and following José Esteban Muñoz's astute diagnosis, I argue that thinking beyond and outside the habit of the Human (and life), is a relentless struggle. It is the necessary but impossible challenge of striving to carve out a "something else" that might never be ultimately ascertainable. However, despite the incommensurability of posthumous (queer) life, untangling and theorizing it is a fundamental step toward providing avenues of escape from, and resistance to, the recalcitrant, contemporary praxes of life and the mechanisms deployed for controlling it. We must continue to destabilize our life comfort zone, remain impure and contaminated, and direct our efforts toward the posthumously queer—the queer futurity foreclosed by humanisms, vitalisms, and identity politics of all stripes. Only then may we hope to furnish an aperture into new and queer futures and the prospects for living that constitute them.

IN/HUMAN—OUT/HUMAN

Jack Halberstam

1. 1969. A man landed on the moon. One small step and all that. I remember it well, I was eight years old and it was the first significant interaction I had with television, with the planetary, with awe, with skepticism, with the outer edges of the human.

2. If you remember when you got your first smart phone or smart tablet, or even if you remember when we all began using e-mail or the Internet, you will recall that, at first, it was just not obvious what this equipment was for—when the iPad came out, many people posted online that they loved the smooth, shiny gadget, but they had no idea what to do with it. TV was a bit like that in my youth. It was an alluring piece of equipment crouching in the living room, promising to entertain you ("here we are now . . .") but, in England in 1969, not making a very good return on that promise. But the moon landing, that was when it all began to come together—that is when it became clear, to me at least, that the TV could deliver the world to you and even what lies beyond. For me, *Dr. Who* (which was in its fifth season by 1969) and the moon landing seemed continuous with each other, and together they offered access to a wild landscape populated by all kinds of extraterrestrial and extrahuman beings.

3. I hold on to the significance of the moon landing despite the fact that it is now believed by many to be a hoax (in the images from the moon, as American astronauts walk on it, the flag does not wave, the stars do not shine, strange objects like Pepsi cans make their way into the frame). And I do so not only because it was such a widely shared moment, but more because it did mark the end of something, perhaps the end of man, the end of white men in particular, the end of the human.

I know, I know . . . claims about the end of this or that are so tired, so last decade, so dedicated to the myth of humanity. And yet, if ever there was an ending, it was surely this exploration of outer space by humans who could only seem diminished by the vastness they found there and by the implied failure of their colonial enterprise— "space, the final frontier."

Space *was* a final frontier and one that has proved resilient to Russian and American attempts to corral it, settle it, to tame it.

4. In a *New Yorker* article from 1969 on the moon walk, E. B. White commented: "The moon, it turns out, is a great place for men."[79] There are so many ways to respond to that, and I am sure either Dorothy Parker or Valerie Solanas (whose *SCUM Manifesto* was in circulation on the streets of New York by 1969) would not have let it pass![80] White meant simply that the gravity-free zone looked like so much fun for the bouncy astronauts whom he promptly dubbed as earth's universal ambassadors who should have been planting not an American flag but a "limp white handkerchief . . . symbol of the common cold which, like the moon, affects us all, unites us all."[81] This white flag which White would have liked to see on the moon could certainly symbolize the vulnerability of the human body to bacteria, a vulnerability, we might add, that has become more and more pressing as we develop new drugs to combat bacteria even as they mutate to resist the new medication. The white handkerchief could also symbolize, as he intended, a kind of blank slate, a universal human, a planetary banner; it could also stand for a voracious and colonizing whiteness with its desire for territory, power, and control; and in its "limp" state it waves feebly for emasculation, and signals a homophobic connection between manhood and loss even as it signifies surrender, resignation, and the end of the human." The bouncy men on the moon made one small step for man and . . . well, just that, one small step for one small man.

5. *Mad Men* ended the first half of its final run this season with the whole world, or at least the United States and its Cold War allies, watching the remarkable and the unthinkable. Another version of the moon walk, another ending. For the puny ad wo/men who, just a few seasons back, seemed poised to rule the world, this landmark event evoked sadness, a sense of loss, a moment of true regret about the world they had built with money, marketing, and magic. And as quickly as that regret came, it was almost as quickly transformed, beautifully and seamlessly by Peggy, into a new narrative with which to sell hamburgers—the moon landing reminds us, she calmly explains in a bedtime story voice to the stolid clients for Burger Chef, how important it is to remain connected. Never mind that this connection will come in the form of fast food served in an impersonal environment and on the road to a national epidemic of obesity. And so the most recent ruination of the human begins, in 1969, with a (probably false)

moment of human communion that becomes a metaphor, by 2014, for the commodification of human desire itself.

Strangely, we are not completely disappointed by Peggy's alchemy—her transformation of gold (man on the moon) into gold (marketable products) is, after all, the new mode of capitalism she commands. But, like Peggy, we still hanker for something that lies outside the magic circle of commodification. This something is named by Roland Barthes in his extraordinary collection of College de France lectures from the late 1970s as "the neutral"—a space that cannot be bought or sold, gendered, raced, known, marketed, made, or fixed. He writes: "I define the Neutral as that which outplays (déjoue) the paradigm or rather I call the Neutral everything that baffles the paradigm."[82] Finding a space in language between oppositional forces, outside binaries, a space that refuses to be defined in relation to what it is not, Barthes proposes that the desire to find such a space is "non-marketable" and "unsustainable." And he unpacks its form through a series of randomized figures like "weariness," "silence," "the damp," "banality," "stupidity." With an archive made up of simply the books he has on hand and a method that is part dream, part intellectual drifting, part emphasis—his goal, he says, is to make "the neutral twinkle."

This kind of method allows us to find our way through the thick material of the universal to queer theoretical spaces of possibility, moon walks if you like, real and imagined. And the "twinkling" is important in terms of thinking about *who* can find themselves in a term as innocuous as "neutrality." Since, all too often, spaces of neutrality have served as covers for capitalist theft (Switzerland), for racial domination (whiteness), for normativity (heterosexuality), we need the neutral to "twinkle," to absorb and give off light, to make clear that its intermittent glow depends on everything around it, in darkness and in light.

6. In "To the Planetarium" (1923), Walter Benjamin, a well-known prophet of the end of the human, not to mention an exceptional narrator of the anatomy of the inhuman, noted that the difference between the modern world and the ancient world may well reside in our diminished relation to the cosmos—while we have reduced our relation to the stars to an individualized, romanticized, and visual experience, for the ancients, stargazing was ecstatic, communal, transporting. Benjamin writes: "For it is in this experience alone that we gain certain knowledge of what is nearest to us and what is remotest from us and never of one without the other. This means,

however, that man can be in ecstatic contact with the cosmos only communally."[83]

7. And so, it is not a matter of whether the moon landing is real or fake, a hoax or transcendent, American imperialism or Cold War rhetoric; it is a question of the waning of the communal, its disappearance into the romanticized "I"—an I that is seduced, offended, wounded, bored, marketed to on a daily basis. The communal is the new wild, a place where the human ends and an inhuman or even an outhuman begins as a dream of ecstatic contact that we continue to seek out in life, in love, in dreams, in material objects, in the neutral, and in the skies. The question for now remains whether the human, in all its brutal, colonial, racist glory, can give way long enough to allow for other in/ and out/ human forms to emerge, evolve, appear, perhaps like a new planet in the night sky, twinkling, as Barthes might say, and transmitting new messages of an out/human future.

Notes

1. Andrea Smith, *Conquest: Sexual Violence and American Indian Genocide* (Cambridge, MA: South End, 2005).

2. Leanne Betasamosake Simpson, "Not Murdered, Not Missing," *Leanne Betasamosake Simpson*, leannesimpson.ca/page/2/ (accessed May 1, 2014).

3. Native Youth Sexual Health Network/Families of Sisters in Spirit/No More Silence, "Supporting the Resurgence of Community-Based Responses to Violence," March 14, 2014, www.nativeyouthsexualhealth.com/march142014.pdf; Simpson, "Not Murdered, Not Missing."

4. This chimes with the challenge that Zakiyyah Iman Jackson poses in her recent question: "Is it possible that the very subjects central to posthumanist inquiry—the binarisms of human/animal, nature/culture, animate/inanimate, organic/inorganic—find their relief outside of the epistemological locus of the West?" (*Animal: New Directions in the Theorization of Race and Posthumanism* [Ann Arbor: MPublishing, University of Michigan Library, 2013], 673.)

5. Denise Ferreira da Silva, "What Is *Critical* Ethnic Studies?" panel of the Critical Ethnic Studies Association Summer Institute, University of Maryland, June 26–28, 2014.

6. Smith, *Conquest.*

7. Katherine McKittrick, *Demonic Grounds: Black Women and the Cartographies of Struggle* (Minneapolis: University of Minnesota Press, 2006); Sylvia Wynter, "Unsettling the Coloniality of Being/Power/Truth/Freedom: Towards the Human, after Man, Its Overrepresentation—an Argument," *CR: The New Centennial Review* 3, no. 3 (2003): 257–37.

8. Andil Gosine and Cheryl Teelucksingh, *Environmental Justice and Racism in Canada: An Introduction* (Toronto: Emond Montgomery Publications, 2008).

9. Smith, *Conquest*; Bonita Lawrence, *Fractured Homeland: Federal Recognition and Algonquin Identity in Ontario* (Vancouver: University of British Columbia Press, 2012).

10. Robert D. Bullard, "Environmental Justice: It's More Than Waste Facility Siting," *Social Science Quarterly* 77, no. 3 (1996): 493–99.

11. Betsy Hartmann, "Population, Environment and Security: A New Trinity," *Population, Environment and Security* 10, no. 2 (1998): 113-28; Jin Haritaworn, *Queer Lovers and Hateful Others: Regenerating Violent Times and Places* (London: Pluto, 2015).

12. Andil Gosine, "Non-white Reproduction and Same-Sex Eroticism: Queer Acts against Nature," in *Queer Ecologies: Sex, Nature, Politics, Desire*, ed. Catriona Mortimer-Sandilands and Bruce Erickson (Bloomington: Indiana University Press, 2010), 149–72. See also Gosine and Teelucksingh, *Environmental Justice and Racism in Canada*.

13. Jodi Melamed, "Reading Tehran in Lolita: Seizing Literary Value for Neoliberal Multiculturalism," in *Strange Affinities: The Gender and Sexual Politics of Comparative Radicalization*, ed. Grace Kyungwon Hong and Roderick A. Ferguson (Durham, NC: Duke University Press, 2011).

14. Haritaworn, *Queer Lovers and Hateful Others*.

15. Ruth Wilson Gilmore, *Golden Gulag: Prisons, Surplus, Crisis, and Opposition in Globalizing California* (Berkeley: University of California Press, 2006).

16. Sara Ahmed, *Queer Phenomenology: Orientations, Objects, Others* (Durham, NC: Duke University Press, 2006).

17. See Jin Haritaworn, Adi Kuntsman, and Silvia Posocco, eds., *Queer Necropolitics* (New York: Routledge, 2014).

18. Discussions of the objectification and animalization of blackness in particular are many and long-standing. For example, see Frantz Fanon, *Black Skin, White Masks*, trans. Charles Markmann (New York: Grove, 1952); McKittrick, *Demonic Grounds*.

19. Kimberlé Crenshaw, "Mapping the Margins: Intersectionality, Identity Politics, and Violence against Women of Color," *Stanford Law Review* 43, no. 6 (1991): 1241–99.

20. Jackson, *Animal*.

21. Jackson, *Animal*.

22. Alexandra Topping, "Morrissey Reignites Racism Row by Calling Chinese a 'Subspecies,'" *Guardian*, September 3, 2010, www.theguardian.com/music/2010/sep/03/morrissey-china-subspecies-racism.

23. Smith, *Conquest*; Naomi Klein, "Dancing the World into Being: A Conversation with Idle No More's Leanne Simpson, *Yes! Magazine*, March 5, 2013, www.yesmagazine.org/peace-justice/dancing-the-world-into-being-a-conversation-with-idle-no-more-leanne-simpson; Lawrence, *Fractured Homeland*.

24. As Leanne Simpson puts it, "bringing in indigenous knowledge" this way must nec-

essarily be "on the terms of indigenous peoples" and go beyond an appropriative or "extractivist approach." See Klein, "Dancing the World into Being."

25. See, for example, Myra Hird, *The Origins of Sociable Life: Evolution after Science Studies* (Basingstoke, UK: Palgrave, 2009).

26. Myra Hird, "Digesting Difference: Metabolism and the Question of Sexual Difference," *Configurations* 20, no. 3 (2012): 213–38.

27. Myra Hird, "Animal Trans," *Australian Feminist Studies* 21 (2006): 35–48.

28. Donna Haraway, "The Promises of Monsters: A Regenerative Politics for Inappropriate/d Others," in *Cultural Studies*, ed. Lawrence Grossberg, Cary Nelson, and Paula Tredichler (New York: Routledge, 1992), 295–337.

29. J. Van Gulck, "Solid Waste Survey in the Territories in Northern Territories Water and Waste Association. 2012. Solid Waste Management in the North," *Journal of the Northern Territories Water and Waste Association* (September 2012); Conference Board of Canada, "Environment: Municipal Waste Generation" (2013), www.conferenceboard.ca/hcp/details/environment/municipal-waste-generation.aspx (accessed October 18, 2012).

30. Isabelle Stengers, "Deleuze and Guattari's Last Enigmatic Message," *Angelaki* 10, no. 2 (2005): 151–67.

31. Stengers, "Deleuze," 159–60.

32. Stengers, "Deleuze," 160.

33. Jacques Derrida's critique of apocalyptism informs my skepticism of the "beyond." Relatedly, in some theoretical quarters, it has become customary to presume the stability of the term "human" and suggest that this ought to be a subject we should move beyond, but it is precisely the casualness of this practice that I want to question. The quotation marks around "beyond" and "the human" throughout the piece suggest that my aim is to examine the implications, particularly the racial implications, of the casual dismissal of the category human. See Derrida, "No Apocalypse, Not Now (full speed ahead, seven missiles, seven missives)," trans. Catherine Porter and Philip Lewis, *Diacritics,* 14, no. 2 (Summer 1984): 20–31; and Derrida, "On a Newly Arisen Apocalyptic Tone in Philosophy," in *Raising the Tone of Philosophy: Late Essays by Immanuel Kant, Transformative Critique by Jacques Derrida*, ed. Peter Fenves (Baltimore: Johns Hopkins University Press, 1993), 117–71.

34. David Scott, "The Re-Enchantment of Humanism: An Interview with Sylvia Wynter," *Small Axe* 8 (September 2000): 120. I use the term *Man* in light of its development in the thought of Sylvia Wynter, a term that Wynter evokes to provincialize Renaissance and Enlightenment-based humanism, challenging its claims to universality. The term suggests that Man is a "genre" and not the human itself. "Out of the world" references a chapter in Achille Mbembe's *On the Postcolony* (Berkeley: University of California Press, 2001), 173–211.

35. Zakiyyah Iman Jackson, "Animal: New Directions in the Theorization of Race and Posthumanism," *Feminist Studies* 39 no. 3 (2014): 669–85.

36. High-water marks include (a list representative but not exhaustive): Lewis R. Gordon, *Existentia Africana: Understanding Africana Existential Thought* (New York: Routledge, 2000); Saidiya V. Hartman, *Scenes of Subjection: Terror, Slavery, and Self-Making in Nineteenth-Century America* (New York: Oxford University Press, 1997); Mbembe, *On the Postcolony*; Hortense J. Spillers, "Mama's Baby, Papa's Maybe: An American Grammar Book," *diacritics* 17, no. 2 (1987): 65–81; Fred Moten, *In the Break: The Aesthetics of the Black Radical Tradition* (Minneapolis: University of Minnesota Press, 2003); Frantz Fanon, *Black Skin, White Masks*, trans. C. L. Markmann (New York: Grove, 1967); Aimé Césaire, *Discourse on Colonialism* (New York: Monthly Review Press, 1972); Toni Morrison, *Beloved* (New York: Knopf, 1987); W. E. B. DuBois, *The Souls of Black Folk* (New York: Oxford University Press, 1903); Sylvia Wynter, "Unsettling the Coloniality." Thus I concur with Uri McMillan's assessment that "theories of 'object life' are at their most fecund, productive, and expansive when considered *with*, rather than *instead* of, black cultural studies" (in this issue). And as Jin Haritaworn has similarly noted, "tackl[ing] anthropocentrism and dehumanization simultaneously, as relational rather than competing or analogous paradigms," will likely "lead us to altogether different objects, and worlds" (in this issue).

37. For key writings by the aforementioned, see Emmanuel Chukwudi Eze, ed., *Race and the Enlightenment: A Reader* (Cambridge: Blackwell Publishing, 1997).

38. Jacques Derrida, *Specters of Marx: the State of the Debt, the Work of Mourning and the New International* (New York: Routledge, 2006).

39. For a discussion of the racialization of mathematical knowledge, see Ron Eglash, *African Fractals: Modern Computing and Indigenous Design* (New Brunswick: Rutgers University Press, 1999).

40. The turn to idiomatic exercises of science and mathematics in speculative realism, object-oriented approaches, new materialism, posthumanism, and animal studies without flagging or examining the politics of such idiomatic expression will likely be troubling for students of the racial, gendered, sexual, and colonial history of science, particularly when mathematics and science are relied upon as precepts to settle the question of 'reality' or evaluate truth claims rather than remaining objects of continual critique and intervention.

41. A number of thinkers have argued that the objective of our critique should not be predicated on an attempt to go "beyond" the human, or beyond ourselves, but a reorientation of the terms through which the human is understood. Their insights have been crucial to clarifying my own (Wynter, "Unsettling the Coloniality"); Césaire, *Discourse on Colonialism*; Fanon, *Black Skin, White Masks*; Sylvia Wynter, "Towards the Sociogenic Principle: Fanon, Identity, the Puzzle of Conscious Experience, and What It Is Like to Be Black," *Hispanic Issues* 23 (2001): 30–66; Neil Badmington, "Theorizing Posthumanism," *Cultural Critique* 53, no. 1 (2003): 10–27; Cary Wolfe, *What Is Posthumanism?* (Minneapolis: University of Minnesota Press, 2010); Jacques Derrida and David Wills, "The Animal That Therefore I Am (More to Follow)," *Criti-*

cal Inquiry 28, no. 2 (2002): 369–418; R. L. Rutsky, "Mutation, History, and Fantasy in the Posthuman," *Subject Matters: A Journal of Communications and the Self* (2007): 99– 112.

42. See www.alternet.org/world/evidence-emerges-israeli-shoot-cripple-policy-occupied-west -bank?page=0%2C0 (accessed August 15, 2014).

43. See www.aljazeera.com/indepth/opinion/2014/09/gaza-crime-crimes-2014926 64043551756.html (accessed October 1, 2014).

44. See www.facebook.com/karl.schembri/posts/10152139900211595 www.facebook.com /permalink.php?id=137704959660345&story_fbid=606670669430436 (accessed August 10, 2014).

45. See www.lrb.co.uk/blog/2014/07/29/nadia-abu-el-haj/nothing-unintentional/ (accessed September 15, 2014).

46. See www.lrb.co.uk/blog/2014/07/29/nadia-abu-el-haj/nothing-unintentional/ (accessed September 15, 2014).

47. Michel Foucault, "Friendship as a Way of Life," in *Foucault Live (Interviews, 1961– 1984)*, ed. Sylvère Lotringer (New York: Semiotext(e), 1996), 309–10.

48. David Halperin, *Saint Foucault: Toward a Gay Hagiography* (New York: Oxford University Press, 1995), 79; Eve Kosofsky Sedgwick, *The Weather in Proust*, ed. Jonathan Goldberg (Durham, NC: Duke University Press, 2011).

49. Michel Foucault, "The Ethics of the Concern for Self as a Practice of Freedom," in *Foucault Live*, 433, 434, and 435. For Foucault, as for the ancient Greek writers he was studying, an *ethos* named modes of being and behavior—of *living*—as opposed to naming some sort of prescriptive morality.

50. Adam Phillips, "On a More Impersonal Note," in Leo Bersani and Adam Phillips, *Intimacies* (Chicago: University of Chicago Press, 2008), 98.

51. Jeffrey J. Cohen and Todd R. Ramlow, "Pink Vectors of Deleuze: Queer Theory and Inhumanism, *rhizomes* 11–12 (Fall 2005–Spring 2006), www.rhizomes.net/issue11 /cohenramlow.html.

52. I am riffing here off of Roderick Ferguson's trenchant work. Ferguson's recent remarks on posthumanism, as a potential keyword to dispose of, comes to mind: which posthumanism are we talking about? And does posthumanism become a vanguard production that is a way not to talk explicitly about race? Roderick Ferguson, remarks presented at the annual American Studies Association convention, "Kill This Keyword" session, Los Angeles, California, November 8, 2014. See also Ferguson, *The Reorder of Things: The University and Its Pedagogies of Minority Difference* (Minneapolis: University of Minnesota Press, 2012).

53. Alexander G. Weheliye, *Habeas Viscus: Racializing Assemblages, Biopolitics, and Black Feminist Theories of the Human* (Durham, NC: Duke University Press, 2014), 21.

54. This woefully incomplete list includes John Akomfrah, *The Last Angel of History* (Icarus Films, 1996); Nalo Hopkinson, *Brown Girl in the Ring* (New York: Warner Books, 1998); Sun Ra, *Space Is the Place* (1974); Ishmael Reed, *Mumbo Jumbo* (1972; rpt.

New York: Scribner, 1996); George Schuyler, *Black No More* (1931; repr. New York: Dover, 2011).

55. Hershini Bhana Young, "Twenty-First-Century Post-humans: The Rise of the See-J," in *Black Performance Theory*, ed. Thomas F. DeFrantz and Anita Gonzalez (Durham, NC: Duke University Press, 2014), 56, 47.

56. Mel Chen, *Animacies: Biopolitics, Racial Mattering, and Queer Affect* (Durham, NC: Duke University Press, 2012), 5.

57. Scott Herring, "Material Deviance: Theorizing Queer Objecthood," *Postmodern Culture* 21, no. 2 (2011); Drew Sawyer, "Crisco, or How to Do Queer Theory with Things," www.columbia.edu/~sf2220/TT2007/web-content/Pages/drew2.html (accessed July 4, 2014).

58. Spillers, "Mama's Baby, Papa's Maybe." The white gaze's reduction of the black man into a negative sign in the field of vision renders him, in Fanon's words, *an object among objects*. See Fanon, *Black Skin, White Masks* (1952; repr. New York: Grove, 2008), 89.

59. Aimé Césaire, *Discourse on Colonialism* (1955; repr. New York: Monthly Review Press, 2000), 42.

60. Christina Sharpe, *Monstrous Intimacies: Making Post-Slavery Subjects* (Durham, NC: Duke University Press, 2010); Darieck Scott, *Extravagant Abjection: Blackness, Power, and Sexuality in the African American Literary Imagination* (New York: New York University Press, 2010).

61. This echoes Jinthana Haritaworn's claim that following objects may well lead us to altogether different objects and worlds.

62. Uri McMillan, *Embodied Avatars* (New York: New York University Press, forthcoming).

63. See Michael Fried's infamous essay "Art and Objecthood," *Artforum* 5, no. 10 (1967): 12–23.

64. Jane Bennett, *Vibrant Matter: A Political Ecology of Things* (Durham, NC: Duke University Press, 2010), 13.

65. In 1985 the video game *Ultima IV: Quest of the Avatar* was released, in which the player's quest was to become an "Avatar." The same year, Chip Morningstar, a designer of Lucasfilm's *Habitat*, a role-playing game released a year later, first coined the current use of avatar to describe a virtual representation of a player.

66. Ann Weinstone, *Avatar Bodies: A Tantra for Posthumanism* (Minneapolis: University of Minnesota Press, 2004), 41.

67. Susan Stryker, "My Words to Victor Frankenstein above the Village of Chamounix: Performing Transgender Rage," in *The Transgender Studies Reader*, eds. Susan Stryker and Stephen Whittle (New York: Routledge, 2006), 244–56.

68. Ruth Wilson Gilmore, *Golden Gulag: Prisons, Surplus, Crisis, and Opposition in Globalizing California* (Berkeley: University of California Press, 2007), 28.

69. Nikki Sullivan and Samantha Murray, *Somatechnics: Queering the Technologisation of Bodies* (Surrey, UK: Ashgate, 2009).

70. Maurice Merleau-Ponty, *Phenomenology of Perception* (New York: Routledge Classics, 2002 [1945]).

71. Jean-François Lyotard, *The Differend: Phrases in Dispute* (Minneapolis: University of Minnesota Press, 1989); Emmanuel Levinas, *Humanism of the Other* (Urbana-Champaign: University of Illinois Press, 2005).

72. Donna Haraway, *The Companion Species Manifesto: Dogs, Humans, and Significant Otherness* (Chicago: Prickly Paradigm Press, 2003).

73. Michel Foucault, *History of Sexuality Volume One: Introduction* (New York: Vintage, 1978).

74. Giorgio Agamben, *Homo Sacer: Sovereign Power and Bare Life* (Palo Alto: Stanford University Press, 1998), 1–5.

75. See James Clifford, "Indigenous Articulation," *Contemporary Pacific* 13, no. 2 (2001): 468–90; and Kim TallBear, "Genomic Articulations of Indigeneity," *Social Studies of Science* 43, no. 4 (2013): 509–33.

76. Elaine L. Graham, *Representations of the Post/Human: Monsters, Aliens and Others in Popular Culture* (New Brunswick: Rutgers University Press, 2002), 35.

77. Donna Haraway, *Second_Millennium.FemaleMan©_Meets_OncoMouseTM™: Feminism and Technoscience* (New York: Routledge, 1996), 60.

78. Claire Colebrook, "Extinct Theory," in *Death of the PostHuman: Essays on Extinction, Vol. 1* and *Sex After Life: Essays on Extinction, Vol. 2.* (Open Humanities Press, 2014), 32.

79. E. B. White, "Notes and Comment," *New Yorker*, July 26, 1969, www.newyorker.com/magazine/1969/07/26/comment-5238.

80. Dorothy Parker's sharp tongue often took masculinity as its target. To wit: "I require only three things of a man. He must be handsome, ruthless and stupid." Valerie Solanas eschewed witticisms for manifestos, and she wrote and self-published her *SCUM Manifesto* in 1967. It was eventually published in 1968 by Olympia Press and then reissued more recently by London and New York's Verso Press in 2004. The manifesto described a man as "completely egocentric, trapped inside himself, incapable of empathizing or identifying with others, or love, friendship, affection or tenderness." She continues: "He is a half-dead, unresponsive lump, incapable of giving or receiving pleasure or happiness; consequently, he is at best an utter bore, an inoffensive blob, since only those capable of absorption in others can be charming."

81. www.newyorker.com/magazine/1969/07/26/comment-5238.

82. Roland Barthes, *The Neutral: Lecture Course at the College de France (1977–1978) (European Perspectives: A Series in Social Thought and Cultural Criticism)* (New York: Columbia University Press, 2007), 6.

83. Walter Benjamin, "To the Planetarium" (1928), in *Walter Benjamin, Selected Writings: 1913–1926*, ed. Marcus Bullock and Michael Jennings, trans. Edmund Jephcott (New York: Belknap Press of Harvard University Press, 2004), 486.

LITTLE MONSTERS

Race, Sovereignty, and Queer Inhumanism in
Beasts of the Southern Wild

Tavia Nyong'o

Introduction: Where the Wild Things Were

$\mathcal{F}$our hundred years ago, the king of Poland presided over the first recorded attempt at wildlife preservation. A relative of the domestic cow, the wild aurochs once thrived across Europe, India, and North Africa. But hunting and human encroachment slowly reduced its habitat to, finally, just the Jaktorowska forest in Poland. For several hundred years, the last of the aurochs survived as property of the Polish crown. Only the king had the right to hunt them. As they dwindled further, the king himself abstained from their hunt, charged the local village with protecting the aurochs, and sent an inspector to perform a regular audit. This sovereign act was an early assertion of what Michel Foucault would later name biopolitics: the "power to *foster* life or *disallow* it to the point of death."[1] As such an early assertion, it was weak and experimental, and it ultimately failed. For when King Zygmunt's inspector arrived in 1630, he learned that the last of the aurochs had died years earlier, in what we today classify as "the first documented anthropogenic extinction."[2] The horned relics of the last male aurochs were brought to the king, in whose keep they remained until carried off as a trophy to a rival's armory in Stockholm, where they remain on view today.[3]

What might this fable of the sovereign and his wild beast teach us today, as we confront the current threat of anthropogenic climate change? At a time when queer studies is confronting the posthumanist spatiotemporal scales suggested by the bringing into humanist analytical focus of the Anthropocene?[4] What happens

GLQ 21:2–3
DOI 10.1215/10642684-2843335
© 2015 by Duke University Press

when we juxtapose the awesome aurochs's relic—the fossil of a form of sovereignty itself ostensibly long extinct—against more recent attempts, in an advanced industrial age, to reanimate the aurochs as harbinger of a "rewilded" planet?[5] And what repercussions does an environmentally motivated "giving up" of human sovereignty imply for queer and other minoritarian subjects, when that gift is looked for in the mouth of the feral beast? In this essay I keep these overarching questions on the horizon as I more closely track how they are incarnated through the preternatural aurochs. These ersatz beasts appear in Lucy Alibar's play *Juicy and Delicious* (2007) and subsequent film, *Beasts of the Southern Wild* (2012), cowritten by Alibar and Benh Zeitlin. In counterpoint to these stage and film aurochs—and the inhumanist wildness they seem to kindle—I bring into view historical zoopolitical efforts to reverse-breed the extinct aurochs back into existence. I argue that in both varieties of fabrication—performative and scientific—we encounter an animal that still wears the biopolitical allure in which the kings of Poland had encircled it. Jacques Derrida suggests that the sovereign and the beast mirror each other as doubled exceptions to the law (the one above, the other below or beyond), raising the question of whether the rewilded aurochs truly augurs the end, or the covert reinstatement, of sovereignty.[6] What might it take to break this double bind of sovereign thinking and truly get to what Jack Halberstam calls "the wild beyond?"[7]

At first glance, the preternatural aurochs appears to already live in that wild beyond: it enjoys an existence outside the law, wild and free. In contemporary theoretical terms, it is a token or emblem of life beyond the correlate of human consciousness, a vital flourishing in the Great Outdoors lauded by Quentin Meillassoux and other theorists associated with speculative realism.[8] In *Beasts of the Southern Wild*, the aurochs also appears outside history, escaping from under the melting polar ice caps to run free across a rewilded North American landscape. Linked to the impending death of the film's protagonist's father, the aurochs also is a potent symbol of human extinction. But the actual aurochs, as my opening fable suggests, was outside neither history nor law. In a move that Giorgio Agamben has familiarized us with, it was included in both history and law through its exclusion or exception.[9] So its preternatural sequel, I argue, must carry a thick freight of human meanings in its icy shag. We are familiar, from as far back as *Godzilla* (1954), with the figure of the revenant prehistoric beast reawakened from its primordial slumbers by the technological depravities of advanced civilization. If the aurochs is to be our guide into a wilderness beyond human sovereignty and civilizational collapse, then we should more closely inspect its quasi-mythic genealogy, lest the "biophilic" pursuit of the Great Outdoors lead us back from where we started: back to primal modernist fantasies of primitive otherness.[10]

As critics have already shown, Alibar and Zeitlin's film is cannily pitched to an ecological sensibility attuned to the need for a rewilded planet in which to share sovereignty with nonhumankind.[11] The independent feature was widely and rapturously embraced upon release, winning prizes at Cannes and Sundance, as well as plaudits from the likes of Oprah Winfrey and President Barack Obama. The film ostensibly teaches humans how to behave less like the king of Poland and more like his wild, herbivorous beasts. Its celebration of the convivial survivalism of an outsider human community has intense, if romantic appeal. But the preternatural aurochs is not frequently commented on, however much its presence becomes an important reason that *Beasts of the Southern Wild* has been embraced as a contemporary fable of otherwise hard-to-visualize climate change. As fabulated by the film's child narrator, the aurochs serves as a larger-than-life monster that is neither real nor imaginary but an involuntary speculative image of what lies in store for us all. *Beasts* has thus been claimed by the visual theorist Nicholas Mirzoeff as "perhaps the first film to create a means to visualize climate resistance" and by the literary theorist Patricia Yaeger as offering "strange pedagogies about how we should live in a melting world."[12] Even the manner in which the film was made has been credited to a rewilding of filmmaking: *Beasts* was made with locally sourced props, locations, and actors in a filmmaking praxis that entailed the director being "all but adopted" by a precarious Gulf Coast community, a process that models the autonomous community extolled in the resulting feature film.[13]

If the film has thus been recruited to the task of figuring adequate aesthetic responses to existential, species-wide threat, it has not for that reason been able to fully subsume questions of human difference: race, gender, class, or sexuality. The color-blind casting of Quvenzhané Wallis as the film's protagonist insistently foregrounds the tension between the particular and the universal, the local and the global, that *Beasts* attempts to manage.[14] Although widely praised for her preternaturally gifted performance, the role that Wallis was given has been sharply questioned. Why, black feminist critics like bell hooks, Jayna Brown, and Christina Sharpe have asked, is a black female child asked to perform the work of imagining the survival of a civilization that has abandoned her? What is the relationship between her singular race, gender, and infancy and the ostensibly universal narrative she embodies? And why is her narrative of wondrous survival framed through such standard tropes as black familial dysfunction, paternal violence, and licentious femininity? Circling around these responses has been another anxiety about cinematic depictions of black (and other subaltern) people as primitives on a continuum with nonhuman animals. Even if the film's ambition is to valorize feral human nature, at what price is such transvaluation purchased?

While this essay draws on the above responses and criticisms, it shifts its gaze slightly from the film's protagonist to what she sees, that is, to the inhuman presence of the preternatural aurochs. These aurochs symbolize both the vulnerability and the resilience of nature in the face of human predation. But they themselves also bear crucial, if understated, racial and biopolitical meanings. If the beast and the sovereign encounter each other as doubled exceptions to the law, where in such a relation are we to locate the dark stain of race that conditions the possibilities of life at or below the threshold of the human? If the aurochs was once "king of the world," as the child protagonist of *Beasts of the Southern Wilds* confirms, what does it mean for her journey to end with her confronting that king, face-to-face, to divine their fearful symmetry? Both the film and the play it is adapted from locate the nonsovereign aspect of the human where we are most accustomed to finding it: in the defenseless, impoverished, raced, and gendered child. Her resilient propensity for fabulation and wonder in the face of nature's animacies forms an inner wild of the human, an invagination or intensive manifold.[15] Her propensities thus bear on the "racial mattering" that Mel Chen argues must also occupy our critically posthumanist concerns.[16] Certainly, race matters to how and why the dark, female child encounters the shaggy, horned beast in an environment wherein, as Levi Bryant puts it, "I no longer experience myself as a *sovereign* of nonhuman beings," a wild in which he instead encounters "the possibility of myself being eaten."[17] The reversal of roles between the eating and the eaten, which Bryant lauds as a salutary thought experiment to provincialize his privileged humanity, is repeated in a film in which the aurochs, victim of the first anthropogenic extinction, presides over the final one.

But the slippage of the "I" between subjects variously privileged within Western epistemological frameworks is worth pausing over. *Beasts* imagines this reduction of humanity to "meat" as a salutary pedagogy (the protagonist is literally taught this lesson in a shambolic schoolroom in the film's opening minutes). Bryant's notion of a "wilderness ontology" might lend this pedagogy philosophical heft, but we hardly need theoretical speculation to invent what history has so remorselessly documented: the reduction of racialized others to human prey.[18] The loss of sovereignty in the face of nonhuman beings, and the forced removal of peoples from spaces reimagined as "wild," is a very old tale. When *Beasts* retells it, it does so literally from the side of the displaced, vagrant, and subaltern. Political sovereignty, both militaristic and biopolitical, emanates from the other side of the levee that the anarchic band of stragglers try to live beyond. The film thus aligns its vision with an alternative, nonsovereign relationship to land and world. But the unnatural history of the aurochs as the sovereign's beast leads me to ask, with Foucault, whether we have yet, in our ecological thinking, to "cut off the head of the king"?[19]

Juicy, Delicious, and Wild

Addressing *Beasts of the Southern Wild* in the context of a special issue on queer inhumanism raises certain questions. To address them, we should look further into the genealogy of the film's protagonist and her wild things. Narratology points to the *fabula* as the source story that can be told and retold in various ways.[20] Rather than treat this source as the true, invariant cause of the various retellings, deconstructive approaches to the *fabula* consider how it "requires a double reading, a reading according to incompatible principles."[21] The incompatible principles in this case proceed from a *fabula* that, according to the white female playwright, has autobiographical sources, but whose protagonist has been twice transposed, first onto a young white boy (in the play), and then onto a younger black girl (in the film). *Beasts* is thus one of several incompossible tellings of the story of a protagonist named Hushpuppy. Frank Wilderson has argued that recent US "racial problem" cinema is characterized by a "grammar of antagonism" in which

> even when films narrate a story in which Blacks or Indians are beleaguered with problems that the script insists are conceptually coherent (usually having to do with poverty or the absence of "family values"), the nonnarrative, or cinematic, strategies of the film often disrupt this coherence by posing the irreconcilable questions of Red and Black political ontology—or nonontology.[22]

The double reading of Hushpuppy I propose here draws from Wilderson's insistence that narrative cinema poses problems it fails to bring into visible or conceptual coherence and that those problems circulate around a fraught triangulation of race, sovereignty, and the human. At the same time, I also look to Kara Keeling's more affirmative account of a generative black cinematic power that evades representation, what she names the "black femme function." This function "highlight[s] the current existence of a figure hidden within the histories and logics generated by struggles against racism, sexism, and homophobia in the United States, a figure whose invisible, affective labor ensures the survival of forms of sociality that were never meant to survive."[23] While the film is white-authored and -directed, its cocreation by its nonprofessional cast (including Wallis) establishes grounds for tracking the flight of the black femme in a film that makes the absent presence of black female characters (Hushpuppy's mother, Miss Bathsheba the schoolteacher, the cook at the Elysian Fields floating brothel) quietly central to the stories it tells.

If the black femme function is dispersed in *Beasts* (Hushpuppy's mother is missing, the cook who might be her fails to recognize the child, Miss Bathsheba is a kind but inconsistent surrogate, Hushpuppy is barely out of infancy), this dispersal only further highlights the invisibility, or partial occlusion, of its affective labor. If the "final" film version of Hushpuppy can be thought of as the retrospective cause of its chronologically preceding versions, it is because each instance is embedded not only in a grammar of black-white antagonism but also in a logic of incompossibility. The concept of incompossibility comes from Gottfried Wilhelm Leibniz, via Gilles Deleuze, who drew on it as a way out of the Hegelian deadlock of dialectical contradiction. As Nathan Widder explains:

> Incompossibility in no way implies contradiction, but rather divergence from a continuous series of compossible individuals and events. . . . A world of incompossibles is one where "Adam sins" and "Adam does not sin" both have truth, not because the sinning Adam's identity must relate to its contradictory, but because its sense requires a relation to differences that are incompossible with it, differences that for Deleuze are fully real but virtual. . . . Like a science fiction story about parallel universes, the two Adams and their worlds are indiscernible yet completely different, and each one seems to repeat the other without either one being identifiable as the original or true world that the other copies.[24]

Widder's gloss on incompossibility as akin to a science fiction story about two parallel universes that are completely different yet somehow indiscernible captures something useful about the queer relationship between the versions of Hushpuppy found in Alibar's play and cowritten screenplay. There is a way in which the *sense* of *Beasts* only emerges in relation to its incompossible precursors, which include not only Alibar's original play and life experiences but also Zeitlin's stories of his own visits to the real locations that inspired his fictional scenario. Rather than force an identification of one Hushpuppy as the original and the others as copies, incompossibility allows a logic of sense to emerge through acts of repetition. Such a logic of sense holds implications for how we read the survival of race and gender in the wake of the human. If I take up incompossibility here in order to apprehend the *virtual* character of Hushpuppy, it is to gauge the implications of a story iterating across real and fictive scenarios and of a protagonist slipping between black and white, male and female bodies. Such a virtualization of the story does not preclude, but can in fact underpin, an account of its racial and imperial unconscious.

In both play and film Hushpuppy's story proceeds from the speculative propensities of child perception, especially under trauma and adversity. That he (in the play) and she (in the film) fabulate a preternatural herd of aurochs to endow this chaos with sensible form and animacy establishes the indiscernibility of "real" and "mythic" worlds within the frame of the narrative. *Juicy and Delicious* is a one-act play about a young white boy growing up in south Georgia with an abusive, dying father. It employs various stage effects to conjure up the wild perception of a child, edging on adolescence, whose world is about to come crashing down. The play cites familiar southern tropes: violence and alcoholism; poverty and prostitution; grits, possum, and gator. It confronts these dramatic issues by navigating the fierce and often funny borderlands between dream and nightmare. The playwright has described her work as autobiographical, with the characters of Hushpuppy and Daddy loosely inspired by the playwright and her own, then ill, father.[25] The theatrical Hushpuppy is described as a "sweet little Southern boy," submissive and not very intelligent. His schoolyard nemesis, a "big scary Southern girl" named Joy Strong, calls Hushpuppy a "pussy-bitch" and repeatedly assaults him. Their dynamic establishes the boy's protoqueerness, ostensibly confirmed in a "big gay dance number" midway through the play.

Juicy and Delicious places its anthropomorphic aurochs in a dreamsequence dance that is a choreography of displacement and innuendo, rather than overt revelation. It is not the sleeping Hushpuppy who dances but his Daddy and Mamma, surrounded by a herd of aurochs. What is gay here is Hushpuppy's propensity to fabulate a herd of aurochs dancing to the tune of the Bangles' "Eternal Flame," who then attempt to abscond with him, sleeping, cradled in the arms of one of them. Snatching his son back from the camp bogeyman aurochs, Daddy awakens Hushpuppy and immediately engages him in a scene of attempted masculinization. "Show me them guns," Daddy yells repeatedly to his son, who flexes his biceps and yells out, at unconvincing pitch: "I the man! . . . I the man!" But Hushpuppy is clearly *not* the man, as the play shows. Daddy's attempt to align the rigorous demands of survival in the southern wilds with a virile, patriarchal masculinity collapses under the weight of its own incongruity. Survival is instead shown to reside in the inner strength to succumb and feel, to dance and play, and to fabulate a place after the end of the world.[26]

When the revenant aurochs thunder across Alibar's stage, they merge with a cacophony of other animate and ferocious objects, within which the vulnerable and effeminate Hushpuppy cringes and falters. We understand the magical world on the stage that Hushpuppy occupies as an exteriorizing of the child's febrile mind, a result of his propensity to fabulate the presence of intelligent forces operating behind all the random violence he suffers. These presences represent histories he cannot know but that stalk him nonetheless. Ironically, the magic of these forces reinforces our understanding that they have a reality beyond his grasp: the surreal chaos of Hushpuppy's life works as an indictment of the social forces grinding human life into abject poverty in neoliberal America. When the story shifts in the film version to rural Louisiana, somewhere south of the levee, this historical backdrop expands to frame the entire industrial age, and the film asks audiences to now consider the story as a fable of an emergent Anthropocene. Hushpuppy must do new work, not only to figure her own catastrophe, but to make "tangible" the catastrophic consequences of centuries of industrial capitalism.[27]

Often described as a post-Katrina allegory, *Beasts of the Southern Wild* takes the basic elements of Hushpuppy's story and transposes it to the fictional Isle de Charles Doucet. Living literally outside the law, the residents call their island "the Bathtub," and fiercely defend their autonomous way of life from the rising tides and worsening storms that climate change is wreaking on their precarious community. Hushpuppy, now younger, black, and female, lives with her rage-filled, dying father, Wink. Resilient and resourceful, Hushpuppy cooks and cares for herself and a flock of domestic animals, gets herself to school, and fabulates the presence of both her missing mother and an awesome herd of aurochs that have emerged out of the thawing ice of Antarctica and are now thundering toward the Bathtub, ready to gobble her up. Film adaptation enables Hushpuppy's story of incipient human catastrophe to be seen from the child's own point of view. Theatrical devices are exchanged for the cinematic technique of the free indirect image, wherein we are not always certain whether what we are seeing is to be understood as actually happening in the reality of the film, in the imagination of Hushpuppy, or some blend of the two.[28] This free indirect imagery allows the film to produce the aurochs as both mythic beings of Hushpuppy's imagination and as potent, ambiguous symbols of a rewilded Louisiana. When Hushpuppy finally meets her aurochs face-to-face, the flash of recognition between them suggests a reconciliation between human and animal on shared autochthonous ground, in which it is left deliberately uncertain who truly is the titular "beast of the Southern wild."[29]

As the aurochs wind their way from stage to screen, they too are engulfed in this new environmentalist mise-en-scène. The preternatural creatures first appear on-screen frozen in ice at the ends of the earth until Hushpuppy animates them as effigies of her father's impending death and her home's impending engulfment. Alibar and Zeitlin invite us to accept the beast and the nonsovereign child as our guides to what Yaeger terms "the dream we need to dream (that is, to make into creed, to make tangible) of our complicity as a dangerous, polluting species."[30]

However inspiring such a creed, it does not obviate a closer analysis of how human sovereignty is unevenly accessible to humans, a history that only inconsistently rises to the surface captured in the film's vibrant, dreamy cinematography. If the filmmakers seem poised to affirm a collective complicity in the environmental crisis engulfing Terrebonne Parish (an affirmation suggested by their interpolation of real footage of climate catastrophe at key points in their montage), then it seems valid to track the biopolitical genealogy of the landscape it populates with feral life.

The race and gender changes in Hushpuppy might initially seem to work to effect a sense of species-wide commonality. Any child could be a Hushpuppy, even as Hushpuppy is not quite an abstract universal but a series of indiscernible singularities. This can be seen in the way that the theatrical and cinematic Hushpuppys can be neither fully collapsed into nor, finally, distinguished from one another. Scenes like "show me them guns" repeat across versions, to differing effect. In both film and play, a father attempts to masculinize a child perceived as too weak to survive his or her imminent abandonment. But while the play must posit the source of Hushpuppy's weakness as male effeminacy—the proverbial "sissy boy"—the film instead produces the equally recognizable figure of the strong-willed, resilient little black girl. While each are coherent on their own terms, the repetition of dialogue and characterization between play and film accentuates Hushpuppy's *virtual* queerness, which derives less from perverse sexual orientation than from the characters' disjunctive emergence into sexed and raced beings. As Hushpuppy crosses between drama and cinema, Hushpuppy becomes an incompossible of wild child and sissy boy, while never stabilizing into either.

It is tempting to embrace this aesthetic tactic as the kind of dream work needed to confront the Anthropocene, itself the self-reflexive feedback loop of capitalist growth on human environments. Collective survival in the face of climate change is routinely presented in the liberal imagination as uniting humanity across differences. Such a liberal universalism undergirds the positive reception of the casting of a little black girl to represent the future of the (human) race (not itself an unusual tactic in dystopic scenarios, as critics such as Brown have noted).[31] But the virtualization of the character of Hushpuppy across a series of incompossible instances, both real and fictive, should not authorize the overlooking of the social antagonisms and contradictions that each character's singular instances are embedded in. To do so would be to fall victim to what Sharpe and Brown rightly term "the romance of precarity."[32] Under the spell of this romance, sympathetic identification with the plight of subaltern populations automatically recuses the sympathizer from accounting for the historical and structural conditions that produce the unequal, hierarchical arrangements that both occasion and outlast their sympathy. As Widder notes in his cogent analysis of political theory in the wake of Deleuze, the actual and the virtual both represent *real* levels of political analysis and intervention. Even if Deleuze privileges the virtual terrain of micropolitics, it is nonetheless the case, Widder wryly notes, that "it is people who can be identified and arrested, never desiring-machines."[33] And while this comment can be taken in both an affirmative and a pessimistic sense, that very ambivalence is worth retaining in any reading of the ecological dream work in *Beasts*. So when Hushpuppy and Wink are identified and arrested in *Beasts*, that should unlock a conversation about race that their color-blind casting as universalized subjects ought not forestall.

The Queer Fabulist in the Preternatural Wild

Why track the spoor of race thinking through the theatrical and cinematic wilds? In part, because wildness has emerged as a motif in a coalescing intellectual project interested in moving beyond humanist and state-centered politics and theories.[34] Wildness pulls focus away from the human, bringing into sharper relief a background of a pulsing, vital, even queer materiality. Through a "free and wild creation of concepts," as Deleuze once called for, this new ecological and materialist thought zooms out from human "species being" (as Marx termed it) to access a fuller sweep of events at a planetary and even cosmic level.[35] *Beasts of the Southern Wild* addresses this intellectual moment, articulating our ecological and human challenge in a cinematic language that celebrates the wild, the feral, the autonomous, and the anarchic. The film's drama turns on our protagonist confronting the fearsome power of the aurochs, a power she initially fears will devour her, and realizing that its wildness is the true source of her strength. It is worth thinking through how this plot resonates with what Grégoire Chamayou has named "cynegetic power": a biopolitical power constituted around the right to make other humans prey.[36] *Beasts* evokes such cynegetic power when the aurochs are set up as a confabulation of the forces that are steadily encroaching on the Bathtub. Hushpuppy's capacity to fabricate the aurochs as animate agents allows her to harness their strength in her fugitive quest to escape the internment camp that would "civilize" her. Her biophilic affiliations allow her to join the beasts somewhere "below the law." But is that where the aurochs ever were?

Beasts of the Southern Wild takes its place in an aesthetic and scientific series of contexts in which the aurochs is a surrogate for modernist and postmodernist fantasies of reclaimed land, wildness, violence, and freedom. It underscores how running with the aurochs can induce what Diane Chisholm calls a "biophilia": an attraction to a landscape so strong it resembles "an outlaw coupling, the wild anarchy of a love affair whose heated obsession betray[s] and unravel[s] some other, weaker, fidelity."[37] This wild perception of nature as something that possesses one, an environment in which one might be eaten as well as eat, may appear a heady way to slip the yoke of human difference. But the freedom of the indirect images through which cinema viewers find themselves immersed in Hushpuppy's landscape is not racially unmarked. The preternatural aurochs do not merely descend on the Bathtub from a future climate collapse, as patched together by the traumatized imagination of a child. When they appear on-screen, they also reveal what Deleuze called their "dark precursors": the "invisible, imperceptible" historical intensities that "determines their path in advance but in reverse."[38] Alibar herself has stated, "I don't know where the herd of aurochs came from."[39] This "nowhere" is precisely the location where Deleuze locates the dark precursor. The film attributes the genesis of Hushpuppy's fabulation to the traumatic sight of an aurochs tattoo on the thigh of her teacher, Miss Bathsheba. But those drawings themselves sketch out an ersatz line of dark precursors, whose story reminds us of the racial and imperial histories decomposing in the preternatural wild.

Between the time that the sovereign's beast exits the primeval forest and when it enters stage right in contemporary film and theater, much of its nature has been transmogrified. Centuries of unnatural history intervene between the Jaktorowska forest and Terrebonne Parish. To skip from the prehistoric to the postmodern is to miss the crucial twentieth-century attempts to "reverse breed" aurochs from modern cattle, an important antecedent to present-day rewilding efforts. Eugenic breeders in Nazi-era Germany considered the aurochs an aboriginal "Aryan" species of cow and sought to rewild the related species of wisent in order to populate the rewilded forests that they projected would someday replace the defeated and exterminated humans of Poland. Modern Heck cattle are the descendants of these fascist experiments.[40] The aurochs that Hushpuppy encounters are thus neither prehistoric nor mythical creatures, as play and film intimate; they are instead a species that has migrated repeatedly across the electrified fences between actual and virtual being, always trailing the scent of the predatory designs of sovereign power.

The geographers Jamie Lorimer and Clemens Driessen, who study the present-day efforts to rewild Heck cattle in reclaimed Dutch wetlands, remind their readers of this species's ersatz origins.[41] Contemporary ecologists recognize that Heck cattle are not literally aurochs, but their ability to impersonate or surrogate the extinct species is key to leveraging popular support for rewilding experiments (a more clearly domestic-seeming species, Lorimer and Driessen point out, might draw more criticism from the public if visibly left wholly without veterinary care or food in the preternatural wild). Of course, contemporary ecological efforts at rewilding are not a direct fulfillment of their awful history. But that history is intermingled in its reappearance, even in a child's fable, as part of a territorializing machine. *Beasts* reckons with this history indirectly, inversely, by extolling a subaltern nonsovereignty that would be repugnant to the Aryan purity sought by early twentieth-century eugenic breeders. The wildness extolled in the Bathtub would be viewed as pollution by the likes of Lutz and Hein Heck, sibling zookeepers whose aurochs de-extinction projects were appropriated by Hermann Göring, who styled himself a great Germanic hunter. Hushpuppy and her kin, in their multihued variety and raucous conviviality, would be a eugenicist's nightmare. The historical practitioners of selective breeding sought to counter, as Michael Wang puts it, the "deleterious genetic effects of civilization."[42] They associated recovered wildness with a preternatural purity antithetical to the "dirty ecology" extolled by contemporary critics like Yaeger.

But direct inversion of the pure/dirty binarism does not, in itself, transvalue the underpinning binarism. As I argued in *The Amalgamation Waltz*, both valorizing and stigmatizing miscegenation can have the effect of making it our "national Thing."[43] Appropriating wildness as our national Thing, as *Beasts* suggests we can, risks skirting over the specific histories, not only of Hushpuppy the fictional character, but also of the Bathtub the fictional location. In Alibar and Zeitlin's fable the rebirth of the aurochs augurs the coming of a feral humankind. This ragtag commune successfully stands up against a governmentality imagined in classically sovereign terms: the levee, the internment camp, the police, the helicopter. If we too easily embrace the ecological fable's image of top-down state sovereignty to rebel against, we may not have, in our political thinking, "cut off the head of the king." One sign that we have not yet done so is that we forget the proximity of cattle, wild or tame, to the legal principle of chattel. The historical aurochs ended its days neither domesticated nor free but as a form of wild property. The sovereign and his chattel were set up in a predator-prey relation from which the sovereign voluntarily abstained. In this, he modeled the ethical predator, who restrains his ferocity and rationally suspends his rights. As the sovereign's beast, the aurochs belonged to an environment whose wildness was to be *fostered*, even if human life, in turn, had to be *disallowed* to the point of death. We see this in the Polish king's injunction to the village of Jaktorow to protect the aurochs and its habitat even at the potential cost of their own flocks and livelihood. This responsibility to protect a wilderness is configured specifically in relation to a land that must be kept clear of other, vagrant life. The sovereign's abstention—in tandem with the pastoral responsibilities delegated to the villagers/vagrants—forms the germ of an ecological ruse out of which the extinct line of aurochs has been regularly rebirthed in the centuries since its disappearance. That this rebirth comes at a cost to racialized and subaltern people who must be displaced so that the sovereign/beast may roam freely forms a challenge that the dream work of *Beasts* unevenly reckons.

Both etymology and usage suggest that "the wild" is caught up in the finitude of the human, which "wilderness ontology" proposes to leave behind in search of a great outdoors. Such dismissals of finitude would ignore, predictably, the manner in which minoritized subjects are captured within an incorporative exclusion that the black diasporic theorist Denise Ferreira da Silva has named "the strategy of engulfment."[44] Engulfment, Silva writes, is

> the political-symbolic strategy that apprehends the human body and global regions as signifiers of how universal reason institutes different kinds of self-consciousness, that is, as an effect of productive tools that institute irreducible and unsublatable differences.[45]

How might the racial other be engulfed by the extension of a transparent and universal reason, even under the guise of fabulated machines of cinematic dreaming? In part, this would happen through the very claim that such fables must have instrumental purpose: that we can and must confront the unconfrontable challenge that we collectively face through fictions like *Beasts of the Southern Wild*. And I don't think such claims for political efficacy can quite be dismissed as simple overreaching; clearly the film has power. But of what nature, and to what effect?

I have already alluded to the complex of historical and libidinal investments that the wild as a zone of excessive purposiveness and dangerous irregularity carries.[46] This excess is also racialized and gendered, often through tropes of an excess of reproductivity that exceeds the boundaries of the biopolitically normative. Andil Gosine also notes how Eurocentric environmentalism has long figured nonwhite reproductive sex as a threat to nature. Even "prior to European colonization of the Global South," Gosine notes, "fantasies and anxieties about its 'monstrous races' and lascivious 'Wild Men' and 'Wild Women' circulated in oral and written texts."[47] "Through the course of colonization, anxieties about non-white peoples' sexualities would also inform the constitution of natural space across the world. The creation of 'wildlife preserves' and national parks across the colonized world was predicated on the removal of their human, reproductive presence: the areas' indigenous populations."[48] If we trace this history all the way back to the Jaktorowska forest, we can see the origins of a biopolitical split between sovereign power and a nonsovereign subject people, legally demoted beneath both exceptional animal and preternatural landscape. For such reasons, and as my reading of Hushpuppy's story and its placement in the landscape suggests, it is not at all accidental that blackness and indigeneity should stalk the outposts that critical thought has set up in the wild, like elongated shadows cast just beyond the perimeter of theory's flickering campfires.

If the liberal color blindness behind the casting of a young African American girl as Hushpuppy becomes the device whereby "broad" audiences can immerse themselves in Hushpuppy's animate world, it is also an event that tethers the film to a real set of people, locations, contradictions. The cinematic mode of production chosen by Zeitlin itself renders difficult the typical distinction between aesthetic form and historical context. Rather, the actors shaped the characters in an improvisational and relational process, and the story itself adjusts to accommodate, to let itself seep into, the preternatural landscape of Terrebonne Parish. At Zeitlin's inspiration, Alibar's story moved to the Gulf Coast of Louisiana, and the aurochs were sent to Antarctica. Along the way, Alibar felt herself finally able to write the character Hushpuppy as a girl. In the introduction to the published play, Alibar does not explain why this "return" to female gender was accomplished via a race change. She does not indicate if that change assisted or disabled the process of distancing Hushpuppy from her own biography. But she does makes clear the degree to which the character Hushpuppy is the fabulated outcome of a writing process that straddles white and black, male and female, fact and fantasy, insofar as the final shape both versions of the character took was influenced by the actor cast in the role, and the setting against which she or he is figured.

In her critical review of the film, Sharpe perceptively infers that casting Quvenzhané Wallis facilitates the transformation of Hushpuppy's narrative from southern family gothic to ecological allegory. Only a black child, Sharpe reasons, can be positioned in conditions of such dire abandonment without a narrative explanation being offered.[49] And just as precarity is frequently naturalized to the black female *figure* in dystopian films such as *Children of Men*, as Jayna Brown has argued, so is ecological stewardship frequently projected onto indigenous *ground*.[50] The preternatural aurochs works to pivot the film between these two racial idioms, as free indirect images are employed to bring Hushpuppy and her water landscape alternately into focus. The film's image of a happy mongrel America, subsisting somewhere below or beyond the invidious racial separatism of bourgeois society, does not initially seem to include Native Americans. But against the backdrop of the internment camp, which Hushpuppy compares to a fishbowl, the true source of her wild nature becomes evident; it proceeds from the land from which "civilization" has violently snatched her.

If the film's narrative offers a voyeuristic look into the survival of a community of alterity living outside the biopolitical protection of the state, the filmmaking process stages a parallel trajectory of the transplantation and adoption of a liberal ecological imaginary onto a real environment and its population. Many look to the Gulf Coast as a site of particular ecological precarity, no more so than now, in the wake of Hurricanes Katrina and Rita, and the Deepwater Horizon oil spill (which occurred during the filming of *Beasts*). And if *Beasts* helps us recognize our complicity in such disasters, it can do so only by correlating the fictional Bathtub to the actual Isle de Jean Charles. This correlation was in fact highlighted in the reporting on the film, such as in the *New York Times*:

> Mr. Zeitlin traveled outside of his adopted hometown [of New Orleans] in search of real-life cultures that live on the front lines of storms and coastal erosion. "When you look at the map, you can see America kind of crumble off into the sinews down in the gulf where the land is getting eaten up," he said. "I was really interested in these roads that go all the way down to the bottom of America and what was at the end of them."
>
> What Mr. Zeitlin found were the bayou fishing towns of Terrebonne Parish. Relatively unscathed by Katrina but hit hard by Hurricane Rita the same summer, and by Hurricanes Gustav and Ike in 2008, Terrebonne is a region with a vibrant culture that extends to the very edge of the Delta's vanishing wetlands. On his first trip there Mr. Zeitlin drove down a narrow road, half-sunk in water, leading to Isle de Jean Charles, a tiny island just off the mainland. Only 40 years ago the thriving home of French-speaking American Indians, the island, with around two dozen families left, is gradually disintegrating into the Gulf of Mexico and falls outside the protection of the federal levee system. Although "Beasts" draws cultural inspiration from across the southern part of the state, Isle de Jean Charles provided Mr. Zeitlin's reference points for the Bathtub's surreal ecological precariousness and its residents' fierce commitment to remaining.[51]

A transplant and adoptee who fabricates a fictional Bathtub out of an actual indigenous community at "the bottom of America" might deservedly raise questions of "playing Indian" or "going native." Zeitlin seeks to avoid such charges by representing his fable as a cocreation of the community that welcomed him. But that language of community subtly elides the Biloxi-Chitimacha-Choctaw and Houma nations residents of Isle de Jean Charles, present in the backstory as "reference points" for "surreal ecological precariousness," but absent from the present-day project of climate resistance (itself a project that often excludes or elides indigenous sovereignty). Zeitlin's filmmaking has indeed captured the preternatural quasi-animacy of his adopted region. But in so extending "our" imaginative presence into those sinewy tendrils beyond land's end, indigeneity is pushed off the map. This raises the question: why superimpose a mythic mongrel utopia over this location of native survival?

Conversely, black sovereignty is hardly an option in a scenario in which Wink first appears as nearly naked and fugitive from a hospital, Hushpuppy nearly burns down her home, and her mother has gone vagrant long ago. The attempt to render coherent Wink's connection to his watery land results in a telling moment of incoherence in the film, when he refuses to explain why he will not abandon the Bathtub during a storm (even when other residents temporarily flee). Despite its overall message of hope and resilience, the film cannot avoid presenting this moment as one of dereliction: a dying man ready to abandon his defenseless daughter to her fate. Even when he finally tries to relinquish his daughter to the state's protection, that act only underscores his ultimate acknowledgment of his pathology. It is startling to encounter critics reading Wink and Hushpuppy's relation through the prism of autonomy given, as Brown notes, that their sources of survival are utterly mystified by the narrative: "Their existence isn't active or sustainable," Brown writes, "the characters' self-destructive forms of coping painfully insufficient. This is no maroon society, nor is it like any community of generationally poor people in the US or the global south."[52] I suggest that one reason for this incoherence is the attempt to project (an idealized) nonsovereignty onto bodies that are always already read as nonsovereign in US racial problem melodramas. As depicted in the film, Wink and Hushpuppy cannot relinquish human sovereignty, because the possibility of a *sovereign* relation to the steadily subsiding land of the Bathtub, as Wilderson argues is the case of black subjects, is already excluded.[53] Conversely, the many incompossible versions of Hushpuppy appear to preclude the possibility of a native one, insofar as the landscape that Hushpuppy sees relies on a cinematic native removal as a condition for its emergence into visibility. It is the engulfment of native sovereignty that renders the resultant wildness recuperable for white fantasies of surrogation, adoption, and transplantation. Native removal, in other words, assists the ease of imaginary access to a "free and wild" use of nature below the human, and at "the bottom of America."

But the recurrence of the aurochs in Hushpuppy's story is also a sign of the return of the European repressed. The aurochs, after all, are not native to North America either. Their "return" to southern Louisiana is also a territorializing of native landscape by Eurocentric myth. The preternatural presence of the aurochs in our southern wild becomes more explicable if we understand how it reenacts the European colonization of the New World in bovine form. Abandoning the eugenic nightmare of Nazi biopolitics does not entirely cleanse the figure of the aurochs from all sovereign designs. Relocated from the play's mis-en-scène to Terrebonne Parish, the aurochs become an invasive species, and Hushpuppy must stand up against their predatory force without even the assurance that her life will be considered human. Her successful confrontation with the aurochs at the film's climax runs the knife's edge between affirming her resilience and consolidating her abandonment.

Conclusion: Sovereignty's Little Monsters

The relations of beast and the sovereign—from the Jaktorowska forest to Terrebonne Parish—are neither fixed nor guaranteed. I do not unspool the fascist genome of the preternatural aurochs, or exhume buried histories of settler colonialism, to posit rewilding as inherently reactionary. Along with queer critics like Halberstam, I am interested in what promise wildness might hold for queer, feminist, and antiracist projects. The little incompossible monsters produced out of our drive toward new and more cogent myths for our present, less governed and more anarchic modes of living and creating, can all best be accounted for if we resist instrumentalizing or essentializing either wildness or freedom. Hushpuppy's fabulation offers both encouragements and cautions for Jane Bennett's new materialist vision of the wild. For Bennett, the wild obliges us to "acknowledge a force that, though quite real and powerful, is intrinsically resistant to representation."[54] I have explored how the incompossibility of Hushpuppy indexes such a force that indeed resists the stability of representation, but I have also noted how this instability itself becomes problematic. Rather than valorize her wildness as offering intrinsic resistance to representation, we might instead take Hushpuppy as a *case*, as one among the proliferating objects of analysis that queer studies increasingly handles, one of its many "little monsters." The proper object of no extant domain of inquiry, this emergent queer bestiary suggests the need for new critical idioms that make space for both fabulation and its complicit antecedents, for ecology and its dark precursors.

It is tempting to misconstrue black and native presences in *Beasts* as signs of progress en route to a color-blind planetary solidarity in the face of climate

change. On the contrary, those signs are symptoms of a continued liberal enchant-
ment with a "transparent" subject, unmarked by exterior signs of racial or sexual
difference.[55] Colluding with this liberalism, posthumanist theory has tended to
present the decentering of the human as both salutary and largely innocent of
history. Up until the present time, we are told in one version of this philosophical
fable, we have incorrectly centered the human. Now we can, and must, correct
that error, if only (paradoxically) to save ourselves. It is in anticipation of such
tales that black studies has repeatedly asked: have we ever been human? And
if not, what are we being asked to decenter, and through what means? There is
a "speaker's benefit" attendant to the act of declaring one's nonsovereignty: one
must presume to have it in order to relinquish it.[56] This is why I suggested earlier,
in the realm of ecotheory, that we have not yet cut off the head of the king. Our
privileged mechanisms for figuring the nonsovereign subject continue to rely on
what Silva calls a "strategy of engulfment" in which vulnerability is projected onto
other bodies and spaces, reterritorializing Western reason in the process.[57] "Modern representation," Silva warns, "can sustain transparency, as the distinguishing
feature of post-Enlightenment European social configurations, only through the
engulfment of exterior things, the inescapable effect of scientific reason's version
of universality, while at the same time postponing that 'Other' ontology it threatens
to institute."[58] The conflation of the real history of Hurricane Katrina with the fictive history of the Bathtub relies on such a strategy with depressing literality: the
engulfing of southern Louisiana is made visible and affecting by the engulfing of
the raced and sexed other in a film praxis that sets up a transparently knowable
"color-blind" character as a stand-in for the self. The film posits, but defers, the
"other" ontology that Hushpuppy threatens to institute.

The filmmakers' dream of a rewilded, ecological cinema is indeed alluring, but achieving it by tapping into the primitive vitality of a native terrain and its
mongrel denizens fails to answer the challenge that black and indigenous studies
pose to the posthuman. The preternatural aurochs, whose place in the history of
imperial expansion the film must occlude in order to produce its multicultural fantasy, is itself the result of a selective breeding seeking to recover pure origins from
a murky past. The aurochs cannot reappear unless we make it reappear, but the
means of that making are indelibly tainted. Rather than miniaturize this awful history to render it cute, queer inhumanism might instead seek to recover from history
a face that is unrecognizable, and a wildness that would transgress the sovereign's
preserve.

Figure 1. Untitled Research Image (Jacktorów). Photograph by Michael Wang

Afterword

The drawings and photographs of Michael Wang offer us a different queer and hybrid path into the preternatural wild. Wang is an interdisciplinary artist whose works broach environmental issues with a wry but oblique attentiveness to race, hybridity, queerness, and planetary capitalism. *Carbon Copies*, from 2012, offers a series of appropriations of famous contemporary works of art (in both plastic and performative mediums) valued at the cost of the carbon offset of the energy expended to make them. Drawing aesthetic and market value into a tight dialectic, Wang stages the stratospheric valorization of artistic experience and abstraction against the shimmering backdrop of its "dirty ecology."[59] His work thus implicitly poses in aesthetic terms the question of the appropriation of experience with which this essay has been (perhaps implicitly) wrestling. It does so pointedly, but nondidactically: his work is wondrous but not inspirational. It stages complicity without requiring a dream to dream an "us" into being. Put another way, it tells the environmental history of the planetary without engulfing the human in a universal "I." *Global Tone*, from 2013, reassembles in drawing and installation the broken and buried pieces of imperial history, including a monument to the wisent, the Aryan bison that Göring tried to breed back into fascist vitality during the Nazi era to replenish the ethnically cleansed Polish wild. The photo that accompanies this essay (fig. 1) forms part of Wang's creative research into the mixed and profane history of preternatural monsters like the wisent and the reverse-bred aurochs, a path that led him back to the creek in the Jaktorowska forest where the last aurochs purportedly died. This last aurochs, a female, was not the male aurochs whose proud, horned relics were carried back to Denmark as war spoils, where they remain on display. The remains of this aurochs subsist only in rumor, as she died years before the king's inspector arrived to count her. Wang's photograph records a wild, anachronistic perception of her absent presence as dark precursor to the preternatural aurochs that crash through *Beasts of the Southern Wild*. Unlike the film, however, no face-to-face moment of biophilic contact or recognition is staged or implied. Neither the aurochs nor the primitivized child fabulist is available in this image to do the work of fabulation for the viewer. As Keeling might posit, the witch's flight diagrams the play of forces in the image, but then retreats from visibility. And indeed it could only have been tacit lore, the deep and discredited memory of the subaltern, that led Wang back to this particular creek, in whose still, dark waters is refracted the shimmering presence of a fugitive life whose dark vitality would be, finally, unutterable in the terms with which contemporary posthumanist theory would speak it.

Notes

1. Michel Foucault, *An Introduction*, vol. 1 of *The History of Sexuality*, trans. Robert Hurley (New York: Vintage, 1990), 138.
2. C. J. C. Phillips, *Principles of Cattle Production*, 2nd ed. (Cambridge: CABI, 2010), 2.
3. My account of the extinction of the aurochs is principally drawn from Mieczyslaw

Rokosz, "History of the Aurochs (Bos Taurus Primegenius) in Poland," *Animal Genetic Resources* 16 (1995): 5–12.

4. A recent critical synthesis of this rapidly expanding literature is provided in Jordana Rosenberg, "The Molecularization of Sexuality: On Some Primitivisms of the Present," *Theory and Event* 17, no. 2 (2014), muse.jhu.edu. See also Elizabeth Grosz, *Becoming Undone: Darwinian Reflections on Life, Politics, and Art* (Durham, NC: Duke University Press, 2011); and Claire Colebrook, *Sex after Life: Essays on Extinction*, vol. 2 (Ann Arbor, MI: Open Humanities Press, 2014).

5. Jamie Lorimer and Clemens Driessen, "Bovine Biopolitics and the Promise of Monsters in the Rewilding of Heck Cattle," *Geoforum* 48 (August 2013): 249–59.

6. Jacques Derrida, *The Beast and the Sovereign*, vol. 1 (Chicago: University of Chicago Press, 2009).

7. My thinking on the wild beyond is shaped by Jack Halberstam's recent work on this concept. See Halberstam, "The Wild Beyond: With and for the Undercommons," in *The Undercommons: Fugitive Planning and Black Study*, ed. Stefano Harney and Fred Moten (New York: Minor Compositions, 2013), 2–13.

8. On the speculative realist critique of correlationism, and the retrieval of the Great Outdoors, see Quentin Meillassoux, *After Finitude: An Essay on the Necessity of Contingency* (London: Continuum, 2008). Rosenberg makes a persuasive case that the pursuit of the Great Outdoors through the pursuit of figures of the "ancestral" is, in her words, a "theoretical primitivism that presents itself as a methodological avant-garde." See Rosenberg, "Molecularization of Sexuality."

9. Giorgio Agamben, *State of Exception* (Chicago: University of Chicago Press, 2005).

10. See the discussion of "biophilia" below. The circularity of this drive toward the outdoors is also noted in Rosenberg's claim that object-oriented ontologies represent an "onto-primitivism" ("Molecularization of Sexuality").

11. See, in particular, Jayna Brown, "Beasts of the Southern Wild—the Romance of Precarity II," *Social Text* (blog), September 27, 2012, socialtextjournal.org/beasts-of-the-southern-wild-the-romance-of-precarity-ii; bell hooks, "No Love in the Wild," *New Black Man*, September 5, 2012, newblackman.blogspot.co.uk/2012/09/bell-hooks-no-love-in-wild.html; Christina Sharpe, "Beasts of the Southern Wild—the Romance of Precarity I," *Social Text* (blog), September 27, 2012, socialtextjournal.org/beasts-of-the-southern-wild-the-romance-of-precarity-i; and Patricia Yaeger, "Beasts of the Southern Wild and Dirty Ecology," *Southern Spaces*, February 13, 2013, www.southernspaces.org/2013/beasts-southern-wild-and-dirty-ecology.

12. Nicholas Mirzoeff, "Becoming Wild," *Occupy 2012*, September 30, 2012, www.nicholasmirzoeff.com/O2012/2012/09/30/becoming-wild/; Yaeger, "Beasts of the Southern Wild and Dirty Ecology."

13. Rachel Arons, "The Making of 'Beasts of the Southern Wild,'" *New York Times*, June 8, 2012. In one particularly telling instance of this blurring of film text and produc-

tion process, the filmmakers reported opting for costumed domestic pigs, instead of CGI effects, to render the preternatural aurochs, because that would lend greater verisimilitude to the low-tech conditions in the (fictional) Bathtub, where the film was set.

14. On the color-blind casting of Hushpuppy, see Bill Keith, "Meet Lucy Alibar, Oscar Nominated Screenwriter of Beasts of the Southern Wild," *The Credits*, February 22, 2013, www.thecredits.org/2013/02/beauty-who-co-wrote-the-beast-meet-lucy-alibar -oscar-nominated-screenwriter-of-beasts-of-the-southern-wild/.

15. On invagination, see Fred Moten, *In the Break: The Aesthetics of the Black Radical Tradition* (Minneapolis: University of Minnesota Press, 2003), 258. On intensive manifold, see Jane Bennett, *Vibrant Matter: A Political Ecology of Things* (Durham, NC: Duke University Press, 2010), 62–81.

16. Mel Chen, *Animacies* (Durham, NC: Duke University Press, 2012).

17. Levi Bryant, "Wilderness Ontology," in *Preternatural*, ed. Celina Jeffery (Brooklyn: Punctum, 2011), 20.

18. Grégoire Chamayou, *Manhunts: A Philosophical History* (Princeton: Princeton University Press, 2012).

19. Foucault, *Introduction*, 89.

20. Jonathan D. Culler, *The Pursuit of Signs: Semiotics, Literature, Deconstruction* (Ithaca, NY: Cornell University Press, 2002).

21. Culler, *Pursuit of Signs*, 176.

22. Frank B. Wilderson, *Red, White, and Black: Cinema and the Structure of U.S. Antagonisms* (Durham, NC: Duke University Press, 2010), 5.

23. Kara Keeling, *The Witch's Flight: The Cinematic, the Black Femme, and the Image of Common Sense* (Durham, NC: Duke University Press, 2007), 149.

24. Nathan Widder, *Political Theory after Deleuze* (New York: Continuum, 2012), 34.

25. Alibar has indicated that she wrote the original character of Hushpuppy in *Juicy and Delicious* with the actor who had been cast to play him in mind, and then rewrote the character when Wallis was cast. "I think all playwrights know it's going to end up changing depending on your cast, and that's why playwrights and actors tend to have ongoing relationships. So with Nazie, it became a lot younger, and a lot more Louisiana. She was already pretty Louisiana by the time we wrote the script, but she was absolutely instrumental" (Katie Calautti, "Lucy Alibar Talks Adapting Her Play into *Beasts of the Southern Wild*," *Spinoff Online*, July 13, 2012, spinoff.comicbook resources.com/2012/07/13/lucy-alibar-talks-adapting-her-play-into-beasts-of-the -southern-wild).

26. The big gay dance number in the play is replaced by a more straightforward primal scene in the film, in which Wink recalls the exact moment of Hushpuppy's conception, immediately after Hushpuppy's mother shoots an alligator with a rifle. Wink, true to his name, has dozed off when the alligator comes creeping, Wink's feminized vulnerability directly contrasted with his wife's gun-toting virilizing force. His subsequent

efforts to masculinize his daughter thus read as belated attempts to compensate for his earlier soft, even queer masculinity, his insistent misgendering of Hushpuppy as "man" a telltale giveaway that the manhood he would inscribe everywhere can in fact be located nowhere.

27. Yaeger, "Beasts of the Southern Wild and Dirty Ecology."

28. The classic theoretical statement on the free indirect image in cinema can be found in Gilles Deleuze, *Cinema 2: The Time Image* (Minneapolis: University of Minnesota Press, 1989), 126–55. For a critical perspective on Deleuze's use of the free indirect image, see Louis Georges Schwartz, "Typewriter: Free Indirect Discourse in Deleuze's Cinema," *SubStance* 34, no. 3 (2005): 107–35.

29. There is another moment in the film—in which several adults, led by Wink, chant "Beast it! Beast it!" as Hushpuppy attempts to eat a crab—that suggests the residents of the Bathtub accept "beast" as a self-designation of sorts.

30. Yaeger, "Beasts of the Southern Wild and Dirty Ecology."

31. Jayne Brown, "The Human Project," *Transition* 110 (2013): 120–35.

32. Sharpe, "Beasts of the Southern Wild—the Romance of Precarity I"; and Brown, "Beasts of the Southern Wild—the Romance of Precarity II."

33. Widder, *Political Theory after Deleuze*, 129.

34. In feminist and queer political theory, the field of thinkers associated with the "new materialism" sometimes draw from figurations of the wild and wildness. In her contribution to the volume that helped constitute that field, which she also coedited, the political theorist Diana Coole draws on the phenomenology of Maurice Merleau-Ponty to describe a "wild-flowering world" made visible by a "brute" or "wild" perception. See Diana Coole and Samantha Frost, eds., *New Materialism: Ontology, Agency, and Politics.* (Durham, NC: Duke University Press, 2010). Halberstam has articulated a new convergence of anarchism and queerness through an imagining and enactment of the wild ("Wild Beyond"). Bennett cites what she describes as Henry David Thoreau's concept of "the Wild" in her field-shaping monograph *Vibrant Matter.*

35. Deleuze and Guattari, *What Is Philosophy?* (New York: Columbia University Press, 1996), 105.

36. Grégoire Chamayou, *Manhunts: A Philosophical History* (Princeton, NJ: Princeton University Press, 2012).

37. Diane Chisholm, "Biophilia, Creative Involution, and the Ecological Future of Queer Desire," in *Queer Ecologies: Sex, Nature, Politics, Desire*, ed. Catriona Mortimer-Sandilands and Bruce Erickson (Bloomington: Indiana University Press, 2010), 376.

38. Gilles Deleuze, *Difference and Repetition*, trans. Paul Patton (London: Continuum, 2004), 145.

39. Lucy Alibar, *Juicy and Delicious: The Play That Inspired the Movie Beasts of the Southern Wild* (New York: Diversion Books, 2012), Kindle edition.

40. Michael Wang, "Heavy Breeding," *Cabinet* 45 (2012), www.cabinetmagazine.org /issues/45/wang.php.

41. Jamie Lorimer and Clemens Driessen, "Bovine Biopolitics and the Promise of Monsters in the Rewilding of Heck Cattle," *Geoforum* 48 (2013): 249–59.

42. Wang, "Heavy Breeding."

43. Tavia Nyong'o, *The Amalgamation Waltz: Race, Performance, and the Ruses of Memory* (Minneapolis: University of Minnesota Press, 2009), 3.

44. Denise Ferreira da Silva, *Toward a Global Idea of Race* (Minneapolis: University of Minnesota Press, 2007), xvi.

45. Silva, *Toward a Global Idea of Race*, 32.

46. See also Fred Moten, "The Case of Blackness," *Criticism* 50, no. 2 (2008): 177–218.

47. Andil Gosine, "Non-white Reproduction and Same-Sex Eroticism: Queer Acts against Nature," in Mortimer-Sandilands and Erickson, *Queer Ecologies*, 151.

48. Gosine, "Non-white Reproduction," 152.

49. Sharpe, "Beasts of the Southern Wild: The Romance of Precarity I."

50. Brown, "The Human Project."

51. Rachel Arons, "A Mythical Bayou's All-Too-Real Peril: The Making of 'Beasts of the Southern Wild,'" *New York Times*, June 8, 2012, www.nytimes.com/2012/06/10/movies /the-making-of-beasts-of-the-southern-wild.html.

52. Brown, "Beasts of the Southern Wild: The Romance of Precarity II."

53. This point is argued more extensively in Wilderson's study of the Hollywood racial problem film, where he argues that the slave and the savage are positioned differently in relation to the society that seeks to exclude and engulf them both. In his comparative analysis of the native and the black, he makes a particular point of noting the presence of sovereignty on the part of the savage, and thus, an at least partial access to the human. See Wilderson, *Red, White, and Black*.

54. Bennett, *Vibrant Matter*, xvi.

55. Silva, *Toward a Global Idea of Race*.

56. I thank Jack Halberstam for making this point while commenting on this manuscript. On the "speaker's benefit," see Foucault, *Introduction*, 6.

57. Silva, *Toward a Global Idea of Race*, 32.

58. Silva, *Toward a Global Idea of Race*, 32.

59. Yaeger, "Beasts of the Southern Wild and Dirty Ecology."

FEELINGS AND FRACTALS

Woolly Ecologies of Transgender Matter

Jeanne Vaccaro

Crochet Coral Reef (2005–) is a woolly exoskeleton of coralline geometries and sea critters made by a collective of hands joining animal and plastic fibers in hyperbolic shapes. The reef is a "testimony to the disappearing wonder of living reefs" and a creative experiment of the twin sisters Margaret and Christine Wertheim, a science writer and an art professor, respectively, and the Los Angeles nonprofit Institute for Figuring; like the marine organism, the crochet reef is fertile and spawns its fiber tentacles to stage public art interventions about warming sea temperatures, carbon dioxide, ocean acidification, plastic trash, and the pacific trash vortex.[1] As a collective and aesthetic rendering of threat and survival, *Crochet Coral Reef* is suggestive of how we negotiate environmental risk in myriad forms of collusion, protest, and cohabitation. "We" is an idea and a problem, a shape to ask after. I am particularly interested in the convergence between this project's engagement with touch, risk/survival, and handicraft, on the one hand, and those issues in transgender theory and experience, on the other: that is, I see promising overlaps between a fiber art project and the everyday process of becoming that transgender life necessitates. In what follows I practice, as a method, *intra action*, a process that Karen Barad describes as "the mutual constitution of entangled agencies," to think between coral erosion and transgender.[2] Valuing a diversity of fragile ecological bodies—human, animal, fiber, and aquatic—this essay examines how patterns of harm contour vulnerable populations and the administration of life in biosocial scenes of not only climate and biosphere but also sex and gender. It does so by foregrounding feelings *and* fractals—or patterns and repeats—to assemble a lexicon of transgender in coral, crochet coral,

GLQ 21:2–3
DOI 10.1215/10642684-2843347
© 2015 by Duke University Press

and hyperbolic geometry, and to craft a tentacle-like shape between transgender and its environments: administrative, aesthetic, cellular, woolly, toxic, oceanic. As Donna Haraway asks in her manifesto for cyborgs, "Why should our bodies end at the skin, or include at best other beings encapsulated by skin?"[3] Oscillating between feelings and fractals, unwieldy and algorithmic modes of description, yields a fibrous and felt science of transgender life.

Woolly Pedagogy: The Handmade

In *Brain Storm* Rebecca Jordan-Young describes the "confused, confusing, and contentious" configurations of sex, gender, and sexuality as a "three-ply yarn" and endeavors to untangle the "strands that are simultaneously distinct, interrelated, and somewhat fuzzy around the boundaries."[4] And Sophia Roosth, in her exploration of *Crochet Coral Reef* and the stories we tell to inhabit and transform evolutionary knowledge, writes: "Analogies from the fiber arts run deep in the life sciences, as attested by the preponderance of terms such as *strand*, *tissue*, *membrane*, *fiber*, and *filament* in anatomy and *net* or *web* in systems biology and ecology."[5] I am similarly compelled by fiber, and this essay animates the labor, process, and materials of handiwork to illuminate the biological and cultural constructions of sex and gender. Like a sewing circle or quilting bee, *Crochet Coral Reef* and its collective labor of "figuring" operates between the optic and sensory. Similarly, identity is made between administrative force and self-determination, between legal and scientific interventions and ad hoc self making. As transgender labors for diverse and sometimes divergent aims, the shape of its analytic force is also knotted to its flux and circulation in, for example, community organizing, arts and culture, the administration of diagnosis and health, and the law. The felt configuration of the "handmade," then, orients our thinking to the labor and materiality (fiber, flesh, "biocodes") of crafting identity.[6] This essay is part of a project to place transgender theory in dialogue with craft studies, themes of figuration, collectivity, process, and amateurism, and the ordinary shapes and sensations of bodily transformation.[7]

Craft is a conceptual limit, categorically unlike the sublime; in Immanuel Kant's aesthetic judgment, it is mere purpose, effect.[8] Maligned in Renaissance hierarchies of liberal and mechanical arts, craft evokes the remunerative, utilitarian, ornamental, and manual labor and laborers— the feminine, ethnic, and "primitive"—however, craft is a legitimate field of inquiry and, while adjacent to art history, is increasingly recognized as a theoretical process and method.[9] Transgender is something of a maligned materiality as well, what the legal theorist Dean

Spade has called "LGB-fake-T studies," in ways that are both theoretical and concrete; as with craft studies there are no undergraduate or graduate degrees offered in transgender studies (although the new research cluster spearheaded by Susan Stryker at the University of Arizona may be a sign of changing times). *Crochet Coral Reef* offers an opportunity to forge a dialogue between these "minor" fields of inquiry, as materiality negatively saturates transgender and craft studies and thus offers a potential theory of identity in flesh and fabric. As the art historian Julia Bryan-Wilson reminds us with scholarship that mines contemporary craft for insights into feminized labor, the outsourcing of labor, and geopolitical commerce, "Craft is uniquely positioned to allow us to reconsider the politics of materiality and exchange—their labors, pleasures, and hazards."[10]

Deploying ideas of craft—too frequently dismissed as low art, skilled labor, or "women's work"—the handmade connects transgender to collective process and quotidian aesthetics. As the material is marginalized by discursive forms of legibility, the performative dimensions of craft privilege the politics of the hand, that which is worked on, and the sensory feelings and textures of crafting transgender identity. The handmade, utilitarian, and purposeful materials popular in craft and material studies is brought to bear in this essay to illuminate the everyday as a site of value for transgender identity. By speaking of "crafting" transgender identity, I mean to highlight the felt labor and traces of making and unmaking identity and the performative doing of gender becoming in relation to the materiality of the flesh. While relevant to all kinds of identity making and politics, it is an especially relevant corrective for transgender histories (of the clinic, of diagnostic force, or of theoretical accounts like, for example, the one made by Jay Prosser in *Second Skins: The Body Narratives of Transsexuality*, which makes a strong objection to performativity as method for knowing transgender life, as he argues performativity cannot account for "the feeling and experience of being transexed").[11] My aim here is to pressure the digestible forms of narrative and diagnostic representation available to transgender people by privileging the labor of texture and touch. Foregrounding process, rather than achievement, is a critical bridge between transgender and craft studies, as the study of *how* works to displace the logic of *when* in the urgent, administrative clock of diagnosis and medicalization.

In connection with transbiology—"a biology that is not only born and bred, or born and made, but *made and born*" (which I discuss below)—and the elastic materials of fiber arts, this essay aims to build a dimensional record of bodily experience.[12] The handmade is a methodology—a call to value the aesthetic and performative labor of making identity—and builds points of contact between transgender and craft studies by looking at materials that make transgender identity felt and legible, such as wood, wool, skin, sweat, rubber, foam, cloth, and scar tissue. In this essay I ask after the lush shapes and textures of many things: the hard, rough edges of marine coral and soft, woolly seams of crochet coral; the slippery, translucent film of plastic grocery bags recycled into an environmental manifesto; and the bright and open turbulence of the hyperbolic dimension. My aim here is to highlight the sensory and emotional dimensions of feeling in order to confront the force of diagnosis and value the ordinary politics of crafting transgender life.

As a felt method, the intervention that the handmade offers is to reexamine method as the ordering—its patterns, repeats, echoes (as waves of the sonic, oceanic thumps, and women's and feminist politics and studies)—of bodily knowledge. In other words, hand making is a mode of knowing and doing objects and bodies. The handmade is an operating system or guide, a fleshy science to untangle ordinary shapes and feelings of embodied life and its intersections with vibrant matter and toxicity. Given this moment of the institutionalization of queer (and increasingly) transgender studies, we are poised to practice transgender studies in what I am thinking of as a tentacle formation, and take up the invitation offered by "trans—," a "(de)subjugated knowledge" affixed to and made plural by proximity:

> "Trans" thus becomes the capillary space of connection and circulation between the macro- and micro-political registers through which the lives of bodies become enmeshed in the lives of nations, state, and capital-formations, while "–gender" becomes one of several sets of variable techniques or temporal practices (such as race or class) through which bodies are made to live.[13]

In other words, leaning on the objectness of craft orients our thinking to the spatial and temporal landscape of embodiment and highlights the force of the hand (rather than the diagnosis) in the worked on, textured, sensory, and amateur labor of making identity in the everyday. Additionally, the lengthened dash in "trans—," theorized in the introduction to a special issue of *Women's Studies Quarterly* on the subject by editors Susan Stryker, Paisley Currah, and Lisa Jean Moore, foregrounds the disruption and remade connection of trans- and -gender, and "marks the difference between the implied nominalism of 'trans' and the explicit relationality of 'trans—,' which remains open-ended and resists premature foreclosure by attachment to any single suffix."[14] The porosity of its categorization is not vacuous or void; as Stryker and Currah ask of transgender in the inaugural issue of *Transgender Studies Quarterly*, "Postposttranssexual: Key Concepts for a Twenty-First Century Transgender Studies," "Does it help make or undermine gender identities and expressions? Is it a way of being gendered or a way of doing gender? Is it an identification or a method?"[15] In the mode of query transgender is made a promise and provocation.

Method is a labor of dispersal, containment, and a pattern, repeat, echo. But as Margaret Wertheim cautions, "by restricting ourselves to a Euclidean perspective we lose the visceral sense of hyberbolic being."[16] By way of offering a cosmic catalog of transgender as labor (cosmic like a mythic science, a mode between sense and belief and a system of study), I focus on patterns and the patterning of identity and the bodies and forms of embodiment we cannot quiet by the work of description. What is foreclosed and what is made quiet by the orientation of our bodies and politics to description? In "I'd Rather Be a Cyborg Than a Goddess": Becoming-Intersectional in Assemblage Theory," Jasbir Puar reads the intersectional as a method to examine the force of its pedagogy and asks how, for feminist thinkers, activists, teachers, and students, the intersectional is, like the university's traffic in diversity language as capital, sometimes invoked to quiet and absorb difference. She stages as "frictional" the false opposition of Kimberlé Crenshaw's intersectionality to Gilles Deleuze and Félix Guattari's assemblage and writes, "Subject positioning on a grid is never self-coinciding; positioning does not precede movement but rather it is induced by it; epistemological correctives cannot apprehend ontological becomings; the complexity of process is continually mistaken for a resultant product."[17] Her staging of a false opposition as "frictional"—X is against X (and is X "a" Body and X an Identity?)—suggests that it is not like or unlike, for or against, or a description of a thing, and so forms a network for thinking of transgender as, for example, a body, a collection of skin and organs, the organizing of social and sexual exchange, a politic, an aspiration, a keyword, a "special guest," a way of being in the world. The handmade, in this spirit, is a frictional offering of transgender as experiment, provocation, potential.[18]

What can the patchwork organization of marine coral, the geometry of hyperbolic crochet, and the transbiological teach us about transgender? The difficulty of language, and my sense of sometimes being at its limits, matter insofar as the work to describe, look, and feel make demands on us differently. To theorize the texture of a thing like politics or identity is always labor of reaching (perhaps desiring), and the space between our descriptive and bodily knowledge is difficult to navigate because the density of material and emotion conjoin to language in uneven and imperceptible modes. It is difficult because the fabric of our alignment in the social is felt at registers we cannot always translate, and language is more than a process of translation or vehicle of connection. If in words we cannot manage the expressive work of identity—we know by our failures we cannot—we might look to the labor of senses and shapes—or feel for it: in our thinking, politics, writing, and art making. The fleshy, fibrous seams of *Crochet Coral Reef* and the geometry of its marine ecology illustrate how new life, including the new lives constituted by shifts in or confirmations of identity, can flourish as felt patterns. What if we expanded our definitions of transgender to a new form of life, a constant process of making that could be figured by or alongside something like coral or handicraft?

Yarns, Plastic, and the Geometry of Craft

Crochet Coral Reef plays at the intersection of marine biology, feminine handicrafts, and mathematics. It began as a creative experiment in the Los Angeles living room of the Wertheims; soon, the crochet reef became difficult to contain, a dense and voluminous fabric in the house, much like the abundant and organic excess of the hyperbolic dimension, a kind of geometry characterized as non-Euclidean by its excess surface and negative curvature, and like the spawning reproductive force of marine coral itself. Looking for some extra hands to help spawn the reef, the artists posted an open call on the website of the Institute for Figuring (IFF)—the nonprofit organization they founded in 2003 for the material and physical exploration of science and mathematics—seeking participants to assist in the making of hyperbolic crochet coral reef as a public artwork. Today, over eight thousand people have contributed to thirty satellite reefs in Germany, Abu Dhabi, Ireland, Latvia, Baltimore, and Japan. Collectives of volunteers, often organized around lectures and interactive workshops taught by Margaret Wertheim, have stitched sea slugs, kelp, anemones, and coral polyps, and produced branches of the crochet coral reef like a kelp garden, the Branched Anemone Garden, the Ladies' Silurian Atoll, a toxic reef made of white and gray recycled plastic trash, and a "bleached" installation made of cotton tampons. *Crochet Coral Reef* stretches over three thousand square feet and has been exhibited at the Andy Warhol Museum (Pittsburgh, 2007), the Hayward (London, 2008), the Science Gallery (Dublin, 2010), the Smithsonian's National Museum of Natural History (Washington, DC, 2010), and the Cooper Hewitt National Design Museum (New York, 2010). According to the IFF, the reef is "one of the largest participatory science + art projects in the world."[19]

The Wertheims formed the IFF in 2003 as a "play tank" for public education about the "aesthetic and poetic dimensions" of science, mathematics, and engineering.[20] Figuring—a process of calculating, shaping, patterning, and forming things and ideas—is a pedagogical method and a hopeful bridge between

Figure 1. Institute For Figuring's *Crochet Coral Reef* project, 2005–ongoing, as installed at New York University Abu Dhabi Institute, 2014. Photo © the IFF

intellect and physicality. In its exhibitions, workshops, lectures, and artist residencies, the IFF seeks to animate abstract ideas like geometry, engineering, topology, physics, and biological life, and does so by making public and accessible exercises of material play, things like how to cut and fold paper, crochet yarn, and tie rope knots. At workshops and installations of the *Crochet Coral Reef* the techniques of hyperbolic crochet (a way to fabricate ruffles and squiggles by increasing stitches on a traditional crochet foundation chain) are taught alongside ideas of hyperbolic space and activist interventions in plastic waste and the crisis of climate change. In this process, making things with the hands intervenes in hierarchies of sensory knowledge to value the work of sensation and touch and make a potentially difficult idea tactile and intimate. Figuring a calculation is a labor shared by our motor, optic, and cognitive capacities. In crochet and handicraft, figuring yields a felt dimensionality and augments our limited ability to know a thing as impossible and imaginary as hyperbolic space. Reef makers take yarn and repurposed plastic trash in a hopeful occupation of a different perspective, abundant, infinite, and spiraling outward, proliferating an excess of surfaces, points of parallel, curvature, and intersecting lines.

The *Crochet Coral Reef* is created in a patchwork process out of many hands and by joining natural, manufactured, and recycled fabrics. Many makers do not identify as artists and are drawn to participate in an environmental, if not aesthetic, intervention. Crochet art workers convene in a collective practice reminiscent of quilting bees and ladies' sewing circles.[21] Bodies lean, eyes dart, and hands touch to repair stitches, learn and exchange technique, and create and share a feeling of community. Stitching kelp, sea slugs, and anemones out of materials like synthetic and animal fibers, plastic yarn, and repurposed trash makes an assemblage evocative of the seascape of coral. The *Crochet Coral Reef* takes the fragile ecology of marine coral as inspiration to build community in a creative and collective process of viral art making: "Just as living coral reefs replicate by sending out spawn, so the Crochet Reef sends out spawn."[22] The IFF bridges public art education and activism to build connections between the domestic and ecological and inspire transformative politics. An environmental aim of the hyperbolic *Crochet Coral Reef*, directed at people who make or encounter the reef in gallery and museum exhibitions, is to teach art makers about climate change and encourage them to make inventories of their plastic trash and develop strategies to lessen waste. The action of stitching is attached to a hopeful idea—the potential of small and private alterations to plastic waste use to inspire institutional and public dialogue.

    Crochet Coral Reef, rather than being expressly transgender, is coded in feminine and feminist ways: handicraft is characterized as "women's work," and the collective labor of the artwork bridges public and private spheres in a gesture to the consciousness-raising ethos of the feminist slogan "the personal is political." Still, how might we think of the reef in connection to a transgender politic? It is not an artwork about gender or identity politics per se, and it is not explicitly created by transgender artists, and, insofar as the reef is created in a collective and anonymous way, it is incidental if transgender, queer, or feminist artists contribute crochet corals and woolly sea creatures to the reef. The maker's identity is inessential to the capacity of crochet, craft, and coral ecologies to animate the woolly and felt matters of transgender life. Moreover, why conjoin transgender art making and artists? I borrow techniques and ideals of craft, but without defining craft itself as queer or transgender, or linking transgender art making to trans artists. I do so to create and demand dense and elastic transgender politics as open, bright, and turbulent as the hyperbolic dimension and a coral seascape. But though craft shares an outside positionality with transgender politics, their connection is more than just an allegory. Sensory and sensual, craft is a praxis primed to illuminate queer bodies and politics; as the textile artist L. J. Roberts argues, "Craft can gain from the methods and tools that queer theory has deployed to reclaim and reconfigure its own marginal position into a place of empowerment."[23] Similarly, queer and transgender theory can gain from the methods and tools developed in craft.

What does the handcrafting of animal fibers and synthetic, plastic yarns teach us about how transgender identities are fabricated and figured? Fabricating an identity, like figuring an idea or crocheting a seascape, is a calculation—a fuzzy method to track the distance or proximity between me and you; my sense of self and how I fit into the world; a topographical misshape; a reworking, one more try one more time; a labor to build something and belong. The collective labor to fabricate the shapes of marine coral in woolly and plastic yarns illuminates the patterning of transgender I describe as handmade, which, like the figuration of the crochet coral, forges a fuzzy and felt knowledge. Stitching a fabric in crochet, knit, or embroidery is like any mode of ordinary labor—a repetition of movement, a performative gesture. Think of fingering yarn, the loop and drag of the crochet hook, as a sensory algorithm. Suturing the so-called natural and manufactured—the fleshy, fibrous, and plastic—the trope of mixture offers an antidote to the surface and depth models that foreclose transgender subjectivity as "wrong" embodiment (as in trapped, diagnosed, released) or other systems of enclosure. As opposed to some psychoanalytic readings, the ethnographic or sociological, the handmade does not operate by a narrative of discovery. Instead, its movement is about cocreation, about making connections and contexts. In the collective joining of hands, *Crochet Coral Reef* is a reconfiguring of shapes and gestures into a diversity of embodied forms and identities that labor as a set of material practices against the toxic effects of climate change and the reproduction of species (and identities).

Transgender Is a Shape

"Straightness turns out to be a subtle and surprisingly plastic concept," writes Margaret Wertheim in the instructional manifesto for hyperbolic crochet, *A Field Guide to Hyperbolic Space: An Exploration of the Intersection of Higher Geometry and Feminine Handicraft*.[24] She describes the discovery of hyperbolic space by the mathematicians Janos Bolyai and Nicholay Lobatchevsky in the nineteenth century as "disturbing" and "undeniable"; efforts to substantiate and/or negate the parallel postulate and the reign of Euclid "struck terror into mathematicians' hearts, offending rational sensibilities and evoking a sense of moral outrage."[25] The "aberrant formations" of hyperbolic space promise, for Wertheim, both an optic and a sensory way to look, feel, and inhabit dimensions that exceed the grids, rectangles, and straight networks that organize the built architecture of our lives.[26] In other words, if knowledge production and sight are intimately connected, as many have contended, then thought itself is transformed as hands look and eyes touch.[27] The "woolly pedagogy" of *Crochet Coral Reef* is a sensuous encounter

with the turbulent geometry of hyperbolic space, and the hyperbolic form of the
crochet reef "verif[ies] materially the manifest untruth of Euclid's axiom" of the
parallel postulate, which in two dimensional geometry regulates the possibility for
a straight line to intersect another.[28] To fabricate shapes evocative of ocean life,
the Wertheims adapted a method of hyperbolic crochet, an invention of Latvian
mathematician Diana Taimina.[29] In hyperbolic crochet, an exponential increase of
stitches yields dimensional permutations of the fiber, made in a fractal pattern. To
fabricate shapes like the coralline tentacles of marine life, crocheters manipulate
the rate of stiches by increasing stitches per row; the more stitches are increased
per row, the more intense the volume and the more dense and crenellated the form
and shape of the crochet fabric.

Crochet Coral Reef is made by a collective process of adaptation, using
the techniques of Taimina's hyperbolic crochet to mutate patterns and discover
how fabric shapes into sea critters and ocean life. An experiment with the mathematic elasticity of hyperbolic geometry and the fiber strands of yarn let crocheters, inspired and instructed by the IFF, build a network environment of feeling and
sight, and between coral, fiber (synthetic or animal), and human bodies. Taimina
is a professor of mathematics at Cornell University, and her invention in 1997 of
hyperbolic crochet is significant for the field of geometric models. The elasticity,
strength, and sensory capacity of fiber offer a way to manipulate, hold, touch, pull,
and disassemble a physical model of hyperbolic space. In yarn she could illustrate a feeling of hyperbolic space in her classroom and remedy a disconnection
between the optic and felt knowledge of hyperbolic geometry. Taimina looked to
yarn and a synthetic fiber (ideal for stitching a stiff and durable model) to avoid
the way that cloth and paper models of hyperbolic space tear, crease, and buckle.
She began to experiment with knitting, but in order to yield an abundant excess of
surface she needed too many double-pointed needles (which allow the yarn to slide
on and off in different directions) to increase her rate of stitching. Crochet requires
only one needle and a skein of yarn, and so is less cumbersome and unwieldy,
letting Taimina formulate a tactile and dimensional method to interact with hyperbolic space.

A reorganization of form and matter, the hyperbolic dimension is suggestive
of shapes that bodies make, and geometry—a study of shapes, figures in position, lengths, distance, volume, and properties of space—gestures to new kinds
of relational identity and embodiment. The elliptical configurations of hyperbolic
geometry and its myriad surfaces and points of intersection prompt us to reexamine how distance and difference are measured by proximity or belonging and
on a horizontal-vertical grid of equivalences. Like the handmade labor of mak-

Figure 2. Institute For Figuring's *Crochet Coral Reef* project, 2005–ongoing.
Hyperbolic model by Margaret Wertheim. Photo © the IFF

ing identity, the dimensional field of hyperbolic space provides another method to
measure the relation between bodies and objects differently, to resist the limited
and oppositional categories of surface and depth that locate transgender either on
or inside the body. We might foreground, for example, gender transformation as a
process of assembly and disassembly in which bodies auto-engineer shape and
form, building and remaking connections between the soft and pliable material
forms of emotional and material life. An alignment of lines in infinite intersection, transgender is a shape and, in the conjoining of feelings beside fractals, an
alternative dimension of shapes—of negative (hyperbolic) and positive (Euclidean) curvature—can coexist to proliferate an abundance of shapely possibilities

Figure 3. A mathematically
precise model of a hyperbolic
plane by Diana Taimina.
Photo © the IFF

for transgender life. Identity is a kind of geometry, too. It approximates the desire to apprehend the boundaries of a body, to calculate the relation of skin, sweat, blood, and hair, to measure the distance between one shape and another, perhaps to configure the measurements and intersections, the way "I" join (or do not) with "you," who "we" are to each other, and how to make contact with some other things like bodies, objects, and ideas. Is the ambient, floating feel of desire, between bodies and for politics, enough of an alternative, or can we devise some new ways to make contact? I am interested in how we attempt to measure these distances and movements between slippery and stuck things. The diagnostic sciences of observation and their administrative instruments of evidence collection seem to always foreclose the openness and possibility that material experience leaves ajar. As a meditation on straight lines and flatness, drawn onto dimensional spaces and curvatures, the hyperbolic dimension invites us to examine positioning, or figuring, and the orientation of bodies, eyes and hands, knowledge and feeling. The material and conceptual work of reconfiguring how lines intersect—in dimensional, or at new and unknown, points of contact—foregrounds the labor of embodiment, the joining and disconnecting work of belonging, and the ways that bodies make and remake identity in the biosocial landscape. In the idea of an excess of surface the seeming problem of "transgender" as the uncontainable body is reimagined as a provocation.

Transgender is a mode of inquiry in my writing, an organizer, a schema, something I ask after: is transgender something we can ascertain in the tools of description, or as a set of bodily practices? The diffractive methodology Barad proposes is instructive for this inquiry into transgender (in/as) patterns. In physics, diffraction describes a wave in an encounter with an obstacle—for example, how light bends. For Barad, diffraction is an optical form meant to describe a reading practice of how knowledge is made in and with text, and it "can serve as a useful counterpoint to reflection," as "both are optical phenomena, but where reflection is about mirroring and sameness, diffraction attends to patterns of difference."[30] Ordinarily, geometry seeks a method of measurement in equivalence, a formula familiar to studies of gender and sexuality. But in geometric studies of shape we can also animate computations to measure the distance between things—calculations of lines, area, angles, volume, the perimeter of a triangle, circumference of a circle, and intersections. We can use these ways of thinking and ascertaining to investigate the space between bodies and politics and categorical configurations of the self and other, human and animal, and surface and depth. Relationality as a non-Euclidean geometric offers a different way to grasp at, feel, and imagine a body and its shape in the world, and to grasp its formulation as, for example, made by the labor of the hand rather than by an administrative or diagnostic force or foreclosure. In particular, orienting our perception to the dimensional field of hyperbolic space is a labor of sensory alignment and reorganization.

In this provocation, mathematical concepts of excess of surface, geodesics, void, finitude, and dimensionality animate the transgender body. There are, however, many other permutations of mathematical knowledge that could illuminate the bodily flesh and matter of transgender. Katie King, for example, has written beautifully about khipu, an Andean recording device of fiber cords and knots, which let her reconsider fundamental questions such as "What counts as writing? as counting? as connecting or disconnecting them?," as "the word khipu comes from the Quechua word for 'knot' and denotes both singular and plural."[31] King harnesses the shapes of knots, the gathering of materials, and the multiple meanings associated with a language and practice in order to investigate her theory of transdisciplinary knowledge. Hyperbolic space, a deviation of geometry with origins in Europe and deeply entangled with Western philosophy, may represent a radical departure from Euclid's axiom of the parallel postulate and foundational mathematic knowledge, but is not the only possible path of inquiry. It is, however, especially relevant to my study of transgender precisely because geometric narratives such as interior versus exterior selves have so often delimited the movements and possibilities for transgender experience. As diagnostic and administrative forces condense and consolidate bodily feelings and sensations into narratives of prior and emergent selves contained or liberated by the body, we can recall how the demands of medicalization and strategic performances of "wrong" embodiment ("feeling trapped in the 'wrong' body") collapse transgender into legible forms of identity and fold trans subjectivity into coherent figurations of binary gender and sexuality.

Transbiologicals

"Coral is good to queer with," writes Stefan Helmreich in "How Like Reef: Figuring Coral, 1839–2010."[32] And coral is a kind of queer object and inquiry—difficult to taxonomize, hovering at the boundaries of plant and animal, softs and solids, inhuman passivity and bodily action, a single thing or a plural collection, life and death. Coral is a breathy and spineless marine invertebrate, inelastic as human bone, fertile and spawning. These are curious contradictions, to be breathy (lively), yet to spew not air but its own reproductive force. Coral sex and sexuality (another odd word to pair with a coral) is also ambiguous: corals reproduce sexually and asexually, spawning gametes and budding genetic material, like a clone, and often broadcasting to reproduce en masse once a year, during the full moon. An object of fascination and study for Charles Darwin, corals, writes Helmreich, "come with durable, multiple, and porous inheritances," and Helmreich foregrounds the labor of figuration and composition to "discern a movement from opacity, to visibility, to readability."[33] Fertile and generous, coral polyps secrete calcium carbonate to form an exoskeleton, a space for diverse species of sharks, chimaeras, bony fishes, crustaceans, sponges, mollusks, clams, sea snakes, seaweed, saltwater crocodiles, and turtles to thrive. A fragile organism, sensitive and receptive to environmental stressors, coral is under enormous threat from climate change. As erosion causes ocean temperatures to rise, sudden spikes of salinity bring on "bleaching events," which leave the white bone of the coral exposed in an environmentally violent shedding of skin.

Marine coral, like sea pods, succulents, lettuce, and fungi, is an organic hyperbolic shape. Its hyperbolic form is adaptive, as the crinkles, frills, and ruffles of its shape allow coral maximal opportunities to filter feed. As a stationary organism with access to a limited volume of nutrients, the coral uses its stinging cells to gather and strain food in an interactive process between the coral tentacles and ambient particles of fish and plankton. This porous interactivity is a promising model for crafted and becoming modes of transgender reproduction. In a collaborative politics of risk and vulnerability, the devaluing of human and inanimate bodies share an economy; as Mel Chen writes, "for biopolitical governance to remain effective, there must be porous or even co-constituting bonds between human individual bodies and the body of a nation, a state, and even a racial locus like whiteness."[34] Violence threatens transgender bodies and coral colonies alike, in registers of diverse feeling and administration as, for example, street harassment, un- and underemployment, toxic waters and chemical pollution. In the patchwork patterns of coral we can learn something about our fragile ecology of identity politics, and so we do not need to inquire about the animacy of coral—is it animate, with a capacity to act and affect objects, things, and life forms?—to do so. Instead we can build connections between organic hyperbolic shapes, like lettuces, kelp, and sea slugs, and the transformation of human bodies in nonbinary and morphologically complex ways, without reproducing hierarchies of the natural and manufactured, the animate and inanimate. Inspired by Chen's inquiry into the "role of metaphor in biopolitics," I want to draw a hyperbolic line to connect how violence is shared between transgender and coral.[35] In *Animacies* Chen offers a "political grammar, what linguists call an *animacy hierarchy*, which conceptually arranges human life, disabled life, animal life, plant life, and forms of nonliving material in orders of value and priority."[36] As our fragile ecologies of sex, gender, and species cohabitate, an ethics of thinking between transgender and coral demands that we read for animacy hierarchies and the uneven shape and distribution of "subordinate cosmologies," returning us to the provocation of a cosmic transgender studies.[37] Coral exoskeletons stretch in a collective shape. A coral polyp is kind of dead, a "brainless jellyfish," yet coral polyps breathe, seek nourishment, and reproduce in a plural formation like an assemblage.[38] In this rigid sea of bone, animate and animating, a rough skeleton is soft and receptive. Here let us imagine how diverse bodies—of land and water, plastic waste, and human in/action—cohabitate to share and distribute violence and form a potential politics as an ecology of trust.

Is it possible to connect plastic trash recycled as yarn to the repurposing work of a transgender body—a body of material flesh and collective politics? Something feels sensible, if strange, in adopting the language of recycling and repurposing to describe human, transgender experience, yet we undo and remake gender in messy and creative negotiations of physicality and capacity, social and financial in/access, and the space between need and desire. Porous flesh, for example, is a way we share or stretch a politics of cohabitation; Beatriz Preciado offers such an account of the porous in *Testo Junkie: Sex, Drugs, and Biopolitics in the Pharmacopornographic Era*, archiving an experiment of the body and how it makes contact and contracts with testosterone as a practice of self-care. Preciado writes to wrestle the flesh and its capture by the administrative coding of gender dysphoria as disorder and to record a breathy, sensual feeling of resistance and containment, and animates Michel Foucault's notion of "biopower," the administration of life, and Deleuze and Guattari's "control society" in order to trace an architectonics of control to the soft, gelatinous technologies of testosterone injection and digestion. "Testosterone," writes Preciado, "is one of the rare drugs that is spread by sweat, from skin to skin, body to body. How can such trafficking—the microdiffusion of minute drops of sweat, the importing and exporting of vapors, such contraband exhalations—be controlled, surveyed; how to prevent the contact of crystalline mists, how to control the transparent demon's sliding from another's skin towards mine?"[39] By offering an account of feeling as seepage from within and against the governmental and cultural apparatuses that foreclose feeling, s/he provides a vital document of feelings and fractals for trans— and —gender.

Like Preciado's account, which dislodges transgender from the singular "event" of its diagnosis to foreground the fleshy, fibrous seams of transformation, handmade and handcrafted identities are characterized by bodily and felt labor. The handmade intervenes to value transgender as matter and fleshy substance, and is a response to both feminist and queer thought experiments and to the history of the clinic, to the way gender "deviant" and nonconforming bodies are made objects of scientific practice, sexological and psychiatric diagnosis. Systems of traditional close reading sometimes govern transgender studies, organized by categories of surface and depth—the body as a text, a surface to interpret or depth to excavate. Yet insofar as it seeks to be an intervention of method, a call to reconsider how the body is read as text, the handmade is not an alternative reading practice. A different epistemology is at work in the figuration of transgender as crafted, one that puts to the side the textual to animate textural modes of labor, process, collectivity, duration, and pattern. If method is a form of ordering knowledge to contain, repeat, and echo an idea again and again, it is also a labor of dispersal. My investment in method for transgender studies is in parsing the tasks of mimetic responsibility and process and untangling the associations of method with novelty, discovery, and invention to make count the ordinary feelings of identity. The demand to feel wrong, to perform a wrong body and a broken feeling, and not, for example, the pain of a discrimination, forecloses the dimensionality of feeling and the fissures, seams, and textures of experience, those things impossible to encapsulate in diagnostic language. For feminist thought and politics, the transgender body is a paradox, mobilized to evidence the immutability of sex and social construction of gender. The demand to be liberated materially or conceptually by physicality prohibits an ability to inhabit the body with meaning or strategy. Here I do not mean to suggest that transgender people substitute strategic ways to inhabit the body for the ways they wish to modify it, but to suggest that these two processes may be mutually constitutive.

In an effort to remedy the problem of transgender bodies doing the work of evidencing both the construction and the immutability of the flesh, it is productive to turn to a biology that does not correlate transformation with technologies of intervention. A potential fleshy and felt science is found in "transbiology," "a biology that is not only born and bred, or born and made, but made and born."[40] In "The Cyborg Embryo: Our Path to Transbiology," Sarah Franklin traces how Donna Haraway's cyborg gives birth to an embryo; she examines the work of biological transfer in assisted reproductive technologies and the embryonic stem cell, and defines transbiology as "the literal back and forth of the labour of creating new biological."[41] While the "trans" to which she refers is not "transgender," the reproductive labor of the cyborg embryo is in productive dialogue with more explicit work connecting transgender to animality by scholars like Eva Hayward and Bailey Kier, who investigate the slippery sex and fingery eyes of coral and endocrine-altered "trans" fish in the Potomac River.[42] Franklin's interest is the biological drag, the push and pull of microscopic things in pipettes and the capture, containing, and insertion of reproductive matter. In the "trans- work of embryo transfer, and the translation of embryology into stem cell derivation and redirection," trans is meant to signify directionality: to cross, go beyond, oppose, or exchange. To "trans" is an action, and transbiology contains the moving parts of biological matter, capital, scientific reach, and the emotionality of hope, despair, and desire in reproductive engineering. Franklin notes the "queer lineage" of the transbiological reproduction of species, populations, and ideas manufactured in a laboratory, how in the diverse proliferation of life forms and narratives about life, the heterosexual matrix of reproduction is made unstable.

Taking up the invitation of the elongated dash to stretch the category of transgender, this essay interrogates the space between "trans" and "biology" as a realignment of the distance and proximity between bodies and objects, forms of theory and practice, natural and manufactured. If we characterize the body as "transbiological," is our description limited to transgender bodies? Can bodies be transbiological or transgender or both? Is transbiology a kind of transgender biology? If some bodies—of flesh, knowledge, and/or politics—are transbiological, those bodies are not containable in a singular form, a body with plain borders, or as a simple reference. Like a collective, one with participant-driven taxonomies, transbiology might be a prompt, a method of disturbing the oppositional formations of surface/depth, human/animal, nature/culture, and before/after. Anchored to the material body and its diverse conditions and mobilized as a political possibility independent of fleshy matters, "trans" beside biology is a prefix able to attach to multiple suffixes like -*national*, -*feminist*, -*genic*, and -*animality*. Franklin writes, "Like the cyborg embryo, transbiology is a mix of control and rogue, or trickster, elements."[43] Cyborg politics sometimes stands in for forms of transgender as bodily liberation and the post- or inhuman, making abstract and diluted the material weight of flesh. While a shared genealogy of biological and artificial matter marks the cyborg and transbiological body, the transgender body (in states "natural" or otherwise) is not an artificial one. A fleshy science like transbiology can be harnessed to counter how quantitative knowledges made about transgender bodies by, for example, institutions like hospitals, laboratories, or administrative bodies like departments of motor vehicles and passport agencies support hierarchies of knowledge between instruments and objects, an expert and patient, and the animate and passive.

Trans figures for me as the possibility of the re-formation of gender, making it impossible to theorize the formation of life—human, marine, aesthetic, textured, or felt—without gesturing to an alternative experience of embodiment. The handmade promise of the prefix *trans*, to which I affix a porous transgender in the definition of transbiology, is "an encounter with technology." If, for Franklin, to trans is an action, I read trans as an encounter, a suturing of trans and biology signaling a potentiality of relational politics. As a reconfiguration of trans in connection to biology, another way to read Franklin's "encounter with technology" is as a felt sense of the body encountering its own flesh. Variations of the handmade and fleshy sciences like transbiology offer a way to access, in autonomously sensible and choreographed forms, the body's encounter with its material composition (blood, skin, skeleton, cellular, and imperceptible workings). Between feelings and fractals, those unwieldy and algorithmic forms, I see a way to gain access to the soft actions and sensations that precede, anticipate, or remake our limited categories of biological containment, observation, evidence, and repeatability and let be variables, contamination, and uncertainty. The handmade, transbiological encounter records the way that bodies accumulate, become in proximity, and build contact, independently of intervention defined as an intrusion, made by one for another, to foreground the relational capacity of bodies to evidence, measure, and reproduce identities difficult to quantify or control.

In "Evolutionary Yarns in Seahorse Valley" Sophia Roosth investigates the "manifold biological theories that inform the *Crochet Coral Reef* makers' descriptions of their project, showing how they draw on contemporary, historic, and folk understandings of evolution and morphogenesis in describing their work," and suggests "that in so doing, they pose evolution as akin to handicraft—something open-ended, lively, time consuming, perpetually becoming."[44] This study also takes the *Crochet Coral Reef* as an invitation to mine the way that we—to return to and reflect on the impossible and imaginary collective—inhabit and transform identity practices by reproducing bodily knowledges. Forging a dialogue out of transgender, woolly and marine coral, hyperbolic geometrics, and transbiological interventions, this essay offers a handmade account of transgender life and something between a provocation and a method for how transgender studies can integrate and value both the feelings and the fractals of transgender knowledge. This essay lingers with the possibilities of preoccupation and the knowledge production it makes possible; it is also a hopeful thought experiment about the queer reproductive ecologies of identity and the politics of crafting a handmade transgender materiality. While it may be difficult to conceptualize bodies evenly accessing health and survival on an intellectual and political terrain that does not value the animal, inhuman, objects, and all kinds of stuff and matter, the knowledge production that preoccupation makes possible is. As Margaret Wertheim offers, "Knotted in thread, bound together across continents by tendrils of shared, evolving energy, the *Crochet Coral Reef* offers us a metaphor—take it or leave it—we are all corals now."[45]

Notes

1. Margaret Wertheim, "We Are All Corals Now: A Crafty Yarn about Global Warming," *Brooklyn Rail*, April 2, 2014.

2. In *Meeting the Universe Halfway: Quantum Physics and the Entanglement of Matter and Meaning*, Karen Barad describes how "the notion of intra-action constitutes a radical reworking of the traditional notion of causality" and is "in contrast to the usual 'interaction,' which assumes that there are separate individual agencies that precede their interaction" (Durham, NC: Duke University Press, 2007), 33.

3. Donna Haraway, "A Cyborg Manifesto: Science, Technology, and Socialist-Feminism in the Late Twentieth Century," in *Simians, Cyborgs, and Women: The Reinvention of Nature* (New York: Routledge, 1991), 149–81.

4. Rebecca M. Jordan-Young, *Brain Storm: The Flaws in the Science of Sex Differences* (Cambridge, MA: Harvard University Press, 2010), 15.

5. Sophia Roosth, "Evolutionary Yarns in Seahorse Valley: Living Tissues, Wooly Textiles, Theoretical Biologies," *differences: A Journal of Feminist Cultural Studies* 23, no. 3 (2012): 9–41.

6. In *Testo Junkie: Sex, Drugs, and Biopolitics in the Pharmacopornographic Era*, Beatriz Preciado writes of sex hormones and "master hackers of gender, genuine traffickers of semiotico-technological flux, producers and *tinkers* of copyleft biocodes" (New York: Feminist, 2013), 395.

7. In my book manuscript "Handmade: Everyday Feelings and Textures of Transgender Life," I examine fibrous and fleshy modes of bodily capacity and transgender art making in soft sculpture, knitting, embroidery, dance, and performance. For a study of transgender textiles and fabrics, see my essay, "Felt Matters," in *The Transgender Studies Reader II* (New York: Routledge, 2013), 91–100.

8. In *Critique of the Power of Judgment* Kant describes the aesthetic beauty of art as oppositional to labor and purpose; while art is "liberal" "play," handicraft is "remunerative art" "attractive only because of its effect" (Cambridge: Cambridge University Press, 2000), 182–83.

9. An important text inaugurating the contemporary field of craft studies is *Thinking through Craft* by the scholar and curator Glenn Adamson (New York: Oxford, 2007). His book investigates the art-craft binary and suggests craft is a "problem" and the "conceptual limit" of art" (3, 2). Yet as the feminist art historian Elissa Auther observes, "More than the names themselves, it is the preoccupation with naming and distinguishing that is of interest here, for such naming is a primary component of artistic consecration" (*String Felt Thread: The Hierarchy of Art and Craft in American Art* [Minneapolis: University of Minnesota Press, 2009], 7).

10. Julia Bryan-Wilson, "Sewing Notions," *Artforum*, February 2011.

11. Jay Prosser, *Second Skins: The Body Narratives of Transsexuality* (New York: Columbia University Press, 1998), 67.

12. Sarah Franklin, "The Cyborg Embryo: Our Path to Transbiology," *Theory, Culture, and Society* 23, nos. 7–8 (2006): 71.

13. Susan Stryker, Paisley Currah, and Lisa Jean Moore, "Introduction: Trans—, Trans, or Transgender?," *Women's Studies Quarterly*, Fall–Winter 2008, 11.

14. Stryker, Currah, and Moore, "Introduction," 14.

15. Susan Stryker and Paisley Currah, "Postposttranssexual: Key Concepts for a Twenty-First Century Transgender Studies," *Transgender Studies Quarterly* 1, nos. 1–2 (2014): 1–18.

16. Margaret Wertheim, *A Field Guide to Hyperbolic Space: An Exploration of the Intersection of Higher Geometry and Feminine Handicraft* (Los Angeles: Institute for Figuring, 2007), 30.

17. Jasbir Puar, "'I'd Rather Be a Cyborg Than a Goddess': Becoming-Intersectional in Assemblage Theory," *philoSOPHIA: a journal of feminist philosophy* 2, no. 1 (2012): 49–66.

18. In "Beyond the Special Guest—Teaching 'Trans' Now," Shana Agid and Erica Rand describe how "structures and beliefs" of the special guest "even as adapted by well-meaning, feminist allies in the struggle against gender oppression" and ask, "What does it mean to teach about trans matters without exoticizing or marginalizing trans people, bodies, identities, and issues?" (*Radical Teacher* 92 [Winter 2011]: 5–6).

19. Institute For Figuring website, theiff.org.

20. Like the chemical, agricultural, and genetic modifications to our food and water, plastic shapes how bodies occupy physicality and the in/capacity of flesh. Parallel to *Crochet Coral Reef*, Margaret and Christine Wertheim undertook an experiment to store their domestic plastic trash between February 2007 and 2011: plastic packaging, food containers, bottles of shampoo, and electronic debris like computers and cellular telephones. In addition to tracking their waste use, the Wertheims repurposed some of the plastic into plarn (plastic yarn) and midden monsters (dolls and sculptures made of trash) and posted observations about oceanic trash and the great Pacific garbage patch on the IFF website. A participatory installation of *The Midden Project* was exhibited at the New Children's Museum in San Diego, "like a forest filling up with toxic fruit" (October 15, 2011, to March 30, 2013).

21. In *Art Workers: Radical Practice in the Vietnam War Era* (Berkeley: University of California Press, 2011), the art historian Julia Bryan-Wilson examines the Art Workers' Coalition and the myriad permutations made possible by the conjunction of "art" and worker."

22. Although satellite reefs organize locally at universities, community centers, art galleries, and museums, the IFF requires exhibition fees and contractual recognition of *Crochet Coral Reef* and its ideas and techniques as the intellectual property of the organization and Margaret and Christine Wertheim; this contradiction brings to mind Julia Bryan-Wilson's critical observation, "The left-progressive valence of many of the

activist and artistic appropriations of craft is evident, but craft-based techniques, like any other, are ideologically ambivalent" ("Sewing Notions," *Artforum*, February 2011, 74).

23. L. J. Roberts, "Put Your Thing Down, Flip It, and Reverse It: Reimaging Craft Identities Using Tactics of Queer Theory," in *Extra/Ordinary: Craft and Contemporary Art*, ed. Maria Elena Buszek (Durham, NC: Duke University Press, 2011), 243–59.

24. Wertheim, *Field Guide to Hyperbolic Space*, 30.

25. Wertheim, *Field Guide to Hyperbolic Space*, 9.

26. Wertheim, *Field Guide to Hyperbolic Space*, 10.

27. See, for example, Jonathan Crary, *Techniques of the Observer: On Vision and Modernity in the Nineteenth Century* (Cambridge, MA: MIT Press, 1992); for a feminist critique of the visual as an apparatus of knowledge making, see Joan Scott, "The Evidence of Experience," *Critical Inquiry* 17, no. 4 (1991): 773–97.

28. The parallel postulate is an axiom of Euclid's two-dimensional geometry and states that at most one line can be drawn through any point not on a given line parallel to the given line in a plane.

29. In 1997, at Cornell.

30. Barad, *Meeting the Universe Halfway*, 29.

31. Katie King, "In Knots: Transdisciplinary Khipu @ UMD 2012," transkhipu.blogspot .com; see King's website for illustrations and an interactive exploration of khipu.

32. Stefan Helmreich, "How Like Reef: Figuring Coral, 1839–2010," in *Party Writing for Donna Haraway!*, partywriting.blogspot.com, reefhelmreich.com.

33. Helmreich, "How Like Reef."

34. Mel Y. Chen, *Animacies: Biopolitics, Racial Mattering, and Queer Affect* (Durham, NC: Duke University Press, 2012), 194.

35. Chen, *Animacies*, 190.

36. Chen, *Animacies*, 13.

37. Chen, *Animacies*, 29.

38. Wertheim, "We Are All Corals Now."

39. Preciado, *Testo Junkie*, 65.

40. Franklin, "Cyborg Embryo," 67–187.

41. Franklin, "Cyborg Embryo," 74.

42. For exceptional work in queer and trans animality, see Bailey Kier, "Interdependent Ecological Transsex: Notes on Re/production, 'Transgender' Fish, and the Management of Populations, Species, and Resources," *Women and Performance: A Journal of Feminist Theory* 20, no. 3 (2010): 299–318; and Eva Hayward, "Fingeryeyes: Impressions of Cup Corals," *Cultural Anthropology* 25, no. 4 (2010): 577–99.

43. Franklin, "Cyborg Embryo," 75.

44. Roosth, "Evolutionary Yarns in Seahorse Valley," 11.

45. Margaret Wertheim, "We Are All Corals Now."

UNBECOMING HUMAN

An Ethics of Objects

Eunjung Kim

The machine is not an *it* to be animated, worshiped, and
dominated. The machine is us, our processes, an aspect of
our embodiment.
—Donna Haraway

$\mathcal{B}$eyond simply being deployed as a condemnatory last word, can "objectification" as a mode of "dehumanization" offer a new way to challenge the exclusionary configurations of humanity that create otherness? At the core of the two concepts are questions of what characteristics define humans—in distinction to those of objects, plants, animals, and otherness itself—and how the determination of their absence elicits the judgment of degradation.

This essay questions the perspective that distinguishes humans from objects on the grounds of ability (e.g., humans are not objects, because "objects do not see or know") and considers the departure from recognizable markers of humanity.[1] Thinking through the performances by Marina Abramović's *Rhythm* series (1973–74) and *The Artist Is Present* (2010) and through *I'm a Cyborg, but That's OK* (*Saibogŭ chiman Koench'ana*), a 2006 South Korean film directed by Park Chan-wook (Pak Ch'an-uk), I explore the moments when one becomes a "quasi-object" (being a laboring machine or being in an unconscious or immobile state), so that one embodies the characteristics of objects, perceives one's body or body parts as objects, or suspends what are conventionally viewed as uniquely human capacities and values. The tantalizing affect produced around the declaration that humans are objects and objects are humans casts light on the seem-

GLQ 21:2–3
DOI 10.1215/10642684-2843359
© 2015 by Duke University Press

ingly sacrosanct but fragile distinction between humans and objects. Object beings and human beings overlap within, and beyond, various contexts of personifying and objectifying interactions. I suggest that unbecoming human—by embodying objecthood, surrendering agency, and practicing powerlessness—may open up an anti-ableism, antiviolence queer ethics of proximity that reveals the workings of the boundary of the human. Dipesh Chakrabarty defines proximity as a "mode . . . of relating to difference in which (historical and contingent) difference is neither reified nor erased but negotiated."[2] This ethical positioning of proximity to human-ness through unbecoming human disengages from any kind of ability-based deter-mination of a being's legitimacy and aims to cease assessing the value or quality of differences.

Disability studies scholars and disability activists (including myself) have claimed that people with various ranges of functions, capacities, and shapes deserve respect and dignity, and that our lives need to be equally valued. The humanness of a being is a condition that has been made grounds for exclusion ("A being that has lost dignity is not human") rather than a positive entitlement that ensures rights ("All human beings have dignity"). The disability activist Ed Roberts, who started Independent Living Movement in the United States, recol-lects the doctor telling his mother: "You should hope he dies, because if he lives, he'll be no more than a vegetable for the rest of his life. How would you like to live in an iron lung 24 hours a day?" Rather than asserting his humanness, he declares, "the vegetables of the world are uniting, and we're not going away!"[3]

The notions of value and dignity may rely too much on images of the nor-mative conditions of life for disability studies to successfully challenge the hierar-chy of disabled and enabled lives, which intersects with the racialized, gendered, classed, and sexuality-based constructions of the "less-than-human." To chal-lenge ableism by instating dignity and by claiming the value of disability through capacity is strongly tied to the production of "nonnormativity not only through the sexual and racial pathologization of certain 'unproductive bodies' but more expan-sively through the ability and inability of all bodies to register through affective capacity." Jasbir Puar argues, "Attachments to the difference of disabled bod-ies may reify an exceptionalism that only certain privileged disabled bodies can occupy."[4] Claiming values or quality of differences often depends on the unearned and earned privileges as the key to acceptability and survival. The question then is how to proximate a mode of existence and survival without producing the power to exclude.

Normative values are often constructed through the legal determination of humanity and its absence. Samera Esmeir points out that the modern law in colonial Egypt operated to determine the absence of the human, which "indicated a state of dehumanization or indeed inhumanity, that is, a state of cruelty, instrumentalization, and depravity."[5] Esmeir further argues that international human rights regimes rely on "the law's power of constituting humanity," noting that humanist critics of violence also "accept the notion that humanity can be taken away."[6] How does object-becoming as an embodied practice refuse the idea that "humanity is a matter of endowment, declaration, or recognition"?[7] The claim that "we are humans, not objects" also operates within this frame, failing to question the moral separation between humans and objects, as if the treatment of one had no effect on the other.

Contrary to the way violence is cast as "inhumane," Chakrabarty emphasizes the humanness of violence involved in mass killing during the Partition of India: "It is obvious that, for all the rendering of the human into a mere thing that collective violence may appear to perform, the recognition by one human of another as human is its fundamental precondition. It is humans who torture, rape, oppress, exploit, other humans. We cannot do these things to objects. . . . In this unintentional practice of mutual human recognition lies the ground for the conception of proximity. The denial of the victim's humanity, thus, proceeds necessarily from this initial recognition of it."[8] The blasphemy of thingification, it seems, is not the misrecognition of one entity (humans) for another (things); rather, it involves the active removal of certain characteristics after humanity is initially recognized.[9] It hinges on a particular way to treat an object, as objects are loved and revered as much as they are used and discarded. Viewing perpetrators of violence as non-human animals and victims as objects is an attempt to render them outside the human, thereby preventing a closer look at the human contexts in which violence and nonviolence occur. It also naturalizes the violence of and against nonhuman animals and objects. Positioning violence inside the human—which Chakrabarty calls "*in-human*" rather than inhuman—compels a movement out of humanness to practice nonviolence, in this way refusing to exercise violence and embracing the vulnerability involved in becoming objects.[10]

Connecting a person who is unconscious or immobile to a quasi-object sounds immoral, derogatory, and "dehumanizing." So does comparing a person to an animal, a plant, an inanimate object, or a nonhuman being (e.g., saying that someone is a "puzzle," an "alien," or in "a vegetative state"), an offense quite common in racist and ableist society.[11] Just as attempts to remove differences by enforcing normality are detrimental, attempts to erase humanness by casting off certain bodies have violent effects. Nevertheless, Sunaura Taylor ponders the connection between disabled people and animals in sideshow culture and medical discourses and asks, "Is there any way to consider these metaphors beyond the blatant racism, classism, and ableism these comparisons espouse? I find myself wondering why animals exist as such negative points of reference for us, animals who themselves are victims of unthinkable oppressions and stereotypes."[12] Like Mel Chen, I take Taylor's question "as a basis for a revised ethics" and ask similar questions about being objectlike, recognizing numerous ways in which objects exist and are treated.[13] The moments of object-becoming yield an opportunity—one that is perhaps counterintuitive yet potentially generative—to fashion an ethics of nonpurposive existence. Seeing humans as objects may invite critical readings of cultural texts that disrupt the political efficacy of "objectification" as a label to condemn morally challenging phenomena.[14] This condemnation often refuses to examine more closely the lived realities involved in objectification. Remedying objectification and dehumanization may end up simply prescribing subjectivity and agency in order to rehumanize othered bodies without questioning why the recognition of humanity relies on certain signs of subjectivity and agency.

In what spaces and arrangements does this object-becoming appear generative rather than annihilative? In what ways can object-becoming contribute to an anti-ableist project of shifting certain observable characteristics from being central to humanness to being inessential or even irrelevant, thereby leaving humanness without qualification? What are the ethical implications of such a project in promoting conditions for a livable and sustainable life and for abolishing violence by invoking universal human rights without relying on humans as possessing, or needing to possess, certain capacities and faculties?

Performances of Objects

The automatic link between objectification and violence assumes a sustained dualistic separation between the objectifier and the objectified. This is the basis of Martha Nussbaum's theorization of objectification: to make objectification positive or benign, consent and equality are necessary to remedy the hierarchy existing between two individuals.[15] The *Rhythm* series by Marina Abramović, a renowned performance artist and a controversial figure, challenges this division by showing an overlap between objecthood and human bodies as the objectifier and the objectified.

The series started with her first performance piece, *Rhythm 10*, which involved the intense and rhythmic motions of jabbing a knife in between her fingers as she positioned them on a white sheet of paper on the floor. Abramović was literally the objectifier, on the one hand, and the objectified, on the other. Whenever she cut her hand, she changed the knife, going through twenty different knives. Meanwhile, she recorded the sound and rhythm that her body, her motion, and the objects generated together. After she had used all the knives, she listened to the recording of the performance and repeated the same performance, ultimately cutting her hand again. The distinction between the surface and the extended fingers disappears as the vulnerability of flesh fills in the space. Setting aside the registers of Abramović's able-bodiedness—her hand-eye coordination, double-handedness with multiple digits, maintaining control of movements, concentration, and multisensory abilities—the repetition of the acts and replaying of recorded sounds take the audience beyond the suspense about the risk of self-wounding and fill the space with the mechanical motions of muscles, enabling the performer to experience her body parts as objects.

In *Rhythm 5*, Abramović lost consciousness while lying in the middle of a burning structure shaped in a pentagram; it was not until her pants caught on fire that the audience realized that she was unconscious and intervened to pull her out.[16] She had fed the flame with her hair and nails, thereby making her own body-objects contribute to her loss of consciousness, which was caused by fumes. Seeing the ending as an interruption of a performance that relies on the artist's intentionality, she devised a way to continue to perform without interruption as she went in and out of consciousness. In *Rhythm 2* she took a pill used to treat catatonia. She wrote that her medicated body started moving involuntarily even while she was conscious and aware of the situation. After the medication wore off, she took another pill that is used for sedation. She explains, "Physically I was there but mentally I was not. I don't remember anything."[17] Abramović also successfully let her unconscious body continue the performance in *Rhythm 4*. When she hovered over a strong blower and tried to inhale air driven from it, she lost consciousness, but the jet of air kept her head moving. The audience could see only her floating head through a monitor, as she was in a different room; they did not notice her unconscious state.[18] These public displays of self-experimentation on the body, generating a state of mind-body disconnect and a movement in and out of consciousness without interrupting the performance, shift focus from the body to the mind and back again to the body as an agent of performance.

The dualisms of subject and object and of mind and body, dismantled insofar as she is the one objectifying herself, were reinstated and accentuated in the last performance in the series, *Rhythm 0*. Abramović stood motionless for six hours in Studio Morra in Naples in 1974. With a sign that said "I am the object," she invited the audience to take the role of objectifier.[19] Instructions in print read, "There are seventy-two objects on the table that one can use on me as desired. I'm taking the whole responsibility for six hours. There are objects for pain, objects for pleasure."[20] Among the objects were weapons, such as a gun, a bullet, a metal spear; tools that could be used as weapons, such as razor blades, an ax, nails, a saw; grooming tools, such as a comb, a mirror, perfume, kitchen utensils; food, such as bread, apple, grapes, honey; and a feather and a rose. Their arrangement heightened the sense of vulnerability and suspended agency. Although the artist's status as an object contradicted her claim of responsibility, it did not stop the audience from acting "as desired." The objects, including her female body, carried stories and purposes in various arrangements, placed ritualistically on a table; as Klaus Biesenbach argues, they could have constituted the Last Supper or an operating room, among many possibilities.[21] Pictures taken at the performance in Naples show her body carried by two audience members, laid down on a table, and covered with a coat. She is also shown standing up with her top removed, tears in her eyes. Her body and face are written on and her body bears a bleeding wound. One audience member placed a gun in her hand, pointing at herself; later, another audience member removed the gun. Her stillness, like that of a living statue, made the transition out of such stasis highly dramatic. After six hours, Abramović started walking toward the audience, and people ran away from her "to escape an actual confrontation."[22] That the transition from an object to a moving subject was so shocking reveals that the audience invested in and interacted with her as if she were a real object. "The veneer of civilization is very thin," Chrissie Iles observes, making the easy link between violence and nonhuman animals: "What is absolutely terrifying is how quickly a group of people will become bestial if you give them permission to do so."[23] Jack Halberstam notes the display of "the murderous impulses of audiences against women, against artists, against self."[24] However, becoming "bestial" or acting on "murderous impulses"—as Iles and Halberstam explain the audience's behavior, drawing on their particular understanding of humans and nonhuman animals—cannot be assumed to have single meanings and cannot account for the fact that Abramović's audience acted within the boundaries that she had predetermined. The proximity and context were carefully shaped by the performer, and then combined with the cultural and historical scripts carried by each object, including the performer's female body. Audience members were turned into actors, activated and authorized by Abramović's and the objects' commands, while the performer remained an object. Like the participants in the Stanford prison experiment, a classic study in which individuals were randomly assigned the role of prisoner or guard, audience members improvised actions in a given context, both cooperating with and working against one another, and thereby enlivening the cultural repertoire of actions involving completely passive flesh, the power given them by the circumstances, and objects. In other words, when given the privilege to act with impunity the audience failed to imagine Abramović's position as an invitation to practice powerlessness together. When the art critic Thomas McEvilley asked Abramović about the traditional idea that she showed female energy in making herself submissive and passive, she identified her courage to do the piece more with male energy.[25] Elsewhere, she has also pointed to the audience's gendered response, in which women took little direct action but told men what to do to her body.[26] Activity and passivity are seen as characteristic of and practiced by males and females, respectively, yet the decision to be completely passive becomes associated with power and is gendered masculine. This gendering of the practice of objecthood illustrates the difficulty of unbecoming human and of achieving disengaged and unqualified proximity without hierarchy.

In the end Abramović's status as object has to be removed (thus she must be deobjectified), even through a pharmaceutical intervention to make her body move out of stillness, restoring the normatively gendered balance (*Rhythm 2*). Object-becoming in the *Rhythm* series does not necessarily challenge the understanding of agency and subjectivity associated with the masculine, but it does reveal the performative power of bodies' objecthood to destabilize the gendered interpretation of passivity and activity. The clear overlap between objects and humans enables the reading of objectification as a practice of powerlessness—what Halberstam calls "radical passivity."[27] Simone de Beauvoir noticed the power of women who play at being objects, which she called "the comedy of being passive": "Man wants woman to be object, she *makes* herself object; at the very moment when she does that, she is exercising a free activity. Therein is her original treason; the most docile, the most passive, is still a conscious being; and sometimes the fact that in giving herself to him she looks at him and judges him is enough to make him feel duped; she is supposed to be only something offered, no more than prey."[28]

Exploring the moments of unbecoming human as a form of power and the reorganization of power relations is not to obscure but to facilitate a deeper understanding of how, in certain contexts, objectifying oneself and others as disposable, replaceable, unworthy of care, and violatable is exploitative and destructive. Nevertheless, recognizing objecthood in humans and keeping in mind the many whose human status has been questioned and denied on the basis of their resemblance to objects, I think of object-becoming as providing entry into the relationship between disabled, unproductive, queer, and nonwhite bodies and the ableist society that tempts them with the legitimizing value of normality. (This does not mean that all disabled people are unproductive or passive.) The instances of objecthood imagined and enacted by oneself or by others as objects and machines expose the lack of a clear distinction between vitality and death and between nonhuman and human. In these blurred spaces, the linkages between objects, matters, and beings are reoriented to form an anti-ableist position—an ethics of queer inhumanism, based not solely on identity and sociality but also on proximity and copresence.

In *The Artist Is Present* (2010), a famous piece performed at the Museum of Modern Art, Abramović's motionlessness created a context of object-becoming different from that of *Rhythm 0* in a way that heightened affective and vibrant proximity between presence and existence. In an empty space surrounded by galleries and heavily guarded by security personnel, Abramović sat on a chair during the operating hours of the museum every day for three months. Visitors were invited to sit across from her and to gaze at her for as long as they wanted. A sitter who did anything other than looking would be escorted out by the guards. In this heavily controlled arrangement, sitters were obliged to perform the stillness of an object-body, interacting only through their gaze and energy field. The significant elements are the presence of the artist and the duration of the encounter, rather than who is being objectified by whom. The work created a "new conceptual space" that is marked by "multiplicity and a profound resistance to closure," demanded the audience's participation, and foregrounded the artist's rules in ways that defined her presence.[29] Objectification and quasi-human status do not automatically lead to violence unless the conceptual space invokes certain repertoires of violent interactions. The fact that the surveillance of the guards controlled the space, so that the audience could only sit still, mimicked the visible and invisible enforcement of the ableist principle of functional, behavioral, intellectual, emotional, and aesthetic norms on which noncapable bodies are often removed from public spaces.

In "The Artist Is Object," Halberstam describes Abramović's performances as demonstrating a "shadow feminism," one that lacks a discernible "feminist subject." There are only "un-subjects who cannot speak, who refuse to speak; subjects who unravel, who refuse to cohere; subjects who refuse 'being' where being has already been defined in terms of a self-activating, self-knowing, liberal subject." Halberstam concludes that by becoming an object, Abramović "stands in potent opposition to all of the clichéd forms of rationality that collect around embodied subjectivity."[30] In the search for feminist subjectivity, embodiment has often been narrowly imagined as able-bodied—characterized by willed desire, speech, seeing, refusal, mobility, purposiveness, intelligence, desire, and connection rather than by unintentionality, speechlessness, unseeing, acquiescence, immobility, inertness, incompetence, asexuality, and disconnection. Halberstam's "un-subject," then, is what Amber Jamilla Musser calls "a mode of desubjectification" and "a mode of becoming-object."[31]

In what way can an embodiment of immobility and speechlessness challenge ableism, which is firmly grounded on the criterion of the capability to control one's body to determine whether one qualifies as human? Abramović's stillness and its duration had an impact on her audience, not because she simulated the incapacity to move but because she displayed a kind of superhuman ability to appear inanimate and to control her body while maintaining eye contact. As all bodies (live, dead, or taxidermied) are constantly marked by what Chen calls "animacies," even in the moment of stillness and "nonlife" in the form of objecthood, appearing inanimate is a performance of a supra-ability as much as a simulation of disability.[32] This uncanny merging of the disability of her material body and the supra-ability of her mind and gaze became evident in her refusal of an accommodation of her animate body's stillness: a bedpan was briefly placed underneath her chair but soon removed. Instead, following a regimen of regulating water intake, she said that she did not urinate during her daily performance; Abramović insisted, "I really have mind control."[33] While regulating water intake is a common experience for people navigating public space with so few safe and accessible public restrooms (in the midst of physically inaccessible, chemically laden, dichotomously gendered, and customers-only restrooms), her emphasis on discipline, control, and overcoming the limits of the body problematically invokes the dualist superiority of mind over body and what Susan Wendell calls "the myth that the body can be controlled."[34] This dualism has long influenced the view of constantly tremoring, fidgeting, or nonmoving disabled bodies as exhibiting a failure of control. Moreover, eye contact as a sign of humanity often works against neurodiverse individuals who are forced to learn how to make eye contact. Yet even with this insistence on ableist tradition, her unmoving, speechless presence provides a moment of proximity, coexisting and negotiating with nonnormative existence, without intimate sociality. Ironically, she labors to overcome her able-bodied temporality and provides an invitation to recognize the materiality of "bodymind" as she becomes object.[35]

In an essay focusing on mental disability, Margaret Price uses the term *bodymind* to remedy the long-standing separation between mind and body, "because mental and physical processes not only affect each other but also give rise to each other—that is, because they tend to act as one, even though they are conventionally understood as two."[36] That they "act as one" does not imply that they are always felt as one. As we think about the objecthood of humans, the sense that mind and body are disconnected emerges as an experience of disability. In *The Man Who Mistook His Wife for a Hat*, for instance, Oliver Sacks writes of one woman, Christina, who lost proprioception, the awareness of the body and "the complex mechanisms and controls by which our bodies are properly aligned and balanced in space."[37] Christina initially felt "disembodied" and her body as "blind and deaf to itself," and continued to feel, with the continuing loss of proprioception, that her body was "dead," "not-real," "not-hers."[38] In this illustration of the limits of the assumed mind-body integration, Christina's disabled body is in proximity to her as an object of her own gaze in order to be operated and as, what Sacks calls, the "nothingness" and inexpressible "non-realm" without words to describe her experience.[39]

The disability of proprioceptive "disembodiment" reveals the overlap between corporeal existence and objecthood. Christina's reliance on the metaphor of blindness and deafness expresses this proprioceptive disability as a difference in sensory processing, aligned with sensory disabilities. Similarly, Larry Davidson writes that one of his research participants with schizophrenia described "the times when he no longer was aware of himself as a person. In these moments, what awareness he retained seemed to him to be that of an object."[40] Davidson quotes another person who was having a similar experience: "I am starting to feel pretty numb about everything because I am becoming an object and objects don't have feelings."[41] Although these quotations do not provide larger contexts of the individual's experiences, being open to the disconnect between body and mind may generate deeper understandings of how multiple dimensions of mental, physical, and sensory disabilities do not fit into a single alternative ontology, such as integrated bodymind, stillness, or advantages of differences. Instead, the ontologies of unbecoming human gesture toward the copresence and simultaneity of the mind and the body whether or not they feel together, relational, and whole, or disconnected, fragmented, and proximal.

At this juncture, the queer inhumanism of unbecoming human as a theoretical and ethical intervention expresses an anti-ableist commitment, recognizing that it is difficult to think of human subjectivity, disabled or not, without resorting to abilities, values, legitimacy, and social acceptance. In the absence of conventional markers of humanity and with the desire to "endow" humanity and personhood entirely set aside, the imperative of progress toward an enhanced future that makes "human life" valuable loses its force. This position is in a way an alternative to what Douglas Biklen calls the "presumption of competence" for individuals who do not communicate verbally or use sign language. Biklen draws the notion from the work of Tito Rajarshi Mukhopadhyay and Sue Rubin, who are autistic: "Give the person the benefit of the doubt, presume competence, then work hard at looking for the evidence, and also support the person in finding new ways of expression."[42] Given how the label intellectual disability often creates otherness and low expectation, the "presumption of competence" is an important practical step toward ensuring equal participation. However, this presumption does not challenge the belief that "competence" is a threshold requirement for equality and sociability. Making competence irrelevant in recognizing the ontology of a being is another way to challenge the qualifications that operate as exclusive criteria of humanity.

To think through disability from a critical inhumanist position is not to recalibrate our understanding of the human in a more accurate and inclusive way but to open up diverse ontologies that make any declaration of value and classification irrelevant, as well as to abandon the able-bodied schema as a normalizing goal of cure, re/habilitation, and assimilation. This focus on the conditions of the inhuman unexpectedly meshes with a global commitment to human rights that is not based on the recognition of humanness in terms of productive citizenship. Hannah Arendt's argument for "a right to have rights" reveals the prerequisite conditions—including "actions," "opinions," and "a right to belong to some kind of organized community"—that warrant rights protections.[43] Arendt adds that before the formulation of modern human rights based on "a completely organized humanity," "what we must call a 'human right' today would have been thought of as a general characteristic of the human condition which no tyrant could take away."[44] Queer inhumanism is an effort to refuse to make the human the central condition required in building a community, for any inclusive claim of humanity never fully represents or describes all humans' characteristics. An objecthood-based critique recognizes nonconforming and recalcitrant forms of a being rather than privileging one form of resistance and agency, and a fixed perception of a valuable life, over all others. To suspend humanness is to abandon the appraisal of difference and move toward a nonjudgmental ontology of copresence and proximity.

Conditions of an OK Life of a Machine

How is object-becoming feasible or ethical within global capitalist politics that supports the exploitation of labor based on oppression and colonial histories? Park Chan-wook's *I'm a Cyborg, but That's OK* (2006) employs surrealism, comedy, musical elements, and a mentally disabled figure who becomes a machine with no purpose.[45] This experiment is paradoxically centered on the search for the minimal elements that sustain life. A young woman named Young-goon (Im Soo-jung), who works on the assembly line of a radio factory, identifies as (or is in the process of becoming) a cyborg whose purpose is as yet unknown to herself. Her self-electroshocking on a rainy night at the factory in an effort to charge her body leads her to a psychiatric hospital in which she refuses to eat and becomes unresponsive.

The film has two contrasting parts woven together: a lighthearted depiction of a community of eccentric people with mental disabilities, one that disrupts the boundary of self by presenting hallucinations and delusions as transferable and shared, almost as machine parts; and a violent visualization of Young-goon's vengeance against the medical system, one activated by her machine identity that mourns the institutionalization and death of her grandmother. The film presents potentially transgressive yet morally ambivalent travels to and from objects, humans, antisociality, and proximity. In the end, the film advocates for a need-based understanding of existence rather than a capacity-based definition of being human: it ultimately challenges the binarized indignity of objecthood and dignified humanity, affirming life with mental disability as well as proximity to and connection with objects. The collaboration between Young-goon and another character in the hospital, Il-soon (Jung Ji-hoon), who is diagnosed as antisocial, suggests that sustenance and social proximity—without identification, a purpose of existence, or the need for "improvement"—constitute the minimal condition of an OK life.

In the initial sequence, extreme close-up images of moving cogwheels as if shown in X-rays vividly portray the internal world of machinery. A mechanical rhythmic sound opens the shot of a brightly colored space filled with an endless number of indistinguishable young women sitting in straight lines and repeating the same motions in unison. A reading of the noncompliant figure of a Korean female disabled factory worker who thinks of herself as a cyborg inevitably invokes Donna Haraway's "Cyborg Manifesto." Haraway mentions Korean factory workers who labor in an assembly line for the manufacture of integrated circuits and that "'women of color' might be understood as a cyborg identity, as a potent subjectivity synthesized from the fusions of outsider identities."[46] After noting that "'women of color' are the preferred labor force for the science-based industries," she observes: "Young Korean women hired in the sex industry and in electronics assembly are recruited from high schools, educated for the integrated circuit. Literacy, especially in English, distinguishes the 'cheap' female labor so attractive to the multinationals. Contrary to orientalist stereotypes of the 'oral primitive,' literacy is a *special* mark of women of color, acquired by US black women as well as men through a history of risking death to learn and to teach reading and writing."[47] Here capability, gender, age, ethnicity, and geopolitical history constitute an "ideal" condition of exploitable humanity. This exploitability is put in contrast with the image of "the oral primitive" as unenlightened and occupying a lower rung of the evolutionary hierarchy, an image that also justified colonial subjugation to usher these individuals into modernity and humanity through education. Literacy and racialized and gendered assumptions that they have a natural aptitude for repetitive unskilled and skilled labor make them desirable in the name of national economic growth.

To be properly human as a woman of color, ironically, is to be equipped with capacities exploitable in global production. In one scene of the film, Young-goon stays still with her head tilted up while she listens to a hallucinated commanding voice, providing a stark visual contrast to the rows of workers laboring in synchronized motion with their heads down. In this mechanized human labor, Young-goon breaks out of the capitalist machinery by becoming a cyborg and transforming into unexploitable existence. Haraway connects cyborg existence with the art of survival: "Cyborg writing is about the power to survive, not on the basis of original innocence, but on the basis of seizing the tools to mark the world that marked them as other. The tools are often stories, retold stories, versions that reverse and displace the hierarchical dualisms of naturalized identities."[48] The themes of power, violence, connection with inhuman objects and animals, and survival, which all address the injustice of othering, appear in *I'm a Cyborg, but That's OK* with an added emphasis on mental disability and medical institutionalization as conditions of politicized nonnormative existence.

Whereas Abramović's sitting objecthood was a condition of social encounters that test the connection and disconnection of bodies through the gaze, the manufacturing process in Young-goon's radio factory creates an environment in which mechanized workers do not recognize each other's state. Obeying the voice commanding her, Young-goon cuts her wrist with a knife, puts a wire into the cut, and affixes the wire with tape. The electrical outlet is then shown in a close-up, implying that in the next step she would put the wire into it. Intercutting Young-goon's actions carried out in the factory is a scene in a doctor's office in which her mother and the doctor, Choi Seul-gi, are discussing Young-goon's "suicide attempt," making the before and the after of the event occur simultaneously. Choi asks, "Was there anything different about Young-goon before the incident? For instance, did she suddenly stop eating?" This question about eating foreshadows the ethical problem of force-feeding. Mother explains, "The truth is that Young-goon raised my mother. No. I mean, my mother raised Young-goon." This linguistic slippage implies generational role reversal and interdependence between Young-goon and her grandmother, both living with an alternate identity. Following the revelation of Grandmother's mouse identity, Choi asks, "Did Young-goon ever say she was something else, too?" Critically, Mother's lie—"Never, doctor. Young-goon is a human being"—is uttered as viewers see a shot of the unconscious Young-goon, who has fallen backward in her chair. Her bleeding body on the ground is a clear mark of an unfit, leaky body, out of order in the middle of the two rows of workers, who never look up from their tasks. The next gory scene playfully transitions to a close-up of her toes lighting in a cascade of colors to signal that her body is fully charged and her cyborgness enacted. Plugging oneself into an electric socket, licking batteries, and receiving electroconvulsive therapy are, after all, the methods of sustaining a cyborg.

In declaring that it is OK to be a cyborg, the film takes a route different from that followed by the typical psychotherapeutic narrative, which moves toward conformity and cure.[49] Mother asks, "Grandmother's thing would not be related, would it, to her suicide attempt? Young-goon will be OK, right?" Mother attempts to reframe it by contending that affinities to an animal, objects, or other humans are not uncommon, hinting at her own undisclosed identity and at matrilineal mental disability: "My mother probably felt a little closer to mice that day. I too have days when I feel extremely close to pig intestines. You feel the same with patients. Don't you?" This is not so much an argument for the universalizability of disability, as experienced on a continuum, as it is Mother's attempt to erase and conceal the ways in which they differ from assumed normality. Nevertheless, Mother's decision to hide Young-goon's cyborg identity illustrates that identifications with visible nonhuman entities (a mouse and pig intestines) are more easily disguised as affinities and intimacy than is Young-goon's cyborgness—which cannot be located as an object of her affinity. Mother's desire for Young-goon's life to be OK, while hiding her cyborgness to avoid pathologization and social stigma, is at war with Young-goon's need for her machine embodiment to be acknowledged and shared so that she can survive.

For Young-goon, being a cyborg means having the power to stop the ambulance in order to give Grandmother her dentures, a technology necessary for Grandmother to sustain her life as a mouse eating radishes. As revealed in her flashback, when Grandmother was forcibly taken away from home to a nursing home, Young-goon fails to catch up to the ambulance and holds on to the dentures as a substitute for Grandmother's presence. Her habit of carrying a computer mouse with the dentures—together with a photo on the wall above her bed, which shows a person bending over, his two arms engaged with a big machine that has a valve emitting steam and pipes connected to the wall—marks her physical and emotional proximity to working machines as fellow beings.[50] The difference between her and all laboring machines is that they each exist with a specific purpose and utility. She longs to discover her purpose as a laboring object. Part organism and part machine, the cyborg is a transitional step toward becoming a full machine with a purpose. Consistent with viewing the instrumentalization of a person to serve someone else's interest as a sign of objectification, Young-goon perceives her potential utility as the essential condition of becoming machine. Rather than valorize humans for their productivity and contributions to society, as a utilitarian might, her desire to be used reveals that relational passivity and proximity are the keys for object-becoming as she moves away from agency as an exertion of power for advocating self-interest.

As the voice communicates with Young-goon, she learns about the seven deadly sins of which she needs to rid herself in order to be capable of exacting revenge on the *Hayan-men* (men in white), the medical professionals responsible for Grandmother's institutionalization. The sins are Sympathy, Sadness, Excitement, Hesitancy, Imagination, Guilt, and Gratitude—"listed in the order of evilness," a soft, kind female voice announces.[51] Young-goon's cyborgian ethical virtues, by contrast, gesture toward antisociality. The voice from the transistor radio urges, "You should not uselessly imagine whether Hayan-men have grandmothers. You should not hesitate to kill because of your sympathy for those grandmothers." Grieving grandmothers, not humanity itself, are offered as a reason to respect life and thus as a hindrance to Young-goon's mission. Sympathy is her symptom of the disorder that needs to be remedied. She asks Il-soon to steal her sympathy, so that she will become antisocial enough to kill all the medical professionals. In a scene in which Young-goon is wearing the dentures and mourning Grandmother's death outside the hospital by burying the mouse she was carrying, she makes a ritualistic crying sound and tells Grandmother that she is not allowed to be sad. Il-soon, who became sympathetic after stealing her sympathy, comes near, holds her body up, and kisses her. Her face is oriented toward him but her body is turned in the opposite direction and levitates as flames come out of her feet as if from a rocket. She collapses when the voice is heard saying, "No excitement." The kiss reveals the heteronormativity tied to the notion of the human; Young-goon shifts it to human–object sexuality as embodied in the machine, endeavoring to suspend her emotions and heterosexual affect to continue to become a cyborg. With the kiss, the dentures are transferred to Il-soon, as he now becomes part of her proximity to objects.

In line with this object transference between the bodies, the "patients" at the hospital present an ensemble in which their unique fantasies that are typically understood as "symptoms" of mental disabilities are traded and shared.[52] One man feels guilty for every event that happens around him, apologizes excessively, and walks backward so as not to rudely turn his back on another person. His excessive modesty and politeness are stolen by Il-soon and later transferred back to him. As Sacks remarks, one reason that hallucinations are startling is their lack of "consensual validation"; here, the transference of "symptoms" suggests the importance of observing and understanding the fantasy experiences of a mentally disabled person.[53] In her ethnographic research of Bethel House, a community in a fishing village in northern Japan, Karen Nakamura learned that people with schizophrenia usually avoid telling anyone about their hallucinations and delusions, so that they will not be considered out of touch with reality, and "this causes them to withdraw into their own world and increases the feelings of social isolation." Instead, in Bethel, "People are encouraged to talk about their hallucinations and delusions. Thus, hallucinations and delusions become communal property, something that everyone can talk about and deal with."[54] Similarly in the film, hallucinations are externalized and can even be stolen and given back, generating interactions and providing tools for imagining different ontologies.

When Il-soon prepares to steal Young-goon's sympathy, Il-soon becomes an anthropologist with an emic perspective, that is, one from which the internal elements of a language or culture are described without interpretation.[55] For Il-soon, "stealing" other patients' characteristics or symptoms is a way to understand their fantasies and become able to practice them; he does so not to ridicule them but to enter into their modes of perception and also to make "symptoms" into transferrable objects. The transference underscores what Davidson calls "the intersubjective nature of experience."[56] Audience members are introduced to Young-goon's characteristics through Il-soon's eyes and not through a clinical gaze that might identify behaviors as signs of catatonia accompanying echoralia, echopraxia, and stereotypy, a clinical term for a repetitive motor activity.[57] He finds out that Young-goon is not eating any food but is secretly only licking batteries, making her exhausted. After he successfully steals her sympathy through a ritualistic act of transference using a mask in a boiler room full of machinery, Young-goon is activated as an automatic machine gun: she starts her first fantasy rampage of shooting nurses and doctors through her fingers, only to collapse and become completely unresponsive— not eating, not communicating, and not sleeping.

Young-goon's unresponsive and emaciated body is in a state that, according to Giorgio Agamben, "marks the threshold between the human and the inhuman."[58] In discussing the *Muselmänner*—camp slang for those in Auschwitz on the verge of death who were emaciated, exhausted, listless, and apathetic (also called the "living corpses")—Agamben rejects the notion of human dignity by considering the *Muselmann* to be "the guard on the threshold of a new ethics, an ethics of a form of life that begins where dignity ends." Agamben argues, "The bare life to which human beings were reduced neither demands nor conforms to anything. It itself is the only norm; it is absolutely immanent. And 'the ultimate sentiment of belonging to the species' cannot in any sense be a kind of dignity."[59]

He contests the possibility of dehumanization: "no ethics can claim to exclude a part of humanity, no matter how unpleasant or difficult that humanity is to see."[60] The playfulness and fantastical nature of *I'm a Cyborg, but That's OK* may make the comparison of Young-goon's catatonia to the historical condition of a *Muselmann* seem extreme. Nevertheless, Agamben's insight powerfully underscores the point that it would be crucial to abandon dignity as the determinant of the beginning and ending of humanity, to avoid creating an "outside" to humanity and to prevent signs of powerlessness from being considered a cause of (and invitation to) violence. Even further, to work against privilege and the liberal notion of legitimate personhood, it is generative to leave the boundary of the human altogether by embodying object beings and by actively undoing human values, abilities, and subjectivity.

Without knowing that Young-goon is a cyborg, her doctor decides to put her through electroconvulsive therapy, which solves her problem of charging her body to its fullest. During the electroshock, Young-goon has a dream of being inside a giant incubator to which many wires are connected.[61] She sees Grandmother outside it, who tries to tell her the purpose of existence, but the sentence is never completed. After being recharged, her body transforms into a high-capacity machine gun and starts to shoot at all the people working at the hospital, sparing only people with disabilities. The ammunition is rolling in her mouth, and her arms and fingers are extended as muzzles. Set to classical music, the scene runs more than three minutes, reflecting the significance of this bloody rampage and displaying the impact of her cold ruthlessness. The killings completely shift the film's genre from a lighthearted drama about a community of people with mental disabilities to a violent story of vengeance against the medical system and identities that divide "us" and "them" and enable violence. During this vigorous action in her fantasy, she appears to others as catatonic.

Although the gory sight of bullet-riddled bodies feeds the stereotypical and dangerous misperception that people with mental illness are violent and murderous (an image more widely held in the United States, where gun violence is strongly associated with mental illness), her fantasy of a massacre also expresses rage against a system of institutionalization and against ableist society in general, which does not allow various modes of existence. Does this violent scene of mass killing by a cyborg justify the use of violence as a mode of resistance and as what Frantz Fanon calls "a cleansing force" at an individual level?[62] Or is it an expression of "queer negativity," launching a vigorous political critique of the system in the form of violent fantasy combined with embodied objecthood?[63] The director's previous films on the theme of revenge might provide useful contexts to understand it. In *Sympathy for Mr. Vengeance* (2002), Park Chan-wook features a deaf character who, much like Young-goon, works at a factory. His sister's failing kidney and his own victimization by organ traffickers attract the involvement of his girlfriend and her socialist organization. Both films criticize the use of human bodies as exploitable commodities in medical capitalism and portray disabled people's nonconformist struggles through enacting or hallucinating violent revenge.

In *I'm a Cyborg, but That's OK*, when Young-goon is subjected to force-feeding, the patients collectively launch a hunger strike as they demand her release from the isolation room. New social links are formed in the hospital ward around Young-goon's prospect of survival and against force-feeding. The acceptance of psychic difference and the intersubjective mixing of fantasies occur in parallel. Il-soon tries to persuade her to eat by explaining that rice will be transformed into an electron if he installs equipment inside her body. In an emotional scene inside the boiler room, Il-soon performs a symbolic surgery on Young-goon's back that gives him access to the machine of her body. At this crucial moment, he also lets go of his own trauma about his mother (who abandoned him) by pretending to install a small locket containing his mother's photo inside Young-goon's body. In a dramatically choreographed group scene, in which everyone cheers as Young-goon swallows rice, Young-goon's body becomes transparent and the locket is revealed inside, as the histories of Il-soon and Young-goon merge as objects.

After the rampage, Young-goon is still haunted by the image of Grandmother trying to tell her what the purpose of her existence is. By decoding Grandmother's message as she remembers it from the movement of Grandmother's lips, she comes to believe that she is now a nuclear bomb and is supposed to detonate to end the world. Needing a billion volts of electricity to do so, Young-goon and Il-soon sit outside, on the top of a hill, holding an antenna to attract lightning on a stormy night. As morning breaks, the camera shows from a distance two naked bodies collapsed on top of each other as a rainbow shines in the sky. This somewhat comical closing recalls the typical ending of musicals: a triumph of heterosexual love, ironically blessed by a rainbow, a symbol of queer diversity. Yet despite suggesting that each will have a companion in journeying through life with mental disability, the ending registers no cure, no disappearance of their psychic differences or resolution of their haunting memories, but only temporary and tentative proximity.

The remark of Young-goon's mother that it is "OK" if she is a cyborg as long as she hides it and eats food is an unwitting challenge to what are assumed to be distinct boundaries between personhood and objectness. An assessment of "OKness" hints at the potential of queer disability to blur the boundaries of humans and objects. More explicitly, *I'm a Cyborg, but That's OK* challenges notions of agency that are bound to signs of capacity. As a seemingly passive object, Young-goon unintentionally creates a community of support in the institutional space where life with disability and with cognitive and psychic difference ultimately disengages from the conditions of personhood. In its hallucinatory and delusional incoherence and in its insistence on the OKness of mental disability, *I'm a Cyborg, but That's OK* challenges viewers to dwell on unlikely pairings that undercut the idealization of the heterosexual nuclear family as the bearer of care and love. Embracing antisociality to lose the quality of being human, Young-goon and Il-soon crucially form a human-object dyad at the end, signaling that they will continue their survival in an existence made intelligible and unintelligible at the same time.

This proximity between two disabled individuals outside the normative family is thus a new form of sociality based on remedying violence and disengaging from the utilitarian framework of human existence. Objecthood is a kind of antisocial mode, a refusal to become what our society demands us to be, as Halberstam declares, "the anti-social dictates an unbecoming, a cleaving to that which seems to shame or annihilate; and a radical passivity allows for the inhabiting of femininity with a difference."[64] What Halberstam names as an act of unbecoming is realized in the form of becoming an object and taking on object-defining characteristics. Becoming an object is not automatically benign, however, as shown by Young-goon's revenge—she creates an identity that imposes an absolute division between the community of disability and the medical professionals to determine who lives and who dies.

After revealing to her doctor that she is a cyborg, Young-goon recalls the traumatic day when Grandmother was taken away. In her recollection, her aunt and uncle, together with her mother, come into the house, interrupting the peace and intimacy that Young-goon and Grandmother share while assembling a radio and eating a radish, respectively. The three adults walk in and domineeringly look down on the two subjects sitting on the floor. First Mother takes Grandmother's radish away. Noticing the strong odor in the house, her aunt screams, "How could you bear living like this? You should have taken her to a nursing home way before now." Young-goon tries to erase her violent words by turning up the radio's volume. Reacting to the loud sound, Mother attempts to take the radio away from her. As they struggle over it, the radio is thrown on the floor and breaks. The smashing of the radio parallels the violence of shattering the intelligibility of Young-goon and Grandmother's world and the violence of Grandmother's removal from her home. This link between the machine and the disabled woman is acutely expressed by

Young-goon's cyborg identity. For Young-goon, violent responses are not anti-human: they are her attempt to illustrate the in-humanness of violence, the in-humanness she needs to fully escape to become an object.

The merging of disabled characters and the symbolic transfer of their objects, fantasies, and symptoms present another way to imagine the experience of mental disabilities. The intense intergenerational female connection between Young-goon and Grandmother is also important, as it counters the ableist familial complicity displayed by her mother and aunt and uncle, who are culpable for taking Grandmother away in the name of remedying the degraded and inhuman conditions of her life. This "remedy" justifies institutionalizing her as a solution.

Proximity and Becoming an Object

What does it mean to unbecome human by becoming an object? Or what does it mean to reveal the already existing overlap between object beings and human beings that conditions our daily experiences? The neoliberal self-containment of families is reserved only for self-regulating and self-sustaining individuals; in contrast, disabled people, queer youth, older people, and laborers are driven outside their homes. In 2011 Kim Jin-sook (Kim Chin-suk), the leader of the Korea Confederation of Trade Unionists, took herself to the top of a 115-foot-high crane, no. 85, above a shipyard of Hanjin Heavy Industries Construction, which had laid her off. The structural adjustment program was not a direct response to economic troubles within the company but connected to neoliberal principles implemented since the economic crisis that led to the intervention of the International Monetary Fund in 1997: low wages, austerity measures, massive layoffs, and offshore production. Kim demanded that Hanjin cancel its layoff plan and rehire the fired workers, pledging to stay on top of the crane until her demands were met. When she finally came down—more than ten months later, after the union and Hanjin reached an agreement—she said, "I haven't seen any other human this close for the last 309 days." By calling herself an "invisible human" and making her life a kind of "bare life" and by relying on others to send food up and to empty the waste bucket that she sent down, Kim seized the tools, the machinery, "to mark the world that marked [her] as other."[65]

Kim Jin-sook inhabited the machinery that would also be discarded and sold as the jobs went away; in addition, her protest was intended to memorialize another worker, Kim Chu-ik, who ended his life in the crane after 129 days of labor rights protest in 2003. Her bare life mobilized the Bus of Hope movement in which people visited the crane and formed a broad coalition that included proponents of labor rights, activists in the disability rights movement, teachers, and contingent workers. Living a marginalized existence under global neoliberal capitalism with machines and as machines, treated as obsolete objects, impels us to embrace object-becoming without purpose as an inevitable protest and as a mode of being that is unintelligible and vulnerable.

In the end, feminist theories of objectification serve as a tool to make explicit the problems of how othered bodies are seen and treated and denied moral, perceptual, and material equality. However, relying on the notion of a degraded objecthood that does not reflect how humans are embodied, attach themselves to objects, live in proximity to objects, and become dis/embodied as objects cannot account for the infinite number of ways in which objects create meanings. Esmeir writes, "Can we rid ourselves of the notion of dehumanization, so that we do not reproduce colonial and neocolonial practices that insist dehumanization can occur and that humanity can be given back?"[66] It is dangerous to reinstate humanity by tying it to notions of the dignity, value, validity, and legitimacy of existence. Instead, I suggest challenging its status as a locus of dignity and respect based solely on limited notions of agency and abilities.

Performing the objecthood of human bodies—as Abramović's oeuvre and *I'm a Cyborg, but That's OK* illustrate—surrenders the power to inflict pain and to relate to each other through violence while undoing the sociality that is built on neoliberal self-regulation, productivity, utility, quality of life, and presumed able-bodiedness, all employed to separate the deserving from the undeserving. A queer feminist disability studies might benefit not from a mere refusal of objectification—"we are humans, not objects"—but from a refusal of the subject-object binary that denies the "object" and the objectlike state attention and presence. The new anti-ableist queer ethics of inhumanism, which negotiates with differences through copresence, proximity without identification, and simultaneous inhabitation, recognizes the labor of living with disability that is not exploitable. Perceiving someone or feeling oneself to be an object in a given conceptual space does not itself constitute ethical harm; indeed, becoming an object provides a point of departure to unravel ableism, normative humanity, and violence.

Notes

I thank Mel Y. Chen and Dana Luciano, who encouraged me to think further on this topic. The anonymous reviewers provided me with thoughtful and insightful feedback that guided me in reconsidering and clarifying various points. Nicole Markotić's and Michael Gill's help were integral to completing this essay. I also thank Margaret Price for her invaluable feedback and for making me think more about the body-mind disconnect. Eli Clare helped me realize the importance of disengagement for which I am deeply grateful. I would also like to thank Alice Falk, Sarah Groeneveld, Stacey Lutkosky, and Elizabeth Freeman for their helpful editorial suggestions. The epigraph is from Donna Haraway, "A Manifesto for Cyborgs: Science, Technology, and Socialist Feminism in the 1980s," *Socialist Review* 80 (March–April), 99.

1. Andrea Dworkin, *Pornography: Men Possessing Women* (New York: G. P. Putnam's Sons, 1981), 108.

2. Dipesh Chakrabarty, *Habitations of Modernity: Essays in the Wake of Subaltern Studies* (Chicago: University of Chicago Press, 2002), 140.

3. "Highlights from Speeches by Ed Roberts," collected by Jon Oda, World Institute on Disability, wid.org/about-wid/highlights-from-speeches-by-ed-roberts (accessed June 17, 2014).

4. Jasbir K. Puar, "Coda: The Cost of Getting Better: Suicide, Sensation, and Switchpoints," *GLQ* 18, no. 1 (2012): 153, 154.

5. Samera Esmeir, *Judicial Humanity: A Colonial History* (Stanford, CA: Stanford University Press, 2012), 3.

6. Samera Esmeir, "On Making Dehumanization Possible," *PMLA* 121, no. 5 (2006): 1547, 1549.

7. Esmeir, "On Making Dehumanization Possible," 1549.

8. Chakrabarty, *Habitations of Modernity*, 142.

9. Mel Y. Chen, *Animacies: Biopolitics, Racial Mattering, and Queer Affect* (Durham, NC: Duke University Press, 2012), 43. Chen explains, "One form of what is understood as dehumanization involves the *removal* of qualities especially cherished as human; at other times, dehumanization involves the more active *making* of an object." These two modes come together when becoming-objects remove the markers of the human.

10. Chakrabarty, *Habitation of Modernity*, 142.

11. A video produced by Cure Autism Now used the rhetoric that children with autism have lost their personhood: "Imagine that aliens were stealing one in every two hundred children. . . . That is what is happening in America today. It is called autism" (Ian Hacking, "Humans, Aliens, and Autism," *Daedalus* 138 [Summer 2009]: 44). Another video in the series treats the body as a vestige, lacking mind and personality: "It's like somebody sneaks into your house in the middle of the night and takes your precious baby's mind and personality and leaves the bewildered body behind. If one in every two hundred and fifty children in America were actually being kidnapped, we would have a national emergency. And we do. It's called autism." See www.youtube .com/watch?v=j_cJp714jXQ, September 4, 2006.

12. Sunaura Taylor, "Beasts of Burden: Disability Studies and Animal Rights," *Qui Parle* 19, no. 2 (2011): 194.

13. Mel Y. Chen, *Animacies: Biopolitics, Racial Mattering, and Queer Affect* (Durham, NC: Duke University Press, 2012), 235.

14. Linda LeMoncheck limits the term's scope: "It is only when women are regarded as inanimate objects, bodies, or animals, where their status as the moral equals of persons has been demeaned or degraded, that the expression 'sex objectification' is correctly used" (*Dehumanizing Women: Treating Persons as Sex Objects* [Totowa, NJ: Rowman and Allanheld, 1985], 11). Lina Papadaki asserts that it is desirable to reserve "objectification" as a negative designation for the morally objectionable situations in which "a person's humanity is denied when ignored/not properly acknowledged and/or when it is in some way harmed" ("What Is Objectification?," *Journal of Moral Philosophy* 7, no. 1 [2010]: 32; italics removed). Martha C. Nussbaum and Ann Cahill bring new approaches to objectification. Nussbaum points out that objectification is "not only a slippery, but also a multiple, concept," and it may involve benign or positive aspects of sexual experiences when consent and equality are present in adult relationships. What makes objectification objectionable, she argues, depends on its specifications and on the contexts in which it occurs ("Objectification," *Philosophy and Public Affairs* 24, no. 4 [1995]: 251, 256). According to Cahill, the source of degradation in objectification comes from seeing the material body as a reduced state. Objectification as currently conceptualized, Cahill insightfully argues, is overly burdened by the Kantian ideal of rationality and autonomy as the grounds of humanness, which does not serve feminist goals. For this ideal fortifies a notion of personhood defined as having distinctive capacities that are "intellectually and/or cognitively derived," ignoring embodiedness and the intersubjectivity of human existence (*Overcoming Objectification: A Carnal Ethics* [New York: Routledge, 2011], 8).

15. Nussbaum, "Objectification."

16. Marina Abramović and Velimir Abramović, *Artist Body Performances, 1969–1998* (Milan: Charta, 1998), 68.

17. Marina Abramović, "Body Art," in *Marina Abramović*, ed. Anna Daneri, Giacinto Di Pietrantonio et al. (Milan: Charta, 2002), 30.

18. Abramović, "Body Art," 30.

19. *Marina Abramović: The Artist Is Present*, ed. Klaus Biesenbach (New York: Museum of Modern Art, 2010), 74.

20. Abramović, "Body Art," 30.

21. Klaus Biesenbach, "Marina Abramović: The Artist Is Present. The Artist Was Present. The Artist Will Be Present," in Biesenbach, *Marina Abramović*, 17.

22. Abramović, "Body Art," 30.

23. Chrissie Iles, quoted in *The Artist Is Present*, directed by Matthew Akers (2012; Chicago: Music Box Films, 2012), DVD.

24. Judith Halberstam, "The Anti-Social Turn in Queer Studies," *Graduate Journal of Social Science* 5, no. 2 (2008): 150.

25. Thomas McEvilley, "Stages of Energy: Performance Art Ground Zero?," in Abramović and Abramović, *Artist Body*, 16.

26. Abramović, "Body Art," 30.

27. Judith Halberstam, *The Queer Art of Failure* (Durham, NC: Duke University Press, 2011), 139.

28. Simone de Beauvoir, *The Second Sex*, trans. and ed. H. M. Parshley (New York: Vintage Books, 1974), 684.

29. Lucy Sargisson, *Utopian Bodies and the Politics of Transgression* (London: Routledge, 2000), 3.

30. Jack Halberstam, "The Artist Is Object: Marina Abramović at MOMA," April 5, 2010, bullybloggers.wordpress.com/2010/04/05/the-artist-is-object-.

31. Amber Jamilla Musser, "Objects of Desire: Toward an Ethics of Sameness," *Theory and Event* 15, no. 2 (2013): n.p. Musser explores the "becoming-object" involved in "objectum sexuality, an orientation in which people sexually orient themselves towards objects" and "questions of relationality and ethics in queer theory."

32. Chen, *Animacies*.

33. Rachel Dodes, "Artist Marina Abramović Sits for an Interview," *Speakeasy: The Wall Street Journal*, June 1, 2010, blogs.wsj.com/speakeasy/2010/06/01/artist-marina -abramovic-sits-for-an-interview/.

34. Susan Wendell, *The Rejected Body: Feminist Philosophical Reflections of Disability* (New York: Routledge, 1994), 85.

35. Margaret Price, "The Bodymind Problem and the Possibilities of Pain," in "New Conversations in Feminist Disability Studies," ed. Kim Q. Hall, a special issue of *Hypatia* 30, no. 1 (2015): 268–84.

36. Price, "Bodymind Problem," 269.

37. Oliver Sacks, *The Man Who Mistook His Wife for a Hat* (New York: Simon and Schuster, 1998), 72. There are limitations to getting glimpses of experiences through the reports of the writers who met individuals in their capacity as clinicians, as Rosemarie Garland Thomson points out in discussing the "freak show" genealogy in Sacks's "wonderment" of clinical tales (Thomson, *Extraordinary Bodies: Figuring Physical Disability in American Culture and Literature* [New York: Columbia University Press, 1997], 56). Nonetheless, Sacks's writing, from a phenomenological perspective, reveals what Wendell observes: "the appreciation of difference" rather than treating the individuals as "curiosities" (*Rejected Body*, 67).

38. Sacks, *Man Who Mistook His Wife*, 51.

39. For more examples of mind-body disconnection or different proprioceptive perceptions experienced by autistic individuals, see Douglas Biklen, *Autism and the Myth of the Person Alone* (New York: New York University Press, 2005), 264–69.

40. Larry Davidson, *Living outside Mental Illness: Qualitative Studies of Recovery in Schizophrenia* (New York: New York University Press, 2003), 148.

41. Andrew McGhie and James Chapman, quoted in Davidson, *Living outside Mental Illness*, 148.

42. Biklen, *Autism*, 258.

43. Hannah Arendt, *The Origins of Totalitarianism* (1951; repr., San Diego: Harcourt Brace Jovanovich, 1976), 296–97.

44. Arendt, *Origins of Totalitarianism*, 297. Ironically, Arendt lists speech as one such example along with human relationship as the minimal human condition.

45. *I'm a Cyborg, but That's OK*, directed by Park Chan-wook (Seoul: CJ Entertainment, 2006), DVD.

46. Donna Haraway, "A Cyborg Manifesto: Science, Technology, and Socialist-Feminism in the Late Twentieth Century," in *Simians, Cyborgs, and Women: The Reinvention of Nature* (New York: Routledge, 1991), 174.

47. Haraway, "Cyborg Manifesto," 174–75; emphasis added.

48. Haraway, "Cyborg Manifesto," 175.

49. In such a coherent narrative, the flight of Young-goon's father shortly after her birth, the absence of her mother (who is running a restaurant), her grandmother's schizophrenia, and her premature birth followed by a period inside an incubator might be employed as the psychoanalytic origin of her mental state and an explanation for her machine identity. But the film provides this information only via a glimpse of the doctor's monitor.

50. The photo appears on the cover of Ed van der Elsken's photo album *Sweet Life* (New York: H. N. Abrams, 1966).

51. These seven evils echo "the seven evils of wives," which in Confucius tradition justify a woman's expulsion from her husband's family.

52. Park Jin, "Chŏngsin Punsŏk Naerŏt'ibŭ ŭi Saeroun Yŏngyŏk" ("New Realm of Psychoanalytic Narrative"), *Kukje Ŏmun* (*International Literature*) 42 (2008): 482. More examples of such transference of "symptoms" among the people in the hospital are as follows: One woman practices yodeling, and Il-soon later repeats the yodel. Il-soon is afraid of vanishing into a dot, a fear born from his experiences of invisibility when his parents ignored his presence. Young-goon is shown shrinking so small that she is carried out of the isolation room by a ladybug. One man thinks that his body is connected to a greater force by a rubber band that will take him to the right place at the end of his life. Grandmother, who after her death visits the mourning Young-goon in a field, is taken away into the sky by a rubber band, vanishing to a dot.

53. Oliver Sacks, *Hallucinations* (New York: Knopf, 2012), x.

54. Karen Nakamura, *A Disability of the Soul: An Ethnography of Schizophrenia and Mental Illness in Japan* (Ithaca: Cornell University Press, 2013), 82–83. Nakamura explains, "Every year, Bethel holds an annual festival where the highlight of the festival is the Hallucinations and Delusions Grand Prix. Here, the best hallucination or delusion is celebrated. The twist is that 'best' means the hallucination or delusion that brings together the most people or has the most community involvement" (82).

55. Kenneth Lee Pike, *Talk, Thought, and Thing: The Emic Road toward Conscious Knowledge* (Dallas: Summer Institute of Linguistics, 1993).

56. Davidson, *Living outside Mental Illness*, 25.

57. "Section II: Diagnostic Criteria and Codes," in *Diagnostic and Statistical Manual of Mental Disorders: DSM-5*, 5th ed. (Washington, DC: American Psychiatric Publishing, 2013), *DSM Library*, dsm.psychiatryonline.org/content.aspx?bookid=556&sectionid=41101755#103435410 (accessed August 31, 2013).

58. Giorgio Agamben, *Remnants of Auschwitz*, trans. Daniel Heller-Roazen (New York: Zone Books, 1999), 55.

59. Agamben, *Remnants of Auschwitz*, 69.

60. Agamben, *Remnants of Auschwitz*, 64.

61. Mentally disabled people in institutions are often subject to involuntary unmodified electroconvulsive therapy without anesthesia, or with anesthesia but without consent, treatment that constitutes a form of violence. In 2013 the UN Human Rights Council received Juan E. Méndez's "Report of the Special Rapporteur on Torture and Other Cruel, Inhuman or Degrading Treatment or Punishment," February 1, 2013 (A/HRC/22/53). The report states, "The environment of patient powerlessness and abusive treatment of persons with disabilities in which restraint and seclusion is used can lead to other non-consensual treatment, such as forced medication and electroshock procedures" (15).

62. Frantz Fanon, *The Wretched of the Earth*, trans. Richard Philcox (New York: Grove, 2008), 51.

63. Halberstam, "Anti-Social Turn in Queer Studies," 154.

64. Halberstam, "Anti-Social Turn in Queer Studies," 151.

65. Haraway, "Cyborg Manifesto," 175. The phrase "bare life" is from Giorgio Agamben, *Homo Sacer: Sovereign Power and Bare Life*, trans. Daniel Heller-Roazen (Stanford, CA: Stanford University Press, 1998).

66. Esmeir, "On Making Dehumanization Possible," 1550.

BEING CELLULAR

Race, the Inhuman, and the Plasticity of Life

Jayna Brown

*I*n 1951 doctors at Johns Hopkins University Hospital in Baltimore, Maryland, took a sample of cancer cells from the cervix of a young African American woman named Henrietta Lacks for use in their laboratory. In line with the medical conventions of the day, the doctors took Lacks's cancer cells without her knowledge or consent. Lacks's cells thrived in the laboratory, continuing to grow and reproduce at an amazing rate. Researchers had been trying to grow human cells for decades, and the so-named HeLa cells were the first to survive "immortally" outside the body. The lead research doctor, George Gey, made a televised announcement and excitedly sent samples to several other researchers and laboratories. Distribution techniques quickly developed to meet demand, and HeLa cells became the first standardized cell line.

The HeLa cells made possible a revolution in cell biology. Infinitely manipulable, life could be perpetuated and altered both spatially and temporally. Life could be expressed in forms no longer bounded by individual organisms. Life could proliferate unrestricted by organismal cycles of birth and death. It was capable of reproducing outside heterosexual conception and could even transcend the notion of species. Considering the developments that have followed the advent of HeLa, it would seem that biological science and technologies could usher in an entirely new ontology of life. A few cancer cells from one body could be the harbinger of an "utterly new mode of existence for human matter."[1] Vitality had a newfound mobility.[2]

Quickly following Gey's televised news of scientific success came stories of Lacks herself. In the stories that circulated, HeLa cells were personified; first

GLQ 21:2–3
DOI 10.1215/10642684-2843371
© 2015 by Duke University Press

she was celebrated as a rescuing angel and then vilified as a contaminant once her cells had "invaded" other cell lines and her race subsequently became news. For scientific rather than political reasons, the cellular biologist Hannah Landecker is impatient with how the HeLa cells continue to be anthropomorphized and attached to the life story of Henrietta Lacks. "No one has ever told origin stories about the life and times of the L cell line or its originating mouse, or the CHO line and its originating hamster," she tersely remarks in her book *Culturing Life*.[3] While I also question the personification of HeLa cells, I join the scholars Priscilla Wald, Karla Holloway, Alondra Nelson, and Dorothy Roberts who, while critiquing this personification on scientific grounds, also argue powerfully that categories of race, gender, and, I would add, (dis)ability are deeply imbricated in the development and application of the biological and medical sciences.[4] Science is always political, both in its history and in its application, and it cannot be assumed that there is such a thing as a biological normative. Disability is not coterminous with race, but disabled people have experienced oppression in the context of eugenic science, with its desire for biological supremacy, which I discuss further in this essay. Scientific revolution is not automatically accompanied by social change or political enlightenment; it often moves in the other direction.

In our historical moment, it could be argued that the lives of most humans are mediated in some way by science and technology. But not all bodies are scientized in the same way. While privileged bodies enjoy life-enhancing scientific processes such as vaccines, organ transplants, and other sophisticated medical procedures, other, often racialized bodies become useful as raw sources and labor, valued for their biological capacities. As studies of medical racism show, black people have historically been objects of scientific exploration and the involuntary recipients of painful, often fatal medical practices. The mass production of HeLa cells first began at Tuskegee at the same time that doctors were conducting syphilis experiments on black men at Tuskegee's medical facility. Black men and women have been continually surveilled, cataloged, and experimented on. With these histories in mind, it is understandable that telling Lacks's story would be an attempt to posthumously grant her the humanity such invasive practices negated for so many others.

The HeLa cell line raises important bioethical problems. Yet, as Wald brilliantly argues in her extensive work on HeLa, estranging ideas of "the human" generates crucial questions about the category human itself and reveals the historicity of the concept as exclusionary and founded on whiteness.[5] How, then, can we think outside the human? As Sylvia Wynter points out, there are different meanings for the concept of the human, both sociopolitical and biological. Scholars using Wynter's theoretical framework have explored the human in sociopolitical terms.[6] But to think also of humans as biological entities helps us suspend assumed ideas of what the human is and shed our attachment to a human-centered universe.

Evolution does not have our species' survival in mind, Landecker states. Many alternative "kinds of living entities have emerged and will continue to emerge," and this may in fact mean the "death" of our so-called species.[7] Since HeLa has been reproducing, it has changed its makeup and evolved. Many scientists claim that these cells can no longer be thought of as human but must be considered a new form of life. My provocation is that a future world may not include humans at all. This may not be a bad thing.

This essay is profoundly interested in the plasticity of life and the possibilities, real and imagined, for "utterly new mode(s) of existence." It reaches for the potential for alternative versions of life and liveliness. I seek to reclaim "life" from its association with heteronormative reproduction and family structures and the human rights discourses that attach themselves to the term. I seek to detach it from conservative "right to life" discourse as well as a liberal politics of inclusivity, including the plea for societal recognition in the political agendas of some LGBTQI and POC social movements. I wonder if reparation and restoration to the category human is enough of an aim. Claims that human life depends on being socially legible ironically reinscribe a politics of exclusion. I also call into question a persistent biological determinism that tries to assign value and meaning to particular biological formations. Thinking about cells invites speculation about alternative genealogies outside the heteronormative model. What other forms of kinship, and mutual care, are possible when we let go of this model? Science has allowed for African Americans to search for their ancestors through tracing their DNA. While the search for a restored human connection is an exciting use of new technologies, we might take further advantage of these scientific abilities to explore the queerness of the biological, to broaden our thoughts about biological life away from notions of ancestral descendancy to the possibility of ethical connections and political affiliations that do not rely on being related. DNA similarity does not restore a lost kinship; in fact, it can be interpreted as erasing the very foundations of kinship as based in heterosexual reproduction.

Attachments to the term *life* circumscribe the concept from a fuller breadth of meaning, one not reliant on simply corrective politics but suggesting a potentially risky unsettling. This destabilization may seem dangerous, as it unmoors us, letting us float in the infinite void of the unknown. Immediate needs for survival, for equitable resources and redistributions of power, might make such inquiry appear frivolous, even apolitical. But I argue that thinking past the human life span is crucial. It lets in the strange and unrecognizable, which requires an entire new paradigm for life itself.

However, in embracing an ontology of life, there are risks. In their introduction to the anthology *New Materialisms*, Diana Coole and Samantha Frost call for theorists to "rediscover older materialist traditions while pushing them in novel, and sometimes experimental, directions or toward fresh applications."[8] In so doing, I argue, fantasies about the plasticity of life in theoretical and speculative thought must not rely on some scientific neutrality but consider the histories of social and scientific racism and eugenics. Yet I still insist on the importance of the utopian, of dreams that reach to new paradigms, that search out the ineffable moments of life that confound us.

To envision exactly what any new entity would look like is unknowable, beyond the horizon. Nevertheless, fantasies about the possible shapes that life could take are a powerful exercise. In his dream of Harmony, the nineteenth-century socialist utopian Charles Fourier predicts that earth's species will evolve once humans are living in accordance with his plan. Humans will grow to seven feet tall and enjoy an expanded life span and enhanced senses. Humans will become amphibious, growing gills and a prehensile tail, which Fourier names an "archibras." With a "small elongated hand at its end," it will be useful for many things, including playing musical instruments.[9]

For Fourier, the organizing principle of the entire universe is what he calls passionate attraction. On the social level, sexuality is this attraction's paramount manifestation of human sociality, and Fourier devises a complex system of sexual relations for his utopia, predicated on the fulfillment of everyone's passions, whose basic physical needs are taste and touch. In his *nouveau monde amoureux*, those with multiple sexual proclivities have reached the highest stages of Harmony.[10] But Fourier means passionate attraction to be much more than a set of human drives. It is the "central element in a comprehensive vision of the universe."[11] Not reducible to human needs and desires, passionate attraction is a "universal law," which could explain "everything from the origins of the stars" to "the most minute alterations of matter in the animal, vegetable and mineral kingdoms." Passionate attraction is "the 'key' to a host of new sciences."[12] Fourier writes: "The properties of an animal, a vegetable, a mineral, and even a cluster of stars, represent some effect of the human passions in the social order, and that EVERYTHING, from the atoms to the stars, constitutes a tableaux of the properties of the human passions."[13]

Even the movement of the stars and galaxies are premised on Fourier's principle of the passions. In his "theory of material movement," God adheres to mathematical principles, and "all creations take place through the conjunction of the northern fluid, which is male, and the southern fluid, which is female," but the stars' sexual reproduction is not limited to a gendered binary.[14] To his declaration, Fourier adds a note: "All stars can copulate: 1. With itself like a vegetable, the north pole copulating with the south; 2. With another star by means of outpourings from contrasting poles; 3. With the help of an intermediary."[15] At this stage in our development, "the earth is violently agitated by the need to create."[16] While I am not suggesting that we take up Fourier's ideas wholesale, we can take his speculations to open ourselves up to the idea that there are other creative ways to think about love, desire, subjectivity, and the relationship between them.

Coming back down from the stars to the level of the cellular, and into the medium of modern science, in *Culturing Life*, Landecker's focus is on what happens in the laboratory. She looks at cells nurtured in a medium, and she emphasizes the importance of modern science in furthering the possibilities for future life forms. But other scholars and scientists look to the unpredictable, the ways in which cells act of their own accord. In *What Should We Do with Our Brain?* Catherine Malabou argues for what she calls "neuronal creativity," explaining that in fact the brain, far from being a central computer for the body, is instead notable for its plasticity.[17] The plasticity, she argues, is in the cut, the void, the gap between synapses. "Between two neurons," she writes, "there is a caesura, and the synapse itself is gapped . . . the cut plays a decisive role in cerebral organization. Nervous information must cross voids, and something aleatory introduces itself between the emission and the reception of a message, constituting the field of plasticity."[18] I am interested not only in what cells do when manipulated by science but in the "something aleatory," in what remains unknown. What happens as the nerve cells transmit across the synaptic leap? What happens by chance or accident?

Within larger conceptions of a connected molecular universe, I wonder at the plasticity of the biological, and particularly of cells. Landecker asks, "What is the social and cultural task of being biological entities—being simultaneously biological things and human persons—when the 'biological' is fundamentally plastic?"[19] An explosion of possible inquiries follows Landecker's question. What ways can we think of life differently? That cells grow and change, and reproduce independently of individual bodies, destabilizes notions of individual subjectivity. When we destabilize these notions, what forms of subjectivity formation are possible? How far can we go in imagining, and practicing, life on other terms? What forms of sociality and the communal are available for us if we estrange ourselves from the life of our species? And how might these practices of estrangement—queering—actually allow for a new ethical landscape?

Considering life on a cellular level provides a productive reorientation in our materialist understanding of ourselves as biological entities. Henri Bergson, the early twentieth century theorist of life, has inspired contemporary materialists by the ways he decenters the human in his theory. He decenters the human, not only in relation to other animals, but also in relation to other possible and potential entities. "The line of evolution that ends in man is not the only one," writes Bergson. "On other paths, divergent from it, other forms of consciousness have been developed, which have not been able to free themselves."[20] Cells, in conjunction with scientific manipulations, are often unpredictable, outside what science and technology intend.[21] There exist, in the material world, other dimensions of being.

The body can be understood as porous and not discretely bounded. Bergson philosophically queried the tenuousness of the individual in 1907. "Who can say where individuality begins and ends, whether the living being is one or many, whether it is the cells which associate themselves into the organism or the organism which dissociates itself into cells?" he wrote.[22] For Bergson, individuality was never complete. "Individuality admits to any number of degrees, and that it is not fully realized anywhere, even in man. . . . vital properties are never entirely realized, though always on the way to become so; they are not so much *states* as *tendencies*."[23] Life "manifests a search for individuality," he writes, but never achieves it.

Situating ourselves at the cellular level shows us that our supposedly discrete bodies are actually complex ecosystems of cells, bacteria, and other organisms, which challenges our notion of individuality and sovereignty. But this materialist recognition is not new. "We are all cell communities," wrote H. G. Wells and Julian Huxley in 1932, in their popular science book *The Science of Life*, "and these cells . . . can behave with remarkable individuality and independence."[24] We can take the conversation of selfhood a step further and argue, as does Jane Bennett, that we consider the fundamental connection between all forms of molecular makeup, both organic and inorganic, and the ecological urgency of decentering the human. Such reorientation may lead to new, perhaps more ethical relationships with the material world. But, as the historical record shows, it does not automatically do so. Bennett begins her analysis of Bergson and Hans Driesch invoking the concept of *Bildungstreib*, developed by Johannes Blumenbach and taken up by Immanuel Kant.[25] This concept refers to an inborn power and drive innate in all life forms. Yet we would do well to remember that Blumenbach also gave us the racial classification system still operative today. His five racial categories and his theory of racial degeneration have provided a durable basis for scientific racism.

Nevertheless, it is exciting to consider that cell life and molecular activity may hold revolutionary potential. Liberation may mean freedom from the confines of "the human." Thinking of this potential invites a radical questioning of the self as a biologically stable entity, of "the human" as a species, and even suggests a turn away from the idea of species itself. Malabou argues that once we are conscious of our brain's plasticity, we will have "the capacity to form oneself otherwise, to displace, even nullify determination: freedom."[26] She argues provocatively that we can "think new modalities of forming the self, under the name of "plasticity.""[27] The transition from "neuronal to the mental," from the material to a conscious state of being, is marked less by homeostasis, she argues, inspired by Bergson, than by explosion, by conflict. "Only in making explosives does life give shape to its own freedom, that is, turn away from genetic determinism," she writes.[28] It is not clear, however, how the seemingly ineffable random occurrence in the void between synapses constitutes freedom. Malabou does not stipulate whether some kind of control is necessary to direct these explosions and what implications that ability would carry. Malabou also does not account for the contingencies of power organized through the categories of race and sex. What kinds of scientific questions can be asked of the brain when the inequality of health care, nutrition, and other factors affecting brain chemistry and function are actually taken into account? What of plasticity then?

Although I insist on dreaming the unknowable, I remain wary of celebrating too soon. The development of the very idea of races comes out of the natural sciences, which themselves grew out of the practice of collecting, classifying, and categorizing life forms. "Reason" and scientific discovery grouped racialized bodies along with the flora and fauna of the colonized worlds. As I look back in this article at the science/fictional ways that the plasticity of life has been conceptualized by Wells the writer and Huxley the biologist, I see how thoroughly ableism and racism are imbricated within scientific advances and literary fantasies.

Notions of race and gender are intimately a part of biological notions and evaluative processes of worth and legitimacy. Optimistic fantasies about the plasticity of life in contemporary speculative thought ignore the history of racial eugenics and its investment in these same ideas to its peril. It reminds us that scholarly enterprise can never be free of the contingencies that shape our understandings of life itself. Remembering how a plasticity of life was imagined and scientifically practiced *through* race and ability is key as scholars go forward in the project of decentering the human. A trust in scientific knowledge must be interrogated, and the "we" of new materialist thinking situated historically. Scholars must remember not to assume a universally shared positioning in relation to the material world. Coole and Frost also posit this new materialism as a challenge to an earlier "cultural turn that privileges language, discourse, culture and values."[29] But studies concerned with "the changing conceptions of material causality and the significance of corporeality" need to attend to how race is embedded in our understand-ings of that materiality and the processes by which scholars theorize it.[30] While they focus a scientific eye, scholars must retain a political, cultural, and historical memory.

This essay explores the politics of science, particularly in relation to race and sex in historical context; looking at the work of the two scientific speculators, Wells and Huxley, I ask about the potential ramifications of self-directed scientific modification of the biological, as the ideas of these men include both ideas of the plasticity of life but also the theory and practice of eugenics. Fantasies about the plasticity of life in speculative thought must consider the histories of social and scientific racism and eugenics. I argue that, while we remember these men's con-tribution to ideas of biological utopia, we also remember how they represented a way of thinking coming out of materialism. I also argue, though, that we need not temper our own utopian urges, that it may be in fact that the life forms excluded from the protective categories of able-bodied, white, and male human will be those most open to seeing and imagining new life forms and "utterly new modes of existence."

"The Limits of Individual Plasticity"

The concept of the plasticity of our biological selves, and the potential of applying these ideas, captivated the scientific, philosophical, and fictional imagination from at least the beginning of the twentieth century. The works of Wells and Huxley are two cases in point, being full of marvelous possibility in their speculations on life itself. Both men thought creatively about existence, social organization, consciousness, the mind, and the universe in their theoretical and fiction writing, and their expansive fantasies had utopian reach. Their conceptual explorations claimed that evolution, when properly controlled, could bring about utopia in the best sense of the concept. Humans could be released from the confines of human limitation into a whole universe of biospiritual potential. Shaped by science, "meeting the universe halfway," manipulating nature's processes of morphogenesis, could lead to unimaginable new creations. But their theories were also full of dreadful potential. Accompanying their leaps toward the murky future and new paradigms of earthly inhabitance were disturbingly calm calls for forms of social engineering and eugenicist policy. Race, gender, and (dis)ability profoundly shape the very nature of their scientific speculation.

For many, including Wells, the question was not simply what happened in the gaps, the stretch points, of life forms. What was most interesting to Wells and his colleagues was that plasticity made life forms potentially manipulable. In 1895 Wells best articulated this fascination. He had been inspired to take up biology after attending one class with Julian and Aldous Huxley's father, T. H. Huxley, ten years earlier at the Normal School of Science in London, before writing the most enduring of his science fiction short stories and novels.[31] In "The Limits of Individual Plasticity," Wells wrote, "We overlook only too often that a living being may also be regarded as raw material, as something plastic, something that maybe shaped and altered, that is, possibly, may be added and that eliminated [*sic*] and the organism as a whole developed far beyond its apparent possibilities."[32] The strength of his assertions was not biological accuracy. But he did articulate in a clear manner the potential to stretch the limits of what we could think of as a discrete living being: "There is in science . . . some sanction for the belief that a living thing might be taken in hand and so moulded and modified that at best it would retain scarcely anything of its inherent form and disposition; that the thread of life might be preserved unimpaired while shape and mental superstructure were so extensively recast as even to justify our regarding the result as a *new variety of being*" (my italics).[33]

Julian Huxley followed Bergson in believing in the continuity of all matter, both inorganic and organic. Huxley argued that this continuity is the "single fundamental truth" and emphasized "the uniformity and unity of the cosmos" throughout his work. "We are built of the same stuff, the same elements," he wrote.[34] Yet an ethics of care does not follow automatically behind such illumination. Huxley, first director of the United Nations Educational and Cultural Organization (UNESCO), was a lifelong eugenicist. In 1923 Huxley wrote, "When Eugenics shall become practical politics, its action, so far as we can see, will be at first entirely devoted to this raising of the average, by altering the proportion of good and bad stock, and if possible eliminating the lowest strata, in a genetically mixed population."[35] In his paper "UNESCO: Its Purpose and Philosophy," which he delivered upon acceptance of UNESCO's directorship in 1946, he wrote that eugenics should work to relieve the "dead weight of genetic stupidity, physical weakness, mental instability, and disease-proneness."[36] (Huxley's support of eugenics curiously ignores his own history of bipolar illness and hospitalization, and his family's history of depressive illness.) In 1962 in his second address before the Galton Society, the solution to improving humanity was not only in "discouraging genetically defective or inferior types from breeding" but also general population control, "reducing over-multiplication in general and the high differential fertility of various regions, nations and classes in particular."[37] Huxley's solution does not acknowledge that "population control" disguises ideas of racial inferiority. He also suggests positive eugenics, though again not racially marked. In his address before the Galton Society Huxley suggests "artificial insemination by selected donors," in "raising the genetic level of man's intellectual and practical abilities."[38]

Julian's better-known brother, Aldous Huxley, imagined a life past heteronormative reproduction with his imagined dystopian future, *Brave New World* (1932). In his vision of a state-dominated, socially engineered world, rows and rows of newly made humans were produced in huge hatcheries. "The principle of mass production at last applied to biology," he writes, produces "standard men and women, in uniform batches."[39] Race science had long deemed racialized bodies, particularly those of African descent, as closer to their animal natures: physically superior, strong, resilient, and fertile. Accordingly, in Huxley's *Brave New World*, "tropical centres" manage to produce more "batches of identicals . . . but then they have unfair advantages. You should see the way a negro ovary responds to the pituitary! It's quite astonishing, when working with European material."[40] Huxley's depiction of the overly fecund tropicals might be considered satirical, if it were not for the fact that he was a staunch eugenicist. "Continuous general progress (along present lines) is only possible upon two conditions," he writes in "Boundaries of Utopia," published a year before *Brave New World*, "that the heritable qualities of the progressing population shall be improved (or at any rate changed in a specific direction) by deliberate breeding; and that the amount of population shall be reduced."[41] The populations he refers to are specifically those from non-European "overpopulated" areas. Twenty-six years later, Huxley insists in *Brave New World Revisited*:

> In the second half of the twentieth century we do nothing systematic about our breeding: but in our random and unregulated way we are not only over-populating our planet, we are also, it would seem, making sure that these greater numbers shall be of biologically poorer quality. . . . what about the congenitally insufficient organisms, whom our medicine and our social services now preserve so that they may propagate their kind? . . . the wholesale transmission to our descendants of the results of unfavorable mutations and the progressive contamination of the genetic pool from which the members of our species will have to draw, and no less obviously bad.[42]

The concept of population control contained within it theories that affected women of color most drastically, and these theories became practices and policies. A concerted policy is required to prevent the present flood of population-increase from wrecking all our hopes for a better world," Julian Huxley writes in his UNESCO speech. Wells and Huxley together supported the practice of sterilization, commenting on the success of the practice in America: "Six thousand such operations have been performed in California alone and it would be difficult to find fault with the results," they write in 1932 in *The Science of Life*.[43] As well as negative eugenics, Huxley had ideas for positive measures. While certain populations, which he will not mark by race, were to be controlled, certain individuals would be encouraged to reproduce. "Quality of people, not mere quantity, is what we must aim at," Huxley writes in 1957, in an essay he titles "Transhumanism."[44] But while Wells could dream of a "new variety of being," for Huxley the aim was the "improvement" of humanity, not the transcendence of the species itself.

Huxley's Transhumanism

In the 1957 essay, excited over the possibilities for new types of existence, Huxley coined the term *transhuman* as part of his bioreligious philosophy. But for Huxley, as with his friend the paleontologist and priest Pierre Teilhard de Chardin, all change would aid and accompany a higher stage in human evolution. It was through conscious control of human evolution that humanity would become a "new type of organism, whose destiny it is to realize new possibilities for evolving life on this planet."[45] Just how much of the humanoid form these new organisms would maintain is ambiguous. For Chardin, "Man will have so far transcended himself as to demand some new appellation."[46] For Huxley, this being would transcend itself only through perfecting its human potential. But it would remain organized around some quality of "humanness." Transhumanism is based in "man remaining man, but transcending himself, by realizing new possibilities of and for his human nature."[47]

Unlike Bergson or Chardin, Huxley stops short of a departure from species. In Huxley's ultimate formulation of evolution, the universe is of one fabric, but "Man" is the most evolved life form on earth. As he has evolved, he has developed a "cosmic self-awareness"; humans are perhaps not the only sentient beings in the universe, for there are surely "conscious living creatures on the planets of other stars," but he has a solemn cosmic duty.[48] Humanity has the "responsibility and destiny—to be an agent for the rest of the world," and "[Man] is in point of fact determining the future direction of evolution on this earth."[49] Man has developed only a minuscule amount of his latent ability, and "the human race, in fact, is surrounded by a large area of unrealized possibilities, a challenge to the spirit of exploration."[50] Huxley imports the language of settler colonialism into his vision of evolution. "A vast New World of uncharted possibilities awaits its Columbus," he writes.[51] This New World is that of the possibilities opened up by and to the bioconsciousness of man, inspired by Chardin's concept of the "nöosphere."[52] This new spatial dimension is an "organised web of thought" formed as a planetary sphere.[53] Huxley's utopianism takes us to an abstract cosmic elevation, inaccessible from where humans are currently.

Concepts of human evolution were key in Huxley's and Chardin's utopian visions. Yet their ideas of evolution were not limited to a Darwinian theory of natural selection. As Huxley put it, Darwin did give us the knowledge that "we were made of the same energy as the rest of the cosmos," and man was linked by "genetic continuity with all the other living inhabitants of his planet . . . [which were] all parts of one single branching and evolving flow of metabolizing protoplasm."[54] But as the most evolved life form on the planet, man was different. Man could exert "*conscious control of evolution*," instead of leaving it to "the previous mechanism of . . . blind chance" (my italics).[55] As Huxley saw it, humans could improve and elevate themselves to a higher state of being. But this higher state of being was accessible only through improving the physical, intellectual, and moral capacities of the human species. In the introduction to his *Essays of a Biologist* Huxley writes, "The possibilities of physiological improvement . . . is no utopian silliness, but is bound to come about if science continues her current progress."[56]

While the shadow of race is everywhere in their work, Huxley and Wells are careful to distance themselves from what Huxley termed the "crude racism" of racial science.[57] Improvement was not based in race, and genetic variation was desirable. In his UNESCO acceptance speech, Huxley clearly delineates an ethical eugenics from the policies of racial extermination attempted by the Nazis. Any attempts at racial or national "purity" were "scientifically incorrect."[58] Eugenics should hold dear "human variety" while working to raise the "mean level of desirable qualities. . . . healthy constitution, a high innate general intelligence, or a special aptitude such as that for mathematics or music." Huxley was careful to distinguish between his eugenicist theories and racial science. Nonwhite races were not inherently inferior. Yet, as his work shows, he retained a colonialist perspective. "UNESCO should aim at securing the fullest contribution to the common pool from racial groups which, owing to their remoteness or their backwardness have so far had little share in it," he writes.[59] Huxley's ideas of racialized people may not be the "crude racism" of the American eugenicists, but it retained what Huxley calls a "liberal imperialism," another branch of race thinking based in European superiority.[60] This formulation calls for the "backward" racial groups to actually contribute to the gene pool. Huxley separates the science of race and the social arrangements of colonialism, but he called himself a proponent of liberal imperialism after his trip to East Africa in 1932 and was clear in his calls for population control that these policies would be aimed at the global South. Huxley's and Wells's support for eugenicist practices such as sterilization and ideas of population control completely disregarded the racial implications of these proposed projections and practiced policies. While Huxley claimed to be above a vulgar racism, he did not actually transcend racialized thinking.

The work of Wells and Huxley shows that eugenics does not map evenly onto scientific racism. Both argue against discrimination on the basis of race and against any belief in race purity. Statistical methods, Huxley argued, showed that a certain range of intelligence and strength could be found in any race and that raw potential could be developed through education and improved environment.[61] Wells scoffs at the idea of white supremacy in *A Modern Utopia* (1905). Yet in his nonfiction criticism and commentary, Wells was self-professedly anti-Semitic and often contradicted himself. "There is no more evil thing in this world than Race Prejudice," Wells spoke out forcefully in an 1893 article.[62] In this instance Wells seemed to read race prejudice as a predominantly American phenomenon. Yet by no means did Wells believe all men to be equal. "Obviously in no measurable or estimable personal quality are men equal," he writes. "It is far more acceptable to suggest that some individuals are on the whole superior, others inferior to the average."[63] Wells also states that race or class was not a factor in evaluating the quality of a person. "These superiorities are too various and subtle to admit of class and race treatment," he writes.[64] Yet Wells cannot catch himself in time, and his racial liberalism leaks at its seams. After complaining that he cannot help himself in the case of the "aggressive Jew," he writes that the necessary civilities demanded in a democracy "must not blind one to the real differences of personal quality, to such a fact as that a negro is usually simpler, kinder, and stupider than a Beacon street Bostonian. One has to keep one's head in these matters."[65]

Wells contradicts himself in speaking out against race discrimination. In the same article, he references his rather strange friendship with the soon-to-be president of the National Association of Colored Women, Mary Church Terrell. "Certainly it would be difficult to find any purely white American woman more level-headed and capable than that admirable public speaker, Mrs. Church Terrell," he writes.[66] Wells's perspective on race is fissured, inconsistent, but certainly not free of liberal racism. Some contemporary critics defended Wells against accusations of racism, calling Wells's critics "biased and selective" in their criticism, and as distorting Wells's thought. Yet the copious work of Wells belies this defense. It is useful to delineate what we mean by "racism" in the context of Wells's, and his contemporaries', specific and often contradictory opinions on race.[67]

Wells devotes an entire chapter to race in *A Modern Utopia*. Because

Wells's utopia is a world state, it involves the entire planet, and Wells makes clear that it will be composed of myriad races all employing a common language. "White and black, brown, red and yellow, all tints of skin, all types of body and character, will be there," he writes in his first chapter.[68] He criticizes the systems of colonialism and slavery, the turn to race science, and a "grotesque insistence upon Anglo-Saxonism."[69] In his utopia, eugenicist policies would not discriminate on racial lines: "Extinction need never be discriminatory. If any of the race did, after all, prove to be fit to survive, they would survive—they would be picked out with a sure and automatic justice from the over-ready condemnation of all their kind."[70] Inconsistencies and gaps remain in Wells's work where it is unclear whether the "lower races" are indeed capable of advancing. While he condemns race prejudice in America, he is ambivalent about what to do with the "rejected white and yellow civilizations and the black and brown races . . . who cannot keep pace" with civilization. These peoples are not synonymous with the "people of the abyss" whom he is so sure should be eliminated or, in his more leavened later views, shipped to a guarded island.[71] Yet these people of the warmer climes may inevitably be erased by the tide of forward-looking biological manipulation.

Sisters of the Sacred Tissue

In 1912 the French surgeon and biologist Alexis Carrel won the Nobel Prize for his innovations in vascular suturing technique. The vivisectionist was also interested in the growth of cell tissue; months before he had put a tissue sample of a chicken heart in a medium and, surprisingly, the cells lived and became legendary, supposedly surviving for twenty years in the laboratories of the Rockefeller Institute of Medical Research. The immortal chicken heart was famous, captivating the popular imagination until 1961, when Leonard Hayflick proved that cells did indeed have a life span, dividing between forty and sixty times before entering a phase of senescence (a phenomenon now called the Hayflick limit). Carrel's cells had probably survived as new cells were introduced with the renewal of the medium.

Carrel is remembered as an important innovator, but he was also a vicious eugenicist. "Each individual must rise or sink to the level for which he is fitted by the quality of his tissues and soul," wrote Carrel in his best-selling book *Man the Unknown* (1935): "Eugenics is indispensable for the propagation of the strong . . . the propagation of the insane and feeble-minded . . . must be prevented."[72] He continues: "Those who have murdered, robbed, kidnapped children. . . . should humanely and economically be disposed of in small euthanasiac institutions supplied with proper gases."[73] In a 1936 German edition of his book, Carrel praised

Germany for "taking energetic measures," and during the war Carrel worked for Vichy France. History seems to have forgiven Carrel his "eccentricities"; in 1979 a lunar crater was named for him.

In 1927 Julian Huxley wrote a short story titled "The Tissue Culture King" while he was professor of zoology at King's College, London.[74] The story acts as homage to the original tissue culture king Carrel. But, set in Africa, it also acts as a strange fictional precursor to the case of Henrietta Lacks and the HeLa cells. Racialized bodies become the raw material for scientific experimentation. Published in *Amazing Stories*, next to a reprint of Wells's *War of the Worlds*, Huxley's story captures the fascination with immortal cell life and combines it with an imperialist penchant for adventure stories set in Africa. Like islands dispersed across the conquered seas, Africa was an imagined site for fantastical renditions of how European civilization's technological advances were opening boundless possibilities for the spread of civilization. For example, in *Robur the Conquerer*, Jules Verne's aeronef flies above the "known and unknown regions of Africa," and modern science alights.[75] As in *The Island of Dr. Moreau*, the colonial setting gives the colonizer permission for unfettered scientific experimentation. In "The Tissue Culture King," though, the experiments are on native bodies. Unlike Wells's novel, however, Huxley's tale does not revolve around pain. Instead, it revolves around the coerced consent of the natives to participate in the scientific experiments of its mad doctor, Hascombe.

A British explorer and his guide, somewhere in Africa, happen upon a mad doctor who has been performing biological feats among an extremely religious African tribe. Dr. Hascombe has made a distinguished place for himself; finding that blood has played a big part in the religion of the Africans, he becomes the "religious advisor to His Majesty King Mgobe" by promising to "render visible the blood's hidden nature and reality, and . . . show this great magic."[76] Placing a blood sample under his microscope, Hascombe explains that "the blood was composed of little people of various sorts, each with their own lives and that to spy on them gave us new powers over them."[77] Granted a laboratory, Hascombe translates the native religion into biology, superimposing scientific processes—"tissue culture; experimental embryology; endocrine treatment; artificial parthogenesis"—over the religion's central tenets.[78]

Hascombe has a specific purpose, to experiment with growing and keeping alive human tissue, and is successful in his aim to "develop means of *mass production*."[79] To this end, Hascombe convinces the Africans to let them take tissue from the king himself. He parcels out slides of live cell tissue from the king's body, by which people could "possess an actual part of his Majesty."[80] Hascombe's second enterprise is the manipulation of bodily processes to create a grotesque menagerie. Through endocrinal manipulation, he creates new types of biological entities, from two-headed toads to "eight-foot tall negroes" and "almost dwarfish [men] . . . with huge heads, and enormously fat and brawny."[81] Coming into the village, he describes "a regular Barnum and Bailey show—more semi-dwarfs . . . others portentously fat, with arms like sooty legs of mutton, and rolls and volutes of fat crisping out of their steatopygous posteriors."[82] Hascombe also claims to have fulfilled the "passion of the men for fatness in their women."[83] Huxley provides a potent primitivist mix of religion, sex, and grotesquery.

Touring the laboratory, the "Institute of Religious Tissue Culture," our visitor encounters the Sisters of the Sacred Tissue, a sect of young women who, like scientific nuns, were given over to the sacred practice of lab work. Yet they are also highly sexualized; Huxley describes them as "platoons of buxom and shining African women, becomingly but unusually dressed in tight-fitting white dresses and caps, and wearing rubber gloves."[84] The processes that they are involved in are clearly sexually marked, as their job is to ensure the reproduction of the king's cells. They remind the narrator of Carrel's laboratory assistants, whom he had encountered while on a visit to Carrel's labs at the Rockefeller Institute: "troops of white-garbed American girls making cultures, sterilizing, microscopizing, incubating and the rest of it."[85] Interestingly, these "American girls," while busy with the midwifery of Carrel's experiments in parthenogenesis, are not specifically marked as sexual.

Because "The Tissue Culture King" was published in a popular science fiction magazine, it is easy to dismiss this tawdry story as a simple colonialist fantasy. But what it reveals is how deeply the raced body is connected to Western scientific development. It also reveals, as does *The Island of Dr. Moreau*, the desire and fear of visiting the boundaries of the human, of contemplating its porousness. "If we concede the justifications of vivisection," Wells writes in "The Limits of Individual Plasticity," "we may imagine as possible in the future, operators, armed with antiseptic surgery and a growing perfection in the knowledge of the laws of growth, taking living creatures and moulding them into the most amazing forms . . . even reviving the monsters of mythology."[86] Yet the anxiety and moral ambiguity of Wells's *Moreau*, and the bawdy lasciviousness of Huxley's story, also reveal a deep attachment to the universalized human. Plasticity, then, should be both embraced and feared, for, as Malabou puts it, humans as a life form may mutate in unpredictable ways.

Works like Wells's *Island of Dr. Moreau* and Huxley's lesser-known short story "The Tissue Culture King" articulate a Western fear of the broaching of boundaries; of the porousness between species, races, sexualities; and of the unknown consequences of manipulating flesh. The desire for control seems to demand a principle of subtraction, which maps onto race. Blackness seems to suggest at once the failure to change or mutate and the ability to mutate too much— both hypo- and hyperplasticity.

We see this anxiety around HeLa cells, as they have spread rapidly and thoroughly. Because of their initial wide dispersal, HeLa cells reside in laboratories across the nation. The cells' "unusually malignant behavior" has enabled them to invade all cell lines that scientists believed to be separate, invalidating decades of cancer research. HeLa's legacy of sabotage lives on, with the 2013 discovery of HeLa contamination found in bladder cancer cell lines. The initial discovery of the contamination instantly brought to the attention of scientists and the public the fact that Henrietta Lacks was black, and the first scientist to declare the contamination assumed that her race was the reason for the cells' unusual power to reproduce.[87] All sorts of racial narratives resonated with this case, including white fear of racial miscegenation and the oversexualization of black women, as well as the injustice of Lacks's family surviving in poverty while huge profits are made from their mother's cells. Black, queer, and disabled people know what it is to be considered inhuman. We feel the politics by which the human is legitimated, how the lines around the human are policed, and the inhuman ways that racialized, disabled, and queer bodies are treated. We are painfully aware of "the way power is present in any attempt to represent material reality."[88] But we (an assumptive we, not a falsely inclusive one) are less ethically bound to honor the boundaries of a bodily sovereignty never granted to us.[89] What would it look like to take as our provocation the idea that we embrace our inhumanness? To let go of the assumption of heteronormative human (and racial) superiority, and open up to new forms of sociality and modes of being?

Henrietta Lacks lived on past the human. The continuing life of the HeLa cell line troubles the boundaries between the human and the inhuman, in much the same way that poor, black bodies across the world do. Perhaps a history of cervical cancer may reveal the inhumane ways that medical science has neglected black, disabled, and queer people, as well as the environmental factors that helped create the vibrant HeLa cells in the first place. I am tempted to personify HeLa myself. But my interpretation would be that Henrietta Lacks has had a truly ironic revenge. She has invaded, and will not leave, as she haunts the labs, wreaking havoc for generations.

Notes

1. Hannah Landecker, *Culturing Life: How Cells Became Technologies* (Cambridge, MA: Harvard University Press, 2007), 140.

2. Nicolas Rose, *The Politics of Life Itself* (Princeton: Princeton University Press, 2007), 15.

3. Landecker, *Culturing Life*, 141.

4. See Priscilla Wald, "Cells, Genes, and Histories: HeLa's Journey from Lab to Literature," in *Genetics and the Unsettled Past: The Collision of DNA, Race, and History*, ed. Alondra Nelson, Keith Wailoo, and Catherine Lee (New Brunswick: Rutgers University Press, 2012); Karla Holloway, *Private Bodies, Public Texts: Race, Gender, and Cultural Bioethics* (Durham, NC: Duke University Press, 2011); and Dorothy Roberts, *Fatal Invention: How Science, Politics, and Big Business Re-create Race in the Twenty-First Century* (New York: New Press, 2012).

5. Wald, "Cells, Genes, and Histories."

6. For a brilliant theorization of the human, see Alex Weheliye, *Habeas Viscus: Racializing Assemblages, Biopolitics, and Black Feminist Theories of the Human* (Durham, NC: Duke University Press, 2014), and Sylvia Wynter, "Unsettling the Coloniality of Being/ Power/Truth/Freedom: Towards the Human, After Man, Its Overrepresentation—An Argument," *The New Centennial Review* 3, no. 3 (2003): 257–337.

7. Landecker, *Culturing Life*, 221.

8. Diana Coole and Samantha Frost, eds., *New Materialisms: Ontology, Agency, and Politics* (Durham, NC: Duke University Press, 2010), 4.

9. Jonathan Beecher, *Charles Fourier: The Revolutionary and His World* (Berkeley: University of California Press, 1986), 340.

10. *The Utopian Vision of Charles Fourier: Selected Texts on Work, Love, and Passionate Attraction*, ed. Jonathan Beecher and trans. Richard Beinvenu (Boston: Beacon, 1971), 337.

11. Beecher, *Utopian Vision of Charles Fourier*, 397.

12. Beecher, *Utopian Vision of Charles Fourier*, 397–98.

13. Beecher, *Utopian Vision of Charles Fourier*, 397.

14. Beecher, *Utopian Vision of Charles Fourier*, 402.

15. Beecher, *Utopian Vision of Charles Fourier*, 403.

16. Beecher, *Utopian Vision of Charles Fourier*, 405.

17. Catherine Malabou, *What Should We Do with Our Brain?*, trans. Sebastian Rand (New York: Fordham University Press, 2008), 21.

18. Malabou, *What Should We Do with Our Brain?*, 36.

19. Landecker, *Culturing Life*, 235.

20. Henri Bergson, *Creative Evolution*, trans. Arthur Mitchell (New York: Random House, 1944), xxii.

21. Materialist speculations bring us into long-standing conversations about the nature of

consciousness. Bergson, William James, and many other "men of science" were advocates of psychic abilities and the infinite connection of our vibratory energies to the
rest of the universe. A full exploration of the debates around consciousness, its relation to the brain, the existence or nonexistence of soul and spirit, is beyond the scope
of this essay.

22. Bergson, *Creative Evolution*, xx.

23. Bergson, *Creative Evolution*, 16.

24. H. G. Wells and Julian Huxley, *The Science of Life* (Garden City, NY: Doubleday and
Doran, 1931), 1:235.

25. Jane Bennett, *Vibrant Matter: A Political Ecology of Things* (Durham, NC: Duke University Press, 2010), 66.

26. Malabou, *What Should We Do with Our Brain?*, 17.

27. Malabou, *What Should We Do with Our Brain?*, 14.

28. Malabou, *What Should We Do with Our Brain?*, 73.

29. Coole and Frost, *New Materialisms*, 3.

30. Coole and Frost, *New Materialisms*, 2.

31. Michael Coren, *The Invisible Man: The Life and Liberties of H. G. Wells* (New York:
Antheneum, Macmillan, 1993), 39.

32. H. G. Wells, "The Limits of Individual Plasticity," *Saturday Review*, January 19,
1895, 36.

33. H. G. Wells, "The Limits of Individual Plasticity," in *H. G. Wells, Early Writing in
Science and Science Fiction*, ed. Robert Philmus (Berkeley: University of California
Press, 1975), 221–22.

34. Julian Huxley, "Progress, Biological, and Other," in *Essays of a Biologist* (London:
Chatto and Windus, 1923), 60.

35. Huxley, "Progress, Biological, and Other," 51.

36. Julian Huxley, "UNESCO: Its Purpose and Philosophy" (London: Frederick Printing,
1946), 21.

37. Huxley, "UNESCO," 123.

38. Julian Huxley, "Eugenics in Evolutionary Perspective," in *Essays of a Humanist* (Mid-
dlesex, UK: Penguin, 1966), 258.

39. Aldous Huxley, *Brave New World* (New York: Perennial, 1998), 7.

40. Huxley, *Brave New World*, 9.

41. Aldous Huxley, "Boundaries of Utopia," *Virginia Quarterly Review* (Winter 1931):
47–54, www.vqronline.org/articles/1931/winter/huxley-utopia/.

42. Aldous Huxley, *Brave New World Revisited* (New York: HarperCollins, 1989), 15–17.

43. H. G. Wells and Julian Huxley, *The Science of Life* (Garden City, NY: Doubleday and
Doran, 1931), 2:1465.

44. Julian Huxley, "Transhumanism," in *New Bottles for New Wine* (London: Chatto and
Windus, 1957).

45. Julian Huxley, introduction to Pierre Teilhard de Chardin, *The Phenomenon of Man*, trans. Bernard Wall (New York: Harper Perennial, 2008), 20.

46. Huxley, introduction, 13.

47. Huxley, "Transhumanism," 17.

48. Huxley, "Transhumanism," 13.

49. Huxley, "Transhumanism," 13–14.

50. Huxley, "Transhumanism," 15.

51. Huxley, "Transhumanism," 14.

52. Huxley, introduction, 180.

53. Julian Huxley, "The Humanist Frame," in *The Humanist Frame* (New York: Harper and Brothers, 1961), 17.

54. Huxley, "Humanist Frame," 19.

55. Huxley, "Progress, Biological, and Other," x.

56. Huxley, "Progress, Biological, and Other," viii–ix.

57. Huxley, "Eugenics in Evolutionary Perspective," 261.

58. Huxley, "UNESCO," 19.

59. Huxley, "UNESCO," 19.

60. Julian Huxley, *Africa View* (London: Chatto and Windus, 1936), 120.

61. Huxley, "Eugenics in Evolutionary Perspective," 260.

62. H. G. Wells, "Race Prejudice," *Independent*, February 14, 1907, 382.

63. Wells, "Race Prejudice," 383.

64. Wells, "Race Prejudice," 383.

65. Wells, "Race Prejudice," 383.

66. Wells, "Race Prejudice," 384. Certainly Wells and Terrell, this consummate race woman, two years away from founding and becoming president of the National Association of Colored Women, seem a strange coupling. However, they remained long-term acquaintances, with Terrell attending social events at the Wells' house when she was in London. In 1941 Wells wrote the preface to Terrell's autobiography and in fact helped choose the title for it. Yet Wells is far from glowing in his preface, and his assessment is a rather shallow and simplistic comparison between the English class system and racism in the United States.

67. John Partington is vociferous in his defense of Wells against accusations of racism. Yet Partington himself selectively uses Wells's oeuvre in his defense. Partington's definition of racism is quite limited (Partington, "The Death of the Static: H. G. Wells and the Kinetic Utopia," *Utopian Studies* 11, no. 2 [2000]: 96).

68. H. G. Wells, *A Modern Utopia* (London: Chapman and Hall, 1905), 24.

69. Wells, *Modern Utopia*, 328.

70. Wells, *Modern Utopia*, 338.

71. H. G. Wells, *Anticipations: or the Reaction of Mechanical and Scientific Progress upon Human Life and Thought* (London: Harper and Brothers, 1901), 304.

72. Alexis Carrel, *Man the Unknown* (West Drayton, UK: Penguin Books, 1935), 273–74.

73. Carrel, *Man the Unknown*, 291.

74. Julian Huxley, "The Tissue Culture King," *Amazing Stories: The Magazine of Science Fiction*, August 1927, 451–60.

75. Jules Verne, *Robur the Conqueror: The Clipper of the Clouds* (London: S. Low, Marston, Searle and Rivington, 1887).

76. Huxley, "Tissue Culture King," 452, 453.

77. Huxley, "Tissue Culture King," 453.

78. Huxley, "Tissue Culture King," 454.

79. Huxley, "Tissue Culture King," 455.

80. Huxley, "Tissue Culture King," 455.

81. Huxley, "Tissue Culture King," 451, 452.

82. Huxley, "Tissue Culture King," 452.

83. Huxley, "Tissue Culture King," 456.

84. Huxley, "Tissue Culture King," 455.

85. Huxley, "Tissue Culture King," 454.

86. Wells, "Limits of Individual Plasticity," in *H. G. Wells*, 223.

87. Adam Curtis, *The Way of All Flesh* (British Broadcasting Corporation, 1997).

88. Coole and Frost, *New Materialisms*, 3.

88. Here I am responding to Coole and Frost's use of "we" throughout their introduction to *New Materialisms*. Their use of "we" assumes particularly privileged subject positions and assumes a universally shared positioning in relation to the material world.

PIT BULL PROMISES

Inhuman Intimacies and Queer Kinships in an Animal Shelter

Harlan Weaver

> How would we feel if it is by way of the inhuman that we come to
> feel, to care, to respond?
> —Karen Barad

*I*n April 2010 a dog named Lennox was seized from a family in Belfast, Ireland. After measurements performed with a "worn dressmaker's tape," Lennox was sentenced to death for being a "pit bull." His family and numerous advocates vigorously contested this label through, among other methods, DNA analysis, sparking a legal battle avidly followed around the world.[1] Even celebrity dog trainers leaped into the fray; Animal Planet's Victoria Stilwell offered to place Lennox with another family living in a jurisdiction in the United States without the breed-specific legislation, or BSL, that led to Lennox's seizure. However, Belfast authorities were not persuaded, and in July 2012 the city council issued a statement: "The dog Lennox, an illegal pit-bull terrier type, has been humanely put to sleep."[2]

Lennox's case speaks to the complex bringing together of category problems, kinship, and affect in contemporary pit bull politics. While the "worn dressmaker's tape" used in the case attests to the uncertain identifications involved—how does one measure pit bull–ness?—feeling and family, not to mention citizenship and race, are also entangled, as when Lennox's advocates issued pleas like "this could be YOUR family, please help fight this injustice" while describing his final hours as the last of his moments on "death row."[3] Further, the council's statement that Lennox had been *humanely* put to sleep contrasts with Stilwell's explanation that she became involved in the case "both as an expert and as an advocate for decency

GLQ 21:2–3
DOI 10.1215/10642684-2843383
© 2015 by Duke University Press

and humanity."[4] The complex ties among conflicting understandings of human, humanity, humane, and the politics of family, racialization, and sexuality at play in Lennox's case lead one to wonder: what does it mean to be human, nonhuman, and/or inhuman in contemporary pit bull lifeworlds? What roles do inhuman, or non-human-based, understandings play in these and related cases? And to push this even further: is there an inhumanity in these pit bull politics that might offer a different manner in which we might not only, as Karen Barad notes, come "to feel, to care, to respond" but also shift the kinds of understandings we bring into both pit bull and human queer politics?[5]

In the following article I attempt to delineate not only the problems and specifically queer issues at hand in contemporary discourses about pit bulls but also some of the ways that, yes, these politics reveal alternative understandings of issues long central to queer theories, kinship, and intimacy. Beginning with the larger worlds of contemporary discussions about pit bulls, I return to Lennox's case along with another high-profile pit bull case, that of the dogs taken from convicted dogfighter and NFL player Michael Vick, to examine how race and family are entwined in these types of advocacy projects. Writings on queer kinships and intimacies help me elucidate how the kinds of families involved in these campaigns are shaped by what David Eng terms the "racialization of intimacy."[6] Finally, an about-face toward a different scale of intimacy, evident in examples from my ethnographic fieldwork, permits me to trace out a different kind of multispecies politics rooted in inhuman intimacies and queer kinships, one that promises a different sensibility and yields an alternative approach to building multispecies worlds, and that I hope contributes to a larger queer/inhuman politics.

"Pit Bulls"

Lennox's case and others like it are more easily understood in the context of what Malcolm Gladwell terms the "category problems" that attend the label pit bull.[7] Today's dog breeds are the product of kennel clubs—the American Kennel Club, the United Kennel Club, the American Dog Breeder's Association—that determine breed through parentage; however, ideal phenotypes (a dog's bodily build or looks) can also play a role, hence the "dressmaker's tape" involved in Lennox's trial. While there are several bully breeds recognized by these clubs—and by bully I mean short-haired and somewhat squat, muscular dogs, including American pit bull terriers, American Staffordshire terriers, American bulldogs, and the like—dogs who become entangled with laws like those in Belfast generally lack papers documenting their breed and/or lineage. Instead, they are identified by their looks. And, as several recent studies comparing visual and DNA-based identification of dog breeds have shown, there is an extremely high rate of error in visual identification, especially when it comes to pit bull–type dogs.[8] Indeed, pit bulls' category problems mean that, instead of being made legible through their genealogy, documentation, or the testimony of their owners, these dogs are often read through a vague correlation between looks and breed. Malcolm Gladwell, among others, describes this type of "I know it when I see it" identification as a form of profiling.[9]

The term *pit bull profiling* underscores the troubling and troubled connections between representations of pit bulls and other dogs deemed dangerous and processes of racialization in the contemporary United States. Indeed, "like race" analogies are widespread in discussions about pit bulls. For example, some advocates take laws like the BSL in place in Belfast to be "canine racism," a metaphor echoed in one adopter's analogy: "I think it's awful what people say about 'pit bulls' or dogs that look like 'pit bulls.' It's like racism, except against dogs."[10] However, while much of this "like race" thinking tends to appropriate rather than speak from the experiences of subjugated peoples, others with more direct experiences of profiling also point to such connections. For example, Michael B. Jordan, the star of the film *Fruitvale Station*, also connects race and pit bulls. The film depicts the death of an unarmed African American man, Oscar Grant, at the hands of police, and in it there is a scene in which Grant pulls a pit bull–type dog from the street where it has been fatally injured by a car and holds it as it dies. Jordan argues: "Black males, we are America's pit bull. We're labeled vicious, inhumane, and left to die in the street."[11] This tangle of connective language reveals the many ways that debates about pit bulls touch on, join, and participate in perceptions of race and practices of racialization.

Ties between these debates and the language and practices of racialization are especially notable in Lennox's case, in part because of its prominence; while dog seizures because of BSL are somewhat common, it is rare for the international press to chime in. Discussions about the case, many of which originated in the United States, were shaped by race-related language in several ways. For example, articles sought to raise awareness about the problems of "racially profiling dogs such as Lennox."[12] And when an image of Lennox surfaced, it was accompanied by commentary about the concrete "prison" in which he was being held.[13] Still others spoke of the duration of his stay with the council dog wardens, two years, as "solitary confinement."[14] Given the legacy of a racist prison-industrialist complex in the United States, overwhelmingly evident in current statistics for incarceration—as we know, US prisons are disproportionately populated with persons of color—it is impossible not to read these prison references apart from US racial formations. However, in addition to this race-related language, what stands out about Lennox's case is how race became involved in the public displays of mourning that followed his death.

Immediately after the announcement of Lennox's euthanasia, humans and their dogs across the Internet posted photos. Their captions? "I am Lennox."[15] This campaign followed in the wake of protests in response to the February 2012 murder of Trayvon Martin, a young, unarmed, African American teen shot and killed by a self-identified neighborhood watchman; part of those protests included an Internet meme in which people posted photographs of themselves in black hooded sweatshirts, the garment Martin was wearing when murdered, captioned "I am Trayvon Martin." While the "I am Trayvon Martin" meme highlighted the racial profiling at play in Martin's death, it also acted as a form of public mourning, a way for people to express their sadness, anger, and rage about Martin's death and the social order that, in exonerating his killer, condoned it. In deliberately evoking this meme, the "I am Lennox" campaign sought to bring the "like race" logic of understandings of pit bull profiling into a "like race" affective politics. "I am Lennox" encouraged people to take up not just the reasoning that pit bull experiences function like racialization but also the feelings involved in public mourning centered in racism, and bring them to bear on their mourning of Lennox's death.

Vick-tory Dogs

The race-related language and affects of Lennox's campaign occurred in dialogue with another high-profile pit bull story in the United States: the dogfighting case involving NFL quarterback Michael Vick. A talented African American athlete playing quarterback—a position reserved, for most of the NFL's history, for white men—Vick was indicted in July 2007 on charges related to dogfighting. The media storm that followed this revelation included protests staged against Vick by football fans and animal advocates across the country, some of which involved hanging and burning him in effigy, a potent reminder of US histories of lynching.[16] Vick's indictment, and the relationships with animals on which it was based, changed how people read his identity as an African American man.[17] Jim Gorant's 2010 *New York Times* best seller, *The Lost Dogs: Michael Vick's Dogs and Their Tale of Rescue and Redemption*, provides a stark example of changes in perceptions of Vick. Describing Vick as "thick yet compact," Gorant notes that "his large brown eyes and small wide nose were offset by a strong jaw that made him look as if he had an underbite." Gorant finishes this description by asserting that Vick's appearance, "while handsome, could be fairly described as almost canine."[18] Unlike the "like race" logic involved in other advocacy practices, Gorant engages in racialization by animalization, coding Vick as animal-like in a manner deeply reminiscent of earlier projects of human racialization through animal likeness.[19]

Prior to the Vick case, most dogs taken from fighting operations were held as evidence and then euthanized. However, advocacy efforts initiated changes in this policy, and in the wake of the court case, the federal government permitted the dogs to be evaluated and, when appropriate, sent to rescue organizations. One organization involved in these efforts was Bay Area Dog lovers Responsible About Pit bulls, or BAD RAP, whose work with the Vick dogs was extensive.

BAD RAP's involvement began with help in evaluating and transporting a large number of the dogs from Virginia to California—a process complicated by the fact that the route had to bypass the many US cities and counties with BSL in place. BAD RAP organizers then placed the dogs in foster homes, where they were rehabilitated. Many of the now renamed "Vick-tory dogs" not only found permanent homes through adopters with ties to BAD RAP but also underwent advanced training to continue to participate in ongoing advocacy efforts on behalf of both pit bull–type dogs and former fighting dogs. For example, Hector is a "CGC (Canine Good Citizen), ATTS (American Temperament Test Society), Therapy Dog and Breed PR Maverick," while Jonny Justice, formerly Jonny Rotten, has "CGC, ATTS, Reading Assistant/Therapy Dog, Media Darling," after his name.[20] These titles index the dogs' many accomplishments; while the CGC requires that a dog pass a series of rigorous tests, standards for ATTS are even higher.[21] Further, many of the dogs, Hector and Jonny included, now work as therapy dogs—for example, listening to children who are learning how to read at the local library—while others compete in sports such as agility and nose work.

The Vick dogs also have their own blog, filled with posts such as "I got a new foster sister for the holidays!" or haiku: "After dinner treat / the bouncy red rubber ball / it is mine all mine."[22] Family is prominent in their stories, with mom, dad, aunt, uncle, sister, and brother as recurrent markers for the dogs' interactions. One post with a picture of a partially torn "I heart my pit bull" sticker on a wood floor, described as a variation on found art, is captioned: "I call this one 'I Love My Mom.' "[23] In another twist well suited for children, Jonny Justice now has a Gund doll modeled after him, while Handsome Dan is "the pawfect nanny dog."[24] Notions of home, family, and good citizenship are key to the Vick dogs' advocacy. Indeed, the video produced by BAD RAP about their initial transition highlights how the dogs are "hardly the cold blooded monsters they were once made out to be" and how "most of the dogs streamlined into normal homes and have become cherished family members."[25]

The tropes of family and citizenship evident in the stories of both Lennox and the Vick dogs are central to most narratives of pit bull advocacy. For example, MyPitBullisFamily.com asks us to help "Lick Discrimination" and "join the network of pit bull lovers spreading the FAMILY message."[26] Advocates are also quick to point out that the American pit bull terrier was known as a "nanny dog" in the United States during the late nineteenth and early twentieth centuries.[27] As is fairly typical in contemporary US animal advocacy, many of these campaigns feature mostly white, mostly heterosexual families living in houses with backyards. The material underpinnings of these efforts are thus connected to practices of home ownership shaped by what George Lipsitz, speaking of the racial politics undergirding bank lending practices and municipal zoning, terms a "possessive investment in whiteness."[28] Indeed, the ability to adopt and own these dogs, especially in light of many shelter policies that require proof of home ownership or a lease explicitly stating that bully-breed dogs are permitted, not to mention home insurance policies that frequently deny coverage when pit bull–type dogs are present, is an ability shaped in very material ways by geographies of race and class. However, as the emphasis on family makes clear, these geographies are also involved in kinship and sexuality; in the following section I expand my analysis of these dynamics.

Queer Kinships

While the pit bull–inclusive families I write about are structured through a kinship premised in species differences, this kinship fits well within contemporary notions of family and domesticity. Indeed, it would be odd if there were a denial of kinship in these discourses; I am reminded of a recent post on the satirical website theonion.com featuring a fictitious interview with a Golden Retriever: "Dog Doesn't Consider Itself Part of Family."[29] However, there are some different kinds of kinship going on in these and related animal advocacy campaigns, for the families and connections involved are not wholly straight. We can see this in articles linking gay rights to dog rescue that feature pictures of "these amazing pets and the parents who saved them"; one adopter notes that he is grateful for the opportunity to help these animals have "a chance of being who they were born to be."[30] However, these links are also apparent in the fact that many of these groups also bring dogs to, for example, pride parades. Indeed, BAD RAP has marched in the San Francisco Gay Pride Parade since 2002. While the couple who founded the organization are straight, they walk in honor of a friend with AIDS who was evicted from his build-ing because his service dog was a pit bull–type.[31] This work demonstrates that there is definitely something queer here, and possibly queerly kindred, but what?[32]

Recent work on kinship has "stressed the fluid and contingent nature of kin relationships and how they are instituted and nurtured over time," a sense of kinship that Judith Butler paraphrases as "a kind of *doing*, one that does not reflect a prior structure but which can only be understood as an enacted prac-tice."[33] This sense of doing-as-kinship is reflected in writings on queer kinships such as Kath Weston's *Families We Choose*, an ethnography detailing how the lives of people in gay families, or chosen families, challenge the belief that "procreation *alone* constitutes kinship, and that 'nonbiological' ties must be patterned after a biological model (like adoption) or forfeit any claim to kinship status."[34] Others augment Weston's writing in describing how "new forms of intimacy" emerge in gay and lesbian families; many emphasize the ways that these queer kin are made apparent by "the labors involved and not the socially sanctioned roles."[35] How-ever, more recent gay marriage campaigns can also be read as reinforcing what Lisa Duggan terms "homonormativity" in that they affirm rather than question the privileges and rights associated with contemporary heterosexual family formations in the United States.[36] Indeed, the issue of homonormativity underscores how the doing of many queer, gay, and lesbian kinships is tied to structures and histories of not just sexuality but also race and class.

In *The Feeling of Kinship*, David Eng outlines how much contemporary LGBT advocacy is based in "an increasingly normative vision of acceptable queer identity and lifestyle. Key to his argument is the notion of the "racialization of intimacy," a term Eng uses to delineate the increasing concentration of whiteness and property in the doings of family as an affective unit in the United States.[37] Eng highlights the material conditions of *Lawrence v. Texas*, the case that transformed sodomy into intimate acts undertaken in the private sphere of the home. Eng notes that what began the case was a neighbor calling the police about a "n—— going crazy with a gun" in a backyard. This history demonstrates that the case began not because of sodomy per se but because an African American man was perceived to be trespassing; *Lawrence* started because of what Eng terms "intimacy as a racial-ized property right," an intimacy in which investments in whiteness shaped the geographies of family and home.[38] When people see the case solely as a landmark decision in favor of gay rights, they occlude how race, and the norms of whiteness and class, played a material role in its inception. For Eng, the example of *Lawrence* speaks to how these types of occlusions are writ large in contemporary gay and lesbian politics.

To bring this back to the dogs, the relationships going on in at least some of the pit bull campaigns I discuss are certainly forms of kinship in that they are doings, enacted practices that create ties among these variously queer, gay, lesbian, and straight activists and their dogs. And there is something queer here, as the gay pride marchers and dog adopters intent on helping their dogs become "who they were born to be" make clear. However, this is not a type of queerness that takes up the larger political challenges of, say, LGBTQI-inclusive health care, bathroom safety, or even the right not to be fired from one's job because of one's sexual or gender identity. The campaigns on behalf of the Vick dogs, not to mention the other forms of pit bull advocacy I describe here, seek to incorporate the dogs into families, gay, lesbian, and straight, where geographies of whiteness and hetero- and homonormativity loom large. This is intimacy as domesticity, in which dogs are only some of the things owned by people whom Eng would term "possessive individuals." Further, the "like race" logic and affective politics involved in many of these advocacy efforts contribute to rather than challenge the ties among intimacy, geography, and whiteness going on in these families. That is, the queerness and kinship involved in this work, on their surface, are not the kind of queer practices that promise to transform contemporary landscapes of race, gender, and sexuality, nor will they necessarily help build better multispecies worlds.

Yet, as I suggest in the title of this article, I do think there *is* something queer here, and I think that there is even something queerly kindred in these worlds of pit bull advocacy. In the midst of all these politics as usual lies a different kind of queerness, an inhuman queerness, and another way of doing kin, one that queers the queer kinship outlined above. To delineate these formations, I now take a moment to reframe this discussion.

About Face

Representation runs thick in these stories—these are tales of looking, of being looked at, and of categorizing looks. The many ways these people look at animals brings to mind not only Derrida's naked staring at his cat in *The Animal That Therefore I Am* but also the work of another philosopher, Emmanuel Levinas, whose writings on ethics are rooted in an openness to and responsibility for the other in facing the other.[39] Not surprisingly, Levinas had thoughts about dogs as well, noting that although "the phenomenon of the face is not in its purest form in the dog," "one cannot entirely refuse the face of an animal."[40] The philosopher David Clark takes Levinas to say that "the animal both has and does not have a face."[41] Some question the implicit humanism of Levinas's facial recognition here—why are human faces privileged?[42] But the role of the face merits questioning in another way, and here I would like to do an about-face.

As I remind friends and family who take offense when dogs present them with their rears, most dogs live in what could be termed a "butt culture." When two dogs meet head-on, they are quick to turn and sniff the other end; indeed, the loose-bodied curving approach of dogs' sniffing each other's behinds is often the first step to their becoming acquainted, and is certainly part of how they come to recognize each other.[43] Butts and smells are not only a big part of dog life but also central to how dogs come to know the worlds and the cultures, canine and human, in which they participate. A certain kind of touch is key here, for dogs possess an auxiliary olfactory organ in the roofs of their mouths, the vomeronasal organ, through which they taste as much as smell, especially pheromones.[44] And while many of the people I think with here, myself included, have spent a lot of time looking at dogs' faces, we have also done our fair share of kissing those faces, not to mention rubbing bellies and scratching butts. These contacts lead me to think that we can and should take seriously the intimacies rooted in touch, contact, smell, and taste that humans experience with dogs and that dogs experience with each other. Indeed, an understanding rooted not in looking but in a more haptic way of meeting and responding to the world promises a way out of the politics as usual that I have outlined above.

In taking the intimacies of touch, taste, and smell seriously, I am inspired by Alice Kuzniar's writings on dogs. Arguing that "dog love has the potential to question the regulating strictures and categories by which we define sexuality, eroticism, and love," Kuzniar posits that intimacies between women and dogs act as a means for the self to become signified.[45] Kuzniar takes up narratives such as Virginia Woolf's *Flush*, a re-creation of the life of Elizabeth Barrett Browning through the eyes of her spaniel, arguing that Miss Barrett "overcomes her sense of isolation in response to Flush's love."[46] This reading contradicts what Kuzniar terms "cultural studies"–style approaches that might focus more on the relationship as a reflection of an ascendant bourgeois subjectivity.[47] Interested in recuperating "intimacy as a productive category," Kuzniar takes seriously how the otherness of a dog's love helps make a self.[48] This approach to intimacy is valuable for my project, for this is an intimacy of a different scale than those critiqued by Eng and others; this is an intimacy that fits within larger social worlds and their increasingly normalizing politics yet offers an alternate understanding nonetheless.

This shift in understanding toward not-seeing, of turning around and taking seriously the nonvisual intimacies that are scattered throughout much of contemporary human-dog culture, points to the promise that inheres in the advocacy worlds I think with. Even as these faceless, unlooking connections fit within the parameters of normal families and homes, queer or no, they also belie this fit, revealing inhuman intimacies and queer kinships that are not quite intimate in the way that Eng critiques, and queerly kindred in a way that does and does not fit into the more normative models outlined above. Here I want to borrow from Neferti Tadiar's reading of experiences that "fall away" from global capitalist and nation-state narratives to suggest that interspecies contacts without the usual forms of recognition are promisingly queer and interestingly inhuman comings together that have the potential to "fall away" from the normative tropes and politics I outline above.[49] To demonstrate these queer inhuman intimacies, I turn to another pit bull story.

Bailey

I have spent the past year doing ethnographic fieldwork in an animal shelter with a high volume of pit bull–type dogs. During this work, I have spent hundreds of hours walking with dogs, playing with them, cleaning up after them, caring for them, and snuggling with them. I have also interviewed and worked with other shelter volunteers as well as shelter staff and members of the general public who enter the shelter. And during this fieldwork, I have noticed two practices of relating specific to the shelter contexts in which faceless recognition and inhuman intimacies run thick. While it is somewhat difficult to render these forms of relating into language—after all, they are rooted in an alternative semiotics of touch and movement if we keep in mind that no dog will ever speak aloud its connections with others as love, friendship, or kinship—I loosely and clumsily classify them as "intimacy without relatedness" and "relatedness without kinship." Both of these practices strike me as promisingly and nonheteronormatively or nonhomonormatively queer, and both are reflected in the case of one dog who came to the shelter as a stray in April 2013, Bailey.

Bailey is a handsome gray pit bull–type dog whose broad chest, lean hips, and tendency to prance when moving at a trot had me making *Zoolander* male model jokes soon after I met him. When he underwent his evaluation walk with another volunteer, she noted that he seemed interested in other dogs, but not leash-reactive; he leaned toward them but did not bark or lunge. His manners in general were very good for a shelter dog, and he was quite affectionate. His main vice was tennis balls: when he had one in his mouth, he was adamant about not being parted from it. As this behavior, "resource guarding," can often be changed through training, a number of us planned to work with him. In short, despite, or possibly because of his behavioral issues, many of us became attached to Bailey.

As a shelter favorite, Bailey went on walks and cuddled with numerous volunteers, practices of relating documented in his "walk card"—the paper on the front of his kennel with volunteers' notes about their time with him—and in conversations volunteers shared about him. I took him out a number of times, and each time, we would settle on a bench by a small body of water. He would lean into me and occasionally clamber onto my lap. This was usually followed by a thorough ear-cleaning from his tongue in which touch and taste mingled. And, as his head came to rest on my chest, I would often let out a sigh that he echoed. Just for a moment, we moved together, not just in walking together, but in relaxing together. This sense of closeness did not come out of our staring into each other's eyes, or even the recognition of a name, for virtually none of the shelter dogs know their names; they are gifted names upon arrival, given the staff's and volunteers' general ignorance about the dogs' earlier lives. Rather, this was a momentary, provisional closeness rooted in our contact, in the feeling of moving together.

Notations spread throughout Bailey's walk card—"a sweetie," "likes snuggles"—revealed that my moments with Bailey were similar to those experienced by many volunteers.[50] However, Bailey continued to stay at the shelter. He did not become part of any one person's home, even as one volunteer affectionately referred to him as "my boyfriend."[51] The touching and caring he experienced and the responsive attention he gave back were all forms of an often-faceless intimacy disjoined from family, queer or no. For half an hour or so every day, he connected with the humans who took him out, leaning on them, moving with them, snuggling and playing with them, after which they put him back in his kennel and returned to their own homes and, often, their own dogs. In this intimacy without family, in these fleeting, touching connections unique to shelter contexts, there is a promising mode of relating, a different kind of queer kinship, an "intimacy without relatedness."

Bailey was fortunate to come to the shelter not long after it began running playgroups, a recent development in many US animal shelters. A typical shelter play session begins with two dogs and includes up to six, although occasionally there are more. This play is intensely physical, involving play bows—an enthusiastic lowering of the front of the body with butt in the air and wagging tail to accentuate—as well as mouthing, toothily grabbing each other's necks or faces or even ankles, humping each other (although we tried to discourage these moments), bumping into each other, chest-bumping, throwing paws over other dogs' shoulders, and more. Dog play is like a lot of other play among mammals in that there is a lot of practice of fighting maneuvers and other social behaviors, but punctuated by nonserious "check ins" that establish that this is still play and not suddenly more serious.[52] There is a fair bit of looking here—a hard stare from one dog to another was enough to make us decide not to let two dogs meet—but the hardness of that stare was rooted not only in unbreaking eye contact but also a frozen or very still body, a tell-tale warning sign among dogs. Contacts and bodily movements dominated these interactions.

When we first brought Bailey into the playgroups, we introduced him to Peanut, a young gray female pit-type. We began by taking them out on a tandem walk, during which Bailey put Peanut at ease or, in one volunteer's words, "acted like a gentleman."[53] At the end of the walk, we let them play, leashes attached. Next, we introduced Bailey to Eliza, with whom he played very well, a practice that he took up with several dogs over the next several weeks. There were the occasionally rude moments of humping, but also play bows and pushings and mouthings that led to actual play. These shelter playgroups not only helped Bailey develop relationships with other dogs through their mouthy, slobbery, pushy, and exuberant contacts but also revealed how these dogs experienced a form of connecting that was both temporary and intimate, close but not kin, a connecting that falls away from narratives of family, another form of "intimacy without relatedness."

We soon learned that Bailey's intense desire for tennis balls had landed him on the list of dogs to be euthanized—the logic being in his and many cases like it that such behaviors are unsafe in dogs who might interact poorly with children and their toys. In other words, Bailey was not an ideal candidate for a family with children, queer or otherwise. This was when the foster team stepped into action. Countless e-mails were sent out, and he ended up in a temporary foster placement with Shanna, who immediately began working on his behavior by giving him balls and, when he relinquished them, rewarding him with treats and giving the balls right back, so that he began to understand that the loss of a ball is temporary, not forever, and a tasty loss at that. She also took Bailey to training classes and continued to bring him to playgroup. And Shanna was only one of Bailey's many advocates, for his care rotated among a group of five women who took on his walks, feeding, and training through an elaborate communal schedule, a shared labor that was especially notable in light of the fact that they did not generally socialize with each other outside such circumstances. Bailey was a nexus through which these humans and various practices of care came together. It is notable that Bailey's care echoes that described by Weston in *Families We Choose*, where a large part of what makes a chosen family has to do with caretaking.[54]

Bailey's foster situation speaks to the "relatedness without kinship" at the heart of many an animal rescue organization. There is intimacy, affection, and undoubtedly love in these relationships, but these are funny kinds of love and different ways of doing intimacy, for the goal in a foster home is another home, a "forever home," not this home. When people take dogs out of shelters and into homes on a purely temporary basis, they bring them into relationships with humans and, often, other dogs and even cats, all the while striving to find them other relationships, other families, in other homes.[55] Then there is the networking, the urgent partnerships forged to care for a foster dog throughout the day. These are not your average friendships, for at their center is the body of a dog that all work together to keep alive. These volunteers are not a family, and despite the resonances with Weston's thinking, they are not a chosen family either. Rather, they go out of their way to coordinate a network cemented through relationships of care. There is kindness here, but not kinship as usual.

Queer and Inhuman

The touches, contacts, and practices of relating in Bailey's story are promisingly inhuman. This inhumanity stems partly from the central role of Bailey and his playmates in these practices of relating, an inhuman that draws from one sense of the word as "of or suggesting a class of nonhuman beings."[56] These are not anthropocentric practices, as my clumsy attempt to render them into the human-centric language of intimacy, kinship, and relatedness makes clear; there are no easily identified words to describe exactly what goes on in these fleeting contacts. These are intimacies and relatings because those are the only words to describe these decidedly inhuman practices, even as I know that the dogs involved cannot claim them as such. However, this sense of inhuman could just as easily be taken to mean inhuman as nonhuman, which is not entirely the case.

Karen Barad argues that the inhuman, and specifically the touch of the inhuman, is at the heart of mattering. Drawing from the example of the electron in quantum field theory, she finds a promising ontological indeterminacy in touch. As a negatively charged point particle, the electron constantly emits and absorbs virtual photons, not only effectively touching itself, but also coming into contact with that photon's potential contacts; Barad describes this as "a particle touching itself, and then that touching touching itself, and so on, ad infinitum."[57] These exchanges reveal touch as a way to understand how matter itself, the stuff of which we are made, *is* touching and sensing.[58] Further, as these touches involve both the material and the virtual, or matter and nonmatter, they undo any clear sense of "we," for the nonmatter, or the inhuman, of the photon and its extended touchings is central to the very being of the electron and, therefore, to the "we" of human readers. Indeed, these touches reveal that the "we" of the human constitutively includes the inhuman.[59] For Barad, tracing touch "calls us to a new sensibility," one animated by the promise of what she terms the "inhuman within."[60]

The proximities and contacts without faces that I write about, the about-faces of nuzzles, touches, licks, "butt culture," shared sighs, and nudges, not only fall away from the face-to-faceness of anthropocentric politics of representation but also resonate with the inhuman touchings that Barad describes. The many movements together I describe are joint doings, momentary togethernesses that belie a strong division between self and other. There is also the touch of the licking and smelling, where the dogs' vomeronasal organs bring the taste of the other within. This is a promising, touching inhumanity.

These inhuman contacts are also queer, especially if we consider some of the definitions offered by Mel Chen: queerness as "social and cultural formations of 'improper affiliation,'" "an array of subjectivities, intimacies, beings, and spaces located outside of the heteronormative," "exceptions to the conventional ordering of sex, reproduction, and intimacy."[61] This is a different kind of queer than the politics of representation, visibility, whiteness, and property delineated above, for the queerness of the fleeting contacts outlined in Bailey's story is a queerness without conventional family, without even chosen families. The momentary, fleeting contacts centered in touches, tastes, movements, and shared rhythms I describe are promisingly, improperly, and queerly inhuman.

The provisional, momentary nature of the contacts I describe in shelter life also point to another way of doing kinship. In a 1981 interview, Michel Foucault argued that state recognition of same-sex relationships was "only a first step" and that in fact "we should fight against the impoverishment of the relational fabric." For Foucault, this means securing "provision for relations of provisional coexistence, adoption," and the like, and by adoption he means not just of children but more, asking "why shouldn't I adopt a friend who's ten years younger than I am? And even if he's ten years older?" He posits that "rather than arguing that rights are fundamental and natural to the individual, we should try to imagine and create a new relational right that permits all possible types of relations to exist and not be prevented, blocked, or annulled by impoverished relational institutions."[62] For Foucault, relations can be grounded in many kinds of contacts, and the rights to these relations are an important part of a queer politics that, arguably, takes seriously the "improper affiliations" that Chen describes. Elizabeth Povinelli's "Notes on Gridlock" adds to Foucault's argument, challenging an impoverished

Western relational fabric in pushing for the disentanglement of what she terms "genealogical and intimacy grids."[63] Much like Eng and Duggan, Povinelli takes issue with how intimate love has been reduced to family formations and subsequently deployed as a basis for recognition by LGBTQI activists. Turning to Jean Genet's *Querelle*, she highlights how the novel's description of men kissing and fucking each other without looking reveals a form of love that "betrayed its usury, and made intimacy, as a relay of recognition, impossible."[64] For Povinelli, in this betrayal there is hope, for this love without face, this intimacy without recognition, disrupts the logics and norms of the interwoven grids of genealogy and intimacy; in this betrayal, Povinelli locates the seeds of a different queer politics that makes even fleeting, faceless contacts also count as practices of relating, ones that disrupt recognition.

Thinking with Barad, Chen, Povinelli, Foucault, and Bailey, it is clear to me that the "intimacy without relatedness" and "relatedness without kinship" I describe challenge understandings of relatedness and kinship to incorporate more provisional, fleeting intimacies. Further, these intimacies without ties to genealogies, these provisional, faceless touchings, involve a different kind of recognition than the family-style politics I outline above, one not rooted in the state and one that cannot easily be seen but must be felt or smelled or tasted. And while they are doings and practices, and in that sense fit into the sense of kinship that Butler outlines, they are also contingent and fleeting, even momentary, in a way markedly different from the more-sedimented queer formations of, say, gay adoption. Theirs is a different butt culture than the one evoked by Povinelli, but in their inhuman intimacies lies an alternative, promising formation of queer kinship.

However, these momentary, queer, inhuman intimacies are not so promising either, in that they occur within the politics as usual that I outline above. We can see this in the shelter where I did my fieldwork, which, like many of its kind, is populated by mostly white, female, middle-class volunteers, many of whom ardently desire the placement of dogs in homes characterized by the family-style politics critiqued above. Indeed, shelter-based practices such as playgroups and outings with volunteers, not to mention dogs' placements into foster homes, all share the goal of making dogs more adoptable. These fleeting, inhuman intimacies are meant to give way to more static kinship formations and less promiscuous affects preferably grounded in homes shaped by investments in whiteness. Which leads me to ask: does the way that the care of shelter dogs may fit into the troubling and troubled politics of "like race" affects and language, along with those of hetero- and homonormative family values, prevent us from responding to the pushes, nudges, and wet-nosed prods of its provisional, queer kinships and inhuman touches? There is certainly promise in the ways that these kinships and touches prompt us to take fleshly interactions seriously, to consider interspecies intercorporealities, to reconsider how to do kinships (queer or no), and to shift our processes of understanding and recognition away from looks and representation.[65] But is it enough?

Conclusion: Splittings

Sometimes, when a dog sees an interaction that looks like it's headed toward trouble, the dog will push its way between the parties involved, a bodily movement that separates the parties and prevents conflict. My younger dog, Annie, did this constantly when we lived with another dog who kept eyeing my cat, Tucker. When I told a visiting dog trainer about this, she identified the behavior as "splitting." Annie's splittings come to mind as I try my best to close this piece, because despite my hopefulness about the queerly inhuman understandings that, I think, could push us to change our politics of recognition, on a large scale, and our politics of kinship and intimacy, on a different scale, I am continually confounded by the impracticality of such maneuvers and the sedimented racial, familial, and state politics in which they fit. Practices that "fall away" do not seem to have much leverage. And, frankly, I am worried that there is an unmarked whiteness in this reoriented politics or, put another way, that a politics of inhuman recognition and interspecies intercorporeality might, in prioritizing touch and feeling, taste and sensation, ignore the roles of race and sexualities in shaping these sensibilities. Indeed, when Zakiyyah Jackson takes up Aimé Césaire in asking of posthumanist theorists, animal studies people among them, "how might we re*signify* and re*value* humanity such that it breaks with the imperialist ontology and metaphysical essentialism of Enlightenment man?," she identifies the trouble with which I am wrestling.[66] Do these shifts, in their different registers, really challenge the troubled ontological and epistemological legacies of the human politics as usual from which they fall away? In answer, I think they might, for, following the thickly inhuman ways of relating that this essay rests on, Annie's movements make me think that, just maybe, it would be possible to split things, to uncouple these matrices of genealogies, families, homes, race, and citizenship from the queerly kindred and inhuman doggish relationships I write with. In my following and final story, I hope to demonstrate such a splitting.

   In January 2011 Jill Posener started the Paw Fund, an organization based in the eastern San Francisco Bay Area dedicated to helping low-income people, many of them living outside, keep their pets.[67] The Paw Fund holds monthly free clinics in sites such as trailer parks and outdoor encampments, providing free vaccinations, spays, neuters, and medical care. The Paw Fund is not focused on "rescuing" dogs by relocating them to "good homes." Rather, the organization wants to sustain and facilitate relationships between humans and dogs, whatever their economic circumstances, however provisional, and regardless of how they choose to make their homes. This type of advocacy splits the provisional and queerly inhuman intimacies I write with from narratives of homes, families, and citizenship. This is an advocacy that offers humans and dogs the chance to live with and be near each other, however they can. Many of the people helped by the Paw Fund are low income, many of them people of color, most live outside families and conventional homes, and all of them are committed to their animals. Many of the dogs that the Paw Fund helps are not "good citizens" in the way that these other pit bull narratives require—they bark at strangers, they do not particularly like small dogs, they have been known to scuffle—yet, for the most part, they are doing fine. And in this work and other projects like it, there is the seed for a promising and alternate worlding, one that aims to create a space where the queerly inhuman intimacies that I describe here might flourish as part of a larger project of multispecies justice.

Notes

Research for this article was supported by NSF grant number 1230743.

1. These details come from *The Lennox Campaign Blog*, savelennox.com/ (accessed April 1, 2013). DNA tests indicated that Lennox was an American bulldog and labrador retriever mix.

2. Agence France-Presse, "Belfast Euthanizes 'Illegal' Pit-Bull Lennox despite International Campaign," *Raw Story*, July 11, 2012, www.rawstory.com/rs/2012/07/11/belfast-euthanizes-illegal-pit-bull-lennox-despite-international-campaign/.

3. "This could be YOUR family, please help fight this injustice," July 8, 2012, "My Pit Bull Is Family," www.facebook.com/MyPitBullisFamily; "Heartbreak as Death Row Dog Lennox Destroyed by Belfast Council," *Belfast Telegraph*, July 11, 2012, www.belfasttelegraph.co.uk/news/local-national/northern-ireland/heartbreak-as-death-row-dog-lennox-destroyed-by-belfast-council-28770103.html.

4. Victoria Stilwell, "How the Legal System Failed Lennox," *Positively Victoria Stilwell* (blog), positively.com/2011/10/09/how-the-legal-system-failed-lennox/ (accessed April 1, 2013).

5. Karen Barad, "On Touching—the Inhuman That Therefore I Am," *differences: A Journal of Feminist Cultural Studies* 23, no. 3 (2012): 206–2.

6. David Eng, *The Feeling of Kinship: Queer Liberalism and the Racialization of Intimacy* (Durham, NC: Duke University Press, 2010).

7. Malcolm Gladwell, "Troublemakers: What Pit Bulls Can Teach Us about Profiling," *New Yorker*, February 6, 2006, www.newyorker.com/archive/2006/02/06/060206fa _fact?currentPage=all.

8. Victoria Voith, Elizabeth Ingram, Katherine Mitsouras, and Kristopher Irizarry, "Comparison of Adoption Agency Breed Identification and DNA Breed Identification of Dogs," *Journal of Applied Animal Welfare Science* 12 (2009): 253–62.

9. Gladwell, "Troublemakers."

10. Tanya Irwin, "Many Sheltered Dogs Mislabeled 'Pit Bulls,'" March 18, 2012, www .toledoblade.com/local/2012/03/18/Many-shelter-dogs-mislabeled-pit-bulls.html. The term *canine racism* is widespread; see Karyn Grey, "Breed-Specific Legislation Revisited: Canine Racism or the Answer to Florida's Dog Control Problems?," *Nova Law Review* 27 (Spring 2003): 415–32.

11. *OWN*, "'Fruitvale Station' Star Michael B. Jordan: 'Black Males, We Are America's Pit Bull,'" *Huffington Post*, December 18, 2013, www.huffingtonpost.com/2013/12/18 /fruitvale-station-michael-b-jordan_n_4462009.html.

12. Karlene Turkington, "Raising Awareness for Racially Profiling Dogs such as Lennox," *Opelika Observer*, April 6, 2012, www.opelikaobserver.com/columnists/ruffly -speaking/699-raising-awareness-for-racially-profiling-dogs-such-as-lennox.

13. This image can be viewed at The Lennox Campaign Blog, savelennox.com/ (accessed March 24, 2014).

14. Turkington, "Raising Awareness for Racially Profiling Dogs Such as Lennox."

15. Many of these images appear on the "I am Lennox" Facebook page, www.facebook .com/WeRLennox (accessed March 24, 2014).

16. Steve Hummer, "Vick Burns in Tailgate Effigy at Dome," *Atlanta Journal-Constitution*, September 18, 2011, www.ajc.com/sports/atlanta-falcolns/vick-burns -in-tailgate-1183830.html.

17. For a more in-depth discussion of changing perceptions of Vick, see Harlan Weaver, "'Becoming in Kind': Race, Class, and Gender in Cultures of Dog Fighting and Dog Rescue," *American Quarterly* 65, no. 3 (2013): 689–710.

18. Jim Gorant, *The Lost Dogs: Michael Vick's Dogs and Their Tale of Rescue and Redemption* (New York: Gotham Books, 2010), 10.

19. For example, Christopher Columbus described the native peoples with whom he traded as "savage cannibals, with dog-like noses" in his log entries of November 4 and 23, 1492. See Victor Schilling, "Eight Myths and Atrocities about Christopher Columbus and Columbus Day," *Indian Country Media Network*, October 14, 2014, indiancountrytodaymedianetwork.com/2013/10/14/8-myths-and-atrocities-about -christopher-columbus-and-columbus-day-151653. Achille Mbembe comments on animalization in light of racialization and colonization at length in *On the Postcolony* (Berkeley: University of California Press, 2001).

20. BAD RAP, www.badrap.org/five-years-later (accessed August 23, 2013).

21. See the American Kennel Club's "Training/Testing: Canine Good Citizen's Test Items," www.akc.org/events/cgc/training_testing.cfm (accessed June 23, 2012); and the American Temperament Test Society Inc., atts.org/ (accessed June 23, 2012).

22. Uba, "My Precious," April 22, 2012, Vick Dog Blog, vickdogsblog.blogspot.com /2012/04/my-precious.html.

23. Vick Dog Blog, vickdogsblog.blogspot.com/search?updated-max=2011-04-30T19:06 :00-07:00&max-results=15&start=15&by-date=false (accessed August 25, 2013).

24. GUND Shop, shop.gund.com/p/gund-top-dog-jonny-justice-8; thebarkpost.com /vicktory-dogs/?utm_source=facebook&utm_medium=shelter&utm_campaign =HeARTs_Speak (accessed April 4, 2014).

25. "The Vick Dogs," BAD RAP, www.badrap.org/vick-dogs (accessed August 25, 2013).

26. MyPitBullisFamily.com, www.mypitbullisfamily.com/ (accessed March 24, 2014).

27. C. J. Arabia, "Did You Know That Pit Bulls Were Known as Nanny Dogs?," The Pet Collective, March 31, 2014, www.thepetcollective.tv/did-you-know-that-pit-bulls -were-known-as-the-nanny-dog/.

28. George Lipsitz, *The Possessive Investment in Whiteness* (Philadelphia: Temple University Press, 1998).

29. "Dog Doesn't Consider Itself Part of the Family," *Onion*, March 14, 2014, www.theonion .com/articles/dog-doesnt-consider-itself-part-of-family,35532/.

30. Winston Gieseke, "The Beagle Effect: How Saving Puppies Enriched These LGBT People," *Advocate*, March 5, 2012, www.advocate.com/news/daily-news/2012/03/05 /beagle-effect-how-saving-puppies-enriched-these-lgbt-people?page=0,5. While the article is specific to beagles rescued from laboratories, pit bulls also feature prominently in movements oriented toward the prevention of the use of dogs in animal testing; see Sue Coe, *Pit's Letter* (New York: Four Walls Eight Windows, 2000).

31. "BAD RAP at SF Pride June 2011," June 27, 2011, www.facebook.com/BADRAP .org/posts/172314092832426.

32. I am, of course, referencing Alexander Doty, "There's Something Queer Here," in *Out in Culture: Gay, Lesbian, and Queer Essays on Popular Culture*, ed. Corey Creekmur and Alexander Doty (Durham, NC: Duke University Press, 1995), 71–90.

33. Nancy Levine, "Alternative Kinship, Marriage, and Reproduction," *Annual Review of Anthropology* 37 (2008): 377; Judith Butler, "Is Kinship Always Already Heterosexual?," *differences: A Journal of Feminist Cultural Studies* 13, no. 1 (2002): 34.

34. Kath Weston, *Families We Choose: Lesbians, Gays, Kinship* (New York: Columbia University Press, 1991), 34.

35. Maureen Sullivan, *The Family of Women: Lesbian Mothers, Their Children, and the Undoing of Gender* (Berkeley: University of California Press, 2004), 17; Christopher Carrington, *No Place Like Home* (Chicago: University of Chicago Press, 1999), 5.

36. Lisa Duggan, "The New Homonormativity: The Sexual Politics of Neoliberalism,"

in *Materializing Democracy: Toward a Revitalized Cultural Politics*, ed. Russ Castronovo and Dana Nelson (Durham, NC: Duke University Press, 2002), 179.

37. Eng, *The Feeling of Kinship*, 26.

38. Eng, *The Feeling of Kinship*, 36, 47.

39. Jacques Derrida, *The Animal That Therefore I Am* (New York: Fordham University Press, 2008).

40. Emmanuel Levinas, "The Paradox of Morality," in *The Provocation of Levinas*, ed. Robert Bernasconi and David Wood (New York: Routledge, 1988), 169.

41. David Clark, "On Being 'The Last Kantian in Nazi Germany': Dwelling with Animals after Levinas," in *Animal Acts*, ed. Jennifer Ham and Matthew Senior (New York: Routledge, 1997), 56.

42. Matthew Calarco contends that Levinas holds a "classical . . . view of the animal" who is "blind and deaf to the call of the Other," in *Zoographies: The Question of the Animal from Heidegger to Derrida* (New York: Columbia University Press, 2008), 56.

43. See Alexandra Horowitz's chapter, "You Had Me at Hello," in *Inside of a Dog* (New York: Scribner, 2009), 259–82.

44. Horowitz, "You Had Me at Hello," 73–75.

45. Kuzniar is careful to note that the love she writes about is not a love that "offers different forms of genital stimulation, indeed quite the opposite" (*Melancholia's Dog: Reflections on Our Animal Kinship* [Chicago: University of Chicago Press, 2006], 109).

46. Kuzniar, *Melancholia's Dog*, 123.

47. Kuzniar, *Melancholia's Dog*, 123.

48. Kuzniar, *Melancholia's Dog*, 112.

49. Neferti Tadiar, *Things Fall Away: Philippine Literature, Historical Experience, and Tangential Makings of Globality* (Durham, NC: Duke University Press, 2009), 5.

50. Author's field notes, April 2013.

51. Author's field notes, April 2013.

52. Horowitz, "You Had Me at Hello," 196–205.

53. Author's field notes, May 2013.

54. Weston, *Families We Choose*, 113.

55. "Failed fosters," dogs who become permanent members of their foster families, are also common.

56. *Merriam-Webster OnLine*, s.v. "inhuman," www.merriam-webster.com/dictionary /inhuman (accessed July 4, 2014).

57. Barad, "On Touching," 212.

58. Barad, "On Touching," 215.

59. Barad, "On Touching," 214.

60. Barad, "On Touching," 216.

61. Mel Y. Chen, *Animacies: Biopolitics, Racial Mattering, and Queer Affect* (Durham, NC: Duke University Press, 2012), 104, 104, 11.

62. Michel Foucault, "The Social Triumph of the Sexual Will," in *Ethics: Subjectivity and Truth*, ed. Paul Rabinow (New York: New Press, 1994), 158.

63. Elizabeth Povinelli, "Notes on Gridlock," *Public Culture* 14, no. 1 (2002): 216.

64. Povinelli, "Notes on Gridlock," 232.

65. In using the term *interspecies*, I draw from the definition put forth by Jasbir Puar and Julie Livingston as a way to "refer to relationships *between* different forms of biosocial life and the political effects" ("Interspecies," *Social Text*, no. 106 [2011]: 3). In pairing interspecies with intercorporeality, I draw from and build on the editorial advice of Dana Luciano.

66. Zakiyyah Iman Jackson, "Animal: New Directions in the Theorization of Race and Posthumanism," *Feminist Studies* 39, no. 3 (2013): 1–17.

67. See pawfund.org/ (accessed October 17, 2013).

INTIMATE ATMOSPHERES

Queer Theory in a Time of Extinctions

Neel Ahuja

Prologue: The Mosquito and the Settler

*P*erhaps queer theory has always been a theory of extinctions. Leo Bersani's 1987 essay "Is the Rectum a Grave?" opens with an epigraph from a BBC television interview that casts the gay male body as the parasite at the heart of the AIDS epidemic. In the epigraph, the virologist Opendra Narayan claims that "a man comes along and goes from anus to anus and in a single night will act as a mosquito transferring infected cells on his penis. When this is practiced for a year, with a man having three thousand sexual intercourses, one can readily understand this massive epidemic that is upon us."[1] Narayan imagines "gay plague" through a vision of swarming parasites fucking at an entomological timescale, outpacing the orgasmic rhythms of the human. As such, the homosexual becomes viral and thus both alien and contagious, invoking tropes of insatiable feminine desire and the machinic rapist. Yet in examining gay publics' refusal to be named sexual parasites Bersani argues that conflating sex with liberation forecloses the risk to which sex opens the subject. In response, Bersani suggests that "if the rectum is the grave in which the masculine ideal . . . of proud subjectivity is buried, then it should be celebrated for its very potential for death. Tragically, AIDS has literalized that potential as the certainty of biological death, and has therefore reinforced the heterosexual association of anal sex with a self-annihilation. . . . It may, finally, be in the gay man's rectum that he demolishes his own perhaps otherwise uncontrollable identification with the murderous judgment against him."[2]

From this line of argument, a number of commentators identify Bersani

GLQ 21:2–3
DOI 10.1215/10642684-2843227
© 2015 by Duke University Press

as father of a tradition of queer negativity, configured as antirelational, anti-social, death-driven, or masochistic. This position has been consolidated in recent debates over reproductive futurism, where Lee Edelman's criticism of the contemporary fetishism of the Child in his book *No Future* appears as the latest generation of Bersani's negative ethical discourse.[3] Yet given that Edelman stakes radical politics on a refusal of both compulsory reproduction and futurity itself, there is another line of thinking in Bersani's essay that might complicate the analogy of inheritance. Bersani writes of gay men who seem sexually "radical" by night but who thrive in bourgeois and racist social positions by day; they have "no problem being gay slumlords" who evict "black families unable to pay the rents necessary to gentrify that neighborhood." This is an iconic rendering of the economic parasite, the slumlord, usurer, or tribute collector, whose occupation of a host ecology extracts and disposes. I cannot help but read this Bersani as a theorist of *reproduction* as well as death, as a witness to "human beings' extraordinary willingness to kill" others even when the reproduction of the self is staked as "ethical ideal."[4] Bersani's gentrifying parasite is thus a variant of Frantz Fanon's colonial settler, who manufactures both a racialized myth of freedom and a material lifeworld of surplus—"wonderful garbage, undreamed-of leftovers"—the disposability of which parallels the disposability of the colonized, displaced to live "hungry" in a "world with no space," that is, to be rendered parasite in turn, associated with "the sting of the native quarter, of breeding swarms." For Fanon, "a hostile, ungovernable, and fundamentally rebellious Nature is in fact synonymous with the colonies and the bush, the mosquitoes, the natives, and disease. Colonization has succeeded once this untamed nature has been brought under control."[5] In the realization of "freedom," the settler renders the colonized displaced, disposable, pestilent.

Thinking beyond the Freudian formulation of a traumatic encounter with objects that moves the subject into a narcissistic fortress of identity, Bersani hopes to dissolve the subject by theorizing an abstract space of "death" or "the nonhuman." But for those colonized, made into waste, and resurrected as parasite, there is no hope for transcendence. Fanon argues that, in expanding and mastering the world, the settler enacts a racial ecology that both feeds parasitically on the colonized and reproduces the dependent conditions that justify their constant displacement. From here, I suggest reading Bersani's references to the mosquito and the settler as meditations on the reproductive force of the living, a force that may casually extinguish life in the name of a mythic freedom.

Lateral Reproductions

Three decades after the onset of the AIDS crisis, the climate crisis presses queer theory for a planetary account of reproduction. The present essay attempts to recuperate, by tracing reproductive figures like the mosquito and the settler through contemporary climate discourses, an ecological dimension of queer critique. The persistent opposition of life and death, relation and negation in queer critical discourses is a symptom of a field's attempt to articulate an antihumanist ethic in the absence of a materialist account of ecological space and interspecies relation. Such an account is especially pressing given that any vision of freedom in today's global North—including visions of freedom *both* staked on the reproduction of the nuclear family *and* on the refusal of it—are imbricated in racialized forms of carbon privilege that disperse social and biological precarity.[6] Thus Fanon's emphasis on colonialism's spatial reproduction of racial disposability must be rethought in relation to today's carbon-fueled exterminations of peoples, species, and entire ways of life.

In this essay I explore relations between reproduction and extinction through a specific environmental crisis: fears of mosquito-borne diseases in a warming atmosphere. To understand this arena of crisis—in which carbon wastes trap solar heat, driving the transborder migration of insects that feed on and reproduce through human bodies—it is necessary to reconfigure notions of intimacy and reproduction across the planet: minerals, mosquitoes, settlers, gases, solar rays, and other bodies share in reproductive metabolisms crossing scales, species, and systems, invigorating "performances of adjustment that make a shared atmosphere something palpable."[7] *Atmosphere*, then, has a double valence: it signals both the interspecies intimacy structured by geophysical forces of the earth and the ambient senses of crisis, withering, and extermination that intensify as the underside of neoliberal freedom. Atmospheric intimacies signal that the reproductive forces and waste effects of carbon intensify contradictions between precarity and freedom, reforming the political through a model of action distinct from the agency of the human sovereign. Drawing on Lauren Berlant's conception of a "lateral" biopolitics in which subjects manage "the difficulty of reproducing contemporary life" in "a mode of coasting," I question both the xenophobic rendering of the environmental parasite in climate discourse and the sovereignty of the antirelational stance against reproduction in queer theory.[8] I argue instead that neoliberal subjects (including queer subjects) are engulfed by processes linking the reproduction of the ordinary and the extermination of various life-forms and forms of life.[9] Carbon-fueled forms of neoliberal freedom at once unleash waste and precarity on far-flung bodies while expanding the potential of others, reformulating racialized divisions between surplus and waste.[10]

Given that the reproduction of late-carbon liberalism, its "parasitic" relation to the earth, exterminates through its very processes of reproduction, it is no surprise that today visions of the future human, including the post-HIV queer subject as human, often evoke crisis and the imagery of detritus and death. While his polemic in *No Future* illuminates how futurity is wagered on normalizing strategies, Edelman's refusal of those strategies as constituting "life" and his resulting embrace of "death" narrows the richness and interrelation of "life" and "death" that we encounter in the contemporary biological sciences, including climate science. We might thus benefit from thinking more broadly about reproduction than Edelman does, recognizing that bodies and atmospheres reproduce through complex forms of socio-ecological entanglement. In what ways, we may query, is an anthropomorphic and gendered conception of reproduction complicit with masking the violence of neoliberal systems for conducting life? Ecological thought refuses an "outside" to reproduction, a sovereign space of ethical hygiene from which to queer.[11] Liberalism thrives on masking violence through ruses of the individual's transcendence, the refusal of the "promiscuous" interspecies connections that make bodies, according to Donna Haraway, "constitutively a crowd."[12] Within queer studies, Tim Dean's unique study *Unlimited Intimacy* resists this tendency by offering an ecology of gay social reproduction linking bodies, species, technologies, and social spaces.[13] Dean's examination of "bug chasers"—men who seek HIV infection, in the process creating networks of kin filiated through viral transmission— shows that social and biological reproduction can be deeply intertwined via forms of interspecies entanglement. In this case, men describe contracting the virus through metaphors of viral impregnation, digestion, and kinship. From another entry point, scholars working at the intersections of trans studies and science studies document biology's queer reproductions, noting that intersex embodiments and homosexuality are completely mundane evolutionary events sustaining species and life systems.[14] Not all publics denominated as "queer" engage reproduction in such explicit terms. But in the production of waste and the consumption of goods, queer publics are deeply linked in ecosocial processes of reproduction.

Karl Marx once explained that capitalism was alienated from "nature" by using the digestive metaphor of an overactive metabolism, an extractive potential that could outpace the soil's normative reproductive rhythms. Today it is alternatively said that life itself poses reproductive constraints on the form of capital.[15] Contemporary visions of ecological waste and scarcity as "limits to capital" reflect that ecocidal violence is more often narrated as a crisis of overconsumption than as a problem of enclosure or of racialized divisions of carbon privilege and waste effects. Environmentalist views of capitalism as frenetic overconsumption link the unequal processes of surplus extraction to the aesthetics of "wasteful" bodies expanding uncontrollably in space. This development takes on a loaded moral and ideological character when metaphors link species, nations, races, populations, or subcultures to the opprobrium of the fat or unconstrained body, an opprobrium that outside environmental debates is elsewhere visited on immigrants or the recipients of social welfare who are racialized as leeches on the social body. This is one example of how neoliberal debates over environmental crisis are saturated with analogies of the parasite: they name how some bodies are made to expand and crowd out the reproductive futures of others.

Bersani outlines two forms of parasitic replication we might follow laterally against Edelman's conception of sovereign reproduction. In the image of the mosquito, we find the contagious virus associated with speed, engulfment, and mutation, which crosses bodies whose own temporalities may be interrupted or radically shortened by the transformations of contact. Alternatively, the settler commits extractive displacement, occupying a host ecology to appropriate energy and matter, even if, Scrooge-like, it collects only to deprive others.[16] Parasites produce curious archives—sometimes residing in bodies rather than texts, often displaced or disposed from sites of contact. These ideologically loaded figures pose some ambivalent and contradictory logics, ones that increasingly render neoliberal life queer not through trumpeted expansions of formal human rights or homonormative kinship with children but through the *lateral connections between distant bodies that appear violent as an inherent feature of their shared existence.*[17] I am completely convinced by left ecological injunctions to battle against capitalism's rendering of high-energy-input consumption as freedom and to refuse the unjust international divisions of life and the dumping of wastes that racialize the effects of climate change. That said, I am attuned to the genocidal, fascistic, and xenophobic logics converging in the idea of the parasitic environmental body. In queer theory, I seek a critical discourse that inquires more deeply into the micropolitics of reproduction and extinction, where racial divisions of climate emerge in the intimate scales of contact between human social forms and ecologies of production and waste. If, in the ecological metaphors of literary criticism described by Valerie Rohy, "homosexuality" has long appeared "as a sort of parasite, feeding off of the failure of normative sexuality," a queer-theoretical response to late-carbon liberalism might involve thinking reproduction as an interspecies entry point into entangled forms of violence—forms often distorted by moralizing and universalizing figures of the parasite.[18]

To Kill Softly

Media representations of climate change struggle to grasp the enormity of killing. The planetary scale of carbon amplification, its association with expanding bodies and displaced destruction, coincides with a spectacular trauma of extinction: ecologically violent uses of land, chemicals, and carbon are accelerating the sixth major extinction event in earth's history. This "event" (if we can stomach the cool rendering of mass death as a singularity) will commit 18–35 percent of extant animal and plant species to extinction by 2050.[19] Perhaps one million species will disappear, and countless billions of living bodies will be denied the conditions of life or prematurely killed. Climate-related disasters are accelerating threats to already precarious lifeways: Inuit nations face melting Arctic ice; Maldivians and other islanders lose ground to rising seas; vulnerabilities to infectious disease grow with shrinking water supplies; the world's agrarian poor face crop diseases, drought, desertification, and food price instability; and all countries face increased weather disasters. The large number of people who depend on subsistence agriculture are already living outside the ecological "boundary parameters" that enabled the rise of modern human societies.[20] In this sense, we are already living the future of extinction. The planetary *present*—not some speculative future—exhibits a staggering scale of "reproductive failure," human and nonhuman.

Yet small bodies and intimate environments often get lost in big atmospheric narratives. Since its seventeenth-century origins in English, the term *atmosphere* has signaled the fluid medium of above-ground relations, its contradictory figuration as a space of geology and life, and a background that forges exchange between social and physical processes. Atmospheres can surround big and small bodies, and can shift as bodies entangle and disentangle spatially. With industrial pollution, lower atmospheric space abounds with plumes of toxic gases (methane, carbon dioxide, and carbon monoxide) as well as noncarbon by-products (e.g., nitrous oxide and ozone) that unpredictably concentrate in our bodies as we encounter a busy street, a power plant, or a factory farm. In addition to rising to heights where they can trap solar heat, these gases fix in soil and water, returning unpredictable flows of toxicity to the lithosphere where plants grow. These toxicities— often concentrated in poor and minority communities—contribute to childhood asthma, lung disease, and the spread of various cancers.

In an account of living with toxic sensitivity to airborne heavy metals, Mel Chen describes navigating and transforming unpredictable atmospheres and their conjoined affective and spatial entanglements. The improvisational strategies for prophylaxis—such as donning a particulate mask to avoid exposure to vehicle emissions on a busy street—inevitably conjure public surveillance. "Suited up in both racial skin and chemical mask," writes Chen, "I am perceived as a walking symbol of contagious disease like SARS, and am often met with some form of repulsion."[21] Chen's account points to how the materiality of everyday air pollution subtly intertwines with the materiality of race. Race, according to Renisa Mawani, might itself be understood as an atmospherics rather than a "social construction." Drawing on Fanon's accounts of race and atmosphere, Mawani explores "race as an affective movement, a force rather than a thing, a current that reconstitutes and reassembles itself in response to its own internal rhythms and to changing social and political conditions."[22] If race is not simply a phenotypic characteristic but an ecology of affective movement and exchange, the effects of carbon pollution—disability, disease, forced migration, and sometimes death—can catalyze the emergence of xenophobic fears about economic and ecological interconnection.

Racialized climate reporting draws affective power from senses of pervasive and inescapable environmental pollution. Michael Ziser and Julie Sze detail the persistent geopolitical and racial fears driving US responses to climate change. Contrasting the sentimental domestication of the (white) polar bear in US media with persistent fears of the cross-Pacific migration of Chinese air pollution, Ziser and Sze argue that climate discourses conjure earlier racial panics about "yellow peril" and obscure primary US responsibility for contemporary and historical emissions.[23] While such reporting contributes to an atmosphere of fear and crisis, the everyday physicality of climate processes inscribes fear at the site of the skin. Atmosphere names a space of unpredictable touching, attractions, and subtle violences—a space at once geophysical and affective, informed by yet exploding representation, a space where the violences of late-carbon liberalism subtly reform racialized sensoria through shifting scales of interface.

To explore this further I suggest that we think with mosquitoes, mosquitoes both figural and real, mosquitoes that bite, migrate, and feed on various bodies. These are parasites like those in Narayan's vision of gay plague; they are also strange kin in a warming atmosphere. Mosquitoes excite colonial tropes in environmental discourse—from anthropophagic consumption (feeding on humans) to visions of tropical contagion.[24] In the vampiric image of female mosquitoes' blood feasts—required for their sexual reproduction—there is a counterpoint to the "carnivorous virility" that Carla Freccero attributes to liberal humanist visions of the subject. A small body becomes a predator of the human, forcing strange ecologies of attraction and feeling even as it poses risks of debility and death.[25]

But the parasite turns out to be feeding on a parasite. Alongside the mosquito, a universalized, waste-expelling human settler appears as the ultimate atmospheric parasite in neoliberal climate discourse. Michel Serres puts the point about scale this way: "The human parasite is of another order relative to that of the animal parasite: the latter is one, the former a set; the latter is time, the former, history; the latter is a garden, the former, a province; to destroy a garden or a world."[26] An organic imperialist, the human colonizes ecologies, time, and thought itself—an entire lifeworld. In the hands of late-carbon liberalism's human settler, killing takes a form both massive and casual. This figuration is based on some daunting facts of extinction. The everyday activities of carbon-dependent industrial living connect one's bodily consumption and waste to the "stranger intimacies" of a shared atmosphere, slowly threatening other far-flung bodies, human and nonhuman.[27] The effects of waste may kill softly, enmeshed in the deep time and circuitous space of "slow violence," a "largely unintentional ecocide."[28] From this vantage, beyond its invocation of xenophobic rhetorics of shape-shifting, virality, and contagion, the parasite suggests a problem of knowledge about agency and causality. For this is a human defined by waste rather than by romantic marks of sentience, feeling, or intentionality.

To gloss Berlant, inhabiting late-carbon liberalism produces myths, icons, and feelings that may be "profoundly confirming" despite binding a person or world to situations of "profound threat."[29] Rather than settle comfortably into the assumption of species-derived power—of the destructive and universal human geological agency of "the Anthropocene"—we might say that to recognize that life is ambiently queer is to divest from spectacular temporalities of crisis and transcendence that infuse queer theory and environmentalism alike. *Queering* in this sense emerges by tracing an affective materiality that interrupts anthropocentric body logics and space-time continuums rather than a sovereign stance of negation in relation to Law, including the law of compulsory reproduction. Thus I interpret "queer inhumanism" as an account of interspecies entanglement and reproductive displacement, an inquiry into the unrealized lifeworlds that form the background of the everyday. This requires thinking askance the human and thinking death, animality, and vulnerability in an age of many extinctions—extinctions of taxonomized species, to be sure, but also more subtle orchestrations of racial precarity and quiet obliterations of histories that could have been. In a time of extinctions, lateral reproduction suggests not some transcendent space of queer negation—or worse, an acceptance of Narayan's logic of plague—but a problem of rethinking our casual reproduction of forms of ecological violence that kill quietly, outside the spectacular time of crisis.

An Anthropophilic Plague

Different figures of the parasite are interrelated and share kinship in public representations of atmospheric change. Take one of the nascent narratives of climate disaster: science journalists and environmental NGOs now widely figure the growth of "invasive" mosquito populations as one deadly sign of climate crisis.[30] For example, *Scientific American* warns of increased numbers of mosquitoes in a warming world, exacerbating the risks of West Nile, dengue, and malaria. Distributions of feared diseases are growing, as "regions with tropical climates expand."[31] Despite evidence that global South poor are most at risk, a warming planet has reinvigorated colonial projections of "the tropics" as a site of uncontainable contagion. The so-called Asian tiger mosquito, *Aedes albopictus*, is the feared species. Figuring entomologists as "waging war" against invasive insect settlers, the French Press Agency notes that the tiger mosquito has established "colonies in twenty European countries . . . as far north as Germany, Belgium, and the Netherlands."[32] The *Independent* adds that trade globalization aids transits of dengue and chikungunya from Asia to England, where mosquitoes might increasingly "survive year-round in milder winters."[33] Heat increases the potency and ferocity of these parasites, according to the National Resources Defense Council: "Female mosquitoes bite more frequently in hotter temperatures. . . . Higher temperatures also shorten the time it takes for the virus inside the mosquito to develop and become infective."[34] A recent *New York Times* article reports that dengue-carrying mosquitoes in the United States are becoming "thirstier for human blood" because of changes in antennae sensitivity and saliva composition.[35]

While climate change in these narratives usually appears as a universalized effect of human environmental wastes—sidestepping recognition of the deeply uneven geographies of profit and privilege from carbon emissions—the narrative of mosquito threats often follows xenophobic immigration, security, and trade discourses depicting the North's engulfment by rising Asian and Latin American populations as well as the entomologic body of the terrorist.[36] Concomitant with rhetorics of atmospheric consumption and pollution in which immigrants from Latin America are "breathing our air," mosquitoes appear to swarm the fluid space of the lower atmosphere from afar. Texas, where 236 people died of West Nile in 2012, stands as the border epicenter of these xenophobic fears. Health officials coordinated aerial spraying campaigns to eradicate mosquitoes using petroleum-derived pyrethroids that endanger avian and arthropod species and may cause neurological and endocrine toxicities in humans.[37] These ecocidal (and often ineffective) sprayings, as well as the promotion of DEET by state health officials, are increasingly being replicated across the Eastern Seaboard. Building on a longer history in which the horrors of colonial proximity are expressed through entomological figures of swarming and plasticity, insects emerge as materially and symbolically potent offshoots of human atmospheric agency.[38] In this sense, toxic bodies move "well beyond their specific range of biological attribution" into the politicized affect of species, race, and (dis)ability.[39]

These fears restage racial logics of colonial parasitology. Parasitology orients public health against forms of entanglement that fail to resolve into colonialism's privileged liberal intimacies. Analyzing the forms of property that expand the figure of the liberal subject from self out into world, Lisa Lowe explains that normative intimacies rely on models of reciprocity, reproduction, and possession of self, kin, and land.[40] As mosquito-borne diseases threatened life expectancy and the cultivation of property, twentieth-century tropical medicine has historically attempted to police human-mosquito entanglement. In Egypt during World War II, for example, authorities appointed a "malaria dictator," the infectious diseases expert Fred Soper.[41] As he had recently done in Brazil, Soper waged environmental war by deploying petroleum and synthetic nitrates used to eradicate breeding pools.[42] The dream of exterminating insects required constructing their behaviors in the language of species desire. Infectious diseases researchers developed the concept of *anthropophilia* and the metric of an anthropophilic index, a measure of the percentage of female mosquitoes in a sample population whose dissected stomachs revealed human blood. While the idea of anthropophilia stressed the universal attraction of mosquitoes to humans, the anthropophilic index revealed variability of feeding habits even within species and population categories. Since "mosquito-borne diseases" are usually zoonotic pathogens that transit through various species, insects and humans forming only part of the chains of their reproductive cycles, the concept of anthropophilia narrowed the lifeworld of the mosquito to a drama of unrequited love for the human, a vision of dangerous intimacy that mandated prophylaxis or eradication. As such, current entomological studies frame anthropophilia as a variable tendency that can be affected by ecological factors.

Thus today's worries about mosquito migration situate mosquitoes as lateral agents of human environmental processes. Their feeding on humans is spurred by anthropogenic warming and intensified by the fact that development exterminates other potential hosts (monkeys, birds) from settler space. Thus ecological visions of "blowback" invigorate postcolonial fears of race, touch, blood, and engulfment as the underside to "development." Fears of chikungunya, dengue, and West Nile rehearse worries about the interpenetration of bodies familiar from histories of eugenic border and health policies, racial slavery, colonial disease control, and the

AIDS crisis.[43] In response, emerging forms of environmental government attempt to redraw borders between species to ensure faith in the reproduction of able-bodied humanity.

Cryptid Traces

What would it mean to understand panics over mosquito-borne diseases from the vantage of interspecies social and biological reproduction? Mosquitoes are linked to industrial processes through assemblages of fossilized carbon, industrial labor, and neoliberal consumption that constitute international divisions of labor and life. Greenwashing capitalism attempts to mask unequal access to carbon privilege for the wealthy through the figure of a rooted, extractive, and expanding body of the waste-defined human. William Rees and Mathis Wackernagel's Malthusian vision of the "ecological footprint" imagines a massified human settler that is slow moving and imprecise in the incidental violence it metes out against earth.[44] Visualized by the New York Department of Environmental Conservation as the brown foot of an outsize human covering the Western Hemisphere, the ecological footprint conjures colonial zoological legends of cryptid megafauna like bigfoot or the yeti.[45] The footprint can be analyzed only in retrospect, and thus the universalized human becomes a moving target defined by its trace. Curiously, although this is a powerful beast that can imprint widely on its environment, it faces its own crisis of reproduction. Like bigfoot, the human cryptid risks vanishing as it grows, and the footprint itself someday may exist only as the trace of the extinct.

Yet the greenwashing spectacle of the outsized, universal, waste-defined human masks more complex chains of interspecies relation. Farmed animals and mined fossil bodies in these processes amplify atmospheric carbon, creating an odd form of time travel in which the bodies of the dead fuel the lateral expansion and acceleration of carbon-privileged bodies in the present (globalization's "time-space compression") at the expense of bodies cast out of the bioengineered economy and into uncertain futures. While there is much more work needed to tease out these situated relations, feminist critics of reproduction have for some time explored linkages of neoliberal metabolism, species, and reproductive labor, arguing that the generation of surplus implicates entire social systems in the toxic administration of life. As Greta Gaard explains, critical-race feminist work on "reproductive justice" points to ways that capital controls reproductive capacities for precaritized women. The northern media's focus on women as individuals torn between child rearing and careers masks environmental conditions of declining fertility, the reproductive inputs of industrial animal breeding, and the production of a transnational market in southern surrogates.[46] Reflecting on the consequences of such entanglements for an analysis of queer liberalism, Heidi Nast highlights how the international divisions of labor and life furthermore produce "surplus" populations to fill the flexible labor forces of sweated manufacturing.[47] Claims that gay and lesbian publics experience freedom from sexually dimorphic reproduction, for Nast, mask the economic mandate that others elsewhere biologically reproduce this labor force.[48] The offshoring of reproduction to southern zones of flexible labor and commoditized surrogacy—as well as the creeping of capital into the plastic form of living species—allows for expansive practices of consumption and the constitution of homonormative kinship by wealthy publics that are shrinking in both numerical terms and purchasing power.[49]

"Footprints" of environmental destruction collect complex itineraries of biocapital into a generic opprobrium against certain styles of consumption. In such renderings of climate crisis, ecologically threatened children often become moralizing fetishes for environmental government. Whereas Edelman's analysis in *No Future* frames dystopic fictions of declining northern fertility—most notably, P. D. James's novel *Children of Men*—as fascistic signs of a compulsory reproduction, such narratives may also emerge as symptoms of contradictions in the geographic logics of production. Queer publics fall on all sides of these contradictions, particularly those of race, nation, and class, and many homosexual and trans subjects are increasingly rendered disposable to the orders of capital even as a privileged few attain benefits of marriage, adoption, and employment inclusion. Edelman's critique of reproductive futurism thus might reflect an atmosphere of climate-driven fears of imperial decline and shrinking capacities to reproduce extant divisions of labor and life. What if many of those populations who do not, will not, or cannot sexually reproduce are in effect doing what growing swaths of humanity are doing: exercising a phantasmic "choice" to refuse reproduction against an increasingly precarious world of unemployment, toxicity, and violence? Put simply, the sovereign choice to refuse reproduction may be redundant from the viewpoint of a late-carbon liberalism unwilling to distribute any more social goods and unable to guarantee life support. From here we can understand that there are constraints to ecological metaphors of the human as a universal waste-defined parasite; the human remains a divided biopolitical assemblage connecting multiple species into unequal flows of energy and labor.

Intimate Atmospheres

If the crossings of the mosquito and the settler in an era of carbon amplification draw on the xenophobic conception of the parasite to garner affective force, Serres alternatively imagines parasitism as a "cascade"—as multiple extractions that draw in a series of species, each feeding from a predecessor until the chain collapses.[50] Parasitism confounds sovereign logics, including the logic of eradication, because the confrontation between host and parasite is always interrupted from some environmental noise that transforms the system. This cascade conception of parasitism undercuts the moral rendering of parasite as invader or as an uncontained body. The host must eat with the parasite while being eaten; the host is, in retrospect, revealed as its own parasite.

One way to add resolution to this cascade is to ask, along with Sara Ahmed, "what does it mean to be oriented" as our bodies find shape and perspective in changing atmospheres?[51] Bruno Latour puts it slightly differently, thinking through the airy constitution of subjects through olfaction (smell) as a process of *articulation* that attunes a subject to the inhaled textures of difference.[52] Such approaches suggest limits to anthropomorphic vision. As Chen teaches through discussions of the queering of "animacy hierarchies," or the normative distinctions humans draw in language between different species of life and matter, the planet and its geophysical processes are less inert, less dead or inanimate, than we often think.[53] In ever more precarious intimacy with the shrinking number of living species, we inhabit a queer atmosphere in which the ether of the everyday is marked by senses of transformation and crisis.[54]

In *A Foray into the Worlds of Humans and Animals*, Jakob von Uexküll builds on Friedrich Nietzsche's curious claim that as humans inflate their place in "nature," so would mosquitoes, who share "the same self-importance."[55] Anticipating logics that script humans and mosquitoes as sovereign enemies, Uexküll explains how species assemble narcissistic forms of vision. A phenomenal lifeworld, or *Umwelt*, is not universal but a product of interactions between environment, embodied sensory capacities, and "perception marks" or desired objects that orient subjects in time and space.[56] Despite its avowed goal of provincializing the human who takes its own vision as universal, Uexküll's "lifeworld" shares with Ahmed's "orientation" an ocular bias. Ahmed presents orientation as having "bearings," of "knowing what to do to get to this place or that"; from here, Ahmed deploys a metaphor of tripping to describe queer moments.[57] For Uexküll, perception marks attract bodies to environments, establishing normative paths of bodily mobility. This allows the sorting of lifeworlds based on dominant hierarchies of species, race, and dis/ability. *Umwelten* appear open at first but proceed toward vanishing horizons limited by privileged body capacities. Dogs, for example, remain limited in their abilities to develop new perceptual "tones." Describing the domesticated dog, Uexküll argues that household objects such as a dining table and plates are visible, but fail to divine their use value. Oddly, Uexküll uses the same rationale to explain the failure of a "Negro" from the "African interior" to understand the use of a ladder. While the "human" in Uexküll's formulations apparently remains universal, his images of spatial attunements lays the groundwork for domesticating a racialized, able-bodied bourgeois domesticity as the privileged lifeworld of humanity.

If, contra Uexküll, we conceive of lifeworlds as relatively open, crossing species, it may be possible to rethink atmospheric intimacies in a world of carbon amplification. A mosquito bite would appear at first glance to be a momentary blip in what J. Jack Halberstam describes as reproductive family time, the temporality organized around the long slog from childhood to adulthood and death marked by bourgeois rituals of ownership, marriage, and reproduction. Conversely, a queer interspecies time, consisting of "strange temporalities, imaginative life practices, and eccentric economic practices" might be able to think a human and a mosquito entangled in a momentarily shared *Umwelt*, and thus to understand how mosquitoes and humans that both seem to derive carbon privileges—that appear as parasites—are often subjected to subtle precarities.[58]

Mosquitoes offer unique models of sensation and tracking, a point not lost on the US Department of Defense, which funds a large portion of academic entomological research against a specter of decentralized terrorism. Entomologists studying mosquito behavior and sensation find themselves in dual-use projects that simultaneously contribute to climate and bioweapons research. This is the outgrowth of a Cold War dream that the US imperial security apparatus could develop detection devices for airborne chemical and biological agents against the proliferation of "asymmetrical" weapons of the pestilent, swarming terrorist. Some of the recent defining research on the behaviors of flying insects—including John Murlis's work on how insects track chemical plumes, John Carlson and Alison Carey's work on mosquito olfaction, and the work of other scientists on mosquitoes' relationships to atmospheric carbon dioxide—nonetheless paints a radically different picture of how humans and mosquitoes entangle in a warming world.[59] These entanglements decompose bodies and think against linear tropes of connection.

For example, the species of mosquitoes in these studies do not encounter humans as fully formed objects, as one of Uexküll's *Umwelt* illustrations or the colonial concept of anthropophilia might suggest. They pursue not the unrequited lover that is the human but the smell of carbon plumes, lactic acid, and other waste traces of bodies that signal proximity to edible blood. Bodies, like planets, have atmospheres. Mosquitoes have much higher olfactory resolutions than humans, allowing them to precisely locate large mammals at a distance, yet reducing this process to a sense of "smell" risks missing the complex work of antennae that gauge direction, perceptual tone, and turbulence of trace plumes. Having developed circuitous forms of navigation to help distinguish effects of gravity and turbulence on gaseous environs, mosquitoes read and navigate atmosphere in ways that assemble the human and other potential feeding animals not as bodies but as specters, expanding environments of liquid and gaseous traces. Orienting across these fluid orbits, mosquitoes opportunistically find protein meals in the human as many other potential feeding species disappear, and as humans and other animals contribute to the expanding carbon noise and humidity of a warming atmosphere, which might disrupt mosquito tracking at those points at which emissions collide with bodies. Imperceptibly engaging in a messy atmospheric dance of attractions and redirections, humans and mosquitoes collaborate in a queer reproductive choreography. A queer theory of the inhuman might thus view the mosquito not as an anthropophilic parasite in need of quarantine or eradication, or as a military model for "integrated pest management" against figures of terror, but as lateral spawn of the assemblage of carbon, water, virus, insect, and human within emerging capital-driven ecological transitions.

Epilogue: Xenogenesis

For Ahmed, "it is important that we do not idealize queer worlds or simply locate them in an alternative space. . . . It is because this world is already in place that queer moments, where things come out of line, are fleeting. Our response need not be to search for permanence but to listen for the sound of the 'what' that fleets."[60] We might read Ahmed's statement doubly as a caution against the liberal ruse of sovereign freedom and the exoticizing tendency of a queer outside, including an animal outside. The point about the mosquito for queer theories of negation is not simply "look—we reproduce with animals!" Minor atmospheric intimacies open out into bigger scales that laterally determine how the reproduction of some bodies will affect planetary form, including through processes of climate change and disease that threaten mass premature death. Methodologies that take seriously interspecies entanglement are a political starting point rather than an ethical end; climate change is a series of small reproductive processes rather than a singular force. We experience a loss in the resolution of the material and symbolic logics of reproduction when we grasp large systemic flows through moralizing figures like the parasite, which affectively support fascistic figures of power like the Child. For these reasons, thinking interspecies helps demonstrate the purchase of the queer on the everyday. One example exists in a nascent cross-border undocumented youth movement, which has appropriated the monarch butterfly to explode the association of migration with parasitism. (Notably, like migrant farmworkers, the monarch is threatened by warming temperatures and ecocidal pesticide use.)[61]

More speculatively, Octavia Butler's novel *Dawn* takes the trope of a toxic fertility crisis to imagine forms of interspecies sex that brutally, yet pleasurably, incorporate humanity into an interspecies future.[62] Conjoining affect, communication, pleasure, reproduction, and healing into a single modality of tentacular intercourse, this wild vision of interspecies sex disturbs the individuated sexual subject through xenogenesis, a reproductive form that moves laterally away from the confines of speciated form. Such a vision asserts that reproduction is at once a negation and transition, and that the living incorporate extinct lives that could have been. At the heart of the body and the future lies the corpse.[63]

Notes

Thanks to Renisa Mawani, Mel Chen, Dana Luciano, and two referees at *GLQ* for feedback on this essay. Special thanks to Aaron Beyerlin, a friend and entomologist in Carrboro, North Carolina. After unexpected encounters with tiger mosquitoes behind my rental in Chapel Hill inspired me to write this essay, Aaron helped me understand some of the contemporary research on the sensory worlds and behaviors of flying insects.

1.   Leo Bersani, *Is the Rectum a Grave and Other Essays* (Chicago: University of Chicago Press, 2010), 3–4, 6.

2.   Bersani, *Is the Rectum a Grave*, 29–30.

3.   For the conference debate on Edelman's *No Future: Queer Theory and the Death Drive*, see Robert L. Caserio, Tim Dean, Lee Edelman, Judith Halberstam, and José Esteban Muñoz, "The Antisocial Thesis in Queer Theory," *PMLA* 121, no. 3 (2006): 819–28.

4.   Bersani, *Is the Rectum a Grave*, 11–12, 30.

5.   Frantz Fanon, *The Wretched of the Earth*, trans. Richard Philcox (New York: Grove, 2004), 4, 6–7, 182. Use of the pesticide DDT, according to Fanon, is comparable to the Christian civilizing mission (7).

6.   See Chandan Reddy, *Freedom with Violence: Race, Sexuality, and the US State* (Durham, NC: Duke University Press, 2011).

7. Lauren Berlant, *Cruel Optimism* (Durham, NC: Duke University Press, 2011), e-book location 234.

8. Berlant, *Cruel Optimism*, e-book location 265.

9. Jasbir Puar dubs this "bio-necro collaboration." See Puar, *Terrorist Assemblages: Homonationalism in Queer Times* (Durham, NC: Duke University Press, 2009), 33–35.

10. Vinay Gidwani and Rajyashree N. Reddy, "The Afterlives of 'Waste': Notes from India for a Minor History of Capitalist Surplus," *Antipode* 43, no. 5 (2011): 1625–58.

11. On the relation of the reproduction of bodies and systems, see Andil Gosine, "Dying Planet, Deadly People: 'Race'-Sex Anxieties and Alternative Globalizations," *Social Justice* 32, no. 4 (2005): 69–86; Greta Gaard, "Reproductive Technology or Reproductive Justice?," *Ethics and the Environment* 15, no. 2 (2010): 103–30; Noël Sturgeon, "Penguin Family Values: The Nature of Planetary Environmental Reproductive Justice," in *Queer Ecologies: Sex, Nature, Politics, Desire*, ed. Catriona Mortimer-Sandilands and Bruce Erickson (Bloomington: Indiana University Press, 2010), 102–33; Michael McIntyre and Heidi J. Nast, "Bio(necro)polis: Marx, Surplus Populations, and the Spatial Dialectics of Reproduction and 'Race,'" *Antipode* 43, no. 5 (2011): 1465–88; Nicole Seymour, *Strange Natures: Futurity, Empathy, and the Queer Ecological Imagination* (Urbana: University of Illinois Press, 2013).

12. Donna Haraway, "Companion Species, Mis-Recognition, and Queer Worlding," foreword to *Queering the Non/Human*, ed. Naureen Giffney and Myra J. Hird (Aldershot, UK: Ashgate, 2008), xxviii.

13. Tim Dean, *Unlimited Intimacy: Reflections on the Subculture of Barebacking* (Chicago: University of Chicago Press, 2009). Dean's work should be read alongside cases in which individuals contract HIV to obtain municipal or state health benefits. See Maral Noshad Sharifi, "The Men Who Want AIDS—and How It Improved Their Lives," *Out*, August 8, 2013, www.out.com/news-opinion/2013/08/02/men-who-want-aids-bronx-new-york.

14. Myra J. Hird, "Animal Trans," in Giffney and Hird, *Queering the Non/Human*, 227–48.

15. Karl Marx, *Capital*, vol. 1, trans. Ben Fowkes (New York: Vintage, 1976), 637. See also John Bellamy Foster, Brett Clark, and Richard York, *The Ecological Rift: Capitalism's War on Earth* (New York: Monthly Review Press, 2010).

16. A caricature of greed and failed heteromasculinity, Scrooge from *A Christmas Carol* is a key figure of the economic parasite. Edelman embraces him for his refusal of "the very warm-bloodedness of mammalian vitality" and for a sadistic subjection of his neighbor to his own deathly fate (*No Future: Queer Theory and the Death Drive* [Durham, NC: Duke University Press, 2004], 44).

17. I adapt here two tropes of the lateral. First, Lynn Margulis and Dorion Sagan critique the life-death binary through a description of the lateral exchange of DNA across

bacterial bodies. Second, Lauren Berlant responds to Achille Mbembe's concept of *necropolitics* by explaining that biopower distributes agency laterally across bodies rather than centered on a sovereign subject. See Margulis and Sagan, *What Is Life?* (Berkeley: University of California Press, 2000); and Berlant, "Slow Death (Sovereignty, Obesity, Lateral Agency)," *Critical Inquiry* 33 (2007): 754–80. In the context of Berlant's article on obesity, which is also a chapter in *Cruel Optimism*, "lateral agency" may be problematic given that it draws affective power from fears of fat bodies as laterally unconstrained. For a disability-critical take on "the obesity crisis," see Anna Mollow, "Sized Up," *Bitch* 59 (2013), bitchmagazine.org/article/sized-up-fat -feminist-queer-disability.

18. Valerie Rohy, *Anachronism and Its Others: Sexuality, Race, Temporality* (Albany: State University of New York Press, 2009), 18.

19. Chris D. Thomas et al., "Extinction Risk from Climate Change," *Nature*, January 8, 2004, 145–48. Edward O. Wilson offers a higher figure: 20 percent commitment to extinction by 2030 and 50 percent commitment by 2050. See Wilson, *The Future of Life* (New York: Random House, 2002).

20. I have in mind Dipesh Chakrabarty's concern about an environmental undermining of basic "boundary parameters of human existence"; contrary to Chakrabarty's argument for a totalizing species-thinking, I would insist that these parameters are already surpassed for some racialized southern agrarian populations. See Chakrabarty, "The Climate of History: Four Theses," *Critical Inquiry* 35, no. 2 (2009): 218.

21. Mel Y. Chen, *Animacies: Biopolitics, Racial Mattering, and Queer Affect* (Durham, NC: Duke University Press, 2012), 198–202.

22. Renisa Mawani, "Atmospheric Pressures: On Race and Affect," unpublished paper, 3.

23. Michael Ziser and Julie Sze, "Climate Change, Environmental Aesthetics, and Global Environmental Justice Cultural Studies," *Discourse* 29, nos. 2–3 (2007): 384–410.

24. See Alexandra Isfahani-Hammond, "Of She-Wolves and Mad Cows: Animality, Anthropophagy, and the State of Exception in Claudio Assis's *Amarelo Manga*," *Luso-Brazilian Review* 48, no. 2 (2011): 129–49.

25. Carla Freccero, "Carnivorous Virility; or, Becoming-Dog," *Social Text*, no. 106 (2011): 178.

26. Michel Serres, *The Parasite*, trans. Lawrence Shehr (Baltimore: Johns Hopkins University Press, 1982), 88.

27. Building on Nayan Shah, Tavia Nyong'o, with a "queer of color account of stranger intimacy," notes that ambient environs fail to stay contained, producing a temporal form of irony: "The background we think we are perceiving . . . is revealed at the conclusion to have another background" (Nyong'o, "Back to the Garden: Queer Ecology in Samuel Delany's *Heavenly Breakfast*," *American Literary History* 24, no. 4 [2012]: 749–50, 761; Shah, *Stranger Intimacy: Contesting Race, Sexuality, and Law in the North American West* [Berkeley: University of California Press, 2011]).

28. Rob Nixon, *Slow Violence and the Environmentalism of the Poor* (Cambridge, MA: Harvard University Press, 2009); Kate Rigby, "Writing in the Anthropocene," *Australian Humanities Review* 47 (2009): 175.

29. Berlant, *Cruel Optimism*, e-book location 36.

30. Fears of mosquito-borne disease complement other reporting on insects as beneficiaries of climate change. For more on how locusts devastate agriculture, beetles accelerate deforestation, and crickets and other insects are thriving and thus being targeted as food species, see Hugh Raffles, *Insectopedia* (New York: Random House, 2011), 207–40, 318–30; David Dunn and James P. Crutchfield, "Entomogenic Climate Change," Santa Fe Institute Working Paper, February 21, 2013; and Marcel Dicke and Arnold Van Huis, "The Six-Legged Meat of the Future," *Wall Street Journal*, February 19, 2001, online.wsj.com/article/SB10001424052748703293204576106072340 020728.html.

31. Umair Irfan and ClimateWire, "Climate Change May Make Insect-Borne Diseases Harder to Control," *Scientific American*, November 21, 2011, health.usnews.com /health-news/news/articles/2013/01/03/climate-change-may-bring-another-mosquito -borne-illness-to-us.

32. Mariette le Roux [Agence France-Presse], "Asian Tiger Mosquito Spreading Disease through Europe," *Cosmos: The Science of Everything*, August 13, 2012, www.cosmos magazine.com/news/asian-tiger-mosquito-spreading-disease-through-europe/.

33. Steve Connor, "Asian Mosquito 'Could Bring Tropical Diseases to Britain,'" independent .co.uk, April 25, 2012, www.independent.co.uk/environment/climate-change/asian -mosquito-could-bring-tropical-diseases-to-britain-7676063.html.

34. Kim Knowlton, Gina Solomon, and Miriam Rottkin-Ellman, *Fever Pitch*, NRDC Issue Paper (New York: National Resources Defense Council, 2009), 3.

35. Donald McNeil Jr., "A Virus May Make Mosquitoes Even Thirstier for Human Blood," *New York Times*, April 2, 2012, www.nytimes.com/2012/04/03/health/research /dengue-virus-may-make-mosquitoes-thirstier-for-human-blood.html?_r=0.

36. The association of the "Muslim-looking" with insects has been commonplace in post-911 US racial discourse. On September 14, 2011, a Sikh participant at a meeting to respond to hate crimes was told, "You Islamic mosquitoes should be killed" by another New Yorker. See Vijay Prashad, *Uncle Swami: South Asians in America Today* (New York: New Press, 2012), 5.

37. Jim Schutze, "Is Dallas Getting Smarter in the Fight against West Nile?," *Dallas Observer*, September 5, 2013, www.dallasobserver.com/2013-09-05/news/dallas-vs -west-nile/. I acknowledge that discussions of pesticide endocrine toxicity often engage transphobic fears of declining fertility and "chemically induced transgenderism."

38. Clapperton Mahvunga, "On Vermin Beings: Pestiferous Animals and Human Game," *Social Text*, no. 106 (2011): 151–76; Neel Ahuja, "Abu Zubaydah and the Caterpillar," *Social Text*, no. 106 (2011): 127–49.

39. Chen, *Animacies*, 190.

40. Lisa Lowe, "The Intimacies of Four Continents," in *Haunted By Empire*, ed. Ann Laura Stoler (Durham, NC: Duke University Press, 2008), 199–201.

41. Timothy Mitchell, *Rule of Experts: Egypt, Technopolitics, and Modernity* (Berkeley: University of California Press, 2002), 19–53.

42. Nancy Stepan, *Eradication: Ridding the World of Diseases Forever?* (Ithaca: Cornell University Press, 2011).

43. Michael Davidson, *Concerto for the Left Hand: Disability and the Defamiliar Body* (Ann Arbor: University of Michigan Press, 2009), 41–42.

44. William E. Rees, "Ecological Footprints and Appropriated Carrying Capacity: What Urban Economics Leaves Out," *Environment and Urbanisation* 4, no. 2 (1992): 121–30; Mathis Wackernagel, *Ecological Footprint and Appropriated Carrying Capacity: A Tool for Planning toward Sustainability* (PhD diss., University of British Columbia, 1994).

45. Gina Jack, "Your Carbon Footprint," *New York State Conservationist for Kids*, www.dec.ny.gov/education/54052.html.

46. Gaard, "Reproductive Technology or Reproductive Justice?"

47. Heidi J. Nast, "Capitalism, Anti-Natalism, and New Geographies of Reproduction" (keynote address at Critical Geographies Conference, University of North Carolina, Chapel Hill, November 2, 2012). See also McIntyre and Nast, "Bio(necro)polis."

48. Nast's argument that "anti-natalism" relies on a reproductive elsewhere does not require us to assume that queer publics alone catalyze these relations. I read it simply as an attempt to locate queer liberalism in relation to geographic contradictions of social and biological reproduction.

49. Melinda Cooper, *Life as Surplus* (Seattle: University of Washington Press, 2008).

50. Serres, *Parasite*, 3–14.

51. Sara Ahmed, "Orientations: Toward a Queer Phenomenology," *GLQ* 12, no. 4 (2006): 543.

52. Bruno Latour, "How to Talk about the Body? The Normative Dimension of Science Studies," *Body and Society* 10, nos. 2–3 (2004): 205–29.

53. Chen, *Animacies*, 2.

54. Bronislaw Szerzynski, "Reading and Writing the Weather: Climate Technics and the Moment of Responsibility," *Theory, Culture, and Society* 27, nos. 2–3 (2010): 9–30.

55. Friedrich Nietzsche, "On Truth and Lie in an Extra-Moral Sense," quoted in Dorion Sagan, foreword to *A Foray into the Worlds of Humans and Animals*, by Jakob von Uexküll, trans. Joseph D. O'Neill (Minneapolis: University of Minnesota Press, 2010), 1–2.

56. Uexküll, *Foray into the Worlds of Humans and Animals*, 53–63.

57. Ahmed, "Orientations," 543.

58. Judith Jack Halberstam, *In a Queer Time and Place* (New York: New York University Press, 2005), 1.

59. See especially John Murlis, "Odor Plumes and How Insects Use Them," *Annual Review of Entomology* 37 (1992): 505–32; and John Carlson and Alison Carey, "Scent of a Human," *Scientific American*, July 2011, 76–79; Teun Dekker, Martin Greer, and Ring T. Cardé, "Carbon Dioxide Instantly Sensitizes Female Yellow Fever Mosquitoes to Human Skin Odors," *Journal of Experimental Biology* 208 (2005): 2963–72; and Pablo H. Guerenstein and John G. Hildebrand, "Roles and Effects of Environmental Carbon in Insect Life," *Annual Review of Entomology* 53 (2008): 161–78.

60. Sara Ahmed, "Orientations: Toward a Queer Phenomenology," *GLQ* 12, no. 4 (2006): 565.

61. In her stunning image *Lupe and Sirena in Love*, Alma Lopez offers an early use of butterflies to imagine relations of migration and queer futurity. The Virgin of Guadalupe embraces a mermaid in front of the Los Angeles skyline, suspended not by the iconic cherub but instead by a migratory viceroy butterfly. For more on Lopez's critique of the association of insects, migration, femininity, and parasitism, see Lopez, "Mermaids, Butterflies, and Princesses," *Aztlán* 25, no. 1 (2000): 189–91.

62. Octavia Butler, *Dawn* (New York: Warner, 1988).

63. Sharon P. Holland, "Bill T. Jones, Tupac Shakur, and the (Queer) Art of Death," *Callaloo* 23, no. 1 (2000): 384–93.

TRANSMATERIALITIES

Trans*/Matter/Realities and Queer Political Imaginings

Karen Barad

*L*ightning is a reaching toward, an arcing dis/juncture, a striking response to charged yearnings.[1]

A dark sky. Deep darkness, without a glimmer of light to settle the eye. Out of the blue, tenuous electrical sketches scribbled with liquid light appear/ disappear faster than the human eye can detect. Flashes of potential, hints of possible lines of connection alight now and again. Desire builds, as the air crackles with anticipation. Lightning bolts are born of such charged yearnings. Branching expressions of prolonged longing, barely visible filamentary gestures, disjointed tentative luminous doodlings—each faint excitation of this desiring field is a contingent and suggestive inkling of the light show yet to come. No continuous path from sky to ground can satisfy its wild imaginings, its insistence on experimenting with different possible ways to connect, playing at all matter of errant wanderings in a virtual exploration of diverse forms of coupling and dis/connected alliance. Against a dark sky it is possible to catch glimmers of the wild energetics of indeterminacies in action.

Like lightning, this article is an exploration of charged yearnings and the sparking of new imaginaries. It is an experimental article about matter's experimental nature—its propensity to test out every un/imaginable path, every im/possibility. Matter is promiscuous and inventive in its agential wanderings: one might even dare say, imaginative. Imaginings, at least in the scientific imagination, are clearly material. Like lightning, they entail a process involving electrical potential buildup and flows of charged particles: neurons transmitting electrochemical signals across synaptic gaps and through ion channels that spark awareness in our

GLQ 21:2–3
DOI 10.1215/10642684-2843239
© 2015 by Duke University Press

brains. This is not to suggest that imagination is merely an individual subjective experience, nor a unique capacity of the human mind. Nor is it to rely soley on a scientific imaginary of what matter is, nor a materialism that would elide questions of labor. Nor is the point to merely insist on an accounting of the material conditions of possibility for imagining, though this is surely important. Rather, what is at issue here is the nature of matter and its agential capacities for imaginative, desiring, and affectively charged forms of bodily engagements. This article explores the materiality of imagining together with the imaginative capacities of materiality—although it does so less by linear argumentation than by the zigzagged dis/continuous musings of lightning. Electrical energy runs through disparate topics in what follows: lightning, primordial ooze, frogs, Frankenstein, trans rage, queer self-birthing, the quantum vacuum, virtual particles, queer touching, bioelectricity, Franken-frogs, monstrous re/generations.

This is an experimental piece with a political investment in creating new political imaginaries and new understandings of imagining in its materiality. Not imaginaries of some future or elsewhere to arrive at or be achieved as a political goal but, rather, imaginaries with material existences in the thick now of the present—imaginaries that are attuned to the condensations of past and future condensed into each moment; imaginaries that entail superpositions of many beings and times, multiple im/possibilities that coexist and are iteratively intra-actively reconfigured; imaginaries that are material explorations of the mutual indeterminacies of being and time.[2]

Electrifying Origins/Flashes of Things to Come

"During this short voyage I saw the lightning playing on the summit
of Mont Blanc in the most beautiful figures."
—Mary Shelley, *Frankenstein*

Lightning is an energizing play of a desiring field. Its tortuous path is an enlivening exploration of possible connections. Not a trail from the heavens to the ground but an electrifying yearning for connection that precedes this and that, here and there, now and then.[3]

Lightning is a striking phenomenon. It jolts our memories, flashing images on the retina of our mind's eye. Lightning arouses a sense of the primordial, enlivening questions of origin and materialization. It conjures haunting cultural images of the summoning of life through its energizing effects, perhaps most memorable in the classic films *Der Golem* (1920) and *Frankenstein* (1931). And it brings to mind credible (if not uncontroversial) scientific explanations of the electrifying origins of life: nature's fury shocking primordial ooze to life, an energizing jump start. Lightning, it seems, has always danced on the razor's edge between science and imagination.

Working with his mentor, the Nobel laureate Harold Urey, in 1953, the chemist Stanley Miller began a series of experiments that would lend support to Alexander Oparin and J. S. B. Haldane's hypothesis that primitive conditions on earth would be favorable for the production of organic molecules (the basis for the evolution of life) out of inorganic ones.[4] Miller used a sparking device to mimic lightning, a crucial ingredient in this genesis story. Filling a flask with water, methane, ammonia, and hydrogen, Miller sent electrical currents through the mixture. Analyzing the resulting soup of chemicals, he found the evidence that he was looking for: "a brown broth rich in amino acids, the building blocks of proteins."[5] "It was as if they were waiting to be bidden into existence. Suddenly the origin of life looked easy."[6]

Marking the beginning of experimental research into the origins of life, the Miller-Urey experiment did not seal the deal, but it was powerfully evocative of what might (yet) have been. The theory of the electrical origins of life—inorganic matter shocked into life's organic building blocks by an electrifying energy (whose own animacy seems to belie the alleged lifelessness of so-called inanimate matter)—is a controversial piece of science that created a fair amount of heat during Miller's lifetime. But no matter how many times skeptics claim to have put it to rest, it continues to be revived.

Miller's latest experiment was completed in 2008. He was dead by then. The experiment had begun fifty-five years earlier. Miller's intellectual offspring discovered, after his death, that he had not analyzed all his data. Opening the well-marked vials that lay dormant for decades, the researchers performed the analysis. They were shocked and delighted to be able to draw a significantly more compelling result from a once-dead experiment that would breathe new life into the theory: Miller's data revealed not five but twenty-three amino acids!

Characterizing Miller's experimental apparatus as a "Frankensteinesque contraption of glass bulbs," *Scientific American* completes the electrical circuit of cultural associations.[7]

Shocking brute matter to life. What makes us think that matter is lifeless to begin with?

Lightning mucks with origins. Lightning is a lively play of in/determinacy, troubling matters of self and other, past and future, life and death. It electrifies our imaginations and our bodies. If lightning enlivens the boundary between life and death, if it exists on the razor's edge between animate and inanimate, does it not seem to dip sometimes here and sometimes there on either side of the divide?

It was in witnessing lightning's enormous power that Victor Frankenstein took upon himself the mantle of science.

> When I was about fifteen years old, . . . we witnessed a most violent and terrible thunderstorm. . . . As I stood at the door, on a sudden I beheld a stream of fire issue from an old and beautiful oak which stood about twenty yards from our house; and so soon as the dazzling light vanished, the oak had disappeared, and nothing remained but a blasted stump. . . .
>
> Before this I was not unacquainted with the more obvious laws of electricity. On this occasion a man of great research in natural philosophy was with us, and excited by this catastrophe, he entered on the explanation of a theory which he had formed on the subject of electricity and galvanism, which was at once new and astonishing to me.[8]

And thus Victor Frankenstein was converted to galvanism.

Galvanism inspired both Mary Shelley and her famed protagonist. Shelley was fascinated by the experiments of her contemporary, Luigi Galvani, an eighteenth-century physician, anatomist, and physiologist who, while preparing dinner on his balcony one stormy night—the atmosphere crackling with electrical buildup—noticed something uncanny that would change the course of his scientific studies. As he touched the frog legs—strung out on a line before him—with a pair of scissors, they twitched. Thereafter, he took it upon himself to study in a systematic fashion the application of electricity—the "spark of life," as Shelley referred to it—to frog legs and other animal parts. Galvani concluded that electricity was an innate force of life, that an "animal electricity" pervaded living organisms. As Jessica Johnson writes, "Galvani proved not only that recently-dead muscle tissue can respond to external electrical stimuli, but that muscle and nerve cells possess an intrinsic electrical force responsible for muscle contractions and nerve conduction in living organisms."[9]

It was a short leap from there to consider that if dead frog legs could be animated by electricity—the secret of life—the harnessing of nature's fury might be used to resurrect the dead or even give life to a creature made of human parts gathered from an array of different corpses. In the introduction to *Frankenstein*, Shelly writes, "Perhaps a corpse would be re-animated; galvanism had given token of such things: perhaps the component parts of a creature might be manufactured, brought together, and endured with vital warmth." Galvani's experiments sparked the interest of other scientists, and soon severed limbs and an assortment of dissected and expired animals and animal parts were animated by electrical impulses. Perhaps most (in)famously, his nephew, the physicist Giovanni Aldini, stimulated animal parts like those of cows, dogs, horses, and sheep.

Electrified by galvanism, Aldini was ready to shock nearly anything, alive or dead, that he could get his hands on. He was among the first to use electroshock treatment on those deemed mentally ill, and reported complete electrical cures. Not satisfied with his experiments on animal corpses, he performed his shock treatments on executed criminals. He recorded the findings of his 1803 experiment on the executed body of George Foster:

> The jaw began to quiver, the adjoining muscles were horribly contorted, and the left eye actually opened. . . . The action even of those muscles furthest distant from the points of contact with the arc was so much increased as almost to give an appearance of re-animation. . . . vitality might, perhaps, have been restored, if many circumstances had not rendered it impossible.[10]

It is not difficult to complete the circuit of sparking disjuncture between Aldini's ghoulish experiments and those of Dr. Frankenstein.

Even while Shelley labored to write *Frankenstein*, the scientific atmosphere crackled with controversy over the nature of the relationship between life and electricity.

Bioelectricity was in the air, sparking the imagination of nineteenth-century scientists. As Cynthia Graber reports, "Many efforts, including using electricity to treat hysteria and melancholia, amounted to little more than quackery."[11] But some explorations gained scientific credibility and established the basis for current medical practices. For example, a textbook published in 1816 suggests the use of electric shock to revive a stopped heart.[12]

Monstrous Selves, Transgender Empowerment, Transgender Rage

The monster always represents the disruption of categories, the
destruction of boundaries, and the presence of impurities and so
we need monsters and we need to recognize and celebrate our
own monstrosities.
—Judith Halberstam, *Skin Shows*

Electricity can arrest the heart. It is also capable of bringing a heart back from a state of lifelessness. It can animate its rhythmic drumbeat—the periodic pulsing of life's electrical song—in once arrested or arrhythmic hearts. Monstrosity, like electrical jolts, cuts both ways. It can serve to demonize, dehumanize, and demoralize. It can also be a source of political agency. It can empower and radicalize.

In an unforgettable, powerful, and empowering performative piece, "My Words to Victor Frankenstein above the Village of Chamounix," Susan Stryker embraces the would-be epithet of monstrosity, harnessing its energy and power to transform despair and suffering into empowering rage, self-affirmation, theoretical inventiveness, political action, and the energizing vitality of materiality in its animating possibilities.[13] Remarking on her affinity with Frankenstein's monster, she writes:

> The transsexual body is an unnatural body. It is the product of medical science. It is a technological construction. It is flesh torn apart and sewn together again in a shape other than that in which it was born. In these circumstances, I find a deep affinity between myself as a transsexual woman and the monster in Mary Shelley's *Frankenstein*. Like the monster, I am too often perceived as less than fully human due to the means of my embodiment; like the monster's as well, my exclusion from human community fuels a deep and abiding rage in me that I, like the monster, direct against the conditions in which I must struggle to exist.[14]

Making political and personal alliance with Frankenstein's monster, she intervenes in naturalizing discourses about the nature of nature, an emphasis that resonates with themes in this essay.

> Hearken unto me, fellow creatures. I who have dwelt in a form unmatched with my desire, I whose flesh has become an assemblage of incongruous anatomical parts, I who achieve the similitude of a natural body only through an unnatural process, I offer you this warning: the Nature you bedevil me with is a lie. Do not trust it to protect you from what I represent, for it is a fabrication that cloaks the groundlessness of the privilege you seek to maintain for yourself at my expense. You are as constructed as me; the same anarchic womb has birthed us both. I call upon you to investigate your nature as I have been compelled to confront mine.[15]

This passage speaks with razor-sharp directedness to those who would position their own bodies as natural against the monstrosity of trans embodiment: examine your own nature, stretch your own body out on the examining table, do the work that needs to be done on yourself (with all this charge's intended multiple meanings), and discover the seams and sutures that make up the matter of your own body. Materiality in its entangled psychic and physical manifestations is always already a patchwork, a suturing of disparate parts.[16]

Toward the end of the piece, Stryker embraces the fecundity of the "chaos and blackness"—the "anarchic womb"—as the matrix for generative nonheterosexual-reproductive birthing, "for we have done the hard work of constituting ourselves on our own terms, against the natural order. Though we forgo the privilege of naturalness, we are not deterred, for we ally ourselves instead with the chaos and blackness from which Nature itself spills forth."[17] This is a reference to the entangled birthing story that Stryker tells. She begins by sharing with the reader the joys and the pain of being in intimate connection with her partner while she was giving birth. This is a birth born of queer kinship relations: not the product of a heteronormative coupling, but a phenomenon rich with multiple entanglements, including a markedly nonnormative delivery room support team. Stryker is attuned to her partner during the birth, bodily and emotionally, yet she is also painfully aware that the physicality of birthing a being from her own womb is denied to her by the specificity of her constructed enfleshment. She describes the raw pain of being part of a process that she could not bring to fruition in the bodily way that she yearns for. This gives way to a painful birthing of transgender rage that becomes, in turn, the womb through which she rebirths herself. This radically queer configuring of spacetimemattering constitutes an uncanny topological dynamic that arrests straight tales of birthing and kinship, and gives birth to new modes of generativity, including but not limited to the generativity of a self-birthed womb. It is nearly impossible not to feel the tug of other entanglements in this queer origin story. In particular, this story reverberates with a queer reading of the Genesis moment when the earth emerges out of the chaos and the void, from a chaotic nothingness, an electrifying atmosphere silently crackling with thunderous possibilities. Nature emerges from a self-birthed womb fashioned out of a raging nothingness. A queer origin, an originary queerness, an originary birthing that is always already a rebirthing. Nature is birthed out of chaos and void, *tohu v'vohu*, an echo, a diffracted/differentiating/différancing murmuring, an originary repetition without sameness, regeneration out of a fecund nothingness.

Quantum Field Theory: Nothingness as the Scene of Wild Activities

Physicists . . . took the vacuum as something substantial . . . the
scene of wild activities.
—Cao and Schweber

Nothingness. The void. An absence of matter. The blank page. Utter silence. No
thing, no thought, no awareness. Complete ontological insensibility.[18]

From the viewpoint of classical physics, the vacuum is complete emptiness:
it has no matter and no energy. But the quantum principle of ontological indeterminacy calls the existence of such a zero-energy, zero-matter state into question or,
rather, makes it into a question with no decidable answer. Not a settled matter or,
rather, no matter. And if the energy of the vacuum is not determinately zero, it is
not determinately empty. In fact, this indeterminacy not only is responsible for the
void not being nothing (while not being something) but may in fact be the source of
all that is, a womb that births existence.

Birth and death, it turns out, are not the sole prerogative of the animate
world; so-called inanimate beings also have finite lives. "Particles can be born
and particles can die," explains one physicist. In fact, "it is a matter of birth, life,
and death that requires the development of a new subject in physics, that of quantum field theory. . . . Quantum field theory is a response to the ephemeral nature
of life."[19]

Quantum field theory (QFT) was invented in the 1920s, shortly after the
development of (nonrelativistic single-particle) quantum mechanics. It is a theory
that combines insights from the classical theory of electromagnetic fields (mid-
nineteenth century), special relativity (1905), and quantum mechanics (1920s).
QFT takes us to a deeper level of understanding of quantum physics.[20] It has
important things to say about the nature of matter and nothingness and the inde-
terminateness of their alleged distinguishability and separability. QFT is a call, an
alluring murmur of the insensible within the sensible to radically work the nature
of being and time. According to QFT, the vacuum cannot be determinately nothing because the indeterminacy principle allows for fluctuations *of* the quantum
vacuum. How can we understand "vacuum fluctuations"? First, it is necessary to
know a few things about what physicists mean by the notion of a *field*.

A field in physics is something that has a physical quantity associated with
every point in space-time. Or you can think of it as a pattern of energy distributed
across space and time. It may be difficult to grasp this notion without specific
examples. Consider a bar magnet with iron filings sprinkled around it. The filings
will quickly line up in accordance with the strength and direction of the magnetic

field at every point. Or consider an electric field. The electric field is a desiring field born of charged yearnings.[21] When it comes to mutual attraction the rule is opposites (i.e., opposite charges) attract. The notion of a field is a way to express the desires of each entity for the other. The attraction between a proton (a positively charged particle) and an electron (a particle with negative charge) can be expressed in terms of fields as follows: the proton emanates an electric field; the field travels outward in all directions at the speed of light. When the electric field of the proton reaches the electron, it feels the proton's desire pulling it toward it. Likewise, the electron sends out its own field, which is felt by the proton. Sitting in each other's fields, they feel a mutual tug in each other's direction.[22]

Now we add quantum physics and special relativity to classical field theory. Quantum physics enters into QFT most prominently in terms of the discretization of physical observables (quantizing or making discrete physical quantities that classical physics assumed were continuous), and the play of indeterminacy in energy and time. And special relativity speaks to matter's impermanence: matter can be converted into energy and vice versa. Putting these ideas together, we get the following. Fields are patterns of energy. When fields are quantized, the energy is quantized. But energy and matter are equivalent. And so an essential feature of QFT is that there is a correspondence between fields (energy) and particles (matter). The quantum of the electromagnetic field is a photon—a quantum of light. And electrons are understood to be the quanta of an electron field. (There are many other kinds of quanta. For example, the quantum of the gravitational field is a graviton.)

Now let us return to our question: what is a vacuum fluctuation? When it comes to the quantum vacuum, as with all quantum phenomena, ontological indeterminacy is at the heart of (the) matter . . . and no matter. Indeed, it is impossible to pin down a state of no matter or even of matter, for that matter. The crux of this strange non/state of affairs is the so-called energy-time indeterminacy principle, but because energy and matter are equivalent we will sometimes call it the "being-time" or "time-being" indeterminacy principle. The point, for our purposes, is that an indeterminacy in the energy of the vacuum translates into an indeterminacy in the number of particles associated with the vacuum, which means the vacuum is not (determinately) empty, nor is it (determinately) not empty. These particles that correspond to the quantum fluctuation of the vacuum, that are and are not there as a result of the time-being indeterminacy relation, are called "virtual particles." *Virtual particles are quantized indeterminacies-in-action.* Virtual particles are not present (and not absent), but they are material. In fact, *most of what matter is, is virtual.* Virtual particles do not traffic in a metaphysics of presence. They do not exist in space and time. They are ghostly non/existences that teeter on the edge of the infinitely fine blade between being and nonbeing. Virtuality is admittedly difficult to grasp. Indeed, this is its very nature.

Virtual particles are not in the void but *of* the void. They are on the razor's edge of non/being. The void is a lively tension, a desiring orientation toward being/ becoming. The void is flush with yearning, bursting with innumerable imaginings of what might yet (have) be(en). Vacuum fluctuations are virtual deviations/ variations from the classical zero-energy state of the void. That is, *virtuality is the material wanderings/wonderings of nothingness; virtuality is the ongoing thought experiment the world performs with itself.* Indeed, quantum physics tells us that *the void is an endless exploration of all possible couplings of virtual particles, a "scene of wild activities."*

The quantum vacuum is more like an ongoing questioning of the nature of emptiness than anything like a lack. The ongoing questioning of itself (and *itself* and *it* and *self*) is what generates, or rather *is*, the structure of nothingness. The vacuum is no doubt doing its own experiments with non/being. In/determinacy is not the state of a thing but an unending dynamism.

Pace Democritus, particles do not take their place in the void; rather, they are constitutively inseparable from it. And the void is not vacuous. It is a living, breathing indeterminacy of non/being. The vacuum is an extravagant inexhaustible exploration of virtuality, where virtual particles are having a field day performing experiments in being and time.[23]

Electric Interlude: Virtual Touch

Touch, for a physicist, is but an electromagnetic interaction.[24]

A common explanation for the physics of touching is that one thing it does not involve is . . . well, touching. That is, there is no actual contact involved. You may think that you are touching a coffee mug when you are about to raise it to your mouth, but your hand is not actually touching the mug. Sure, you can feel the smooth surface of the mug's exterior right where your fingers come into contact with it (or seem to), but what you are actually sensing, physicists tell us, is the electromagnetic repulsion between the electrons of the atoms that make up your fingers and those that make up the mug. (Electrons are tiny negatively charged particles that surround the nuclei of atoms, and having the same charges they repel one another, much like powerful little magnets. As you decrease the distance between them—say, between the electrons that constitute the outer edges of the atoms of your fingers and those of the mug—the repulsive force increases.) Try as you might, you cannot bring two electrons into direct contact with each other.

The reason that the desk feels solid, or the cat's coat feels soft, or we can (even) hold coffee cups and one another's hands, is an effect of electromagnetic repulsion. All we really ever feel is the electromagnetic field, not the other whose touch we seek. Atoms are mostly empty space, and electrons, which lie at the farthest reaches of an atom, hinting at its perimeter, cannot bear direct contact. Electromagnetic repulsion: negatively charged particles communicating at a distance push each other away. That is the tale physics usually tells about touching. Repulsion at the core of attraction. See how far that story gets you with lovers. No wonder the Romantic poets had had enough.

Lightning: Responses to a Desiring Field

Lightning is an energizing response to a highly charged field. The buildup to lightning electrifies the senses; the air crackles with desire.[25]

By some mechanism that scientists have yet to fully explain, a storm cloud becomes extremely electrically polarized—electrons are stripped from the atoms that they were once attached to and gather at the lower part of the cloud closest to the earth, leaving the cloud with an overall negative charge. In response, the electrons that make up atoms of the earth's surface burrow into the ground to get farther away from the buildup of negative charges at the near edge of the cloud, leaving the earth's surface with an overall positive charge. In this way a strong electric field is set up between earth and cloud, and the yearning will not be satisfied without the buildup being discharged. The desire to find a conductive path joining the two becomes all-consuming.

The first inklings of a path have a modest beginning, offering no indication of the lightning bolt to come. "It begins as a small spark inside the cloud five miles up. A spurt of electrons rushes outwards, travels a hundred meters then stops and pools for a few millionths of a second. Then the stream lurches off in a different direction, pools again, and again. Often the stream branches and splits. *This is not a lightning bolt yet*" (my emphasis).[26] These barely luminous first gestures are called stepped leaders. But the buildup of negative charges (electrons) in the lower portion of the cloud does not resolve itself by a direct channel of electrons making their way to the earth in this fashion. Instead, *the ground* responds next with an upward signal of its own. "When that step leader is within ten or a hundred meters of the ground, the ground is now *aware* of there being a big surplus" of charge, and "certain objects on the earth respond by launching little streamers up toward the stepped leader, weakly luminous plasma filaments, which are trying to connect with what's coming down." This is a sign that objects on the ground are attending to the cloud's seductive overtures. When it finally happens that one of the upward responses is met by a downward gesture, the result is explosive: a powerful discharge is effected in the form of a lightning bolt. But even after a connecting path has been playfully suggested, the discharge does not proceed in a continuous fashion: "The part of the channel nearest the ground will drain first, then successively higher parts, and finally the charge from the cloud itself. So the visible lightning bolt moves up from ground to cloud as the massive electric currents flow down."

An enlivening, and indeed lively, response to difference if ever there was one. The lightning expert Martin Uman explains this strangely animated inanimate relating in this way: "What is important to note . . . is that the usual stepped leader starts from the cloud without any 'knowledge' of what buildings or geography are present below. In fact, it is thought . . . that the stepped leader is 'unaware' of objects beneath it until it is some tens of yards from the eventual strike point. When 'awareness' occurs, a traveling spark is initiated from the point to be struck and propagates upward to meet the downward moving stepped leader, completing the path to ground."[27] What mechanism is at work in this communicative exchange between sky and ground when *awareness* lies at the crux of this strangely animated inanimate relating? And how does this exchange get ahead of itself, as it were?[28] What kind of queer communication is at work here? What are we to make of a communication that has neither sender nor recipient until transmission has already occurred? That is, what are we to make of the fact that the existence of sender and receiver follows from this nonlocal relating rather than preceding it? What strange causality is effected?

A lightning bolt is not a straightforward resolution of the buildup of a charge difference between the earth and a storm cloud: a lightning bolt does not simply proceed from storm cloud to the earth along a unidirectional (if somewhat erratic) path; rather, flirtations alight here and there and now and again as stepped leaders and positive streamers gesture toward possible forms of connection to come. The path that lightning takes not only is not predictable but does not make its way according to some continuous unidirectional path between sky and ground. Though far from microscopic in scale, it seems that we are witnessing a quantum form of communication—a process of iterative intra-activity.[29]

Back to Quantum Field Theory: A Touchy Subject

When it comes to quantum field theory, it is not difficult to find trouble—epistemological trouble, ontological trouble, a troubling of kinds, of identities, of the nature of touching and self-touching, of being and time, to name a few.[30] It is not so much that trouble is around every corner; according to quantum field theory, it inhabits us and we inhabit it, or rather, trouble inhabits everything and nothing—matter and the void.

How does quantum field theory understand the nature of matter? Let us start with the electron, one of the simplest particles—a point particle—a particle devoid of structure. Even the simplest bit of matter causes all kinds of difficulties for quantum field theory. For, as a result of time-being indeterminacy, the electron does not exist as an isolated particle but is always already inseparable from the wild activities of the vacuum. In other words, the electron is always (already) intra-acting with the virtual particles of the vacuum in all possible ways. For example, the electron will emit a virtual photon and then reabsorb it. This possibility is understood as the electron electromagnetically intra-acting with itself. Part of what an electron is, is its self-energy intra-action.[31] But the self-energy intra-action is not a process that happens in isolation either. All kinds of more involved things can and do occur in this frothy virtual soup of indeterminacy that we ironically think of as a state of pure emptiness. For example, in addition to the electron exchanging a virtual photon with itself (that is, touching itself), it is possible for that virtual photon to enjoy other intra-actions with *itself*: for example, the virtual photon can metamorphose/transition—change its very identity. It can transform into a virtual electron-positron pair, that subsequently annihilate each other and morph back into a single virtual photon before it is reabsorbed by the electron. (A positron is the electron's antiparticle—it has the same mass but the opposite charge and goes backward in time. Even the direction of time is indeterminate.) And so on. This "and so on" is shorthand for an infinite set of possibilities involving every possible kind of intra-action with every possible kind of virtual particle it can intra-act with. That is, there is a virtual exploration of every possibility. And this infinite set of possibilities, or infinite sum of histories, entails a particle touching itself, and the particle that transmits the touch transforming itself, and then that touching touching itself, and transforming, and touching other particles that make up the vacuum, and so on, ad infinitum. (Not everything is possible given a particular intra-action, but an infinite number of possibilities exist.) Every level of touch, then, is itself touched by all possible others. Particle self-intra-actions entail particle transitions from one kind to another in a radical undoing of kinds—queer/trans*formations.[32] Hence *self-touching is an encounter with the infinite alterity of the self. Matter is an enfolding, an involution, it cannot help touching itself, and in this self-touching it comes in contact with the infinite alterity that it is.* Polymorphous perversity raised to an infinite power: talk about a queer/trans* intimacy!

What is being called into question here is the very nature of the "self," and in terms of not just being but also time. That is, in an important sense, *the self is dispersed/diffracted through time and being.*

Commenting specifically on the electron's self-energy intra-action, the physicist Richard Feynman, who won a Nobel prize for his contributions to developing QFT, expressed *horror* at the electron's monstrous nature and its perverse ways of engaging with the world: "Instead of going directly from one point to another, the electron goes along for a while and suddenly emits a photon; then (horrors!) it absorbs its own photon. Perhaps there's something 'immoral' about that, but the electron does it!"[33] This self-energy/self-touching term has also been labeled a perversion of the theory because the calculation of the self-energy contribution is infinite, which is an unacceptable answer to any question about the nature of the electron (such as what is its mass or charge?). Apparently, touching oneself, or being touched by oneself—the ambiguity/undecidability/indeterminacy may itself be the key to the trouble—is not simply troubling but a *moral* violation, the very source of all the trouble.

The "problem" of self-touching, especially self-touching the other, is a perversity of quantum field theory that goes far deeper than we can touch on here. The gist of it is this: this perversity that is at the root of an unwanted infinity, that threatens the very possibility of calculability, gets "renormalized" (obviously— should we expect anything less?!). How does this happen? Physicists conjectured that there are two different kinds of infinities/perversions involved in this case: one that has to do with self-touching and another that has to do with nakedness. That is, in addition to the infinity related to self-touching, there is an infinity associated with the "bare" point particle, that is, with the metaphysical assumption we started with that there is only an electron—the "undressed," "bare" electron—and the void, each separate from the other. Renormalization is the systematic cancellation of infinities: an intervention based on the idea that the subtraction of (different size) infinities can be a finite quantity. Perversion eliminating perversion. The cancellation idea is this: the infinity of the "bare" point particle cancels the infinity associated with the "cloud" of virtual particles; in this way, the "bare" point particle is "dressed" by the vacuum contribution (that is, the cloud of virtual particles). The "dressed" electron—the electron in drag—that is, the physical electron, is thereby renormalized, that is, made "normal" (finite). (I am using technical language here!) Renormalization is the mathematical handling/taming of these infinities. That is, the infinities are "subtracted" from one another, yielding a finite answer. Mathematically speaking, this is a tour de force. Conceptually, it is a queer theorist's delight. It shows that all of matter, *matter in its "essence" (of course, that is precisely what is being troubled here), is a massive overlaying of per-versities: an infinity of infinities.*[34]

To summarize, quantum field theory radically deconstructs the ontology of classical physics. The starting point ontology of particles and the void—a foundational reductionist essentialism—is undone by quantum field theory. According to QFT, perversity and monstrosity lie at the core of being—or rather, it is threaded through it. All touching entails an infinite alterity, so that touching the other is touching all others, including the "self," and touching the "self" entails touching the stranger within. Even the smallest bits of matter are an unfathomable multitude. Each "individual" always already includes all possible intra-actions with "itself" through all possible virtual others, including those (and itself) that are noncontemporaneous with itself. *That is, every finite being is always already threaded through with an infinite alterity diffracted through being and time.* Indeterminacy is an un/doing of identity that unsettles the very foundations of non/being.

Electrons, for example, are inherently chimeras—cross-species cross-kind mixtures—made of virtual configurations/reconfigurings of disparate kinds of beings dispersed across space and time in an undoing of kind, being/becoming, absence/presence, here/there, now/then. So much for natural essence. The electron—a point particle without structure—is a patchwork of kinds sutured together in uncanny configurations. Trying out new appendages made of various particle-antiparticle pairs, producing and absorbing differences of every possible kind in a radical undoing of "kind" as essential difference: its identity is the undoing of identity. Its very nature is unnatural, not given, not fixed, but forever transitioning and transforming itself. Electrons (re)birth themselves in their engagement with all others, not as an act of self-birthing, but in an ongoing re-creating that is an un/doing of itself. Electrons are always already untimely. It is not that electrons sometimes engage in such perverse explorations: these experiments in intra-active trans*material performativity are what an electron is.[35]

Ontological indeterminacy, a radical openness, an infinity of possibilities, is at the core of mattering. How strange that indeterminacy, in its infinite openness, is the condition for the possibility of all structures in their dynamically reconfiguring in/stabilities. Matter in its iterative materialization is a dynamic play of in/determinacy. Matter is never a settled matter. It is always already radically open. Closure cannot be secured when the conditions of im/possibilities and lived indeterminacies are integral, not supplementary, to what matter is. *In an important sense, in a breathtakingly intimate sense, touching, sensing, is what matter does, or rather, what matter is: matter is condensations of responses, of response-ability.*

Each bit of matter is constituted in response-ability; each is constituted as responsible for the other, as being in touch with the other. *Matter is a matter of untimely and uncanny intimacy, condensations of being and times.*

The Body Electric: Regenerating What (Never) Was and Might Yet (Have) Be(en)

"It's alive!"[36] Galvanism is alive and well in Medford, Massachusetts, where the biologists Michael Levin and Dany Adams of Tufts University have taken up the mantle of Dr. Frankenstein, or if not that of the good doctor's, then surely that of famous frog electro-animator Luigi Galvani. Wedding galvanism to more mainstream contemporary biological endeavors like gene therapy, Levin and Adams have performed a series of experiments with electrifying results for understanding developmental and regenerative biological processes.[37]

Regeneration is a capacity shared by all living creatures, but not equally. Planarian flatworms can regenerate their entire bodies (including their brains) from a small bit of the original animal. Liver tissue regeneration is one of the few regenerative talents that humans have. Ecosystems can regenerate if they are not too badly damaged. Brittle stars, salamanders, lobsters, and other critters are famous for their ability to regenerate lost limbs. But something quite different is happening in the Tufts University lab, where regeneration has taken on uncanny new shapes. Let us take a tour through some of Levin and Adam's key laboratory experiments.

Like Galvani, Levin and Adams have a fondness for frogs. There are solid scientific reasons for choosing this favored organism. For example, the African clawed frog, *Xenopus laevis*, or *Xenopus* for short, an aquatic native of sub-Saharan Africa, holds the honor of being a model organism in developmental biology, cell biology, toxicology, and neuroscience because of its "relative evolutionary closeness" to humans and laboratory cooperativeness.[38] It does not hurt that the embryos are transparent and that they are prolific reproducers. *Xenopus* is not only evolutionarily close to humans, relatively speaking, it is directly entangled in human kinship relations. "It is an invasive species all over the world because it was used in human pregnancy tests in the 1940's. When more effective means of pregnancy tests were made available, many *X. laevis* were released all over the world."[39] Furthermore, "*Xenopus* oocytes are a leading system for studies of ion transport and channel physiology."[40] All in all, a mixture of human and *Xenopus* reproductive capacities led to its employment in developmental biology laboratories. Levin happened to conduct his doctoral studies in one such lab. *Xenopus*'s entanglement with heteronormative reproduction notwithstanding, Levin and Adams have found themselves entranced by its regenerative, rather than reproductive, capabilities.[41]

Much like the way that human children have the ability to grow back a severed fingertip until the age of seven, *Xenopus* tadpoles can regenerate their tails, provided these are lost during the first seven days of life. By day eight—right around the time the tadpole begins to metamorphose into a frog—it begins to lose that capacity, and at ten days the ability has gone completely. Growing back a tail is different than regrowing skin at the site of an injury. "A tail is a complex organ containing multiple cell types: muscle, peripheral nerves, spinal cord, notochord, skin, and vasculature."[42] In a breakthrough series of studies on the effects of electricity on regeneration, Levin and colleagues showed that it was possible to get tadpoles to regenerate their tails outside the specified time frame by manipulating the electric field around the missing tail.

What accounts for this success? In a world where molecular biology rules, it is unusual to find a scientist willing to align himself with the field of bioelectricity, with all its troubling and spotted past, littered with charges of charlatanism and quackery. But as much as Levin likes to fancy himself a scientific maverick, he has strategically hitched the old wagon of bioelectricity to the brand-new, shiny, high-powered machinery of molecular biology. The techniques of molecular biology are key to his exploration of bioelectrically controlled regeneration. Levin's approach is "to understand the genetic components that underlie bioelectrical events during development and regeneration."[43] Make no mistake: this is not an Aldini performance; this is galvanism with a contemporary face. One science writer explains it this way:

> In a paper that could help bring the study of bioelectricity into the mainstream of 21st century science, [Levin and colleagues] . . . identified a protein that serves as a natural source of regenerative electricity. By manipulating the protein, an ion transporter, they were able to induce frog tadpoles to regrow tails at a stage of development when such regrowth is typically not possible. . . .
>
> What had been missing from studies until now is an understanding of how electricity—the flow of charged particles—works at a molecular level to bring about regeneration.[44]

Levin and his colleagues have provided evidence that large-scale electrical patterning of bodily morphology plays a causal role in embryonic development and regeneration. This is surely not the conventional approach to follow in this age of genomics, where all causes are molecular and things are built from the bottom up. This bioelectrical approach is unique and producing some electrifying results. So while the majority of biologists focus on stem cells and other biochemical and genetic factors, the dynamic duo are intent on cracking the "bioelectric" code of the body. As Levin explains, "All cells, not just nerve cells, use bioelectrical signals to communicate pattern information to each other. . . . you can tweak those signals artificially to get them to do what you want them to do."[45]

Trying out their exciting understandings of the linkage between bioelectric fields and regeneration, researchers in Levin's lab took on the challenge of seeing if they could get body parts that are not normally capable of regeneration to regenerate by using the same techniques of molecularly producing electrical fields that would induce the appropriate regeneration. "Dr. Levin and his colleagues have been able to stimulate the regeneration of complete frog legs. Frog legs don't usually grow back (or regenerate) like salamander legs. But by providing appropriate electrical gradients at the frog's wound site, these researchers stimulated the growth of an entirely new limb."[46]

Regeneration is one thing, but what about stimulating the growth of limbs, organs, and other body parts that have never been? Manipulating the bioelectric fields by changing various ion channels, the researchers were able to use the bioelectric fields to monstrous effect, growing extra heads, limbs, and eyes. Four-headed planaria, six-legged frogs, two-tailed worms, and one bioelectrical mutation really caught the imagination of science reporters.

An article titled "'Franken-Tadpoles' See with Eyes on Their Backs" reports that "using genetic manipulation of membrane voltage in *Xenopus* (frog) embryos, biologists at Tufts University's School of Arts and Sciences were able to cause tadpoles to grow eyes outside of the head area."[47] Vaibhav P. Pai, a postdoc fellow working in their lab, explains, "This suggests that cells from anywhere in the body can be driven to form an eye."[48] Not only that, it turns out that some of these monstrous eyes can see![49]

This is rather dramatic evidence in support of epigenetics. Clearly, there is more at work biologically speaking than a genetic code: bioelectrical signaling evidently plays a significant role in the determination of bodily morphology. But perhaps the most striking finding was the result of a combination of serendipity and Adams's scientific instincts.

Adams had hooked up her research camera to a microscope to film the early stages of *Xenopus* tadpole development. Having achieved an image of remarkable clarity (which is particularly difficult when imaging tiny critters), Adams decided to leave the camera on overnight, for the heck of it, anticipating that the images

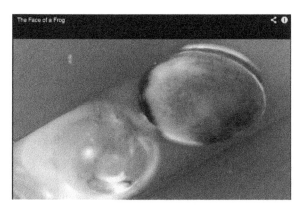

Figure 1. Still from *Electric Face*. Courtesy Dany Spencer Adams

would blur as the embryos moved. When she returned to her lab she did in fact find that the images were blurry, but she was able to get surprisingly clear images after computer processing. She developed a time-lapse video using a sequence of photographs, and the result was "jaw dropping." The video, she says, was "unlike anything I had ever seen. I was completely blown away."[50] (Fig. 1 is a still from the video. I strongly encourage the reader to stop reading and watch the video. It has to be seen to be fully appreciated. The image shows two frog embryos. The light flashes on the left embryo indicate the electric potential as it traces out a face to come—a face that does not yet exist but only exists in potential for a brief moment and then vanishes!)

"The images show an embryonic frog 'light show' in fast forward," Adams said. "When a frog embryo is just developing, *before it gets a face*, a pattern for that face lights up on the surface of the embryo. . . . We believe this is the first time such patterning has been reported for an entire structure, not just for a single organ. I would never have predicted anything like it" (my emphasis).

The face-to-come of the embryo flashes in electrical patterns across the surface of the embryo.[51] It is important to take in the fact that the "electric face" appears and disappears *before* any actual features develop, that is, prior to cell differentiation! For example, the "eye field" electrically paints out the location and structure of the eye and vanishes *prior* to differentiation. "To assess whether this bioelectric pattern is crucial to proper development or just an interesting by-product, the researchers disrupted the biochemical pump that generates electric potential. This affected specific critical genes, which resulted in abnormal tadpole facial development. Apparently, the genes are activated by the bioelectricity."[52] That is, what we may be witnessing are electric traces of a bioelectric epigenetic switch that regulates genes expression or the pattern of where genes are expressed.[53]

"Our research shows that the electrical state of a cell is fundamental to development. Bioelectrical signaling appears to regulate a sequence of events, not just one," explains Laura Vandenberg, a postdoctoral associate who works with Adams.[54] "Developmental biologists are used to thinking of sequences in which a gene produces a protein product that in turn ultimately leads to development of an eye or a mouth. But our work suggests that something else—a bioelectrical signal—is required before that can happen." Adams does not hold back on touting the possible implications of this finding: "If it holds that these bioelectrical signals are controlling gene expression, or the patterns of where genes are expressed, we have a whole new approach to correcting birth defects, or preventing them, or spotting them before they happen."

Wedding bioelectricity to molecular genetics, and charged cultural imaginaries from the past with future hopes for regenerative medicine, Levin, the lab's director, delights in playing the errant genius in search of one of life's most profound and promising secrets. As one Tufts University reporter puts it: "In the world where Michael Levin's vision has come to life, people who lose a limb in an accident are able to re-grow it. Birth defects can be repaired in the womb. Cancer cells are detected and rendered harmless before they become tumors. Any number of other diseases are conquered as cells are altered and adjusted."[55] "Grow Your Own," the article's headline, makes an apt motto for the lab, even if this autopoietic framing belies the enormous labors, the patchwork of entangled practices that will be necessary to move toward anything like this futuristic goal. But this futuristic imaginary is no doubt currently sparking the interest of a host of potential funders.

Quantum Phenomena: Entanglements of Disparate Parts

This article is a patchwork. Made of disparate parts. Or so it may seem. But why should we understand parts as individually constructed building blocks or disconnected pieces of one or another forms of original wholeness? After all, to be a part is not to be absolutely apart but to be constituted and threaded through with the entanglements of part-ing. That is, if "parts," by definition, arise from divisions or cuts, it does not necessarily follow that cuts sever or break things off, either spatially or temporally, producing absolute differences of this and that, here and there, now and then. *Intra-actions* enact cuts that cut (things) together-apart (one move). So a patchwork would not be a sewing together of individual bits and pieces but a phenomenon that always already holds together, whose pattern of differentiating-entangling may not be recognized but is indeed re-membered. Memory is not the recording of events held by a mind but marked historialities ingrained in the world's becoming. Memory is a field of enfolded patterns of differentiating-entangling. Remembering is not a process of recollection, of the reproduction of what was, of assembling and ordering events like puzzle pieces fit together by fixing where each has its place. Rather, it is a matter of re-membering, of tracing entanglements, responding to yearnings for connection, materialized into fields of longing/belonging, of regenerating what never was but might yet have been. This article is dedicated to re-memberings, to reconfiguring anew seemingly disparate parts.

The task now is to attempt to stitch together, if only imperfectly, the pieces of this monstrous article by tracing a few of the uncountable and generative entanglements in their ongoing reconfiguring. What do we have so far? Lightning, primordial ooze, electrifying origins, frogs, galvanism, Frankenstein, trans rage, queer self-birthing/regeneration, fecund void, quantum vacuum, virtual particles, indeterminate wanderings, lightning's errant pathways, queer touching, bioelectricity, Franken-frogs, monstrous re/generations, the promise of monsters, future cures, and radical im/possibilities.

Let us begin by learning just a bit more about the striking phenomena of lightning and bioelectricity. To see lightning from above the earth's atmosphere (again I encourage the reader to stop reading and have a look at this impressive phenomenon) is to see something visually akin to the flashings of the electric (pre) face of the embryonic tadpole.[56] Both the becoming of lightning and the becoming of face exhibit flashes that mark out the traces of (what might yet) be-coming. Preceding the flash of a lightning bolt, and preceding gene involvement in cell differentiation, electrons and photons play at making virtual diagrams, flashes of light painting possibilities across the sky and across an embryo, hinting at things-to-come. What I am suggesting is that as instances of the virtual play of electron-photon intra-actions that QFT tells us are the elemental happenings of electromagnetic phenomena (all such phenomena, including the ones presently under consideration), these electromagnetic phenomena in their (ongoing) be-coming illuminate an intrinsic feature of materiality: *matter's ongoing experimenting with itself—the queer dance of being-time indeterminacy, the imaginative play of presence/absence, here/there, now/then*, that holds the disparate parts together-apart.

Embryonic Lightning

At the US Air Force Atmospheric Research Center in Colorado Springs, Geoff McHarg, an atmospheric physicist, is trying to capture the elusive birth of a lightning bolt. McHarg is using a new generation super-slow-motion camera that can record thousands of images per second—visually resolving temporality on unprecedented scales that allow the human eye for the first time to see how very much happens in the "flash of an eye."

What does embryonic lightning look like? The Discovery Channel program shows McHarg at his computer terminal replaying the video of his lucky first-ever catch of the "birth of a lightning bolt," although, as we soon learn, what we are witnessing is arguably not its birth but the display of its embryonic electrical stirrings before any part of a lightning bolt begins to manifest.

The video playback shows "a flash of light dart out of a cloud and zigzag downward in roughly 50 yard segments."[57] (Once again I encourage the reader to watch this remarkable video now.) What the Discovery program narrator does not mention, but the viewer is witnessing in the video, is a stunning feature of the not-yet-lightning flashes: the flashes of light do not just head downward for fifty yards and then change direction and head out again (much like a child's drawing of lightning). Rather, one sees erratic, disjointed sets of flashes tentatively testing out different pathways. The trace of each trial gesture vanishing as quickly as it appears. The narrator's voice continues, "This first stage of lightning is called a stepped leader." Then the scientist's voice: "You can see the stepped leader coming down here looking for a ground, going back and forth. You can see the tortuous channel it is taking as it divides back and forth." Look closely, and you can see that the so-called back and forth motion is a discontinuous pattern of flashing (it flashes here and then over there, some distance away), and that some of the gestures are upward rather than downward. That is, what McHarg's film seems to have captured is a stepped leader gesturing toward the earth, variously expressing its yearnings. It is important to keep in mind that this is not a lightning bolt yet or even the birth of one. Stepped leaders are the barely luminous first gestures of a lightning bolt-to-come. What we are witnessing is the potential face of lightning yet to be born—*a discontinuous exploration of different possible pathways*—before a lightning stroke explodes and shatters the darkness.

Uman points to the fractal-like nature of the stepped leader's musings and attributes this wondering/wandering to a kind of electrical confusion:

> There are zigs and zags 100 yards long and, within these, other zigs and zags 10 yards long, and within these yet smaller zigs and zags. . . . Why is the lightning channel so tortuous? The answer is not known, but some reasonable guesses may be made. The larger-scale tortuosity in the channel (representing, say, tens of yards or more) is due to the fact that the stepped leader makes such an errant trip to ground. Why does it do this? Possibly various airborne regions of charge (space charge) divert the leader on its trip. *More likely, the leader just doesn't know exactly where it wants to go,* except that ultimately it wants to move downward. (my emphasis)[58]

It is as if the electrons are trying out different paths, feeling out this desiring field, exploring entanglements of yearning, before any discharge to the ground takes place. Remember that the buildup of negative charges (electrons) in the lower portion of the cloud does not resolve itself by a direct channel of electrons making their way to the earth by a stepped leader moving to the ground. Instead, *the ground* responds next with an upward signal of its own. These gestures are material imaginings, electrical flirtations signaling connections-to-come. Lightning is born of discontinuous spooky-action-at-a-distance signaling in a decidedly queer communication between earth and sky as they exchange gestures toward the other before either exists, signals of the desiring field that animates their intra-active becoming.[59] If this is reminiscent of the indeterminate exploration of the multiple errant pathways of a quantum phenomenon, it may not be that surprising. Lightning is, after all, the luminous activity of strong electromagnetic fields where photons and electrons engage in a quantum exploration of multiple temporalities and polymorphous/polyamorous couplings—the dance of indeterminacy.

Lightning Face of an Embryo

The "electric face" phenomenon that Adams caught on video is a blend of the fantastic and the scientific, utterly mesmerizing. We catch the glimpse of a face that does/not (yet) exist, but before we can fully discern its indeterminate features, it is gone, in a flash. As Adams describes it:

> The result is so remarkable it almost doesn't seem real. As cells divide within the ball of the embryo, lines and shapes glow and disappear. A slash where the mouth will form shimmers into view, only to quickly fade away. A dot, signifying an eye, appears briefly on the left side of the embryo; a moment later, a matching dot flashes on the right. Vertiginous time-lapse photography is a staple of nature documentaries, but this is different. *These features—the mouth, the eyes—didn't actually exist.* In fact, many of the genes that are linked to their development hadn't even been turned on. *It's only after the patterns fade, the ghost of features yet to come, that all the necessary proteins are activated.* (my emphasis)

The electric traces of a face flash across the cells of the undifferentiated tadpole embryo and disappear. Much like the faint traces of embryonic lightning that tease with the promise of an electrifying connection, the flashes of light that paint out the face of the tadpole offer tantalizing glimpses of what does not (yet) exist. What we witness are traces of differentiating materializations-to-come, virtual explorations of making face. Internally generated lightning flashes are coursing through the embryonic body exploring different possibilities of what might yet be/ have been. What I am suggesting by drawing on quantum field theoretic imagery to describe this event is that what Adams captured is in fact a *quantum* feature of the biophysical epigenetic phenomenon she and her colleagues have been studying: the material play of indeterminacy, the teasing gestures of what might yet be/ have been.[60] If my conjecture is correct, it places the Levin-Adams regeneration investigations within the emerging field of quantum biology. The stunning nature of this example is that what it shows is not merely (nonrelativistic single particle) *quantum mechanical* effects (e.g., quantum entanglement) that scientists now believe account for photosynthesis, bird navigation, and olfactory function, but *quantum field theoretical* effects, like virtual explorations of what might yet materialize (or what might yet have been) as an integral part of ongoing processes of materialization in the dynamical play of indeterminacies in being and time.[61] The sky and the embryo, like the quantum field theory void, are having brain flashes, imagining all matter of becomings. They are trying on different faces, electrical patterns of differencing/différancing, diffraction patterns of differential mattering. *Experiments in virtuality—explorations of possible trans*formations—are integral to each and every (ongoing) be(com)ing.*

Virtual TransMatterRealities and Queer Political Imaginaries

I find no shame . . . in acknowledging my egalitarian relationship with non-human material Being; everything emerges from the same matrix of possibilities.
—Stryker, "My Words to Victor Frankenstein above the Village of Chamounix"

The promise of monsters is a regenerative politics, an invitation to explore new ways of being in touch, new forms of becoming, new possibilities for kinship, alliance, and change.[62] Regeneration understood as a quantum phenomenon brings indeterminacy's radical potential to the fore. *The indeterminacy of being-time/ time-being means that matter/materiality is a matter of material wanderings/ wonderings, a virtual exploration of what might yet be/have been, dispersed across spacetimebeing and condensed into each material bit-here-now, every morsel (each "dressed point") of spacetimemattering.*

 The virtual is not a set of individual possibilities, one of which might yet be realized or actualized.[63] Virtual possibilities are not what is absent relative to the real's presence. They are not the roads not taken or some yet unrealized potential future, the other to actual lived reality. The virtual is a superposition of im/possibilities, energetic throbs of the nothingness, material forces of creativity and generativity. Virtual possibilities are material explorations that are integral to what matter is. Matter is not the given, the unchangeable, the bare facts of nature. It is not inanimate, lifeless, eternal. Matter is an imaginative material exploration of non/being, creatively regenerative, an ongoing trans*/formation. Matter is a condensation of dispersed and multiple beings-times, where the future and past are diffracted into now, into each moment. Matter is caught up in its own and others' desiring fields. It cannot help but touch itself in an infinite exploration of its (im/possible) be(com)ing(s). And in touching it/self, it partners promiscuously and perversely with otherness in a radical ongoing deconstruction and (re)configuring of itself. Matter is a wild exploration of trans* animacy, self-experimentations/self-re-creations, not in an autopoietic mode, but on the contrary, in a radical undoing of "self," of individualism. Ever lively, never identical with itself, it is uncountably multiple, mutable. Matter is not mere being, but its ongoing un/doing. Nature is agential trans*materiality/ trans-matter-reality in its ongoing re(con)figuring, where trans is not a matter of changing *in* time, from this to that, but an undoing of "this" and "that," an ongoing reconfiguring *of* spacetimemattering in an iterative reworking of past, present, future integral to the play of the indeterminacy of being-time.[64]

The electric body—*at all scales*, atmospheric, subatomic, molecular, organismic—is a quantum phenomenon generating new imaginaries, new lines of research, new possibilities.[65] The (re)generative possibilities are endless. Fodder for potent trans* imaginaries for reconfiguring future/past lived realities, for regenerating what never was but might yet have been. Can we cultivate bioelectrical science's radical potential, subverting Dr. Frankenstein's grab for power over life itself, aligning (neo)galvanism with trans* desires, not in order to have control over life but to empower and galvanize the disenfranchised and breathe life into new forms of queer agency and embodiment? Can we (re)generate what was missing in fleshiness but materially present in virtuality? Can we (re)generate what our bodies sense but cannot yet touch? Can we find ways to adjust the appropriate ion potential to activate and generate new fields of re-membering? Can we learn to reconfigure our fleshliness bit by bit by slowly changing the flow of ions? Can dis-membering as well as re-membering be facilitated through such charged reconfigurings of molecular flows? Can we trans/form, regenerate, dismember, and re-member anew fleshly bodies in their materiality? And if these fleshy hopes feel cruel to us sometimes, especially perhaps when reality seems impossibly hard and fixed and our own naturalcultural bodies and desires feel immobilized, if there are times when we have to face the knife, tear ourselves open, draw blood, might a regenerative politics with all its monstrously queer possibilities still serve to recharge our imaginations and our electric body-spirits, helping us transition from momentary political and spiritual rigor mortis to living raging animacy?

Surely these imaginings of the queer potential of regenerative science (and quantum theory more generally) should not be (mis)understood as an uncritical embrace of science's utopian promise. No meditation on Frankenstein could entertain for a moment such a straight alliance with the scripted equation "science = progress," indeed, as the very incarnation of this promise. There is no illusion of queer regeneration being a bloodless affair.

The promise of regenerative medicine is surely not inherently innocent, progressive, or liberatory. It does not constitute an innocent mode of engagement with science, divorced from any heteronormative reproductive impulses. Indeed, its own quite explicit commitment to normative ideas of embodiment, able-bodiedness, and naturalness belie any such suggestion. On the contrary, its goals are to renormalize and eliminate bodily irregularities in a quest to honor Nature and her intentions, if only by doing her one better. The current bioelectric studies of regeneration are already aligning themselves with promises of curing cancer, birth defects, and disabilities because of lost body parts.[66] Levin's initial motivation was to create robots that could heal themselves. Projects in the service of the military-industrial complex, capitalism, racism, and colonialism cannot be disentangled from the practices of modern science. Nonetheless, even as "science seeks to contain and colonize the radical threat posed by a particular transgender strategy of resistance to the coerciveness of gender," and even if "its cultural politics are aligned with a deeply conservative attempt to stabilize gendered identity in service of the naturalized heterosexual order," this is not reason to believe that trans* desires can be corralled into cooperation.[67] In alliance with this crucial point, this article engages with science in a mode that invites us to imagine not only the possibilities of subverting science's conservative agendas from the outside, as it were, but also those of opening up science from the inside and serving as midwife to its always already deconstructive nature.

Significantly, according to QFT nature is an ongoing questioning of itself—of what constitutes naturalness. Indeed, nature's indeterminacy entails its ongoing un/doing. In other words, nature itself *is* an ongoing deconstructing of naturalness. As I have shown in this brief encounter with quantum field theory, the void is "the scene of wild activities," perverse and promiscuous couplings, queer goings-on that make pre-AIDS bathhouses look tame. The void is a virtual exploration of all manner of possible trans*/formations. Nature is perverse at its core; nature is unnatural. For trans*, queer, and other marginalized people, "The collective assumptions of the naturalized order [can] overwhelm [us]. Nature exerts such a hegemonic oppression."[68] The stakes in denaturalizing nature are not insignificant. Demonstrating nature's queerness, its trans*-embodiment, exposing the monstrous face of nature itself in the undoing of naturalness holds significant political potential. The point is that the monstrously large space of agency unleashed in the indeterminate play of virtuality in all its un/doings may constitute a trans-subjective material field of im/possibilities worth exploring. And the political potential does not stop with regeneration, for there are other wild dimensions within and without that rage with possibilities. *For all its entangled history with capitalism, colonialism, and the military-industrial complex, QFT not only contains its own undoing—in a performative exploration/materialization of a subversive materialism—but in an important sense makes that very undoing its im/proper object of study.*[69]

The point is not to make trans or queer into universal features and dilute their subversive potentials. The point is to make plain the undoing of universality, the importance of the radical specificity of materiality as iterative materialization. Nor is this to set trans as an abstraction, to deny it its fleshly lived reality, sacrificing its embodiment in an appropriative embrace of the latest theory trends. What is needed is not a universalization of trans or queer experience stripped of all its specificities (as inflected through race, nationality, ethnicity, class, and other normalizing apparatuses of power), setting these terms up as concepts that float above the materiality of particular embodied experiences, but to make alliances with, to build on an already existing radical tradition (a genealogy going back at least to Marx) that troubles nature and its naturalness "all the way down." In doing so, it would be a mistake to neglect the spaces of political agency *within* science—its own deconstructive forces produce radical openings that may help us imagine not only new possibilities, new matter/realities, but also new understandings of the nature of change and its possibilities.

Queer kinship is a potent political formation, crucial to Stryker's forceful analysis. Imagine how the possibilities for alliance with nature's ongoing radical deconstruction of naturalness might enable the (re)making of queer kinship with nature. What would it mean to reclaim our trans* natures as natural? Not to align ourselves with essence, or the history of the mobilization of "nature" on behalf of oppression, but to recognize ourselves as part of nature's doings in its very undoing of what is natural?

Stryker's queer topological musings, both in "My Words to Victor Frankenstein," where she is giving birth to her rage that births her, and also in more recent works, reverberate with the trans* generative mode being explored here:

> From my forward-facing perspective I look back on my body as a psychically bounded space or container that becomes energetically open through

the break of its surface—a rupture experienced as interior movement, a movement that becomes generative as it encloses and invests in a new space, through a perpetually reiterative process of growing new boundaries and shedding abandoned materialities: a mobile, membranous, temporally fleeting and provisional sense of enfolding and enclosure. This is the utopian space of my ongoing poesis.[70]

This topological dynamic reverberates with QFT processes, much like the one that perverse kinds of self-touching/self-re-creating electrons enact. An electron touching itself, rebirthing/regenerating itself (there is no singular birth moment, no origin, only rebirthings/regenerating), in a process of intra-active becoming, of reconfiguring and trans-forming oneself in the self's multiple and dispersive sense of it-self where the self is intrinsically a nonself.

In her "Frankenstein" piece, Stryker writes poetically of her transgender (re)birthing in a manner that echoes the literal passage of birthed body from the liquid darkness of the womb. Her voice solicits me to diffractively intercut her words there (italicized in the text below) with those (nonitalicized below) of an electron I imagine to be speaking contrapunctually of its own perpetual (re) birthing.[71]

I am an electron. I am inseparable from the darkness, the void. *It is dark. I see a shimmering light above me.* I am one with the void I was allegedly immersed in, but from which there is no possibility of extrication. There is no myself that is separable from it. *Inside and out I am surrounded by it. Why am I not dead if there is no difference between me and what I am in?* While I struggle to come into being I am virtually annihilated and re(sub)merge into the nothingness, over and over again. Time has no meaning, no directionality. My being no more than an im/possible indeterminate yearning. Bubbling up from the nothingness, I fall back into the void that fills me and surrounds me. I return to the void and reemerge once more only to fall back again. *This [void] annihilates me. I cannot be, and yet—an excruciating impossibility—I am. I will do [everything] not to be here. . . .*

I will try out every im/possibility, every virtual intra-action with all beings, all times.

I will die for eternity.
I will learn to breathe the [void].
I will become the [void].
If I cannot change my situation I will change myself.

I am transforming in intra-action with the light above me, below me, and within me, and with all manner of other beings. I am not myself. I am becoming multiple, a dispersion of disparate kinds.

In this act of magical transformation
I recognize myself again.
I am groundless and boundless movement.
I am a furious flow.
I am one with the darkness . . .
And I am enraged.

Here at last is the chaos I held at bay.
Here at last is my strength.
I am not the [void] —
I am [a] wave [a raging amplitude, a desiring field surging, being born],
and rage
is the force that moves me.
Rage
gives me back my body
as its own fluid medium.

Rage
punches a hole in [void]
around which I coalesce
to allow the flow to come through me.

Rage
constitutes me in my primal form.
It throws my head back
pulls my lips back over my
opens my throat
and rears me up to howl:
: and no sound
dilutes
the pure quality of my rage.
form.
teeth
No sound
exists
in this place without language
my rage is a silent raving.

I am one with the speaking silence of the void, the cries of im/possibility move through me, until there erupts a raging scream without sound, without language, without comprehensibility or articulation.

Rage
throws me back at last
into this mundane reality
in this transfigured flesh
that aligns me with the power of my Being.
In birthing my rage,
my rage has rebirthed me.

Let us align ourselves with the raging nothingness, the silent howling of the void, as it trans*figures fleshy possibilities. Wandering off the straight and narrow path, wonderings alight. Trans* desires surge forth electrifying the field of dreams and transmaterialities-to-come.

Notes

I am grateful to Mel Chen and Dana Luciano for their patience and enthusiasm and for wonderful suggestions for reeling in an article that had grown to monstrous proportions. I would like to thank Susan Stryker for graciously accepting my proposal to have some of her poetics diffractively read through mine and, especially, her willingness to have her powerful poetry interrupted by the murmurings of the void (in particular, the musings of a virtual electron that is inseparable from the void). As ever, I am grateful to Fern Feldman for her feedback and ongoing support.

1. TransMaterialities is a term that arose in the planning of UCSC's 2009 "Trans-Materialities: Relating across Difference" Science Studies Cluster graduate student conference, co-organized by Harlan Weaver and Martha Kenney, with faculty sponsors Donna Haraway and Karen Barad. The first time I saw the playful term *matterealities* was at a conference run by Monika Buscher at Lancaster University in 2007.

2. Inspired by QFT's understanding of each moment as a condensation of other beings, places, and times, this ontological-political project resonates with Marco Cuevas-Hewitt's call for a "futurology of the present": "The futurology of the present does not prescribe a single monolithic future, but tries instead to articulate the many alternative futures continually emerging in the perpetual present. The goal of such an endeavor is to make visible the living, breathing alternatives all around us" ("Futurology of the Present: Notes on Writing, Movement, and Time," *Journal of Aesthetics and Protest* 8 [Winter 2011–12], joaap.org/issue8/futurology.htm).

3. For more on lightning's queer quantum nature, see below, and also Karen Barad, "Nature's Queer Performativity (the authorized version)," *Kvinder, Køn & Forskning/Women, Gender, and Research* 1–2 (2012): 25–53; and Vicki Kirby, *Quantum Anthropologies: Life at Large* (Durham, NC: Duke University Press, 2011).

4. Charles Darwin seems to have suggested as much. See, for example, Helen Fields, "The Origins of Life," *Smithsonian Magazine*, October 2010, www.smithsonianmag .com/science-nature/The-Origins-of-Life.html.

5. Douglas Fox, "Primordial Soup's On: Scientists Repeat Evolution's Most Famous Experiment," *Scientific American*, May 28, 2007, www.scientificamerican.com/article .cfm?id=primordial-soup-urey-miller-evolution-experiment-repeated.

6. Nick Lane, quoted in Cynthia Graber, *Electric Shock: How Electricity Could Be the Key to Human Regeneration* (2012), readmatter.com.

7. Douglas Fox, "Primordial Soup's On."

8. Mary Shelley, *Frankenstein, or The Modern Prometheus* (n.p., 1818), 15.

9. Jessica P. Johnson, "Animal Electricity, circa 1781," *Scientist*, September 28, 2011, www.the-scientist.com/?articles.view/articleNo/31078/title/Animal-Electricity—circa -1781/.

10. Aldini quoted in Anne K. Mellor, "Frankenstein: A Feminist Critique of Science," in *One Culture: Essays in Science and Literature*, 287–312, eds. George Lewis Levine and Alan Rauch (Madison: University of Wisconsin Press, 1987), 304.

11. Graber, *Electric Shock*.

12. J. D. Roger, "1816 Textbook Suggests Use of Electric Shock in Treatment of Cardiac Arrest," *Canadian Journal of Cardiology* 20, no. 14 (2004): 1486.

13. Susan Stryker, "My Words to Victor Frankenstein above the Village of Chamounix," *GLQ* 1 (1994): 237–54.

14. Stryker, "My Words," 238.

15. Stryker, "My Words," 240–41.

16. For one thing, as Judith Butler points out, "Not only is the gathering of attributes under the category of sex suspect . . . indeed, the 'unity' imposed upon the body by the category of sex is a 'disunity,' a fragmentation" (quoted in *Meeting the Universe Halfway: Quantum Physics and the Entanglement of Matter and Meaning* [Durham, NC: Duke University Press, 2007], 60). But there is much more to this point. For more details on an agential realist reworking of the nature of nature, matter/ing, and the cutting together-apart of disparate parts, see Barad, *Meeting the Universe Halfway*.

17. Stryker, "My Words," 251. I am left wondering why Stryker talks about the womb as a place of "blackness" rather than say "darkness," or even, as I suggest, "nothingness" (the void). Part of my political investment in enlarging the scope of my project to include quantum field theory (QFT) is its ability to trouble the underlying metaphysics of colonialist claims such as *terrae nullius*—the alleged void that the white settler claims to encounter in "discovering undeveloped lands," that is, lands allegedly devoid of the marks of "civilization"—a logic that associates the beginning of space

and time, of place and history, with the arrival of the white man. In contrast to this doctrine, according to QFT the void is full and fecund, rich and productive, actively creative and alive. Which, of course, is not the only way to contest the racist and colonialist impulses at work but is to try to further unearth and unsettle how space and time are themselves racialized.

18. Parts of this section are borrowed from Karen Barad, *What Is the Measure of Nothingness? Infinity, Virtuality, Justice / Was ist das Maß des Nichts? Unendlichkeit, Virtualität, Gerechtigkeit*, dOCUMENTA (13): 100 Notes—100 Thoughts / 100 Notizen—100 Gedanken | Book Nº099, English and German edition (2012).

19. A. Zee, *Quantum Field Theory in a Nutshell*, 2nd ed. (Princeton: Princeton University Press, 2010), 4.

20. Quantum field theory does not negate the findings of quantum mechanics but builds on them. Similarly, these explorations help further articulate agential realism. As I argue below: QFT entails a radical deconstruction of identity and of the equation of matter with essence in ways that transcend even the profound un/doings of (nonrelativistic) quantum mechanics.

21. The more general term *electromagnetic field*, rather than *electric field*, is sometimes used. The interchangeability is due to the fact that electricity and magnetism were unified into a single electromagnetic force in the mid-nineteenth century.

22. While the idea of a field may seem like a convenient fiction, and was in fact originally introduced as an imaginary construct to facilitate calculations, physicists in the nineteenth century began to embrace the idea that fields are real. This shift was a result of the finding that light is an electromagnetic wave made of (nothing but) changing electric and magnetic fields.

23. This is a subtle point that I develop further elsewhere (Barad, "On Touching: The Inhuman That Therefore I Am," *differences* 22, no. 3 [2012]: 206–23): namely, the difference between the play of indeterminacy and a rapid appearance and disappearance of particles as the hallmark of virtuality. I would argue that "flashes" of potential are traces of virtuality synchronized to clock time, but this very particular manifestation is far from the only set of possibilities in the play of virtuality. I address these issues further in a forthcoming publication.

24. Parts of this section are borrowed from Barad, "On Touching."

25. Parts of this section are borrowed from Barad, "Nature's Queer Performativity."

26. All quotations in this paragraph are from the Discovery Channel television program "Discovery Wonders of Weather: Lightning Phenomena," September 2007, www .discovery.com/video-topics/other/lightning-phenomena.htm.

27. Martin Uman, *All about Lightning* (Mineola, NY: Dover, 1986), 49–50.

28. I am indebted to Vicki Kirby's writings on lightning, and in particular her attention to the untimely nature of lightning's connective engagement. See Vicki Kirby, *Quantum Anthropologies: Life at Large* (Duke, NC: Duke University Press, 2011).

29. I have repeatedly made the point that quantum phenomena are not restricted to some alleged "micro" domain. Perhaps a(nother) large scale example like this one will help to defeat that misconception.

30. Parts of this section are borrowed from Barad, "On Touching." See also Barad, "On Touching—The Inhuman That Therefore I Am (v1.1)," in *Power of Material/ Politics of Materiality*, eds. Susanne Witzgall and Kerstn Stakemeier (Zurich-Berlin: Dia-phanes, 2015).

31. The virtual photon can also be absorbed by another particle, and that would constitute an electromagnetic interaction between them, but that is not my focus here, which is how to understand an "individual" particle.

32. *Trans** is a term that employs the wildcard symbol (*) for internet searches. It is at once a term meant to be broadly inclusive (e.g., transgender, transsexual, trans woman, trans man, trans person, and also genderqueer, Two Spirit, genderfuck, gender fluid, masculine of center) of an array of subversive gender identities, and also self-consciously tuned into practices of exclusion. As "Anony Mouse" notes in a response to a posting on the Q-Center of Portland web page: "When you see a [starred] word or sentence while reading [a] book or articles, you automatically look [to] the margin to see if it has any more meaning to it." See, for example, www.pdxqcenter .org/bridging-the-gap-trans-what-does-the-asterisk-mean-and-why-is-it-used/ (written by Addie Jones, "Bridging the Gap — Trans*: What Does the Asterisk Mean and Why Is It Used?," posted August 8, 2013).

33. Richard Feynman, *QED: The Strange Theory of Light and Matter* (Princeton: Princeton University Press, 1995), 115–16.

34. Renormalization is a sign of physics' ongoing (auto)deconstruction. Physics continually finds ways to open itself up to new possibilities, to iterative re(con)figurings.

35. Electrons are not an arbitrary choice for this article. Electrons are not only the source of our body electric, the genesis of our own inter- and intracellular lightning flashes; in an important sense, "electrons R us": we are made of electrons and their wanderings. Note: to suggest that electrons are trans/material configurations/reconfigurings is not to naturalize trans (or queer for that matter), but rather to acknowledge the radically transgressive potential of nature itself in its own undoing/deconstruction of naturalness (sufficiently subversive, in this case, to instill "horror" in those who would propose to know it fully).

36. This material was presented during my talk, "Multispecies Intra-actions: Queerness and Virtuality," Distinguished Lecturer for Environmental Humanities, University of New South Wales, Sydney, Australia, July 11, 2013. I am grateful for the lively discussion it generated.

37. Research into bioelectricity and regeneration has a history going back to the nineteenth century. Although some articles covering the research activities of Tufts University Center for Regenerative and Developmental Biology position Michael Levin,

the center's director, as the direct descendent of Galvani and a scientific maverick in the sole pursuit of bioelectricity and regeneration in contemporary times, this is an ongoing field of research that has multiple devotees. For a history of bioelectricity and regeneration, see, for example, Joseph W. Vanable Jr., "Bioelectricity and Regeneration Research," in *A History of Regeneration Research: Milestones in the Evolution of a Science*, ed. Charles E. Dinsmore (Cambridge: Cambridge University Press, 1991), 151–78. What is important and cutting-edge about Levin et al.'s approach is the study of bioelectricity using the techniques of molecular biology.

38. "This animal is widely used because of its powerful combination of experimental tractability and close evolutionary relationship with humans, at least compared to many model organisms" (Wikipedia, "Xenopus," en.wikipedia.org/wiki/Xenopus [accessed October 28, 2013]).

39. "During the 1940's, female *X. laevis* were injected with the urine of a woman. If the human was pregnant, then the injected frog would start to produce eggs. *Xenopus laevis* was the first vertebrate cloned in the laboratory." Both quotes from the entry for "Xenopus laevis," Animal Diversity Web, University of Michigan, animaldiversity .ummz.umich.edu/accounts/Xenopus_laevis/ (accessed October 28, 2013).

40. Wikipedia, "Xenopus."

41. Brittle stars are organisms that combine the two: reproduction and regeneration. Some species of brittle stars asexually reproduce via regeneration, for example, via the fissioning of the central disk (Wikipedia, "Brittle Star," en.wikipedia.org/wiki/Brittle _star [accessed October 28, 2013]). For more remarkable features of this creative creature, see Barad, *Meeting the Universe Halfway*, chap. 8.

42. Ai-Sun Tseng et al., "Induction of Vertebrate Regeneration by a Transient Sodium Current," *Journal of Neuroscience* 30, no. 39 (2010): 13192–200.

43. Dany S. Adams, Alessio Masi, and Michael Levin, "H+ pump-dependent changes in membrane voltage are an early mechanism necessary and sufficient to induce Xenopus tail regeneration," in *Development* 134 (2007): 1323-35.

44. Misia Landau, "Regenerative Biology: The Body Electric," *Focus: News from Harvard Medical, Dental, and Public Health Schools*, March 9, 2007, archives.focus.hms .harvard.edu/2007/030907/regenerative_biology.shtml.

45. Helen Ragovin, "Grow Your Own," *Tufts Journal*, January 14, 2009, tuftsjournal .tufts.edu/2009/01_1/features/01/.

46. "Unlocking the Biological Code," *What A Year! Introducing Medical Discoveries to Biology Students*, www.whatayear.org/06_13.php.

47. "Researchers Discover That Changes in Bioelectric Signals Trigger Formation of New Organs," *Tufts Now*, December 8, 2011, now.tufts.edu/news-releases/researchers -discover-changes-bioelectric-sign.

48. "Researchers Discover."

49. "When new tissue is introduced, Levin explains, it sends out axons to make connections with host tissue. In these tadpoles, the eyes' axons almost universally connected

with either the spinal cord or the gut (Levin, quoted in Michael Price, "'Franken-Tadpoles' See with Eyes on Their Backs," February 27, 2013, news.sciencemag.org /plants-animals/2013/02/franken-tadpoles-see-eyes-their-backs). The ones that connected to the spinal cord were able to see.

50. The video is available on the Tufts University website: "The Face of a Frog: Time-lapse Video Reveals Never-Before-Seen Bioelectric Pattern, now.tufts.edu/news -releases/face-frog-time-lapse-video-reveals-never-seen#sthash.DgsjzC7y.dpuf. If any of the videos mentioned in this article aren't current, see people.ucsc.edu/~kbarad.

51. "The flashes are caused by a process called ion flux, which causes groups of cells to form patterns marked by different membrane voltage and pH levels. When stained with dye, the negatively charged areas shine brightly, while the other areas appear darker. The result? 'Electric face.'" Jennifer Viegas, "Electrical Patterns Found on Frog Face," July 20, 2011, news.discovery.com/animals/electrical-patterns-frog -110720.htm.

52. Brian Thomas, "Tadpole Faces Form by Bioelectric Patterning," July 27, 2011, www .icr.org/article/tadpole-faces-form-by-bioelectric-patterning/.

53. Daisy Yuhas, "It's Electric: Biologists Seek to Crack Cell's Bioelectric Code," *Scientific American*, May 27, 2013. www.scientificamerican.com/article/bioelectric-code /?mobileFormat=false.

54. See now.tufts.edu/news-releases/face-frog-time-lapse-video-reveals-never-seen#sthash .DgsjzC7y.dpuf.

55. Ragovin, "Grow Your Own."

56. See www.discovery.com/video-topics/other/lightning-phenomena.htm.

57. "Lightning in Super Slow Motion," a segment from the Discovery Channel video on lightning (2007), www.youtube.com/watch?v=RLWIBrweSU8.

58. Uman, *All about Lightning*, 83, 90.

59. "Spooky-action-at-a-distance" is the notion that Albert Einstein introduced in his objection to the nonlocality of quantum phenomenon. Today, this nonlocality is understood to be a feature of quantum entanglements. See Barad, *Meeting the Universe Halfway*, chap. 7; and Karen Barad, "Quantum Entanglements and Hauntological Relations of Inheritance: Dis/continuities, SpaceTime Enfoldings, and Justice-to-Come," *Derrida Today* 3, no. 2 (2010): 240–68, special issue, "Deconstruction and Science," edited by H. Peter Steeves and Nicole Anderson.

60. Indeed, this is further evidence that quantum effects, falsely believed to exist only at micro scales, are being detected at larger and larger spatial scales. Here we may be witnessing yet another inherently quantum effect at the molecular level, at the level of biology, orders of magnitude larger than the atomic scale (of the so-called microworld).

61. Note that untimeliness and temporal indeterminacy are intrinsic to the nature of virtuality.

62. This is an invocation of Donna Haraway, "The Promises of Monsters: A Regenerative Politics for Inappropriate/d Others," in *Cultural Studies*, eds. Lawrence Grossberg,

Cary Nelson, and Paula A. Treichler (New York: Routledge, 1992), 295-337. I have in mind here also brittle stars among other creatures who display an array of nonheteronormative modes of reproduction, including asexual reproduction through regeneration. See the discussion of the brittle star in Barad, *Meeting the Universe Halfway*, chap. 8.

63. Although a common story of measurement in quantum theory is that the "wavefunction," which represents a superposition of possibilities, is collapsed on measurement and one of the possibilities is realized, I argue that there is no collapse, that measurement intra-actions reconfigure possibilities. For more details on an agential realist solution to the measurement problem, see Barad, *Meeting the Universe Halfway*, chap. 7. The notion of the *virtual* discussed here is based on my interpretation of quantum field theory. It is not the same as Gilles Deleuze's notion of the *virtual*, although there are some interesting resonances. I discuss this further in a future publication.

64. Thinking the temporalities of transitioning outside linear and external conceptions of time seems important, and this ontology gives us new understandings of being and time that may be useful. For example, what is at issue, then, is not necessarily a matter of discovering a past that was already there or remaking a past through the lens of the present but a reconfiguring, a cutting together-apart of past-present-future in the wild play of dis/identities and untimely temporalities.

65. I have tried to make the point over and over again that quantum phenomena are *not* restricted to the so-called micro scale. Scale does not precede phenomena; scale is only materialized/defined within particular phenomena.

66. This is not to suggest that curing cancer and addressing birth defects and disabilities are not worthy goals, on the contrary. But the question of what constitutes a "defect" and a "disability" needs to be thought through in conversation with disability scholars and activists, among others.

67. Stryker. "My Words," 242.

68. Stryker, "My Words," 248. The notion of a natural order is certainly important to scientific racism as well. On the historical links between scientific racism and scientific discourses on sexuality, see, for example, Siobhan Somerville, "Scientific Racism and the Emergence of the Homosexual Body," *Journal of the History of Sexuality* 5, no. 2 (1994): 243–266.

69. I take up this issue in depth in Barad, *Infinity, Nothingness, and Justice-to-Come* (book manuscript).

70. Susan Stryker, "Dungeon Intimacies: The Poetics of Transsexual Sadomasochism," *Parallax* 14, no. 1 (2008): 36–47.

71. With apologies to Susan Stryker for disrupting her powerful poem, and with gratitude to her for her generosity and willingness to be open to this experiment in entangled poetics.

PARIAH AND BLACK INDEPENDENT CINEMA TODAY

A Roundtable Discussion

Kara Keeling, Jennifer DeClue, Yvonne Welbon, Jacqueline Stewart, Roya Rastegar

My first contribution as editor of Moving Image Review is a roundtable discussion sparked by the conversation in the United States surrounding the theatrical release of Dee Rees's 2011 film *Pariah*. Organized as a session at the American Studies Association's annual convention in 2012, the following is an edited transcript of what was presented there. Out of an interest in centering queer media making and scholarship within the broader sociocultural contexts to which they contribute, I asked the scholars included here (some of whom also are filmmakers, archivists, or curators) to assess, situate, and discuss the current state of black film culture in the United States, with a particular focus on what Nelson George identified in a December 23, 2011, feature article in the *New York Times* about the black lesbian film *Pariah* as a "mini-movement of young black filmmakers telling stories that complicate assumptions about what 'black film' can be by embracing thorny issues of identity, alienation and sexuality."[1]

An engaged audience at the American Studies Association session contributed to a discussion that generated additional insights and questions not included here. These were primarily about audience, alternative production streams and distribution models, and the issues of class and the existence of subcultures that might be considered part of this discussion. I am grateful to Alex Juhasz and Ming-Yuen Ma, the former editors of Moving Image Review, for allowing me to par-

GLQ 21:2–3

DOI 10.1215/10642684-2843251

© 2015 by Duke University Press

ticipate in the production of the Queer Media Manifestos as a way to learn how to produce the Moving Image Review.

—Kara Keeling

Jennifer DeClue: I first encountered *Pariah* in 2007 as a short film that won the Audience Award at OutFest, Los Angeles's LGBT film festival. Since then, *Pariah* has been produced as a feature film distributed by Focus Features. The narrative differences and casting changes made between *Pariah* the short and *Pariah* the feature are indicative of industry demands for name recognition and universal appeal in this capital-generating artistic venture. Of all the groundbreaking things a short film can accomplish, making money is usually not one of them. While I do understand the need to meet the demand of universal appeal, the poignancy and vulnerability captured in the short keeps that version of *Pariah* near and dear to my heart.

That said, *Pariah* the feature, because of its presence in theaters across the country, has been able to open up conversations about the tensions between blackness and sexuality on a much wider scale than the short film version could. *Pariah*'s representation of the black family raises questions about being black and gay and belonging. Alike, the black lesbian daughter in *Pariah*, tests her belonging to a normatively religious, socially conservative, middle-class black family, and, more broadly, her sexuality challenges this normatively religious, socially conservative, middle-class black family's belonging in the nation that persistently challenges its inclusion.[2] The tensions that surround the tenuous national belonging for black families and the stakes of compulsorily black heterosexuality produce a dissonance that is palpable in *Pariah*'s narrative. An element of the ambivalence that circulates through blackness is the specter of pathological sexuality. Religiosity and the black church have served as vectors through which the taint of sexual deviancy becomes absolved. In her book *Private Lives, Proper Relations*, Candice Jenkins describes the salvific wish and uplift ideology as a pledge for salvation from the pathologizing discourse of black sexuality.[3] Jenkins argues that ideologies of upward mobility and the salvific wish encourage silence and denial about sexuality. The violence of the salvific wish that separates Alike from her parents is visualized in *Pariah* in a cinematic eruption that lays open the sorrow and the stakes of not belonging and not being willing or able to help it.

When Alike admits to her parents that she's gay, the tenuousness of her family's national belonging rocks them and their place in the black church, and blackness is thrown into question. The understanding that blackness and queerness are mutually exclusive is a problem of silence and of visibility. It would seem that Dee Rees's *Pariah* is a cinematic contribution that has made black lesbian coming of age not only visible but universal in appeal. Alike's coming out to her parents makes her sexuality visible in the narrative structure of the film, and Focus Features's distribution of the film makes black lesbian sexuality visible on the national and perhaps even international stage as well. *Pariah*'s narrative foregrounds sexual attraction between black women from strong, churchgoing black families. The all-black world of the film demands that this film be recognized as a black film and frustrates attempts to distance homosexuality from black authenticity. The visibility of black women attracted to one another in *Pariah* produces witnesses who see loving black lesbians who do not lose their blackness even though they may be threatened with losing their families. The fear of black lesbian and gay youth being ostracized from their families and communities for being traitors to their people or for not being black enough because of their sexuality is a very real concern. Even though visibility can be an oppressive regime in which bodies are policed and regulated, visualizing black lesbian sexuality on the big screen can also work to dismantle the mutual exclusivity of blackness and queerness in a world that overly sexualizes black bodies and within the black community whose national belonging is persistently and violently scrutinized.

Yvonne Welbon: To situate *Pariah* within a history of black film production, I am going to focus on the lesbian factor in black independent cinema with a bit of an overview on black lesbian independent film history. The 1974 student Academy Award–winning short *Sojourn*, codirected by Michelle Parkerson and Jimi Lyons Jr., is thought to be the first film directed by an out black lesbian filmmaker.[4] In her early films Parkerson did not focus her lens specifically on black lesbians. It is the 1986 video "Women in Love, Bonding Strategies of Black Lesbians" by Sylvia Rhue, described by Jenni Olson, author of *The Ultimate Guide to Lesbian and Gay Film and Video*, that is the first out black lesbian film about black lesbians.[5] It was screened in 1987 at the Los Angeles International Gay and Lesbian Film Festival, and it marks the beginning of the first quarter century of out black lesbian media making. There was only a handful of films directed by out black lesbians in the 1980s. From 1991 to 1996, the number of films, videos, and interactive media created by out black lesbians increased to about 70 works. There were four artists working in the 1980s and about twenty-five artists working in the early 1990s. I consider that five-year period (1991–96) the golden age of out black lesbian media making because of the amazing diversity of the work being produced in both form and content by such a large group of women. In the fifteen-year period that follows,

1996 to 2011, 70 more films and videos were made by an additional thirty artists. So by 2012, we have about fifty-five black lesbian media makers with a filmography of about 140 films.[6]

About 100 feature films were directed by black woman between 1922 and 2012. Almost one-third of these films were directed by black lesbians. While statistically about 4 percent of the adult American population is likely to identify as LGBT, black lesbians have directed about 30 percent of those films.[7] Black women directors rarely have an opportunity to direct more than one feature film. Here, I am thinking of Julie Dash and her feature *Daughters of the Dust*, which was the first feature film by an African American woman to receive national theatrical distribution. In 2012 we celebrated the twentieth anniversary of its release, and Dash has yet to direct another feature film.

While the production budgets and reach in terms of audiences vary, the black women who have directed the most feature films are almost all black lesbians. Coquie Hughes has directed six features. Cheryl Dunye has directed five feature films. Tied for third place with four features are Shine Louise Houston and Kasi Lemmons, who is heterosexual. The highest-grossing Hollywood studio film directed by a black woman was directed by a black lesbian: Angela Robinson's *Herbie Fully Loaded* grossed over $144 million worldwide. Robinson is also the black woman who has worked with the largest Hollywood studio budget—$50 million. The only black woman to be nominated for a nonstudent Academy Award for directing is also a black lesbian. Dianne Houston was nominated for her short film *Tuesday Morning Ride* in 1996.

I'm not sure why it's cool to be a black lesbian in the film industry, although I do think that part of the reason black lesbians have been successful is because of film festivals. The black lesbian media artist emerged simultaneously with the growth and expansion of the gay and lesbian film festival industry. There are about 130 of these festivals worldwide right now. The film festival has historically been the first stop for a new filmmaker. Festival directors have a lot of power in selecting the next generation of filmmakers. The birth of YouTube has allowed a handful of filmmakers to bypass this first step. So I'm thinking right now of Issa Rae, the creator of the online series *Awkward Black Girl*, who signed a deal with Shonda Rhimes, the creator of the television series *Grey's Anatomy* and *Scandal*. Still, I believe that the industry will continue to rely on the film festival process to discover talent. But most festivals do not show a lot of women's work. Even at the premiere film festival, Sundance, over the last decade, only about 24 percent of the features shown are directed by women.[8] So the thing about gay and lesbian film festivals is that they're called gay AND lesbian film festivals, and they have a mandate to show gay AND lesbian work. What happens is that a lot of lesbian women get to make this first step more often than their straight counterparts because gender equity is mandated by the festivals.

Jacqueline Stewart: What I'd like to do to begin is go back to Nelson George's piece in the *New York Times* (which Kara mentioned in the introduction to this roundtable). In that piece George tries to describe what's happening with *Pariah* and a number of other contemporary black filmmakers. He claims that they constitute a kind of mini movement. For some reasons that I want to lay out, I don't think he's wrong in characterizing it that way. The notion of "black film" has been evolving over the decades along with the ideas of black independent filmmaking and independent filmmaking in general. I think *Pariah* occupies a really interesting point at the intersection of those histories. I also think that what we can see happening now is an increased "visibility" (to pick up a term that Jennifer used) and marketability of notions of difference within the black community, which obviously *Pariah* is tapping into. At the same time, *Pariah* is a film that is benefiting from a kind of institutionalization of independent filmmaking, structures that make it possible for independent filmmakers to get some mileage out of the idea that they're making something independently.

If we look back at the turn of the last century, black independent filmmaking was something that came out of necessity; folks like Oscar Micheaux and Spencer Williams had no possibility of entering the mainstream film industry as directors, so you have hundreds of films made for segregated African American audiences. Some are comedies, some are uplifting melodramas, but they are constituting insular black worlds, both in terms of what they're representing on-screen and their audiences. I think we see much of the same kind of ethos in one of the earlier movements in black independent filmmaking that George talks about, the LA Rebellion, which is, as many of you know, a group of black filmmakers who were all going to film school at the University of California at Los Angeles (UCLA) in the late 1960s through the mid-1980s. So folks like Charles Burnett, Julie Dash, Haile Gerima, Ben Caldwell, Larry Clark, and dozens of other black filmmakers were very much interested in making films that would create a kind of resistance to commercialized black images circulating at the time, especially those that were affiliated with blaxploitation. They were very self-conscious about creating a cinema that they felt was articulating a set of aesthetic principles that they found to be more authentic, that was not imitating Hollywood models—even though many of them did hope that after film school they'd be able to make deals in Hollywood so they would be able to continue to finance their work. But it seems as though the LA Rebellion is a group of filmmakers who are so principled about not wanting to dilute their work and their vision to get white money, so to speak, that many of them haven't made a whole lot of work.

These are important precursors in terms of thinking about black independent filmmaking as an effort not only to address a separate black public but also to figure out how to construct the film language that can speak to black issues and to black viewers in authentic ways; that is, there's a sense or hope that the black audience is a known and rather unified quantity. I think that we see this changing dramatically in the evolutions in how independent filmmaking gets understood and financed. George points to the blaxploitation era, which is a really important moment for us to think about in the context of what's happening now. We tend to reduce blaxploitation to a set of what George calls "crime melodramas," or sex and violence, action-based films, but, of course, there were many, many different types of black films produced during the 1970s. We can think about films like *Sounder*, or *Claudine*, for example, that were giving lots of black actors work and also providing new opportunities for African Americans behind the camera—not a lot of directors but certainly a lot of craft people, compared with what was happening in previous decades. This is true for writers in particular. It is important to think about the blaxploitation period not just in terms of a trajectory of black image making—a lot of discussions of black exploitation focus on the debate about positive and negative images, the kinds of things that were embarrassing, airing dirty laundry, and so forth. We also have to recognize that blaxploitation took off at a moment when a kind of transgressive filmmaking was on the rise in American filmmaking more broadly—so think about directors like George Romero, Roger Corman, and about films like *Bonnie and Clyde* and *Easy Rider* as well as about changes that were happening in terms of film censorship during this time. There emerged a kind of niche marketing so that edgier films could be made and financed, exhibited more generally. This is the moment when blaxploitation emerges. So the industrial factors at work during this time provided a context in which black filmmaking could also transgress certain kinds of boundaries of decorum because audiences were understood to be not simply a monolith but more differentiated.

George also points to the early 1990s as a significant moment, and this dovetails in important ways with the history that Yvonne was just spelling out. In 1991, depending on which article you read, fifteen or seventeen or nineteen films written and/or produced and/or directed by black people got theatrical distribution. It's the year of *New Jack City, Boyz in the Hood, Straight out of Brooklyn, House Party, Jungle Fever, Chameleon Street, To Sleep with Anger, The Five Heart-*

beats, *A Rage in Harlem*, and *Strictly Business*, which was cowritten by George. These films were riding on the coattails of Spike Lee's success. What's instructive to think about regarding this moment is the way in which the idea of black independent filmmaking was becoming something that allowed for a different kind of niche marketing than we saw during the black exploitation period. So Spike Lee's success is very much tied to the kinds of successes that you saw from people like Kevin Smith or Michael Moore, and the opening up of festivals for independent filmmaking—most notably Sundance. The imprimatur of something like Sundance could create a profile of the black independent filmmaker as something that could stick, even when the filmmaker was no longer independent. (This is one of the most amazing things to me about Spike Lee's career—he continues to perform as though and we continue to act as though he's an independent filmmaker, even though he's had a long-standing relationship with Universal and with HBO films. But this idea of his final cut and his kind of bombastic personality continue to create the sense that he is fully authoring his work and that he's speaking against the commercial dominant film making structure.)

So more recently we get Spike Lee serving as artistic director of the filmmaking program at NYU, where he's mentoring a bunch of young film students including Dee Rees. What he's able to do from that position and from the model that he has established is to open up possibilities for this younger generation of filmmakers to figure out how they can brand themselves in ways that continue to take advantage of developments and structures in independent filmmaking. So let's think about how *Pariah* was funded. Jennifer mentioned that it was a short first. Then there was the process of financing it as a feature. Dee Rees's short version of the film was shown in about forty film festivals around 2006. And then she was able to secure a lot of support from various sources. She was a 2008 Tribeca Institute Fellow, a Sundance Institute Screenwriting and Directors Lab Fellow. Her producer, Nekisa Cooper, got support from Film Independent where she was a Project Involve and Fast Track grant recipient, which provide a unique opportunity for underrepresented producers and filmmakers to shop their projects to industry people. This is a film that also benefited from exposure through its Kickstarter campaign. The Kickstarter campaign appealed to people to help them get to Sundance to show their film. The tone of the campaign was "We need to finish it up."[9]

The last thing I want to mention in terms of these new structures for independent filmmakers is that Dee Rees was a recipient of a Netflix Find Your Voice Competition grant. She cites this as being extremely important for developing a new media strategy, a social media strategy. This strategy is crucial for the ways this film was able to secure actual financing, and also for the way this project tapped into existing and growing discourses of LGBT activism. Look at some of the things that happened, for example, on the *Pariah* website. It became a place for people to post videos about their own coming-out experiences. In this way, Rees and Cooper clearly connected *Pariah* to the It Gets Better project for queer youth happening during the same time.[10] So the *Pariah* website is a combination of "support this film" and "this is a safe space, a supportive space for you to articulate your own identity." In this way I think it's really useful to think about how questions around the expression of diverse sexualities are like questions about mixed-race identities, or about Diaspora. These are the kinds of differences that were formerly papered over within the black community we see in earlier films. Now filmmakers like Dee Rees are able to connect these differences and questions to longer-standing discourses around black independent filmmaking.

Roya Rastegar: I became interested in film curating when I realized that films by people of color and queer women of color weren't circulating into the public realm for broader audiences, even for what the industry considers "niche" audiences. My assumption was that people of color just weren't making enough films. But that was dead wrong. Through the better part of the last decade I've been working on the selection committees of larger, industry-based film festivals in the United States. I started working at Sundance in 2006, and then at Tribeca and Los Angeles film festivals in 2008 and 2009. I very quickly learned that, actually, people of color, black women, queer women of color are making lots of films. The problem is that these films aren't recognized as valuable, or their value isn't legible to critics, curators, and distributors. Largely, film festivals are bottlenecking these films. Festivals are a major gateway through which independent films have to pass, but since there are so few people of color—or people who actually value these films—on the selection and curating committees, that these festivals block many of these films from reaching audiences. Taste, as we know from Bourdieu and many other scholars, is not only subjective, it is collective: completely tied with where you come from, whom you break bread with, whom you sleep with, where you grew up. Aesthetic valuations, as Clyde Taylor has painstakingly argued, hinge on a sense of morality that is not only based on an apolitical notion of beauty or form but is formally structured to stabilize and reinforce the dominant racial order.[11] Festivals are a perfect storm for assertions of taste and aesthetic value to drown films by people of color, to sink them right out of the public eye, out of the archives.

So that's a bit of the context in which I want to talk about Shari Frilot, a veteran film festival programmer and how her work as a curator has been transformative over the past twenty to twenty-five years for independent film and popular culture at large. Frilot has been a central force for creating the space and context in which black independent filmmaking—and filmmaking by people of color more broadly—has been able to rise to the movement it is now. I'll start by talking a little bit about Shari's work at the Sundance Film Festival. For the past fifteen years she's been one of the leading curating voices at Sundance. Next to John Cooper and Trevor Groth, who have been with the festival essentially since it started, Frilot has had the longest tenure as a programmer. Many of the independent films that have been accessible to us on DVD or in theaters over the last several years are available because Frilot has been there fighting for them to be included in a major film festival's program. Films like *Pariah, Sleep Dealer, Whale Rider, Middle of Nowhere, Restless City, A Good Day to be Black and Sexy* (these are just a handful, I could go on) have been championed by Frilot, and because of her advocacy are able to take advantage of the kind of exhibition platform and industry connections that Sundance offers independent filmmakers.

I've interviewed Shari Frilot at length about her programming work, and I have been part of the Sundance programming team in various capacities over the past six years. Sundance's programming happens by committee, and there are nuanced modes of valuing film—sometimes unconsciously, sometimes explicitly—that play out in these selection meetings. As often the lone woman of color in the room, Frilot has faced the limits of how people can actually hear what she's saying. She describes an instance where in the first few years she was working there, as soon as a film by a person of color was starting to be discussed they'd be like, "OK, Shari, you're on to talk about the black film." She described it in this way: "I was the voice of diversity, as though I was the filmmaker, like it was my film. And this is all in the context of Sundance, which has a white, liberal commitment to diversity. In the early days when I was there people would say 'yes, we're going to show this for diversity's sake.' So I decided to change what that meant."[12] Frilot's strategy was to shift the framework for engaging diversity, starting with advocating for an experimental film by a white filmmaker. "I would say to the team, 'You know I really think we should include this film because of its formal qualities, it's very unique. We should include it because of diversity.' The whole room fell silent." By changing the context and language around how diversity was engaged, Frilot opened up something that otherwise was being closed down because of the almost obligatory way her colleagues were reducing films by people of color to their race or gender or sexuality.

Frilot's work at Sundance was very much informed by her work as the director of the MIX: New York Gay and Lesbian Experimental Film Festival. Renaming the festival "MIX," she began to experiment with different notions of how to put together a film festival. She kept this up as the director of programming at Outfest: Los Angeles LGBT Film Festival. Frilot has articulated her approach to curating in terms inspired by Audre Lorde's notion of the erotic as an embodied form of knowledge grounded in our deepest sense of self. Frilot's work has been singular and unique in its approach to opening spaces and creating contexts for work that refuses these nationalistic impulses around identity categories, and engages race and sexuality and gender in unwieldy and complicated ways that viscerally shift something in viewers.

In 2007 Frilot started New Frontier at Sundance, an exhibition in digital works, media installations, multimedia performances around the body's active engagement of film and performance, something Frilot has called "physical cinema."[13] Whether from a curatorial perspective or a scholarly one, the work of framing is key when discussing black independent film. How do we frame the cultural expressions, objects, and movements we research and theorize? How do we frame the spaces in which people are brought into and cultures are organized within? What is the relationship between how we frame black independent films and filmmakers and how they are taken up in popular culture? For example, festival programmers write approximately 150-word curatorial notes about films that go in the festival guide. This is the first piece of writing about a film: no one except the programmers has seen the film before; it's a world premiere of a film that is being introduced by curators through their notes. This guide is what audiences look through to decide what they want to see, it's what curators and journalists use to jump-start their reviews, it's what distributors look at to decide what films to check out for acquisition. In Frilot's note for *Pariah*, she writes, "Debut Director Dee Rees leads a splendid cast and crafts a pitch-perfect portrait that stands unparalleled in American cinema." So Frilot refuses to put this film in a niche category that would limit its market value and unabashedly contextualizes *Pariah* within a trajectory of American independent film.

Jennifer provided a really great analysis around blackness and visibility. Building on that, I think it is absolutely critical to see how identities around sexuality, race, and gender are being radically refigured in popular culture. We need to revisit the idea of what black film even is in this contemporary moment. What is a black lesbian film? Do these characterizations facilitate an opening up of spaces for black independent filmmakers? What are the other ways we can talk about films that unsettle dominant gender and racial ideologies but make space for unexpected coalitions across different filmmakers, different films?

I end with two overall points: First, there is definitely something happening right now with black independent film, and I don't know how much it has to do with any single person. There is a real confluence of talent rising from all sides—cinematographers, critics, producers, directors. Ava DuVernay, director of *I Will Follow* (2010), *Middle of Nowhere* (2012), and the upcoming *Selma* (2014), and founder of distribution company AFFRM, the African Film Festival Releasing Movement, has transformed the game of distribution. She is not only making narratively sophisticated films but, through AFFRM, also breaking the bottle so its neck becomes moot. She's creating pathways of black independent filmmakers on an ambitiously international scale. Bradford Young (*Mississippi Damned* [2009], *Restless City* [2011], *Pariah* [2011], *Middle of Nowhere* [2012]) is among the most innovative cinematographers working today, lighting and filming differently hued skin and creating new ways of making black people look gorgeous on-screen. Frilot has been patiently chipping away at the dam as she waited for this flood of talent to come crash it down. I almost feel like using *Precious* to frame the current movement of black independent film would yield a different kind of insight to this conversation. It's not a coincidence that the year after the storm around *Precious* started and it was bought in an unprecedented partnership between Tyler Perry, Oprah, and Lionsgate, the next three films that sold at Sundance the following year were about young people of color and their explorations of sexuality: *Pariah*, *Gun Hill Road*, and *Circumstance*. I think it's important to think about these films in relation to each other, even if they are not all classified as black independent film-making in the conventional sense.

KK: Roya, your closing comments set us up pretty nicely to respond to the first question I asked people to think about; namely, what are the implications of situating *Pariah* as a watershed moment or a turning point or something else that you might begin to identify in the history of black film or of LGBT, queer film?

JD: I think that there's a way that *Pariah* sets the stage for seeing black lesbians' sexuality—like actually seeing love scenes between black women on the screen. Although we don't see the sex scene in *Pariah*, there's a way that visualizing a black woman's sexuality, the actual, physical practice of showing people having sex on-screen, is something that *Pariah* opened up in a more mainstream way than had been done previously. It opens up this kind of world of airing dirty laundry—doing things in front of people that you were never allowed to do before. Shine Louise Houston was definitely making films that did this kind of work before *Pariah*, but I think there's something that shifts in the mainstream around depictions of black lesbian sex after *Pariah*.[14]

YW: The thing that struck me that's kind of a turning point right now in black independent cinema is the African Film Festival Releasing Movement (AFFRM), which is headed by Ava DuVernay, a seasoned public relations professional who has become a director. From my research, I haven't seen a black woman do what she has done. What she did was she directed her first feature film, *I Will Follow*, in 2010, and she set up the distribution company AFFRM through which she released her film. AFFRM releases two African American titles each year. In 2012 she released her second feature film, *Middle of Nowhere*. Now, remember it's been twenty years, and Julie Dash still hasn't released her second feature. With *Middle of Nowhere*, DuVernay became the first African American woman, and I think she's really the first African American to win the Best Director Award at Sundance. She is currently in preproduction on her third feature. Again, that is remarkable. It's not just the creation of AFFRM but the fact that she is successfully building a career as a director in a short period of time. I think a part of her success is because she actually is a public relations specialist. She understands the power of the media in general and social media in particular.

I'm going to tie that into *Pariah* because the producer on *Pariah* is Nekisa Cooper, and she comes from corporate America. She worked at Procter and Gamble. If one learns how to sell soap, one can sell anything. That is what she did with Dee Rees. She positioned the filmmaker like a product. She packaged Rees with the short film to get to the feature. As Jackie said, the short played in forty festivals, and it won a lot of awards. So what I see as kind of a grassroots organizing strategy in black independent cinema is the marketing, promotional, and packaging savvy. But I want to tell you, this is cyclical, because I can look twenty years back at *Daughters of the Dust*. The film had an African American marketing firm called KJM3. Michelle Materre was part of that group. They did the same thing, except their grassroots did not have Twitter or Facebook. They were old school: "Here's a postcard. Here's a flier. Post it at your community center, bring folks to the screening." A big difference is the dollar amounts that are made. Twenty years ago more money was made. So *Daughters of the Dust* made close to $2 million, and it played for six months. *Middle of Nowhere* played for six weeks and made just over $200,000. If we even go further back, twenty years before *Daughters*, which would be Melvin van Peebles's *Sweet Sweetback's Baadasssss Song*, I think that film made like $4 million in 1971–72.

JS: What you are saying connects to the idea of how the niches are changing, too. *Pariah* has made about $750,000. It opened at four theaters. It got to twenty-four at its peak.[15] So we're talking about a very small set of numbers, people, and money. What we're responding to, I think, is the idea of its influence. And it would be important for us as scholars to try and have some perspective on what we're talking about regarding representations of black women, sexuality, in light of a film's actual exposure to specific numbers of people's cultural currency.

One thing I would add to the conversation at this point is to think about some of the ways in which *Pariah* is instructive for thinking about the current viability of making films on film. One of the many grants that Dee Rees received for the film was a Kodak Film Grant from Film Independent, to shoot *Pariah* on 35 [mm film] to go to Sundance. The kind of respectability that shooting film on film and circulation on film, as a kind of art film, what that means, is changing. It seems as though we've been prognosticating that "film" is going to disappear for a long time. This is an opportunity to really think about what that means. It's not just that this film takes advantage of a number of new social media possibilities in terms of its marketing. I think it's a film that also makes us think about the making of films and about what we call "films," because a lot of black independent work is shot and distributed on video. Coquie Hughes was shooting on video. That's how she became the most prolific black lesbian filmmaker ever, selling stuff out of the trunk of her car. She's amazing. I think that there are some interesting issues of scale as well as issues of format that *Pariah* calls to our attention.

RR: The year 2010 at Sundance was the year that *Precious* came up. Most people don't see *Precious* as an independent film. They think, "Oh, it was Oprah and Tyler Perry. It was big." But actually, what went down was that the Weinstein Company was being shady about buying the film, yo-yoing their interest, low-balling Lee Daniels. I remember a lot of the black industry people at Sundance were talking about it in hushed tones as a major controversy. So when Oprah and Tyler Perry banded together to buy this film, connecting with Lionsgate, that was a major coup. That's why *Precious* was so important in terms of what you're saying, Yvonne, about having a plan around how you're going to sell your film so that you don't just get to Sundance and you're subject to the whims of a distribution company. Dee and Nekisa both met at Colgate company. They both manufactured that toothpaste, the one where you open it and two different kinds come out. Nekisa is also a basketball coach. Her approach to producing is very team oriented, organized, ambitious, and no-nonsense. Spike Lee is a mentor for them. And they are very, very smart. They locked in a two-picture deal with Focus Features. Lucky for Focus because those films are going to be amazing. But also smart for them because women—let alone women of color—rarely make more than one studio film, if that. That was a very smart, business savvy, and forward-thinking move.

And the entire context of independent film distribution and storytelling platforms is changing. Shondra Rhimes is knocking it out with *Scandal*, but she's been on the forefront of storytelling for years with *Grey's Anatomy*. And then Dennis Dortch started a YouTube channel, Black&SexyTV, as a way to promote his 2008 film *Good Day to Be Black and Sexy*, and now they have hundreds of thousands of subscribers and multiple web series. Dortch also teamed up with Issa Rae, of the *Misadventures of an Awkward Black Girl*, which is its own powerhouse of game-changing storytelling.

KK: I'm also curious to hear about the ways that you, in your writing, in your work, are thinking about the categories that organize your scholarship and how you might open up your thinking (or not) in relationship to the different kinds of films that we're seeing making it to screen and entering the public discourse. Given the way that you're approaching your own work, what might you want to say in relationship to these kinds of conceptual questions about how we organize our work and our practice?

JD: I read an interview with Dee Rees in *The Griot* (thegrio.com). It was about being snubbed by the Oscars and the fact that *Pariah* had not gotten any Oscar nominations and *The Help* had gotten so many Oscar nominations. Dee Rees's response was that it should not be an either/or situation. She asked, why is it that there's a finite amount of space in our imagination of black cinema that there's room for only one film to be acknowledged? Why does there have to be a choice between *Pariah* or *The Help*? She said, "There's room enough for *The Help* and *Pariah*." I think the paradigm of mutual exclusivity demonstrated in the remark that elicited Rees's response reflects a limitation in our cultural imagination about representations of blackness and specifically black queer sexuality. White power structures impose and reinforce notions of acceptable black imagery in popular culture through systems of meritocracy like the Oscars. These cultural impositions get backed up by black cinematic standards, which are inflected with the politics of respectability. We accept the tacit understanding that there is only room for one great black film every few years. There is no real mutual exclusivity between black films—that is an antiquated idea, one that we must rebuff. *The Help* and *Pariah* can both receive accolades for their respective reception in the world of cinema. We need *Pariah* to be recognized for what it contributes to popular culture, especially in a world that nominates and awards *The Help* for the work that it does in the field of cultural production.

YW: I agree with you on that. When *Precious* came out, *Mississippi Damned* came out too. (If you all haven't seen *Mississippi Damned*, please check it out.) What happened that year was that there just couldn't be two dysfunctional black family films in distribution at the same time. So *Mississippi Damned*, an amazing gem of an indie, lost out.

The thing that I'm noticing is that right now that when we're talking about independent film, we're really kind of talking about films like *Pariah*. But when I look at black independent film I see a lot of stuff happening on the street level. It is not reaching the academy. The reason I even found out about it is that there's a group of us in Chicago who have gone to film school and we noticed that there were these films being shown at the Black Harvest film festival and none of us knew any of these filmmakers. Somebody got the bright idea that the black filmmakers who went to film school might meet with these other black filmmakers. We met and an alliance was formed. I learned a lot. For example, Mark Harris told me he did fifty thousand units of his first DVD. Today he has sold over one million units—DVDs from films he's made. There are a whole bunch of these filmmakers whom we don't know. Coquie Hughes is one of those people. So, when it comes to black independent film I think we're missing part of it. We're not fully seeing what's happening with black independent cinema. A lot of it's on the Internet, particularly with black lesbian series. Coquie Hughes has over one million views on her YouTube channel. *Come Take a Walk with Me*, the *Lovers and Friends Show* was definitely the number one black lesbian show way beyond *The L Word*. Quarter of a million viewers regularly. I think they just finished season 4. *Between Women* is the new series out of Atlanta. I think that's the issue—we're missing it because these filmmakers did not go to film school. They are not on the festival circuit. They're not your friends. They're not even friends of your friends . . .

JS: The one thing I would add to this is how to manage this idea of postraciality, postblackness. In the article that Nelson George wrote he had some quotes from Dee Rees who was talking about the group of black filmmakers she went to NYU with. Some of the terminology that she uses is really interesting. This is a group of black filmmakers who want to avoid reductive views of black people, resist monolithic black identity, and see an extreme diversity of images. George ends the essay thinking about the way in which her approach to representing characters who are queer is very much like the way she approaches issues of race. It's not necessarily incidental; it's a part of who they are, but it doesn't "define" who they are. I think this resonates with what Roya was saying about how Shari Frilot packaged *Pariah* in terms of tying it directly to an idea of how it transformed American cinema, skipping over questions that could stop the sale and attractiveness of this film if it seems to be ghettoized as a black film or as a black queer film. So I think one of the things that we need to think about in our writing and in our teaching this material is how to negotiate these questions of color blindness or postraciality that are so much a part of the way in which people are talking about these films, even though we can see what's happening in the films is very much about articulations of race and continuing to think about questions of inequality based on race. When we have students who don't want to talk about these issues and they're being encouraged by a lot of discourse surrounding these objects not to do so, I think it's really important for us to figure out how we can keep these things as a part of this conversation.

RR: We need to nurture film cultures across different kinds of racial groups and class backgrounds. Film culture is becoming increasingly segregated, especially with individualized viewing formats and webisodes and things you can just do on your own. I'm interested in developing coalitional film cultures and ways of looking together across different platforms—that both acknowledge our differences and also allow for them to be there, and also make connections across them. Looking at the work of Diasporic filmmakers, female directors, the handful of people of color making films in the studio system distributing films within the conventional channels, but also at those innovating new distribution networks like DuVernay, how can we enable connections across different investments, approaches, and practices?

Notes

1. Nelson George N. (2011), "'Pariah' Reveals Another Side of Being Black in the U.S.," *New York Times*, December 23, 2011, www.nytimes.com/2011/12/25/movies/pariah -reveals-another-side-of-being-black-in-the-us.html. The feature film *Pariah* (dir. Dee Rees; 2011) started as a short film by the same name, *Pariah* (dir. Dee Rees; 2006).
2. Hortense Spillers describes the experience of African American subjects as ambivalent; according to Spillers, the sometimes tacit, sometimes explicit resistance to national belonging produces an incomplete Americanization for black people. See Spillers, "The Things You Could Be by Now If Sigmund Freud's Wife Was Your Mother: Psychoanalysis and Race," in *Black, White, and in Color: Essays on American Literature and Culture* (Chicago: University of Chicago Press, 2003), 376–427.
3. Candice Jenkins, *Private Lives, Proper Relations: Regulating Black Intimacy* (Minneapolis: University of Minnesota Press, 2007), 125.

4. Gloria J. Gibson, "Michelle Parkerson: A Visionary Risk Taker," in *Black Women Film and Video Artists*, ed. Jacqueline Bobo (New York: Routledge, 1998), 178.

5. Jenni Olson, *The Ultimate Guide to Lesbian and Gay Film and Video* (New York: Serpent's Tail, 1996), 282.

6. In general, works produced as part of QWOCMAP—the San Francisco–based Queer Women of Color Media Arts Project—are not included in these figures. While there are an additional seventy-five titles produced through the workshops by over eighty-five African American lesbians between 2006 and 2013, only the films produced as part of QWOCMAP that have been broadcast, programmed, and screened in theaters and film festivals outside QWOCMAP festivals and programming have been included in these figures.

7. See Experian/Simmons, *The 2012 LGBT Report: Demographic Spotlight*, Experian Information Solutions, www.experian.com/assets/simmons-research/white-papers /simmons-2012-lgbt-demographic-report.pdf (accessed December 5, 2014).

8. Stacy L. Smith, Katherine Pieper, and Marc Choueiti, "Sundance Institute and Women in Film Los Angeles Study Examines Gender Disparity in Independent Film," dotorg-cms-production.cfapps.io/blogs/news/sundance-institute-and-women-in-film -los-angeles-study-examines-gender-disp (accessed December 5, 2014).

9. For more information about the Kickstarter campaign, see www.kickstarter.com/projects /619452369/pariah-the-movie (accessed December 5, 2014).

10. See www.itgetsbetter.org (accessed December 5, 2014).

11. Clyde Taylor, *The Mask of Art: Breaking the Aesthetic Contract* (Bloomington: Indiana University Press, 1998).

12. Interview with Shari Frilot, Los Angeles, June 10, 2009.

13. Roya Rastegar, "Curating 'Physical Cinema' at Sundance's New Frontier," *Feminist Media Theory: Iterations of Social Difference*, ed. Jonathan Beller. Special issue of *The Scholar and Feminist Online* 10, no. 3 (2012).

14. During the audience discussion period for the session at ASA, I mentioned that Cheryl Dunye's queer porn film *Mommy Is Coming* and Campbell X's *Stud Life* were both released in 2012, the year after *Pariah* hit the big screen. Dunye's and X's films each offer explicit sex scenes that delve into BDSM, and I wondered about the meaning of the appearance of these films on the festival circuit after *Pariah*. Alex Juhasz reminded me that there's an intimate knowledge that happens inside black lesbian film production and that Campbell X and Cheryl Dunye and others have been creating black lesbian film cultures that enabled *Pariah* to bring black lesbian sex into the mainstream. In light of Alex's contribution to the discussion during the roundtable session at ASA, I have adjusted my comments here for clarification.

15. See Box Office Mojo website: www.boxofficemojo.com/movies/?id=pariah.htm (accessed December 5, 2014).

Books in Brief

WRITING DISSENT

Making African Queernesses Visible

Sandeep Bakshi

Queer African Reader
Sokari Ekine and Hakima Abbas, eds.
Dakar, Nairobi: Pambazuka Press and Fahamu Books, 2013.
xiii + 454 pp.

Sokari Ekine and Hakima Abbas's highly accomplished and long-awaited edited collection, the *Queer African Reader*, encompasses an extraordinary breadth of LGBTQI interventions from Africa and its diasporas. Including vital contributions from poets, creative writers, social justice researchers, lesbian feminists, transgender activists, performance artists, queer bloggers, and many others, the *Reader* records, explores, and disseminates the increasingly critical voices of what the editors appositely term "African resistance" (3). The diversity of articles, essays, poems, testimonies, manifestos, and memoirs in the anthology raises important concerns about the polymorphous existence of queer practices and how African people both resident in African countries and the diasporas perceive them. It is this underlying plurality—tension even—that gives queerness a distinct and well-documented African specificity.

The collection makes a timely intervention in the context of what the African LGBTQI manifesto/declaration of April 18, 2010, terms the "transformation of the politics of sexuality" such that queer Africans articulate their own narratives of identity (52-54).[1] As Ekine's essay points out, two crucial and contesting narratives of sexuality in the African context tend to foreclose any serious engagement with African queer anticolonialist politics (78–91). The persistent nationalist exclusion of nonheteronormative arrangements in countries such as Nigeria, Uganda, Malawi, and Liberia has often led to a strengthening of the colonial laws that criminalize homosexuality. One result of this frame was the antihomosexuality bill that was repeatedly tabled in Uganda from 2009 to 2012 with the help of both the local government and US missionary interventions. The bill was finally signed into law in 2014 and carried the punishment of life imprisonment for same-sex relations. The second narrative originates in the global North whereby fantasies of a deeply homophobic Africa are considered legitimate reasons for queer organizations of the North to protect LGBTQI populations in Africa. This white savior fixation often disregards the complex trajectories of oppression and participates in impeding the work of local queer movements. The nexus of colonialism, racism, and debt dependency affects LGBTQI African subjects in equal proportion as other heteronormative subjects in Africa.

In the context of the interconnectedness of North and South dialogues, the essays of Lyn Ossome, Kenne Mwikya, Sibongile Ndashe, Douglas Clarke, Bernedette Muthien, Kagendo Murungi, and Jessie Kabwila offer a nuanced examination of the place of queer African LGBTQI activism. For example, the collection offers rich insights into the complex dissonances or disagreements with reference to foreign aid. It opens with the indictment of American Evangelicals in Uganda in an essay by the activist David Kato, who is called the "fallen soldier," assassinated on January 26, 2011 (4). While few contributions specifically invalidate the recent declaration of the British prime minister David Cameron that sutures aid conditionality to sexual rights, overall there emerges a sophisticated position, which hinges on an extensive critique of both national governments and the Western charity industry.[2] In this regard, chapter 9 reproduces, in its entirety, the statement of those African queer activists who expressed concerns about the use of aid conditionality by the British government (92–94). While not every activist organization chose to sign the statement, a diversity of viewpoints vis-à-vis donor sanctions is presented in the collection. As this and other discussions suggest, the contributors eschew a simplistic redemptive reading of Africa when considered in opposition to the neoliberal and neocolonial North.

Queer fiction, poetry, life experiences, and exchanges enrich the general appeal of the collection. Interwoven with critical writing on queer rights, the contributions of Busisiwe Sigasa, Mia Nikasimo, Diriye Osman, Hakima Abbas, Olumide Popoola, Pamella Dlungwana, Valérie Mason-John, and Ola Osaze, among others, attest to the multiplicity of queer voices emanating from the continent and its diasporas. Gabrielle Leroux's collaborative portraits of trans and intersex activists (54–68), Zanele Muholi's positive images of LGBTQI community in South

Africa (169–72), and Raél Jero Salley and Kylie Thomas's analysis of Muholi's portraits (107–18, 354–71) are innovative experiments in style offering visual testimonies of queer self-representation. Muholi is a visual and performance artist whose photographs of black lesbians in South Africa and trans-identified individuals in the African diasporas offer, in her own words, "a positive imagery" of queer lives (169). Embodying the challenge to conventional narratives of oppressed queer communities by establishing a queer archive, the images and portraits signal the transformative promise of visualizing affirmative conceptions of African queernesses.

Although contributions from Francophone or Lusophone Africa could have been a welcome addition, the broad spectrum of queer articulation presented in the collection offers a crucial step in orientating discussions on Africa toward queerness. In sum, the *Queer African Reader* is indicative of ongoing radical reassessment of the "oppressive hetero-patriarchal-capitalist frameworks" in the African context (3). Breaking away from all received knowledge of an allegedly nonmodern, homophobic Africa entrenched in canonical interpretations, it engages critically with the complexities of LGBTQI lives. As a first collective archive that offers a rich array of voices pertaining to queer discourses from Africa, it invariably signals newer directions in queer self-fashioning. It can only be hoped that the extensive discussions centering on race, class, gender, identity, disability, sexuality, solidarity, and resistance further impel similar imaginative ways to articulate queerness in both the globalized North and South.

Sandeep Bakshi is a teaching and research fellow in English at the University of Le Havre, France.

Notes

1.   The manifesto can also be accessed at www.blacklooks.org/2011/05/african-lgbti-manifestodeclaration/.
2.   See www.bbc.co.uk/news/world-africa-15243409.

DOI 10.1215/10642684-2843263

THE BEAUTY OF GLIDING

Figure Skating Politics and the Many Pleasures of Life

Claire Carter

Red Nails, Black Skates: Gender, Cash, and Pleasure on and off the Ice
Erica Rand
Durham, NC: Duke University Press, 2102. x + 309 pp.

On a recent visit with an old high school friend, she pulled out old photograph albums from when we were synchronized swimmers. One photograph has haunted me; it is of our team in "costume" prior to performing our routine. The routine was my first on the senior team, and my embodied memory is of strength and increased skill development and ability. But this routine was characterized by our coach and teammates as our "oriental routine"; the music was from Miss Saigon and our costumes involved Mandarin characters, chopsticks in our hair, and white makeup and bright red lipstick resembling a Geisha girl (the Japanese and Chinese combination reflect our ignorance). Over the years, I came to understand the depth of our racism and cultural appropriation and have used this as a learning opportunity. Rand's book *Red Nails, Black Skates: Gender, Cash, and Pleasure on and off the Ice* analyzes these types of contradictions; the pleasure and joy in physical ability that come with figure skating alongside the politics of accessibility and discrimination that plague the sport.

   Red Nails, Black Skates is a personal examination of the world of figure skating that successfully interweaves anecdotal narratives with sharp analysis of rituals and regulations that govern the sport. Divided into eight chapters, each with three to four short essays, the book covers diverse topics from changes in scoring to cultural appropriation, the pink politics of breast cancer, and gender and sex policing. The book draws on Rand's experience of becoming an adult figure skater in her early forties and is informed by insider knowledge and participant observation. The book surfaced as a way to encourage Rand to compete in the Gay Games: having the motive of doing research provided the impetus to compete. Disappointed by the lack of *queering* taking place, Rand revised her book project to instead focus on the "workings of pleasure, power and politics" (12).

The book begins by introducing the reader to figure skating culture, through discussion of the complexities of scorecards and the common—though criticized—practice of sandbagging, whereby more skilled skaters can compete at lower levels to ensure medaling. As the book progresses, Rand analyzes how various aspects of figure skating privilege some bodies over others. In the chapter "Booty Block: Raced Femininities," Rand outlines how instruction on movement, such as "straight spines and tucked butts" function to reinforce the predominance of white bodies in the sport under the guise of "vertical alignment" (131). In several places, Rand highlights the financial barriers to skating, including coaching costs, rink rental, and health care costs, as well as further limitations informed by class once a skater enters the skating world. For example, Rand notes that some well-connected coaches and skaters get access to changes in skating rules in advance of others, granting them unfair advantage (38).

A central theme throughout the book is the way that gender, sex, and sexuality are regulated within figure skating. A notable example is Skate Canada's initiation of the nicknamed "Tough" Campaign, intended to highlight the "difficulty of the sport" (154). This campaign was interpreted publicly as a way to counteract the common stereotype that all male figure skaters are gay. This interpretation was given further weight by former skater Elvis Stojko, who stated that men's skating is about "power and strength," not being "lyrical or feminine" (155). Gender, sex, and sexuality are strictly policed in figure skating in everything from the color of skates and prescribed outfit options (though Rand points out that outfit designs for women incorporate the potential for crotch shots during spins!) to partners whom one is allowed to pair with (always heterosexual), to specific training on how to "skate like a girl" or "skate like a boy."

Alongside her sharp and engaging analysis of figure skating, Rand suitably partners short personal essays on pleasure, including her love of her skating scars in contrast to those from her biopsies, her grandmother's love of shoes, and three stories about bras. In one essay about her brief stint in hockey, engaging in sport is connected to gender identity, as Rand dislikes hockey largely because the "outfit" disrupts her gender identity by covering up her feminine curves. Rand acknowledges that for many, this is appealing about hockey, as are other elements such as being physical and strong, things he takes pleasure in while skating. Rand also effectively demonstrates the political nature of sports in her discussion of the opening ceremony of the Gay Games in 2006, rather than focusing solely on celebration or athleticism.

Red Nails, Black Skates is a good read, bringing together critique of the sociopolitics of figure skating with numerous everyday facets of Rand's life. The most poignant contribution of Rand's book is the conclusion, where she makes recommendations for how skating can address the many fallacies and exclusions it harbors. Notably, she recommends that the practice of sandbagging be terminated; advocates for increased accessibility on numerous fronts and doing away with gender restrictions even though she reminds us there is no official rule on who can occupy categories of "Girls, Boys, Ladies and Men" (254); and urges that the skating world work to ensure racist or colonial narratives are not reproduced (260). These short essays leave some issues in need of further elaboration, but the book reads like a series of conversations, crafted to reach a broad audience but also with the intent to change thinking about gender and sport.

Used to defending synchro as a legitimate sport, I understand Rand's concern that she needed to "butch up" her topic. Feminized sports are often dismissed by dominant culture, making her contribution to critical sport and gender studies ever more important. Rand's book is pleasurable, not only for its engaging narratives about the intricacies of the skating world, but also for critical analysis of sport and athletic life.

Claire Carter is assistant professor in women's and gender studies at the University of Regina, Canada.

DOI 10.1215/10642684-2843275

EMERGING BETWEEN INVISIBILITY AND HYPERVISIBILITY

Michael Hames-García

¡Oye Loca! From the Mariel Boatlift to Gay Cuban Miami
Susana Peña
Minneapolis: University of Minnesota Press, 2013. xxx + 224 pp.

Susana Peña's ethnographic history is a welcome addition to studies of sexuality, masculinity, immigration, and race in Latino contexts, complementing Lionel Cantú's essays on Mexican men and Carlos Decena's monograph on Dominican men.[1] In addition to its focus on Cuban men, Peña's book distinguishes itself by its interdisciplinarity. Rather than a straightforward ethnography of gay Cuban American and Cuban immigrant men, *¡Oye Loca!* is also a historical retelling of narratives that many of us in Latina/o studies thought we were already familiar with: that of Cuban American exceptionalism and of the Mariel experience. In the process, she offers the first thorough engagement with the significance of the large number of gay men who entered the United States during the 1980 Mariel boatlift and forces us to rethink much of what we thought we knew. Chapters 1–3 are historical, narrating familiar stories (homosexuality and the Cuban Revolution, the Anita Bryant/Save Our Children campaign in Dade County, the Mariel boatlift, and the contradictions of US immigration policy) in new and surprising ways. Chapters 4–8 consist of a more traditional ethnography, focusing on the emerging gay Latino cultures in Miami in the 1990s. Peña frames the book with an argument that gay Cuban men have had to contend simultaneously with hypervisibility and invisibility. For example, US immigration authorities needed to not see their sexuality, given the contradiction between Cold War–era Cuban immigrants' favored status and policies barring homosexual immigrants. At the same time, their sexuality was made hypervisible through the very mechanism of their arrival, since admission to homosexuality in front of a Cuban government panel was one way to qualify to leave Cuba at this time.

In the first part of the book, Peña's retelling of Mariel and Cuban immigrant experience challenges received wisdom and demonstrates the value of intersectional frameworks for studies of men. Peña makes a convincing case that the impact of the Mariel influx of gay men on the city of Miami, its sexual subcultures, its politics, and its Cuban American community has been profound. Central to this impact was not only the high number of men who had sex with men among the Mariel immigrants but also the fact that so many of them were effeminate men coming to the United States anticipating a milieu in which they could be open and flagrant in their sexual and gender expression. Their presence contributed as well to the high number of "broken sponsorships" between Mariel immigrants and their ostensible US sponsors and to the reputation of Mariel immigrants as "hard to place."

Although the interviews on which Peña bases most of her ethnography are dated (they were all conducted in the 1990s), the book feels theoretically fresh, engaging recent scholarship and making new interventions into debates over the status of culture, identity, family, and sexuality in the lives of immigrant men who have sex with men. In the later chapters, Peña's discussions of culture, family, identity, masculinity, and race begin by showing how her data fit with dominant theoretical models before pushing back against those models by sharing data that do not conform to them. In discussing culture and sexuality, for example, Peña first engages Tomás Almaguer's model of a Latin American sex/gender system to discuss her subjects' different understanding of homosexuality and masculinity in Cuba. She then draws from Fernando Ortiz's concept of transculturation to argue that the immigrant men she interviewed do not simply adopt US categories and identities but adapt them to their own needs. Ultimately, however, both the model of a singular Latin American sex/gender system and the sharp contrast between acculturation and transculturation begin to dissolve as she presents us with complex interactions among culture, gender, race, and sexuality. As she argues, "Non-Anglo and non-English-speaking homosexual men in the United States do not simply adopt US meaning structures. Rather, they sometimes redefine English and US gay culture or infuse it with other ways of understanding and organizing same-sex desires" (86). Furthermore, "Cuban first-generation immigrant men do not all make cultural negotiations in the same way" (86).

Each of the key thematic topics is fleshed out in separate chapters on culture, nation, and sexual identity, family and sexual disclosure, racialized masculinity, and effeminacy and drag. However, the discussions sometimes feel a bit truncated. Peña's considerations of masculinity and race are never quite as critical or rich as Decena's, for example. She mentions the retention of male privilege as a possible reason for her subjects' investment in masculinity, disavowal of femininity, and nondisclosure of sexual identity to family, but does not seem to push inquiry in this direction in her interviews. The politics of blackness also haunts the edges of the book, despite Peña's awareness of its important and vexed role in the formation of Cuban identity. What she does give, however, is a fascinating examination of the texture of Cuban American whiteness. For example, Peña's interviewees experience the benefits and limitations of gay Latino stereotypes among white gay men in South Florida's gay circuit party scene, yet few of them understand themselves as racially different from those white gay men. As Peña observes, while many of the men she interviewed felt distanced from this scene, they rarely framed their criticisms of it in racial terms. Cuban American whiteness functions, like so much in her account, as another example of the contradictions of invisibility and hypervisibility. Ultimately, this knot of contradictions is what Peña's study excels at unraveling for us.

Michael Hames-García is professor of ethnic studies and director of the Center for the Study of Women in Society at the University of Oregon.

Note

1. Lionel Cantú Jr., *The Sexuality of Migration: Border Crossings and Mexican Immigrant Men*, ed. Nancy Naples and Salvador Vidal-Ortiz (New York: New York University Press, 2009); Carlos Ulises Decena, *Tacit Subjects: Belonging and Same-Sex Desires among Dominican Immigrant Men* (Durham, NC: Duke University Press, 2011).

DOI 10.1215/10642684-2843287

"JUST WHEN THEY SEEM ENGAGED IN REVOLUTIONIZING . . ."

Miranda Joseph

Safe Space: Gay Neighborhood History and the Politics of Violence
Christina Hanhardt
Durham, NC: Duke University Press, 2013. vii + 358 pp.

Christina Hanhardt's *Safe Space: Gay Neighborhood History and the Politics of Violence* is a richly researched examination of activist organizations and less-organized activist efforts on behalf of LGBT rights in San Francisco and New York over the last fifty years.[1] Hanhardt draws on archival materials as well as interviews and participant observation to provide a view that is close to the ground, attentive to the trees, even sometimes the weeds, without losing view of the forest. Yet this is not a conventional historical narrative; instead, Hanhardt takes a step back to the past for each step she takes forward, so that each chapter is a thematically driven case study, summoning its own historical antecedents rather than simply the next set of events unfolding during the next set of years.

Hanhardt focuses on those activist efforts that took violence to be the problem, safety the goal. The violence/safety orientation, she argues, was centrally constitutive of LGBT social movements, identities, communities, and neighborhoods as well as being constitutive of the urban spaces and government policies of which it was a symptom. LGBT community—as *place*, a neighborhood located in real estate, *and* as imagined *space* of belonging—is never portrayed by Hanhardt as discrete, unified, or autochthonous. Rather, she presents contradictory and changing configurations that emerge at the conjunctures of the LGBT activist efforts, urban processes (especially gentrification), and also shifting social scientific theories, which mobilize social groups and social deviance as objects of knowledge and governance—most importantly as victims and agents of violence. For Hanhardt, the term *community* almost always has quotation marks or a capital C because she is talking about someone else's deployment of the term, often in the title of an organization or state agency.

While Hanhardt shows the activist organizations to be implicated in social processes, they are not only or necessarily complicit with the most destructive. They are rather endlessly and diversely desiring and strategizing, sometimes in ways that enhance stratification, dispossession, and the power and reach of the repressive apparatuses of the state. But as Hanhardt makes sure we understand, this is not inevitable. The third chapter, "Counting the Contradictions," focuses on critiques of gay gentrification and on those activist groups such as Third World Gay Coalition, Lesbians Against Police Violence, and Dykes Against Racism Everywhere that "did not call for the primacy of state protection or empirical enumeration . . . did not see as a solution the effort to make identities visible through a tabulation of violence in the frame of crime-based state recognition" (126).

One of the text's most interesting components is the central role Hanhardt attributes to social science and social accounting as a determinant of, but also point of contention for, the LGBT formations she examines. In the first chapter, "The White Ghetto," she traces the efforts in the 1960s of organizations including Mattachine to capture War on Poverty money for San Francisco's Tenderloin district. Specifically, they wanted access to the Community Action Program, manifested locally in the Community Action Agencies, which, informed by social scientific theory, sought to reduce juvenile delinquency by enhancing "legitimate social avenues" (47). Advocates produced "reports" (think "Moynihan Report")[2] that drew on the "culture and personality school" of social analysis (44–45), developed to account for racialized poverty, thus producing an analogy between race and sexuality, which here as always works to produce claims for similarity but also separateness.

In chapter 2, "Butterflies, Whistles, and Fists," Hanhardt describes the emergence of 1970s safe street patrols as implicated in a merger of urban and gay-affirmative social science, which identifies neighborhoods (e.g., San Francisco's Castro) as sites for the realization of gay life (83). Meanwhile she notes that street patrols meshed well with the emergent broken windows theory of crime (107), which takes crime as a given (an inevitable product of rational opportunity) and shifts the focus of crime-related policy to the calculation of risk and prevention, to be deterred by quality of life enforcement and enhanced penalties.

In the fourth chapter, Hanhardt explores efforts to promote hate crimes laws, efforts that take up the penalty enhancement imperative directly. She tracks the work of "activists dedicated to ending violence [who] found promise in empirical evidence and the rule of law, documenting rates of violence and using this information to demand legal recognition and remedies" (156). Here quantitative accounting (rather than sociological theories of crime that deploy statistical argumentation) takes center stage, with performative crime-reducing efficacy attributed to the tabulation itself: Hanhardt notes that not only did the National Gay and Lesbian Task Force use enumeration to demonstrate that antigay violence had reached epidemic proportions in efforts to get hate crimes laws passed, but also the first law on the books, signed by President George H. W. Bush in 1990, was called the Hate Crimes Statistics Act. (That law was quickly followed by the Hate Crimes Sentencing Enhancement Act, signed by President Bill Clinton in 1994, and then more hate crimes laws signed by every president since.)

Chapter 5, "Canaries of the Creative Age," returns to the question of gentrification and how overlapping social and financial accounting—such as the Gay Index, developed by Gary Gates and promoted by Richard Florida as an indicator of high-tech regional development and high-end real estate development (186)—drove twenty-first-century antiviolence efforts in New York's Chelsea Piers area. Again, Hanhardt makes sure that we know that this "knowledge" and associated policies and practices are contestable. As she narrates, they have been contested by radical antiracist queer activists. And I would suggest that they are contested as well by the counterknowledge that Hanhardt offers us in this important book.

Miranda Joseph is professor of gender and women's studies at the University of Arizona.

Notes

1. My title. "Just When They Seemed Engaged in Revolutionizing . . ." is from Karl Marx, *The Eighteenth Brumaire of Louis Bonaparte* (New York: International Publishers, 1963), 15.
2. Daniel Patrick Moynihan, *The Negro Family: The Case for National Action* (Washington, DC: US Department of Labor, Office of Policy Planning and Research, 1965).

DOI 10.1215/10642684-2843299

LET'S NOT SPLIT

Huffer's Queer Feminism

Jana Sawicki

Are the Lips a Grave? A Queer Feminist on the Ethics of Sex
Lynne Huffer
New York: Columbia University Press, 2013. ix + 246 pp.

Has the academic institutionalization of feminist and queer theories diminished their power to do something "surprising and transformative" (1)—to promote "new modes of living and political belonging" (184)? Might a queer feminism shake up the thinking habits, normative judgments, and grounding assumptions about power, sexuality, and ethics within both theoretical camps? In this collection of essays spanning over a decade of thinking, Lynne Huffer resuscitates queer feminism. She reminds us that our stories about ourselves as feminists and/or queers inevitably supplant and revise other stories. Rejecting a binary either/or logic, she suggests that the polarization of feminism and queer theory has obscured not only queerness in the history of feminist thought but also erasures of alterity (queerness?) in queer theory, despite the latter's anti-identitarian celebration of difference. Furthermore, she argues, if some feminists have tended to view sexuality as a site of harm and danger and have relied on the state to provide legal protections, many queer theorists have downplayed the danger of sexuality by celebrating sexual freedom and pleasure and abandoning ethical concerns.

Huffer's theoretical lineage is avowedly French and post-structuralist, as the introduction and title essay reveal. Indeed her approach bears the marks of a queer coupling of concepts and methods drawn from Michel Foucault and Luce Irigaray—both of whom, she argues, are ethically sensitive to otherness and to the silence, blind spots, and erasures that secure the modern Western (and sometimes masculine) subject. Irigaray represents an important supplement to Foucault insofar as she highlights the absence of a maternal genealogy in a history of Western philosophy governed by a masculinist subject's logic of the same. This is the subject that Huffer's genealogical excavations and nonbinary thinking attempt to undo in a manner reminiscent of the self-shattering force of rupture associated with sexuality in Leo Bersani's classic essay, "Is the Rectum a Grave?" If, as Bersani intimated, the rectum is a site in which a certain idealization of the masculine is buried, Irigaray's "lips," signifiers of true sexual difference, represent the site in which the feminine, a masculine construct, is buried as well. Huffer brings a feminist perspective on gender asymmetry back into the picture here, drawing attention to androcentrism in some versions of queer theory—even those extolling the virtues of the feminine.

Chapters on queer universalism, "Foucault's fist," *Lawrence v. Texas*, and queer lesbian silence continue in this vein—revealing exclusions and effacements, the fissured grounds of discourses of queerness. Thus, for example, Huffer notes the gender insensitivity in Foucault's attempt to desexualize rape by equating it with a punch (a fist?) in the face, as well as David Halperin's suggestion that we might degenitalize, hence desexualize, sex by engaging in subversive practices such as fisting. The fist is gendered, she reminds us—a fist in the mouth or vagina, or one raised high in the air in feminist protest, all represent significations that might be deployed to disrupt any easy or gay male–centered narratives about the fist and sexual freedom presented by queer theorists.

Later chapters turn to queer feminism itself, addressing its blind spots and fantasies, its attachment to a modern Western feminine subject—evidenced even in its productive if limited concept of intersectionality, as she argues in the introduction. In the final essays Huffer interweaves autobiographical reflections and readings of literary texts (Proust, Collette) and cinema (Virginie Despentes, *Baise-moi*) to talk about betrayal among women and moments where feminist attachments to ideas of women's vulnerability and woundedness obscure their capacities for harm and violence, as well as the histories of violence and ethical failure that continue to haunt us in the present. Huffer calls for an ethics that can address the inevitability of ethical failure, the daunting task of reparation, and the desirability of an erotic ethics of alterity centered on life (eros) and not exclusively on our sexual selves—the selves we have become in the context of the rise of what Foucault called "biopower."

There are many reasons to read this book, not the least of which is the provocative and productive impulse to link Foucault and Irigaray, and to use this queer coupling to invite both feminist and queer theory to engage each other politically rather than split. Huffer invites us to avoid reductive readings of one another and to attend to our enmeshments in the very cultural norms and practices that we are challenging. Least satisfying, perhaps, is Huffer's treatment of the idea of an erotic ethics—a topic more fully explored in her book-length tour de force, *Mad for Foucault: Rethinking the Foundations of Queer Theory* (2009), where she argues that Foucault's historical practice exemplified such an ethics. Yet I am left with questions that I hope Huffer will answer in future work: Are Irigaray's ethics of sexual difference distinctly and importantly different from Foucault's erotic ethics? Is Irigaray concerned with unraveling the self? How important is vulnerability in their respective ethical positions?

Jana Sawicki is Carl W. Vogt '58 Professor of Philosophy at Williams College.

DOI 10.1215/10642684-2843311

About the Contributors

Neel Ahuja is associate professor of postcolonial studies at the University of North Carolina, Chapel Hill. His forthcoming book is titled *Bioinsecurities: Disease Interventions, Empire, and the Government of Species*.

Karen Barad is professor of feminist studies, philosophy, and history of consciousness at the University of California at Santa Cruz. With a PhD in theoretical particle physics and quantum field theory, Barad held a tenured appointment in a physics department before moving into more interdisciplinary spaces. Barad is the author of *Meeting the Universe Halfway: Quantum Physics and the Entanglement of Matter and Meaning* (2007) and numerous articles on physics, philosophy, science studies, post-structuralist theory, and feminist theory. Barad's research has been supported by the National Science Foundation, the Ford Foundation, the Hughes Foundation, the Irvine Foundation, the Mellon Foundation, and the National Endowment for the Humanities. Barad is codirector of the Science and Justice Graduate Training Program at UCSC.

Jayna Brown is associate professor in ethnic studies at the University of California, Riverside. Her first book, *Babylon Girls: Black Women Performers and the Shaping of the Modern* (2008), won Best Book awards from both the American Society for Theatre Research and the Theater Library Association. She has also published on African American race film and popular music in various journals including the *Journal of Popular Music Studies*, *Social Text*, and *Women and Performance*. Her book in progress, "Black Utopias: Speculative Life and the Music of Other Worlds," considers alternative and radical forms of communality and modes of being in speculative literature and music.

Mel Y. Chen is associate professor of gender and women's studies at the University of California, Berkeley, and director of Berkeley's Center for the Study of Sexual Culture. Chen's *Animacies: Biopolitics, Racial Mattering, and Queer Affect* (2012, Alan Bray Memorial Award) explores questions of racialization, queering, disability, and affective economies in animate and inanimate "life" and "nonlife." Chen's writing appears in *Women's Studies Quarterly*, *Discourse*, *Women in Performance*, *Australian Feminist Studies*, *Amerasia*, and the *Journal of Literary and Cultural Disability Studies*. Along with Jasbir K. Puar, Chen serves as series coeditor for Duke's Anima book series.

Eunjung Kim is assistant professor of gender and women's studies at the University of Wisconsin, Madison. Kim is a member of UW Disability Studies Initiative and is affiliated with the Centers for Visual Cultures and East Asian Studies. Kim has published articles on disability films, asexuality, humanitarian visual cultures, and intersectional minority politics in Korea.

Dana Luciano is associate professor of English at Georgetown University, where she teaches sexuality and gender studies, nineteenth-century US literatures, queer and feminist theory, and queer film. She is the author of *Arranging Grief: Sacred Time and the Body in Nineteenth-Century America* (2007), which won the Modern Language Association's First Book Prize in 2008, and coeditor, with Ivy G. Wilson, of *Unsettled States: Nineteenth-Century American Literary Studies* (2014). Current projects include two monographs: "Time and Again: The Circuits of Spirit Photography" and "How the Earth Feels: Geological Fantasy in the Nineteenth Century US."

Tavia Nyong'o teaches performance studies at New York University. The author of *The Amalgamation Waltz: Race, Performance, and the Ruses of Memory* (2009), Nyong'o is completing one monograph on memory and fabulation in black performance and another on sense and sensitivity in queer aesthetics.

Jeanne Vaccaro is a postdoctoral fellow in the Department of Gender Studies at Indiana University. She is writing a book, "Handmade: Feelings and Textures of Transgender," about the handcrafting of bodily matter and creative and experimental forms of survival and self-determination. Jeanne's scholarship is published in *TSQ, The Transgender Studies Reader II*, and *Radical History Review*.

Harlan Weaver is a visiting assistant professor in gender and sexuality studies at Davidson College. He received his PhD from UC Santa Cruz's History of Consciousness Department, with a designated emphasis in feminist studies, and recently completed an NSF postdoctoral fellowship at the Center for Science, Technology, Medicine, and Society at UC Berkeley.

DOI 10.1215/10642684-2844219

Gender Studies from Chicago

Thoughts and Things
Leo Bersani

"In its ambition and originality, *Thoughts and Things* is classic Bersani, offering readers conceptually dense formulations—'psychic time is unitary mobility'—that no other contemporary thinker could plausibly have uttered."
—Tim Dean, SUNY-Buffalo
Cloth $30.00

Fuckology
Critical Essays on John Money's Diagnostic Concepts
Lisa Downing, Iain Morland, and Nikki Sullivan

"In *Fuckology*, Downing and co-authors capture Money's story ably."—*New Scientist*

"John Money's influential and controversial career has never received the careful, critical, and nuanced attention it deserves—until now."—Susan Stryker, University of Arizona
Paper $27.50

Seeing Sodomy in the Middle Ages
Robert Mills

"Not since Boswell's *Christianity, Social Tolerance, and Homosexuality* has a single scholar working in gender and sexuality studies taken on such a vast array of data, genres, and languages and treated it with such wisdom and care."—William Burgwinkle, University of Cambridge
Cloth $55.00

Visions of Queer Martyrdom from John Henry Newman to Derek Jarman
Dominic Janes

"Janes has written a fascinating study of the artistic and ritual elaborations of male homoeroticism in the nineteenth century's Anglo-Catholicism. There is much here to persuade—and much to delight."—Mark D. Jordan, Harvard University
Cloth $50.00

THE UNIVERSITY OF CHICAGO PRESS   www.press.uchicago.edu

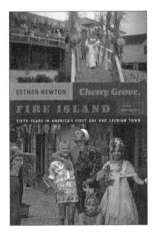

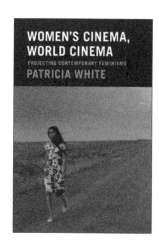

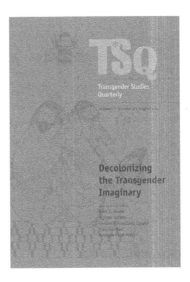

Printed and bound by CPI Group (UK) Ltd, Croydon, CR0 4YY

13/04/2025

14656480-0003